SYMBOLISM AND RITUAL IN A ONE-PARTY REGIME

D1287833

SYMBOLISM
AND RITUAL IN
A ONE-PARTY
REGIME

Unveiling Mexico's Political Culture

Larissa Adler-Lomnitz,
Rodrigo Salazar-Elena,
and Ilya Adler

Translated by Susanne A. Wagner

The University of Arizona Press   Tucson

The University of Arizona Press
© 2010 The Arizona Board of Regents
All rights reserved

www.uapress.arizona.edu

Library of Congress Cataloging-in-Publication Data
Lomnitz, Larissa Adler de.
[Simbolismo y ritual en la política mexicana. Englis
Symbolism and ritual in a one-party regime : unveiling Mexico's political
culture / Larissa Adler-Lomnitz, Rodrigo Salazar-Elena, and Ilya Adler ;
translated by Susanne A. Wagner.
p. cm.
Includes bibliographical references and index.
ISBN 978-0-8165-2753-3
1. Political campaigns—Mexico. 2. Elections—Mexico. 3. Communication
policy—Mexico. I. Salazar Elena, Rodrigo. II. Adler, Ilya. III. Title.
JL1281.L639   2010
324.972—dc22   200904428

Manufactured in the United States of America on acid-free,
archival-quality paper and processed chlorine free.

15   14   13   12   11   6   5   4   3   2

In Memory of Ilya Adler
Beloved Brother, Colleague, and Co-author of this book
Sensitive, caring, and committed to humanity,
his untimely passing pained all who
had the fortune of knowing him

Contents

Tables

Preface

Electoral campaigns are associated with competition between parties for popular approval: resources and work teams are mobilized and efforts are made to access the greatest number of votes possible that will allow a candidate or a party to win over another. Electoral campaigns are supposed to determine who will be the victor. However, not all campaigns function in this way. In Mexico, for example, during most of the twentieth century, the winner was known to all even before the elections took place. Nevertheless, electoral campaigns were held and were taken very seriously. This book addresses the question of what purpose electoral campaigns serve when the outcome is determined beforehand.

In 1987, a team was formed that provided an ethnographic follow-up of Carlos Salinas's presidential campaign, literally starting the moment that his candidacy was announced publicly. The team was composed of Larissa Adler-Lomnitz, Claudio Lomnitz, and Ilya Adler, who were supported by Guillermina Grisel Castro Nieto, María del Carmen Hernández Beltrán, and Alberto Lomnitz. Fieldwork was carried out in the states of Tabasco, Yucatán, Coahuila, Puebla, Veracruz, Jalisco, Chihuahua, Hidalgo, and Mexico City. The group was primarily made up of anthropologists using techniques from their discipline—such as participatory observation in campaign events and the conducting of hundreds of open interviews with various organizers, assistants, party members, leaders, and others. The Institutional Revolutionary Party's (Partido Revolucionario Institucional–PRI) cooperation was essential for the completion of this work.

By dealing with this topic from an anthropological perspective, the campaign can be seen as a rite of passage that allows us to understand the political culture of the country—an approach shared by Larissa Adler-Lomnitz and Claudio Lomnitz. Ilya Adler added a perspective from the field of communications, identifying an important sphere of competition for power. The initial outcome of this teamwork was an article entitled "El fondo de la forma: Actos públicos de la campaña

presidencial del Partido Revolucionario Institucional, México 1988"
[The depth of forms: Public events in the presidential campaign of the
Institutional Revolutionary Party, Mexico 1988] (Adler-Lomnitz, Lomnitz, and Adler 1993). This book is the result of a second phase of analysis
of the information, interviews, and field notes gathered at the time, and
it approaches the topic in an interdisciplinary manner representative of
the group. This was particularly important, since it became clear that
the topic under study had to be handled as a process (the presidential
succession) that pertained to a particular political system. As such, the
authors followed an anthropological (Larissa Adler-Lomnitz), political
science (Rodrigo Salazar), and communications approach (Ilya Adler).
Previous articles written by Larissa Adler-Lomnitz with the historian
Frida Gorbach were also incorporated, such as "Entre la continuidad
y el cambio: El ritual de la sucesión presidencial" [Between continuity
and change: The ritual of presidential succession] (Adler-Lomnitz and
Gorbach 1998). As the authors were able to distance themselves from
the events over time, they were able to delve further into the topic: it
can now be asserted that the succession process of 1987–1988 was the last
electoral event that reproduced those cultural patterns that had been
formulated over decades, while it was also the first to demonstrate that
these patterns could no longer be adequately adjusted to the new social
realities that had emerged.

The primary thrust of the book continues to be anthropological.
Starting with the ethnographic data gathered during the PRI presidential
candidate's campaigns throughout the federal states and the phases that
preceded elections, this study represents a case study of the ritualistic and
symbolic content found in campaigns within a specific cultural and political context. From this point of view, the electoral campaign expresses
while simultaneously reproducing a national culture and a dominant
order. These dimensions of Mexican politics were more evident in times
of crisis, such as when there was a change in leadership. Our analysis of
campaign events is meant to demonstrate this duality (expressive and
reproductive) found within the Mexican political ritual.

For many Mexican readers, particularly younger ones, the description provided herein of the campaign rituals will give the impression
that they are living in another country. Mexico has changed in several
aspects since this field research was completed. Specifically, there has
been a change from a non-competitive political system with a hegemonic and corporatist party to a multi-party system in which political

parties compete against each other to gain a majority of votes. The president no longer has the tremendous power he once had. A vast majority of experts as well as most of the general public agree that the opposition movement launched by Cuauhtémoc Cárdenas in 1988 gave rise to this change. Apparently, and according to PRI versions, the information system that handled voting results failed during the 1988 elections, which most likely had an impact on the final and official electoral results. This failure of the system has led to a broad range of studies on the dynamics of electoral competition and regime change.

However, an understanding of this phenomenon from an inter-party dimension can be complemented with greater knowledge of the characteristics that defined the relationship of the president with his party. Our study was meant to understand what the substance of "authoritarianism" was during those years. We especially intended to show the resources of power available that led to the population's voluntary integration under hegemonic rule.

The transformations of the political regime have provided an opportunity to compare current mechanisms to those in existence prior to competitive elections. This has led to a recent interest by several political scientists in the functioning of the PRI system from a neo-institutional and incentive-based perspective. Although we attempted to incorporate this perspective to provide a complete scope of reference, we placed a greater emphasis on informal rules, interpersonal relationships, and the dominant symbolic and cultural system as indispensable factors in explaining the behavior that we observed during the succession process of 1987–1988.

As stated, this was the last of the processes that had the general characteristics of the traditional model, at least in reference to the presidential designation of his successor and the format of the campaign. Afterward, political violence, PRI's rebellion against the technocracy, and the requirements imposed by competition altered this model. On the one hand, the analysis of this process shows the cultural aspects that made the campaign indispensable for the political regime's stability. On the other hand, the analysis demonstrates the perpetual tensions that existed between the demands for change and the need for continuity. Along these lines, the fact that the campaign adhered to the rules of the past despite the changed social environment helps us understand the factors that failed in providing the PRI with a guaranteed and indisputable electoral victory.

From an international perspective, the existence of hegemonic party systems is not a thing of the past. While Mexico began a transition toward democracy, authoritarian leaders in dozens of countries simply pretended to adopt democratic practices. Even though our research was limited to Mexico under the PRI, we hope that our findings will lead to comparable studies of the relationship between the formal and informal rules, the relative weight of co-optation and repression, and the complexity of internal unifying mechanisms of the group in power in these types of regimes.

Culture is persistent, and its relationship with the political system is complex. Sometimes cultural changes have an impact on institutions; in other instances, transformations brought about by political elites have to confront the population's adverse predispositions and attitudes toward change. Our research into the succession process provides a photograph of the political culture of the time. It does not measure the frequency or the degree of support for a democratic regime or of preferences vis-à-vis strong leaderships, but instead looks for relational characteristics and the subjective ties of these relationships, as well as their immersion into the political system. The current competitive democratic regime within the bounds of a country that is now closer to its legal structure has to confront the more persistent features of society. This is even truer at a time when the reduced degree of power available to the president is perceived as impotence and the dispersion of political power among different parties is viewed as leading to paralysis. We hope that this analysis will help individuals gain a greater awareness of those forces that are clamoring for a new balance between continuity and change.

The book is organized into four sections. The first serves as an introduction to the Mexican political system of 1988 and the relationship that existed at the time between the president and the PRI. The second part focuses on the activities that took place prior to the announcement of the crucial decision that the sitting president made every six years: who would be his successor. The third part deals with the activities that the PRI presidential candidate and the party participated in during the electoral campaign. In the fourth part, we discuss, first, the mechanisms used in the 1988 campaign to meet the PRI's diverse goals (geared toward reestablishing stability within the political system). Then, we provide some reflections on the cultural aspects of change within the political game that have taken place since the 1988 elections and continue to find expression within Mexico's political culture as illustrated by the 2006 presidential campaign.

Appendix A lists some of the most important events in the 1987–1988 succession process in chronological order. In Appendix B, we present a list of institutions and names of individuals that played an important role in our history. We added a brief description of the institutions and of the role played by the individuals during the succession process, as well as the fate they faced during Salinas's term.

Mexican political jargon is colorful. In order to preserve this property as much as possible, we use the idiosyncratic expressions in original Spanish. The first time each expression is used, we provide the literal translation within brackets. Appendix C, the Glossary of Spanish Terms, explains the meaning of each expression in more detail.

PART I

THE MEXICAN POLITICAL SYSTEM AND ITS ACTORS

The Mexican political system is characterized, among other factors, by the tension that exists between the formal and informal rules of conduct. This tension was clearly evident throughout the 1988 presidential campaign. While most political actors abided by the established and "official" or formal rules, they also followed informal and informal behavioral norms based on Mexico's national culture. These two sets of rules frequently worked toward opposite ends.[1]

The Political Constitution of the United Mexican States of 1917 established Mexico as a representative, democratic, and federal republic. The constitution also calls for the separation of powers, by which the "supreme power of the federation" is divided into the executive, legislative, and judicial branches. Territorial powers are separated between the national government and the states of the Mexican federation.

Executive power is held by a president elected through a system of direct vote. Presidential terms are six years long without any possibility for reelection. The president alone has the power to select the members of his/her cabinet. Legislative power resides with the Mexican Congress, composed of the Chamber of Deputies and the Senate. Judicial power is exercised by the Supreme Court. In other words, like many other modern democracies, Mexico's formal institutional structures are based on a presidential political system—a political model that has its origins within the U.S. constitution.

Nevertheless, for many decades, Mexico's political system did not follow these formal regulatory structures and was not a democracy, nor was there a separation of powers as described above. A commentator once stated: "In general terms, Mexico has similar formal political structures as other countries. However, it is imbued with a functional particularity derived from Mexico's political culture that is unique, and which distinguishes it from those countries that served as the inspiration for its political system" (Garcia Castro 1997, 32).

These particularities have resulted from a host of informal rules that have lived side-by-side with the established norms and that have "defined orderly conduct, served as guidelines for political actors, and determined what types of behaviors were compatible with the overall goals of the government" (Serrano 1998, 17). These informal rules and cultural expressions forged a government different from the one described in formal and official terms.

The processes surrounding presidential succession can not be fully explained without an understanding of the interaction between these two sets of rules. Existing laws guided political actors throughout the political process, while informal rules of "real" politics and cultural norms constituted the contextual framework on which political actors based their behavior. Thus, rules were interpreted within a specific contextual circumstance.

Despite this duality, politicians tried to avoid straying too far from the established rules. Processes of presidential succession were not simply implemented to comply with a legal requirement or to give a democratic appearance to Mexico. Throughout this study, it became evident that in the 1987–1988 succession process too many human and financial resources were mobilized and too much effort and competition went into the campaign than were necessary to simply "safeguard appearances." It also demonstrated that political actors believed in the campaign's value beyond its legal framework and felt that it served an irreplaceable symbolic purpose and as a mechanism to reproduce the political system.

The first part of this book describes the political and cultural context within which the succession process of 1987–1988 took place. Chapter 1 looks at the three elements that comprised the Mexican political system: the political regime, the party system, and the political culture. Their interactions demonstrate that political rituals were central to the behavior of Mexico's political class, despite the existence of formal representative institutions and the absence of a truly democratic essence.

The chapter explains that the political system neither prevented conflicts nor allowed for their open expression, leading to their veiled and ritualistic manifestations within the political battle. This could be seen in newspapers and campaign activities. The presidential campaign was simultaneously a symbolic expression of national unity and the arena for voicing and resolving conflicts among diverse groups within the hegemonic party.

Chapter 2 describes the political system's dominant actors. On the one hand, the presidential figure is reexamined. The president wielded enormous power, despite constitutional restrictions, that was seen as almost divine by the general public. On the other hand, the president's party—the Institutional Revolutionary Party (Partido Revolucionario Institucional–PRI)—is analyzed with a specific focus on its organizational characteristics (corporatism) and its peculiar submissive relationship vis-à-vis the sitting president. This description will aid in understanding the actors and their relationships when looking at the two main phases of Mexico's presidential succession: the period preceding the *destape* (unveiling) of PRI's official candidate and the stage of the actual presidential campaign.

1

The Mexican Political System

A Structural Analysis

To understand the political system of any given society, one has to analyze its component parts. For the purposes of this study, we have chosen three essential factors within the Mexican political system: (1) the political regime and its relationship to elections; (b) the party system and the interactions of the hegemonic party with opposition parties; and (c) Mexico's political culture and its political rituals, which is the central theme of this book.

The Political Regime, Elections, and Mexico's Party System

The process of holding periodic federal elections was central to the Mexican political system as seen in the 1987–1988 period. Also of great importance were the personnel changes that occurred within the executive and legislative branches once electoral results had been announced. Political actors have taken uninterrupted and periodic elections for granted since the 1910–1917 Mexican Revolution and as established within the Mexican constitution. This phenomenon has largely contributed to Mexico's political stability.

However, this is only one piece of the puzzle. The behavior of political actors during presidential campaigns would largely go unexplained without an analysis of other aspects of Mexican politics, such as the regime and the party system. These have greatly defined the character of Mexico's electoral processes.

The Mexican political system can be termed a variation of an authoritarian regime. It allowed the formation of relatively independent opposition parties, which, however, essentially participated in non-competitive elections.

General Considerations

Political regime or political rule is generally understood as "a group of formal and informal procedures that serve to select the national leadership and determine public policies" (Geddes 1999, 18). Accordingly, holding periodic elections is *a*, but not *the*, only condition of democracy. In a "true" democracy, elections must be competitive and have the following characteristics: there can not be a predetermined winner; electoral results can not be reverted; and there is an absolute certainty that future elections will take place as did past ones (Przeworski et al. 2000, 16–18).[1]

In principle, regimes can be considered authoritarian if they do not hold elections or if electoral processes are not competitive. Electoral processes can be considered non-competitive when only one political party participates or when opposition parties can not defeat the ruling party through elections. In other words, in these cases, electoral processes do not determine who will exercise political power (Hermet 1982, 26; Fernández Baeza and Nohlen 2000). The difference is that in democracies "political parties lose elections," and in authoritarian regimes, "*opposition parties* lose elections" (Schedler 2002, 47).

The aforementioned electoral processes have a different impact on the configuration of the group in power and on political actors participating in either one of these types of regimes. This is particularly true with regard to the certainty of political outcomes. In democracies, ". . . there is no group whose preferences and resources enable it to predict outcomes with any degree of certainty" (Przeworski 1995, 81). Political actors may be able to calculate probable outcomes, but do not *know* if they will actually win or lose. Democracy therefore "is a system of regulated open-ended outcomes or of organized uncertainty" (Przeworski 1995, 19).

In contrast, authoritarian regimes provide a high level of certainty in a negative sense with regard to electoral outcomes. "Opponents among government officials will not replace the ruling party," and "public policies that are not accepted by those in power will not be implemented" (Colomer 2000, 127). Outcomes that are undesirable are excluded from the political process. Actions that could lead up to these outcomes are prohibited. When undesirable and/or unwanted outcomes result from political processes, they are annulled.

In the case of Mexico, we refer to a regime in which opposition exists, but that is authoritarian through its hegemonic party system as defined by Sartori (1999b). This type of authoritarianism is more sophisticated than those that directly prohibit the existence of opposition parties. In these cases, it is more difficult to clearly determine whether or not these regimes are democratic.[2] Their institutions are the same as those found in electoral democracies, and they include genuine opposition parties and civilian and dissident populations that enjoy substantial freedoms, at least when compared to governments with one-party rule (Diamond 1997, 16–18). These are regimes that "appear to be democratic, since they allow opposition parties and the holding of public offices as a result of elections. They are not democratic in the sense that opposition parties can not access public office as a result of elections . . . some [of these regimes] hold elections knowing that the opposition can not win, while others, where opposition parties could come to power, do not allow these to take office" (Przeworski et al. 2000, 27). Under these conditions, the ruling party maintains its control and "assigns a portion of its power to subordinate groups at its own discretion" (Sartori 1999b, 276–77).

This study focuses on the mechanisms by which the Mexican political system reproduced and strengthened existing loyalties toward the ruling party. However, since we are dealing with a hegemonic party system (almost an original model of this type of rule),[3] it is important to discuss what motivates an authoritarian coalition to take the risk of decreasing its own power by allowing the existence of autonomous opposition groups that can appeal to society through electoral processes.[4]

Authoritarian regimes, unlike democracies, are extremely vulnerable to expressions of social discontent (strikes, protest marches, etc.), since these threaten the regime's stability (Przeworski et al. 2000, 212–13). Citizens can not satisfy their demands for public policy changes by simply choosing to elect a different government. As a result, their discontent is directed toward those who regulate access to political power and decision making, i.e., the political regime (Linz and Stepan 1996, 49; Huntington 1994, 232–38). Where electoral processes exist, citizens who are discontent are more likely to express their grievance through the ballot box than by using other collective means for change—especially since alternatives could be more risky even if they are probably more effective.[5]

Even if expressions of social discontent are limited, opposition parties hope to introduce greater political reforms and a possible, even if slow, transition to democracy by taking advantage of the spaces made available to them by the hegemonic party (Colomer 2000, chap. 2).[6] By opening up some limited spaces to the opposition, authoritarian regimes hope to increase their political stability, which is at times simply defined as "the predictable capacity . . . to endure over time" (Morlino 1991, 533).

Non-competitive Elections

The Mexican electoral system, throughout the period of the Institutional Revolutionary Party's (Partido Revolucionario Institucional–PRI) hegemony, was non-competitive. Formal rules worked in conjunction with informal and culturally based regulations, which allowed the official party to recur to fraud when electoral results were unfavorable.

One source of guaranteed votes for the official party came from its client-based (clientelistic) ties, which existed at all levels of society. These resulted from the exchange of goods and services for electoral support.[7] The client-based nature of Mexican society depended on the nurturing of long-term loyalties, which were also manifested within the informal structure of Mexico's political culture.

Formal rules regulating electoral processes, their organization, and the validity of electoral results tended to favor the PRI. Beginning in 1946, the Federal Commission for Electoral Vigilance (Comisión Federal de Vigilancia Electoral) was charged with organizing elections. This commission later became the Federal Electoral Commission (Comisión Federal Electoral–CFE). The rules that guided the appointment of members to this entity clearly guaranteed that participants had a vested interest in the regime's continuity. For the 1988 elections, the PRI had sixteen representatives within CFE, while all other parties combined had only thirteen. Each congressional group also voted for a representative to CFE selected by a majority vote, which meant that this person would belong to the PRI since the PRI always held a majority in Congress. The secretary of the interior, also a member of PRI, presided over the CFE.

Elections were ratified by a political rather than a judicial government entity. Members elected from the Chamber of Deputies formed an electoral college. The electoral college was the only authority and the ultimate decision-making body with regard to the legality of all electoral results—the president's and their own. The electoral college was the only entity that could challenge electoral results.[8]

There were no guarantees that electoral processes would be fair and equitable, especially considering the biased nature with which elections were organized. Additionally, electoral results, as stated, could not be challenged through legal processes and according to established and formal norms. Thus, electoral fraud, even if not necessarily a frequent practice, became a permanent possibility. In other words, if the hegemonic party won by a clear majority of votes based solely on its campaign appeal, elections were clean—or most likely not fraudulent. When the opposite occurred, election results could always be modified. In some circumstances, electoral fraud was used even when it was not necessarily required to achieve specific electoral outcomes. Sometimes, fraud was practiced in response to internal power struggles and to ensure that the presidential candidate would be indebted to the party (Gómez Tagle 1986). At the regional level, PRI leaders inflated the number of votes in their favor to show that their political power was greater than that of other political parties.

Fraud was practiced in various forms, and different types of fraud were described with a specific terminology. This is clearly shown in a colorful summary given by a commentator: "Electoral fraud can be defined as different irregularities that leave different types of imprints: changes in the voting ledgers; the organization of wandering voters (*carruseles*) [carrousels]; the stealing and/or burning of ballot boxes; the expulsion of a voting booth representative; the closing down or opening up of voting booths without prior notice (*ratón loco*) [crazy mouse]; the stuffing of ballot boxes prior to the initiation of elections (*urnas embarazadas*) [pregnant ballot boxes]; one voter submitting various ballots (*taqueo de votos*) [making tacos of votes], etc. (Lujambio 2000b, 108)."

The Hegemonic Party System[9]

In Mexico, the hegemonic party system had its origin in 1929 when 148 parties were joined together (Nacif 1996, 3) under the umbrella of the National Revolutionary Party (Partido Nacional Revolucionario–PNR).[10] The idea initially was to achieve a presidential nomination by consensus of all political actors, especially regionally based caciques, known as strongmen, whose power rested on the role they played during the 1910–1917 Mexican Revolution. At the regional level, these parties were often the only ones in existence or were without a doubt the most dominant one. By uniting all parties under one specific party umbrella, the victory of its candidates was guaranteed. As a result, the nomination of candidates became central to the political battle. Frequently, candidates who lost the bid for the presidential nomination would run as independents or in representation of a hastily created new party. This practice was common for all elections, including presidential ones, and is seen as a dynamic of opposition candidates as illustrated in the cases of Tejeda (1934), Almazán (1940), Padilla (1946), and Henríquez (1952).

These realities led to the creation of complementary mechanisms that included substituting party primaries for a system of conventions in 1937; prohibiting candidates from running as independents; barring local parties from participating in federal elections; and requiring in 1946 that political parties be created at least a year before the elections that they planned on participating in.[11] Such regulations ensured that politicians who had their own power base but did not become presidential candidates could not run as independents with local support or with the help of a local party nor form their own opposition party (Nacif 1996, 11–12). In other words, all exit strategies for those with grievances were annulled. Running as a candidate for an already registered opposition party meant a guaranteed defeat.

Several groups did try to challenge through elections what had become a state party. Some of these parties, such as the Mexican Liberal Party, the National Agrarian Party, and the Communist Party were assimilated into the official party during the Cárdenas regime. The Popular Force Party (Partido Fuerza Popular), which had its origins as the National Synarchist Union party, and Miguel Henríquez' Federation of Parties of the Mexican People (Federación de Partidos del Pueblo Mexicano), among others, enjoyed a large enough social base to represent a real threat. In both cases, the National Electoral Commission exerted its power to deny these parties their registration in an effort to "sweep" dangerous enemies from Mexican territory.[12]

In the early 1960s, there were only three parties that competed against the official party in elections. All of them were offshoots of the revolutionary family: the Popular Socialist Party (Partido Popular Socialista–PPS); the Authentic Party of the Mexican Revolution (Partido Auténtico de la Revolución Mexicana–PARM); and the National Action Party (Partido Acción Nacional–PAN).[13] Both the PPS and PARM eventually became junior partners of the official party. They supported the presidential candidate as if he was of their own choosing and defended the hegemonic party's position in Congress and before CFE. For decades, PAN was the only true opposition party. However, it suffered tremendous internal divisions since it had to participate in elections that were wrought by unfair rules (Loaeza 1999).

The Mexican party system was very much a one-party rule throughout this time. In 1961, the PRI was the only party capable of nominating candidates for all electoral districts. It became more and more difficult for opposition parties to recruit members, since their electoral participation required investment of energy and time and often of personal funds when the chances of a victory were practically non-existent (Nacif 1996, 14–15). Generally, PAN gained access to between four and six congressional seats in each election. For the most part, the PRI conceded these to PAN, and they were not won through the electoral process (Lujambio and Marván Laborde 1997, 44–45). In 1958 and 1961, PAN ordered its congressional candidates to reject their seats, but in both cases, the orders were ignored (Nacif 1996, 17; Lujambio and Marván Laborde 1997, 52).

The fact that PAN could potentially abandon the electoral battle, which would have left the ideological right without a voice, led to decisions that would give Mexico its hegemonic party system. Beginning with the 1964 federal elections and with only a few variations over time, the composition of the Chamber of Deputies was determined by a system of majority rule with proportional representation.[14] Invariably, the PRI always held an absolute majority of seats, ensuring that only a few slots would be delegated to minor parties through proportional representation.

In 1964, the electoral system guaranteed that only fifteen congressional seats would be shared among the three opposition parties. In the end, this was enough for PAN to continue participating in elections. In the famous 1977 electoral reforms, the Communist Party was granted its registry. Reforms also allowed for one hundred out of a total of four hundred seats to be occupied by smaller parties. In 1988, possibly to protect the PRI against a decrease in electoral votes, it was decided that the party that received the highest number of votes (relative majority) would automatically receive sufficient seats in the Chamber of Deputies to hold an absolute majority, while proportional representation was upheld for all other parties. This reform was termed the "governability clause."

These reforms were meant to stimulate greater party participation. From this moment on, between seven to nine parties competed in elections, although they all knew that the PRI would continue to hold an absolute majority in Congress and would win the presidential elections. In the long history of PRI electoral reforms, there is not a single registered case in which an opposition party refused to participate in elections when given the opportunity or abandoned the electoral arena voluntarily when in Congress, even when threatening to do so.

Between 1946 and 1985, the PRI received between 65 and 94 percent of the votes, thus guaranteeing for itself a minimum of two-thirds of the seats in Congress. It lost only one senatorial seat and always triumphed in all elections for governorships and the presidency. Opposition parties held a subsidiary position and were further divided between those parties that actually opposed the PRI and those that were the PRI's allies.[15]

By the time the 1988 elections came around, structural changes within Mexican society had had an impact on voting patterns with regard to the PRI. Juan Molinar Horcasitas (1991, 137–46) argues that tendencies specifically associated with modernization—such as education, income, and urbanization—led to relative losses in votes for the PRI.[16] He further argues that these tendencies and their potential consequences were perfectly visible to any observer even prior to the initiation of the electoral process, which, according to Molinar Horcasitas, was of even greater significance.

From 1964 to 1985, the PRI votes had been reduced by twenty-one percentage points. However, this did not necessarily imply a dismantling of the hegemonic party structure. In 1985, the PRI still received 65 percent of the votes and won almost all of the districts with a majority. Thus, the PRI held almost two-thirds of all the seats in Congress. The National Action Party was fifty percentage points behind the PRI, a distance that would be difficult to bridge in a three-year time period.

As a result, no one expected a complete electoral overturn for the 1988 elections. Some may have expected that the PRI would receive less than 60 or maybe even 50 percent of the votes, but no one seriously questioned that the PRI would continue to receive a majority of the votes. Currently, with all the information that has been attained regarding the 1988 elections, it is difficult to fathom that the political actors were unable to foresee the dramatic results of these elections. They did foresee that there would be important modifications in electoral behavior. Their subjective analysis of the hegemonic party system, however, misled them into believing that the most essential parts of the system would remain intact. That there was a complete lack of understanding of how profound electoral changes really were is clearly illustrated by the fact that Carlos Salinas based his campaign on a traditional, noncompetitive model just as his predecessors had done.

All of these factors provide a contextual framework within which the succession process of 1987–1988 took place. Although periodic elections with the presence of opposition parties were a regular feature of the Mexican political system, the truly fundamental characteristic of this system—which was known and accepted by all political actors of the time—was the certainty that the PRI would continue to control the electoral process.

This certainty, in turn, influenced the political behavior of all political actors (Lujambio 2000a, 4).

The Mexican Political Culture

Following the model proposed by Adler-Lomnitz and Melnick (2000), political culture is defined as a "language." Like a language, it is composed of a grammatical structure (the *langue*) or a "set of categories and rules that represent the continuity of a culture" and its oral manifestation (the *parole*), which is its "linguistic behavior that by its very nature is variable." Defined in this way, political culture is a function of (1) the structure of social networks and their interaction with political power, and (2) the symbolic system that is integrated by such elements as speeches, political rituals, language, architecture, myths, emblems, and the use of space and time, among others. They legitimize and feed into the social network structure and often represent the basis of nationalist ideology. The following section discusses the structure of social networks that exist in Mexico in an effort to explain the corresponding symbolic system.

Patron/Client Relations and the Issue of Loyalty

When analyzing different campaign activities, it becomes evident that each one has a basic characteristic. On the one hand, even when participation is not necessarily free in liberal-democratic terms, all campaigns try to convince everyone to collaborate and participate, emphasizing voluntary participation without the use of repressive mechanisms. On the other hand, participation seems to be motivated primarily by moral obligations (loyalty) fostered through long-standing patron-client relationships rather than by convictions. Ultimately, loyalty was the essence that allowed the immense machinery of presidential campaigns to function. From the cultural perspective, vertical loyalty was the typical and permanent social relationship that characterized the Mexican political system.

In a specific kind of social relationship, loyalty functions as an ethical code that is established for the purpose of an informal exchange of resources.[17] In any given society, individuals are part of a personal network of relations, which they potentially use for the exchange of resources. These relations can either be horizontal or vertical, depending on the social distance that exists between an individual and his/her counterpart.

Individuals' positions within a social structure are a function of (1) the type of resources they control (money, political power, employment, loyalty); (2) the level and amounts of these at their disposal; (3) whether resources are exchanged along vertical or horizontal lines; and (4) the formal or informal agreements that are reached with those groups that control the resources. Depending on how these variables play out, each person represents a "node" within the social mosaic.

Relations with friends and family members of the same social hierarchy are considered horizontal. The vertical dimension is made up of relations established with "inferiors," for whom one represents the figure of the "boss," and a "superior," in which case the individual becomes a client.

Horizontal relations are egalitarian, composed of people of the same social ranking who exchange favors according to the rules of reciprocity. Vertical relations are characterized by unequal resources or power, which nevertheless lead to the creation of personal, long-term relationships. The asymmetry in these relations leads to a dependency of the "inferior" vis-à-vis the "superior," which in turn creates a clientelistic structure. "Patron-client relations are a type of reciprocity in which the benefits to subordinates are negotiated in return for loyalty and power" (Adler-Lomnitz 1994, 143). In these types of relationships, the patron provides resources such as employment, protection, public service, or bureaucratic sponsorship. In return, the client provides work and political support. For those involved in patron-client relations, the system represents a "luck of the draw" primitive mechanism for the redistribution of wealth. It complements and eventually even substitutes the formal, impersonal public policies and systems of social assistance.

Horizontal and vertical relationships are informal. Exchanges of resources that take place within this structure fall outside established legal norms. Compliance with this system and its continuity largely depend on unwritten ethical codes that represent cultural values. In this way, the ethical code of solidarity regulates horizontal relations. What counts is not the actual payment of a favor—since occasionally the resources may not be available for a party to comply with his/her obligations—but the permanent willingness of people who trust each other to exchange favors.

Patron-client relations exist as a result of and for the continuous flow of resources. Their temporary suspension does not end mutual obligations between both sides. There must be a certainty that individual interests will be sacrificed solely to uphold the relationship, even if such a sacrifice is required only under exceptional circumstances. In these cases, obligations derive from a sense of loyalty. It should be noted that loyalty goes both ways. The client owes the patron loyalty, and under the established informal ethical codes, the patron has responsibilities toward the client. Consequently, clientelism has been associated with paternalism since patrons must take care of their clients.

One can compare reciprocal and hierarchical relations with those of formal and informal market interactions. In markets, resources are exchanged in an absence of personal relationships. Demand and supply laws substitute for moral, implicit obligations.

On the macro-social level, the political culture of a collectivity is defined by the social relations that dominate the collectivity's social interactions. When there is a predominance of horizontal relations, social classes are structured in an egalitarian manner.[18] Societies where vertical relationships predominate are, in turn, seen as more hierarchical (Adler-Lomnitz and Melnick 2000, 7–11).[19]

Despite recent and accelerated social transformations, the Mexican political system associated with the PRI's hegemony was built on the foundations of the Mexican vertical clientelistic social structure. This model can be described as a conglomerate of pyramids that compete among each other for resources, status, and power. At the top of each pyramid, there is a boss (patron) who distributes resources to his/her subordinates and who, in turn, is subject to a higher authority. Thus, the boss acts as an intermediary who exchanges resources for loyalty, which can be political or labor related in nature.

The internal structure of the pyramid is determined by the closeness of its members to the leader. Immediately below the leader we find the "trusted people" (gente de confianza). These are succeeded by the next level of dedicated loyal people, who are slightly further removed from the leader's circle of trust. In this manner, the pyramidal levels go all the way down to the base.

Another factor that determines individuals' power is their horizontal relations with other pyramidal structures that allow them to obtain additional resources. This increases their usefulness vis-à-vis their immediate superior and increases chances for upward mobility within the pyramid.

Within the vertical dimension of the pyramid, resources (capital and power) are funneled from the top down, while work, loyalty, and political support radiate from the bottom up. Every person provides loyalty and services to a superior while receiving the same from his/her subordinates; thus, a member of a pyramid "receives material compensation and power from his/her superior and provides material compensation and power to his/her subordinates. The amount of material benefits and power an individual controls determines his/her position as an intermediary within the structure" (Adler-Lomnitz 1994, 254).

The top-down distribution of resources and the bottom-up flow of loyalty forge the social cohesion or solidarity of each group within a pyramid. The level of solidarity in turn determines the efficiency of the group, since it relates to the leader's ability to obtain more resources. In contrast, leaders within the same hierarchical grouping are loyal to the same superior and therefore compete with others of similar rank for the same resources. Thus, this type of social structure concentrates power at the top, while fragmenting it toward the bottom.

This ingrained social structure meant that democratic and constitutionally based practices in Mexico could not rely on an individualistically structured society. In Mexico, society was conceived of as an organic whole composed of hierarchically interrelated segments. Representation was based on negotiated agreements reached between these segments. The negotiated results were of greater importance than the legally sanctioned individual rights.[20] The segmentation of the dominant party was, after all, a historical manner by which the constitutionally based liberal-democratic ideology could be accommodated within a structure of spontaneous, holistic, and relational practices that have always been so much a part of Mexican society.

In the twentieth century, political power was built in such a way that it basically formalized Mexico's pyramidal social structure. The ruling party incorporated workers, peasants, and civil society and forged a system of corporatist rule.[21]

In Mexico's traditional political system, every politician relied on a group of loyal followers who shared his/her political fate. These followers accompanied him/her in every administrative position he/she held. Generally, these groups are known as "camarillas" or power groups. However, we prefer to call them "political networks," since the term power group implies a small, homogenous, closed, and inflexible group. The concept of network, however, refers to a group with a broad range of action, in which relationships of trust are of essence. Additionally, positions within political networks are based on professional abilities required for specific tasks so that people exiting and entering each networks can enjoy internal mobility depending on relationships of trust and links that exist between different networks. Thus, a power group may be at the core of the political network without necessarily encompassing the whole.[22]

At higher levels, each minister and deputy minister heads a group whose members are linked by ties of personal loyalty to their common patron. Several of these, in turn, head another group of loyal subordinates. The members of each group would have had an interest in supporting their leader's capacity for negotiation. When negotiation through formal paths was not possible, followers might have had to make use of their own personal relationships in an effort to gain access to the resources held by another group.

Even when followers were assigned to different governmental agencies as a result of administrative changes at the top, they continued functioning as a loyal faction vis-à-vis their original leader. If loyalty persevered in challenging times, followers were rewarded when a member of their own faction gained access to a position of political power.

Within this system, no one fully controlled his/her formal subordinates; factional bosses often placed some of their loyal followers within the ranks of their clients' subordinates. These, in turn, would more likely follow the instructions of their informal rather than their formal bosses. The power of factional leader was largely determined by the number of loyal followers they could position within the official organizational chart of their administrative entities—the people they could trust (Smith 1979, 317–18; Chapela 1983). "The degree of control exerted by a factional leader over his/her subordinates is in inverse relation to the degree of trust and loyalty that exists among them; in this way, the power of a subordinate is compensation for his/her loyalty to the factional head" (Adler-Lomnitz 1994, 149). Thus, there was a partial overlap between the bureaucratic structure and the informal hierarchies determined by complex relations of relative power exerted by political actors.

At lower levels within the hierarchy, intermediaries were increasingly charged with implementing compromise solutions and negotiations that had been agreed upon within higher ranks. They were charged with implementing negotiated agreements with positive outcomes. As an example, members at the bottom of the pyramid were rewarded with a constant influx of vital resources such as electrification projects or land distribution in rural areas. The amount of resources members received depended on their ability to mobilize people for certain protest marches or in support of a specific candidate.

Even though the potential for violence to break out always existed, members at the grassroots level of this structure believed in the system. They saw it as materially important and morally right. Consequently, the Mexican political system made selective rather than systematic use of repressive mechanisms. The PRI incorporated these structures into the hegemonic party system, becoming an enormous social organization capable of covering social needs with its own resources or with resources obtained from its privileged access to government agencies. This was particularly true at the local level.

Patron-client relationships, despite their unequal and hierarchical nature, are not relationships of subjugation or imposition. Clients bring available resources that are deemed useful by the patron into these relations. This allows the client to negotiate some terms and conditions of the relationship to a certain degree. Generally, the client avoids direct confrontations when in disagreement with the patron and instead uses forms of passive resistance, such as not complying with a previously agreed upon obligation without even notifying the patron. In this manner, the client shows the patron how necessary his/her services really are.

Those patrons with a clear understanding of the nature of patron-client relationships tend to negotiate terms and conditions of their clientelistic relationships. Far from being arrogant and tyrannical, the patron upholds all social protocols of respect when negotiating the conditions of a relationship. Thus, the voluntary nature of the relationship is further highlighted.

Mexico's vertical political system incorporated at least two mechanisms that explain its long-lasting stability. Overall, the system discouraged the formation of large coalitions of discontents. Regardless of their political ambitions, powerful politicians were forced to accept a presidential change every six years, which came with a concomitant rotation of people within the highest administrative positions. Each newly elected president designated a new group of people to positions of power. Those groups relegated to inferior positions and/or those who were displeased with the new government waited patiently for the next favorable six-year change, which could happen at any time. Leaders who did not benefit from the positions assigned by the president would often gain access to other high-ranking positions (Centeno 1997, 150). This allowed them to stand by comfortably while they bided their time.

The system's ability to create hope for the fulfillment of future expectations is one of the variables that best explains the longevity of the PRI's rule. Without this or another similar stabilizing mechanism in place, the system would have suffered from structural instability (Przeworski 1995, 30). Along these lines, Mexico also followed the "no reelection" rule, which will be discussed later.

If we apply Hirschman's model (1970) to Mexico's political situation, in which the social structure is vertical and relationships are based on loyalty from the bottom to the top of the pyramid, the political regime creates a subjective and affective barrier that impedes discontent from being translated immediately into support for the opposition (the exit). A group of followers who have momentarily lost the implicit benefits of their patron will not establish a new and more beneficial patron-client relationship since this would be seen as mercantile. The group will not form an independent union nor take over rural lands by force. On the contrary, the group's members negotiate with their patron, who persuades them to be patient by either highlighting past benefits, appealing to their sense of personal loyalty, or giving them some material good. During political crises, the regime had time reserves that allowed it to recuperate and reestablish the status quo thanks to the aggregate impact of multiple relationships based on personal loyalties—not always necessarily vis-à-vis the government—that forged the foundations of the system. This was clearly evident in the union uprisings of the seventies, the student movement of 1968, and even more important, during the 1982–1983 economic crisis that the sucessors to the López Portillo government inherited.

The importance of this point is clearly illustrated when we compare the actual fall of the PRI regime with the fall of the Communist regimes of Eastern Europe, Poland, and Czechoslovakia. Although the PRI suffered a shock in 1988, it really lost its power only twelve years later. When the Soviet Union did not intervene, the entire political systems of Eastern Germany, Poland, and Czechoslovakia collapsed at the first signs of political crisis. This can largely be attributed to the fact that the people within these systems had no affective relationships or moral obligations toward the regime and were therefore willing to permit its instant demise.

Clientelistic relationships have a flexibility that is substantiated by those obligations generated through direct personal dealings. Even so, they are relationships of exchange and require a continuous inflow of resources. When resource input has been interrupted, participants within the structure expect that the flow of resources will be restored shortly. The Mexican political system in 1988 depended on two factors to ensure its stability: (1) political elites participated in a rotational system that convinced each faction that it could gain access to a portion of political power; and (2) popular classes received resources to satisfy their demands, which in turn required relatively prolonged periods of economic growth (Serrano 1998, 19).

The above discussion describes the factors that forged the Mexican political system and its activities during the years of PRI hegemony. Even with the existence of an independent opposition that was organized and capable of gaining votes, elections did not determine who would be a part of government and what future direction the government would take. The existence of different political parties apart from the dominant PRI, and periodic elections as established in the 1917 constitution, did not fulfill democratic functions. On the contrary, since true electoral competition was non-existent, these elements were an integral part of an authoritarian structure that was based on a hegemonic party system.

Even though there were strong tendencies that put the regime's long-term stability in jeopardy, central actors within the system were careful to implement institutional modifications necessary to avoid any immediate surprises. The opposition had no choice but to accept these changes if it wanted to continue to participate within the political arena.

Continuity was further guaranteed by the past's "dead weight." The vertical political culture that was based on loyalty and PRI hegemony reinforced one another. It generated practices, relationships, and values that solidified the system and gave it a certain degree of predictability when it came to relationships between power groups. This was true both internally and toward society in general.

In real politics, mandatory decisions are made for the entire society. In the case of Mexico, these decisions were taken within the governing coalition that was made up of the president, his cabinet, and the distinguished members of the party and the sectors that they represented. This is what Brandenburg (1964) termed "the revolutionary family."

As mentioned, the pyramidal hierarchical structure was characterized by competition among groups for scarce resources and particularly for political power. Competition implies conflicts of interest and political clashes. In Mexico, political elites did not voice these conflicts openly in their competition for votes. They were also not manifested as public social demands of organized grassroots groups. But these conflicts did exist and had to be expressed in some way. Members of political networks and organized workers' groups would not voluntarily join a political order if they did not at least have the expectation that they would be able to influence those political decisions that had a direct impact on their own personal existence. The alternative of simply waiting for resources to fall from the heavens was not a sufficiently attractive alternative within a political system that preferred cooptation over repression. As described earlier, the open and public expression of discontent and conflict is contrary to the principles of an authoritarian system. Consequently, in Mexico, these were manifested in a codified and ritualistic manner. Each social group—working class or political class—expressed its conflicts in different arenas.

The Symbolic System: Interpretation and Political Rituals

According to the democratic model, citizens are equal in exercising their rights and there is a representative relationship between the people's interests and their collective decisions, which is fostered by an open competition among political elites through the free vote of the citizens.[23] Candidates to political positions will anticipate future reactions of the electorate and, in an effort to promote their own interests, will try to ensure that their decisions will warrant them the political position they desire. This takes place when the following conditions are met: (1) the electorate is free to form its own opinions with regard to political issues and cast its votes accordingly, (2) politicians compete among each other to obtain the majority of votes, and (3) politicians gain access to positions that allow them to make decisions that have an impact on issues that are important to the population. This process is known as a representative political system and has recently also been called a system of accountability. In this model, open discussions, particularly in the media, fulfill the task of informing voters in a pluralistic manner using many voices and perspectives and various criteria to evaluate government performance and the state of public affairs. Governments are made aware of citizens' satisfaction with their performance and take this into account when making decisions for the future. Freedom of expression and the open and informed discussion about political matters are essential to the functioning of a representative relationship.

The democratic-egalitarian model can not function in a vertically structured authoritarian social system with a non-competitive government. Without an effective electoral mechanism, representation loses its incentives. Hierarchies are based on clientelistic relationships that promote the interests of subordinates to a certain extent. However, it does not contemplate the possibility that the subordinates ultimately judge political performance to determine whether the benefits they have received are satisfactory or whether they should opt for another political alternative. While a representative is periodically submitted to performance evaluations and reelection, a political "godfather" is in principle irreplaceable. Mechanisms for open collective discussions about political issues are generally lacking at national and regional levels, as well as within specific sectors.

From an anthropological point of view, Claudio Lomnitz (2000) has demonstrated the impact of inexistent representative mechanisms and conditions.[24] In Mexico, open discussions of political events, autonomous organization, and mediation of collective demands so that these can be incorporated at the decision-making levels have been nonexistent since colonial times. They have been substituted by political rituals "as political battlefields in which political decisions are negotiated and incorporated. . . . [T]he correlation between political rituals and public discussions is negative." Political rituals occupy a more central position proportionate to the decrease in importance of public discussions (Lomnitz 2000, 242). Political rituals lead to pragmatic arrangements and negotiations that do not require the involvement of legal formalities or commitments made to the public. Instead of open decision-oriented processes that resolve conflicts of interest, political rituals offer a means by which political demands are expressed, interpreted, and resolved. Negotiations do not take place in an open manner, nor do they incorporate explicit exchanges among the parties involved. Instead, they become over-dramatized and take place in public spaces designated for other purposes. Politicians enact their external roles, which are interpreted and given an implicit significance depending on their access to resources and position within the vertical hierarchy.

Public acts, such as bullfights, civic ceremonies, religious feasts, and political campaigns, have both explicit and implicit purposes. At the explicit level, their purpose is to entertain, honor heroes, perform religious rites, or recruit political personnel via elections. As political rituals, these events are evaluated on the use of time and space, gestures, physical distances between those in attendance, the specific use of words, and overall behaviors from which alliances, ruptures, and agreements between power groups can be inferred. These signals are interpreted as much by protagonists as by spectators based on their shared understanding of political codes. Protagonists are consciously aware of what they are "truly" expressing and communicating. Spectators are "informed" about power relationships within the higher levels of the political hierarchy, as well as their own position within that hierarchy by the role played by their own patron.

When rituals take on a festive character, they serve to reiterate the validity and continuity of patron-client relationships. By paying for the celebration's costs—whether with public or private funds—local leaders reaffirm their commitment to the redistribution of the benefits gained by their positions of power to subordinates in return for their continued loyalty. Simultaneously, they demonstrate the vitality of the collective group that they control to those in superior positions within the hierarchy.

The communications functions of political rituals in Mexico were based on a mixture of an institutional republican democratic framework and a vertical social reality with a non-competitive government. Public actions and declarations had to be adjusted to democratic formalities. Real negotiations and important information could not be openly shown in behavior and words, but rather had to be hidden behind formal processes. "In Mexican politics there are few actions while interpretations proliferate" (Adler-Lomnitz, Lomnitz, and Adler 1993, 242). A code of the hermeneutic reading of political rituals (the press will be discussed later) was used by political participants to communicate among each other and with the population.

Democratic formalities and rites did not express the reality of political relationships. However, they were the only openly observable manifestations of these relationships. As a result, those who were in search of information tried to identify the invisible behind the visible. The ascription of hidden meanings to political rituals took place at all political public acts. "[T]he weakness of the public national sphere in Mexico has guaranteed that political events are interpreted in a symbolic manner: its expressive dimensions are equally or more important than its instrumental dimensions" (Lomnitz 2000, 266).

Imagine a luncheon or feast that celebrates the creation of a new workers' union or the birthday of a bureaucrat. Observers do not see a luncheon. They see the people at the event and look at those seated closest to the most powerful person in attendance and try to figure out why some are allowed into the "inner circle" while others are excluded. They observe who talks with the leader attentively and who receives a pat on the back. They also try to determine what motivates certain observable behaviors. The leader, fully aware that gestures and behaviors are being interpreted and are seen as the only source of information, will purposefully control the messages that he/she intends to convey through actions. Others in attendance will become aware of their position through the perceived messages and may actually end up competing with others to become the beneficiaries of these symbolic expressions, even when these are in reality trivial. They may end up fighting over the seats closest to the leader, and the actual luncheon or feast ultimately is the least important aspect.

The legal framework, combined with the authoritarian characteristics of the regime, resulted in a shared and accepted code of conduct. Thus, it was of utmost importance to abide by the "rules of conduct" that were so typical of the PRI culture, which explains why these behavioral norms persisted for such a long time. Since the rules of conduct determined the content of the indirect message, any variation from the accepted guidelines could lead to unnecessary confusion or erroneous signals.

Newspapers tend to decrease uncertainties in communications and convey political intentionality with greater accuracy. Since it was physically impossible for politicians to participate in all public events to identify the "truly significant messages" conveyed at such events, politicians became avid readers of newspapers.[25]

In contrast to the role played by print media in liberal democracies discussed earlier, during those years the Mexican press did not serve to form a free public opinion. Regardless of content and of the control mechanisms in place vis-à-vis print media, their circulation was extremely limited, barely reaching one million readers, despite the fact that there were many newspapers and magazines (more than fifteen daily newspapers in Mexico City alone, for example). However, the press did not function as a propaganda machine or for indoctrination purposes either, as is common in totalitarian systems.

Advertisements are vital to the survival of most media, and the government was the largest buyer of advertising space, which became an indirect means of controlling the press. The government would threaten—and at times follow through with the threat—to withdraw advertising funds from a communications medium, which greatly limited the independence of the press.[26] A further mechanism of indirect control existed in the monopolistic government ownership of paper supplies. Its subsidized purchase was an absolute necessity for the continued survival of the majority of newspapers.

Journalists often received payments from politicians taken from public coffers, known as *embute* (stuffing) or *chayote* (mirliton), which represented one form of direct control. Journalists were motivated to accept these payments, since their salaries were low. Newspaper publishers, although not actively encouraging these practices, allowed them to take place. They also protected their financial arrangements with the government by strictly controlling the political orientation of each journalistic piece.[27]

The close ties established between the press and the government limited news coverage that contained political criticisms. In a systematized analysis of fifteen newspapers over a six-month period in 1984 and 1985, it became evident that not a single story criticized the president. A total of 95 percent of articles that talked about a particular government ministry were either neutral or positive.

The remaining 5 percent of articles that contained some criticism served in part to pressure a specific ministry to pay arrears, including embutes, or to renew services that had been cancelled due to financial restraints. However, the majority of stories that contained criticisms must be seen as the media's participatory role in political battles between political groups and as a means of communication among members of the political class.

The government's cooptation of the press did not take place as part of the overall structure. Every institution had to create its own relationships with the media and with specific journalists separately. In this way, different factions used the media they controlled to launch attacks against members of competing factions. Through criticisms, the media voiced the struggles that took place within the political class publicly and indirectly. Such expressions could also be a sign of new coalitions forming, especially when criticisms were issued by different factions and directed against a common enemy. Politicians who needed to be updated on these rivalries and alliances used the press as their main source of information.

Political actors in turn designated significant resources to upholding their relationships with the press, not only to launch attacks against their adversaries but also to ensure that they would receive favorable coverage. This was particularly true for people with presidential ambitions. Usually, institutions that were criticized in the press and the people in charge of those institutions were seen as incapable of controlling the press, since the objective of attaining favorable coverage was seen as achievable. The damage caused to a politician's image by unfavorable coverage could have an impact on the president, who might decide to interrupt the official's political career—thus becoming politically *quemado* (burnt).

The reaction that the media could provoke in readership was limited, and thus there was no justification, in that sense, for the obsessive attention that politicians paid to the print media. On the one hand, as stated, the readership of newspapers was small, and on the other hand, audience preferences did not influence the composition of government. The only readership that was affected by media criticism was made up of high-ranking political officeholders and political groups. Political allies and competitors alike, they represented a minority of approximately one hundred thousand people who carefully read the newspapers daily. The communication formats used by print media can convey more adequately certain types of complex information than electronic media can (Sartori 1998). As a result, politicians tacitly agreed that the press represented the center for the transmission and reception of messages. "In this way, government institutions use the press to communicate with other members of the 'dominant coalition' rather than with the more widely spread 'public opinion'" (Adler 1993b, 20).

Members of every faction informally agreed to use newspapers as the arena for their political battles, and they understood that newspapers contained information about these battles. However, the fact that government was not an open system meant that these struggles were expressed in an indirect manner, which made an exact decoding of the messages contained in the news difficult. It was necessary to read between the lines without reading the actual information, utilizing techniques and skills that could be gained only from experience and familiarity with the political environment. In those years, it was difficult for the general public to understand the language and style used by the press when dealing with government-related topics. There is evidence that criticisms were interpreted differently among bureaucrats. Interpretations became more indirect and sophisticated the longer a bureaucrat's political career was.

Within this framework, the real (not electoral) competition for greater power took place between political groups that formed the Mexican political class. It included the relationship of the hegemonic PRI with opposition parties; loyalty as the predominant factor underlying political relations that were marked by an inequality between parties; the ritualistic nature of public acts as an expression of power relations; and the creation of a codified language to interpret correctly meanings hidden behind visible actions. All of these elements created the context within which presidential successions took place.

Tensions between the need for change as expressed by the president and the imperative for continuity of the party system were displayed in all of these processes. This takes us to the two principal actors within the Mexican traditional political system: the president, who was elected every six years, and the party, which continuously nominated the victorious candidates. This is the theme of the next chapter. The particular nature of the Mexican presidential system explains the problems that government change engendered and shows how democratic formalities were used by the political system to overcome these challenges. It also illustrates the extent of informal authority enjoyed by the candidate who formally was most likely to become the next president.

2
The President and His Party
Informal Networks in a Formal System

The Mexican presidential system was unique. It oscillated between an individualistic dictatorship similar to that of Porfirio Díaz, the militaristic type of rule that proliferated throughout South America, and a party-based dictatorship similar to the Soviet regime. Simultaneously, it maintained certain democratic formalities. Because of its many informal realities, the Mexican political system with its constitutionally based balance of power was able to coexist with an exceptionally strong presidency. The president was able to implement his projects without any major social opposition and without a veto from constitutionally appointed powers.

The Institutional Revolutionary Party (Partido Revolucionario Institucional–PRI) oversaw all institutions capable of limiting the president's power (Congress, the state governments, the judiciary) and was able to mobilize the population through the corporatist union structure under its control.

It can be argued that the PRI and the presidency had an informal agreement in which each side reduced its own power with regard to the other in exchange for concrete benefits. The president was supported by the party on the most crucial decisions and was assured social control and subordination. In turn, he renounced any possibility of extending his presidential term beyond the six years set by the Mexican constitution and refrained from modifying the party's hegemony and its internal balance so essential for its functioning. The party was guaranteed (1) control over state governments, where its members held all key decision-making positions, (2) access to resources for distribution among its multiple client-based networks to ensure their continued support, (3) personal gain in terms of wealth and power for political officials and union leaders loyal to the party, and (4) the expectation among those within the upper echelons of the PRI bureaucracy of political career benefits that would not be affected by sudden interruptions other than experiencing the normal ups and downs that came with every six-year electoral cycle.

This arrangement was accepted because of the following realities: (1) the certainty that the PRI would always win elections; (2) the president's direct and indirect control over the PRI's future; and (3) the rule of "no reelection," which created movements within and among political networks and provided an expectation of future political promotion. The party's organization and its control over the branches of government guaranteed that the president would uphold his side of the agreement. The formal republican structure did not comply with its purported purpose of restricting presidential power, but instead served as the framework within which the informal norms and real politics ruled. The informal realities forged a basis in which party discipline vis-à-vis the president prevailed.

The "Weak" Presidency

From a strictly constitutional perspective, the Mexican presidency faces potential vetoes at all levels where there is a separation of power. Theoretically, the president cannot enforce decisions when he disagrees with Congress. The Mexican Constitution of 1917 allocated executive power by establishing a "pure" presidential government. This means that (1) the population elects the president and legislature (Congress) separately, (2) both have fixed terms so that the legislature can not end a presidential term with a vote of no confidence and the president can not dissolve the legislative assembly and call for early elections, and (3) the president holds absolute power to elect and remove cabinet members (Shugart and Carey 1992, 19). The Mexican president is elected every six years through popular vote. For the period under discussion, the president designated the cabinet secretaries, the heads of the administrative departments,[1] and the attorney general (Carpizo 1978, 117–18) at his discretion.

The Mexican presidential system was inspired by the United States's model of checks and balances. This model creates equilibrium between the powers by requiring that actions be approved by two separate entities and/or by giving one branch exceptional powers that usually pertain to another. Because of these provisions, presidential systems of this type have the peculiar distinction of functioning with divided majorities. So, for example, the party or coalition that won the presidency may not have an absolute majority in Congress. In these cases, opposition parties have few incentives to cooperate with the president and may actually prefer to block his/her initiatives and proposals in the hopes of benefiting in the next electoral cycle (Linz 1997).

Recent research on presidential systems has concluded that a president's power is in large part a function of the resources that he/she is allocated constitutionally to intervene in the legislature. This is especially true when the most important government decisions have to pass through the legislative branch for approval and when this government organ has final decision-making power (Shugart and Carey 1992; Shugart and Mainwaring 1997; Shugart and Haggard 2001).

According to the indicators used in this research, the Mexican president's legislative power is relatively weak compared to that in other presidential systems.[2] In general terms, the Mexican presidency lacks certain constitutional tools to impose on a legislature that opposes public policies requiring its approval, at least to a greater degree than in other presidential systems.[3]

There are two additional characteristics imbedded in Mexico's institutional design that limit the president's power. One is the two-chamber structure of the legislature (the Chamber of Deputies and the Senate). Both chambers act as legislators, and all legislation has to be approved by a majority first in one chamber and then in the other. Under these terms, the president's projects have to confront not one but two potential vetoes before laws can be approved.[4]

The Mexican federal system further limits the president's power. Federal states as constitutional entities have several functions, attributes, and rights in which central powers can not intervene, while they simultaneously are allowed to participate in some fundamental national decisions, such as constitutional reforms (Dahl 1983; García Pelayo 1993, 232–39). The federal system incorporates a vertical dimension into the horizontal separation of powers among the executive, legislative, and judicial branches in the form of the division between the central government and member states.

Until 1997, when the government was divided for the first time since the creation of the hegemonic party, the rate of congressional approval of legislative initiatives remanded by the executive was close to 100 percent (Casar 1999, 96–97). A similar pattern existed regarding the annual budget (Weldon 2002, 400). Presidential initiatives were approved without any modifications during the majority of the period and with only minimal modifications in 1982 and 1987 (Díaz Cayeros and Magaloni 1998). Until 1988, all bicameral commissions were headed by PRI legislators.

The hegemonic party thus enjoyed formal rights and the institutional space to impose decisions on the president, with the ability—in principle—to create a party-based dictatorship.[5] However, the party entered into a relationship of submission vis-à-vis the president by informally renouncing its legislative authority and thus making the executive a legislator without opposition.

The same dynamic existed for nonlegislative decisions in which Congress was involved. Among these, the Senate's intervention in removing state governors and in naming the heads of the judiciary stands out. The Senate formally determined the conditions under which the powers of a federal state "disappeared." In these cases, the Senate named an interim governor selected from a list of potential candidates submitted by the president.[6] Because of the extent of real presidential power in Mexico, it is obvious that the Senate initiated these processes on the president's behalf (Weldon 1997, 253–55). Between 1917 and 1935, the senatorial power to remove governors was a tool used in the president's struggle against local strongmen (caciques). The use of this tool diminished over time, however, and by 1988, thirteen years had passed since the last governor was removed by the Senate. Instead, the process changed to one in which governors who had fallen from grace would resign from their positions. The fact that governors would pay attention to the "insinuations" coming from the federal executive (Carpizo 1978, 198) shows that the president exerted substantial control over their future political careers. They also believed that they would lose their dignity in a constitutionally based process of impeachment.[7] Even though governors enjoyed tremendous power within their own states, their subordination to the national executive was a matter of political survival.

The highest organ of the judiciary, the Supreme Court of Justice of the Nation (Suprema Corte de Justicia de la Nación), was composed of twenty-one ministers designated by the president and ratified by the Senate with a majority vote. This method of designating Supreme Court justices is seen in the United States as guaranteeing a minimum of impartiality. This was not true for Mexico, where the PRI held all positions within the Senate. Even though Supreme Court justices were elected to life-long terms, the president could have them removed through the Chamber of Deputies by claiming "misconduct." It made them susceptible to the same "insinuations" that led to the resignation of governors (Cossío 2001, 88–91). The executive's control over the judges saved him from facing a potential veto arising from decisions made within the legislative branches of government, since the judicial power could revoke presidential deci-sions or specific legal applications ratified by the legislature by claiming that they were unconstitutional.[8] As a by-product of the judiciary's sub-jugation to the executive, a theory of constitutional interpretation devel-oped that promoted the superiority of the social goals of the state, which had their origins in the 1910–1917 Mexican Revolution, over individual guarantees as expressed in the liberal tradition (Cossío 1998, 46–51).

The unwillingness of the PRI to reduce the executive's power vis-à-vis Congress was in and of itself a means of increasing presidential power at the expense of the legislature. It also served as a tool to prevent potential vetoes from being issued by the judiciary and the federal states. As María Amparo Casar (1999, 2002) explains, the PRI as the hegemonic party occupied institutional positions—basically Congress, governor-ships, and local legislatures—and delegated the powers that formally belonged to them as members of these institutions to the president in an informal way. This practice was extended to the internal functioning of the party, where the president held the ultimate decision-making power in assigning leadership positions and nominating candidates to the vari-ous popularly elected government positions.

The Corporatist Structure of the PRI

Above all else, PRI was a powerful organization at the disposal of the presi-dent. In it, the vertical nature of society and the non-competitive character of the political system conjoined in a government apparatus used primar-ily for social rather than electoral control. On the one hand, this control was based on a leadership that was not accountable (in the democratic sense) and on vertically organized sectarian groups. On the other hand, it used cooptation based on the inclusion of a corporatist structure. The corporatist nature of the party, which made it populist, meshed with an integration of regional elites and technocrats. This created a highly hetero-geneous governing coalition, whose members shared an acceptance of the political rules and a general vision of Mexico's goals for economic devel-opment. These included an active participation of the public sector and the promotion of economic and social advancement of the less-privileged sectors (Cook, Middlebrook, and Molinar Horcasitas 1996, 52). Historic, political, and national cultural issues were expressed in a permanent orga-nization that represented continuity despite the political power change that took place every six years at the federal bureaucratic level.

In 1936, Lázaro Cárdenas introduced a corporatist element into Mexico's political regime. This was the year he transformed the National Revolutionary Party (Partido Nacional Revolucionario–PNR) into the Authentic Party of the Mexican Revolution (Partido Auténtico de la Revolución Mexicana–PARM), with the explicit purpose of ensuring that the people were organized in defense of the social programs implemented by the state (in essence the new labor laws and the collective ownership of land). The corporatist structure would far outlive his more radical aspirations of social transformation. The call to transformation, the statutes, and other documents related to the re-establishment of the party are imbued with a strongly anti-individualist, pro-state, and organically oriented rhetoric (Córdova 1974, chap. 6), illustrative of the ideological foundations of the revolutionary party.

The four sectors of the PRI (workers, peasants, public employees or the "popular" sector, and the military [which was later suppressed])[9] retained autonomy in activities related to their "specific purpose" and in their internal organization. In return, they agreed not to partake in electoral activities outside of the party. In the case of the workers and peasants sectors, each renounced the ability to integrate members from the other (Córdova 1974, 163–65; Garrido 1982, 247). The corporatist nature of the party was evident in the fact that it emphasized that individuals belonging to any of these organizations would be collectively affiliated to the party (Garrido 1982, 248). By law, workers in specific industries had to become members of the company's union, which meant that they automatically also became members of the party. To be a member of the party, in turn, it was essential to belong to one of the sectors, and individual affiliations, although in existence, had to be made through the popular sector (González Compeán, Lomelí, and Salmerón Sanginés 2000, 157–58).

Each sector had an equal number of representatives in the National Council (Consejo Nacional), an organ formally in charge of naming candidates to the decision-making entity of PRI—the National Executive Committee (Comité Ejecutivo Nacional–CEN). These party organizations were reproduced at the state and district level, and even at the electoral sections within each district. The organizational network was and continues to be composed of the direct or territorial expanse of the party that coexists with the sectarian, corporatist structure.

The workers sector had the greatest degree of organizational autonomy upon the re-establishment of the official party and enjoyed a greater negotiating capacity than the other sectors. The Confederation of Mexican Workers (Confederación de Trabajadores de México–CTM) was originally incorporated into the official party as part of a negotiation that took place between two independent actors with a mutual need (León and Marván 1985).[10]

The CTM is primarily made up of national industrial unions and unions composed of corporations grouped together at the regional, local, or state levels. In every affiliated industrial plant, there is a local union with its corresponding general delegate and delegates within every section of the plant. At a higher level, the regional representation has an executive committee and different commissions (Adler-Lomnitz 1994, 237–39). As such, the workers sector was grouped together in a pyramidal structure that ran from the factory to the confederation of unions, giving its leadership significant social power. The immersion of organized labor into the state structure gave its leadership some influence in economic policy decisions. Thus, it served to guarantee a minimum of social services provided to the working class; representation at the factory level for individual workers; employment stability through open-ended employment contracts; firing policies with stringent limits; promotions based on seniority; salary levels established by categories; work obligations with detailed specifications; and restrictions on internal mobility (de la Garza Toledo 1996).

The National Confederation of Peasants (Confederación Nacional Campesina–CNC) is organized into four hierarchical tiers: local, regional, state, and national. This structure was created in response to Article 27 of the Mexican Constitution and agrarian legislation requirements for communal landholdings'(ejidos)[11] representation before judiciary and state authorities. Specifically, the law stated that each ejido had to have an elected commissioner who represented the ejido's interests legally and executed the agreements made in the assembly. This organization in turn headed the executive committee of the CNC in the ejido. Grouped into regions, the president and secretary of the ejido commission elected ten to twenty regional peasant committees from each state. In turn, these regional committees chose five leaders from their respective states as representatives in the League of Agrarian Communities (Liga de Comunidades Agrarias) and Peasants' Unions (Sindicatos Campesinos). The 160-member leadership of these committees represented the thirty-two states to form the National Convention of the CNC, which in turn designated the leaders who made up the National Executive Committee of the CNC (González Compeán, Lomelí, and Salmerón Sanginés 2000, 185–86).

In the same way that the CTM and other less powerful workers' unions that belonged to the workers sector of the hegemonic party automatically gained industrial workers' representation, the CNC, based on the ejido system, attributed to itself the membership of practically every peasant with communally owned lands. The central committee, which was a part of the PRI, monopolized the access to the government's agrarian bureaucracy and controlled the foundations of peasant subsistence: "When reforms to the agrarian legislation made land donations and redistribution ever more complicated, peasants had no means of formalizing processes outside of the CNC" (González Compeán, Lomelí, and Salmerón Sanginés 2000, 187).

The profile of the National Federation of Popular Organizations (Confederación Nacional de Organizaciones Populares–CNOP) was very heterogeneous since it was designed to group together the middle and popular classes of Mexico. Among its most outstanding members was the state employees' union—the Federation of Unions of Workers in the Service of the State (Federación de Sindicatos de Trabajadores al Servicio del Estado–FSTSE). Here, unions with moderate negotiating ability participate, such as those representing lower levels of the government bureaucracy. It also includes the most powerful union in Mexico, the National Union of Workers in Education (Sindicato Nacional de Trabajadores de la Educación–SNTE). The CNOP hoped to cover a large portion of the middle class even though its operational mechanisms resemble those found in the workers sector. Other members of the popular sector were semi-organized groups. They included the organizations working with the informal sector and the small and even marginal property owners who had submitted a request for subsidized housing. The former demonstrates that even the informal sector was incorporated into the corporatist structure.

President Ávila Camacho used the CNOP to appeal to those middle sectors most likely to support the 1940 opposition candidate Juan A. Almazán, and also to expand the social base of the party. The organization also functioned as a buffer between the executive and the workers and peasants sectors, which at the time were pressuring the president to continue with Cárdenas's social program (Garrido 1982; González Compeán, Lomelí, and Salmerón Sanginés 2000).

In this way, the corporatist structure combined (1) legal mechanisms that made it obligatory for individuals to pertain to a primary structure, such as a union or ejido, in order to have access to a minimum of material goods (social security, land), and (2) the incorporation of these structures into a bureaucratic, hierarchical union tied to the state through its membership in the hegemonic party.

Corporatism and clientelism have certain common characteristics, in particular, the unequal nature of relations, in which the less powerful side obtains resources (in this case employment stability and land) in exchange for political support. However, important differences exist when one looks at the true-life experience found in each circumstance. In the patron-client relationship, direct negotiations take place that appeal to the personal nature of the relationship. Loyalty is not spontaneously evoked, but is born out of the daily interactions between the two parties. In a corporatist organization, the bureaucratic hierarchy replaces the personal relationship, while the formal codified and legal obligations replace loyalty. In this way, corporatism can be seen as the formalization of clientelist relations in which the weakest actors lose negotiating capacity. Political support takes on a more mandatory character, even if in practice clientelist personal relations were created within the corporatist structure between workers and union leaders at the factory level, for example. In these cases, the "patron" justified workers' absences and/or tardiness and distributed workloads and overtime, etc., as personal favors (de la Garza Toledo 1996, 408).[12]

By 1978, the mechanisms of obligatory or quasi-obligatory affiliation provided the PRI with 7,726,060 party members through the peasants sector; 3,275,610 through the workers sector; and 2,250,615 through the popular sector (Langston 2002). These data are not only representative of the power within each sector but also demonstrative of the PRI's enormous numerical advantage in relation to its competitors. In 1986, the PRI had a membership of some sixteen million (Centeno 1997, 51), while the National Action Party (Partido Acción Nacional–PAN), the strongest opposition party, had only forty-nine thousand members in 1988 (Heredia 2002, 215).

In principle, the problems of collective action had been resolved through the great number of workers who through corporatism could obtain benefits by class (Olson 1992). The hegemonic party's corporatist structure gave it resources to massively mobilize workers, who could express themselves in favor of policies that went against the chosen capitalist model. However, one must note that despite the large amount of land redistributed during Cárdenas's government (1934–1940) and the attainment of some of the elements that make up a benefactor state (minimum wage, collective contracts, social security, housing programs), the governments that arose from the PRI were able to discard the workers' objectives for social improvements since workers renounced their right to use the unions to pressure the government in times of economic instability (Middlebrook 1996, 38).[13]

In part, there is an ideological explanation for this submission. Juan Linz (2000, 208–17) points out that the rhetoric of corporatist governments appeals to a sense of national unity, which is conceived of as an organic whole whose parts are subordinate to the government. From this perspective, the interests of each part should not be antagonistic, and it is the state's duty to bring them into harmony for the well-being of the collectivity, which is of superior value. The pursuit of personal benefits is seen as divisive behavior vis-à-vis the social order. It has already been stated that the vertical structure of Mexican society overshadowed individualism in a collectivist ideology. For the PRI, unity (of the party, the country) was perhaps the most important value and the ideological weapon used most often to discredit adversaries. As the interests of social groups were systematically sacrificed to meet the economic policy needs of the moment, the initial demands of "workers" and "proletarians" for a socialist order were replaced by the broader and, to some extent, innocuous ideology that became known as revolutionary nationalism.

One must add that the ideological posture used to avoid conflict was accompanied by the system's reliance on the resources available to the president to garner loyalty and subordination.

Presidential Power

The presidency was able to take over party control largely due to the resources it had at its disposal. With these, the president satisfied individual interests as a reward for the loyalty demonstrated by party members. Notably, the presidency had discretionary power over the public coffers. He made public investment decisions, which allowed him to designate funds to groups whose behavior warranted "rewards." More important, however, the existence of certain specific electoral rules gave the president control over the future political career of PRI members.

Benito Nacif (1996, 2002) demonstrates how significant the concept of non-consecutive reelection within the legislature, implemented in 1932, really was. Legislators at the national and local levels could neither hold important positions within opposition parties nor forge an independent base with a nucleus of permanent voters within their own electoral districts. Since they had no possibility of continuing with a legislative career, their only choice for immediate permanence became to accept an appointment to a position within the federal bureaucracy. These appointments were directly or indirectly controlled by the president.

The party discipline that had thus been achieved was reinforced in 1949 by substituting primaries with a system of conventions to nominate candidates to elected government positions. It has been shown that interparty competition gives legislators an incentive to act more responsibly toward their constituents than toward the leadership of their respective parties (Shugart and Haggard 2001, 85–88). As per the PRI, the system of conventions was obligatory. The call for nominations was consequently left in the hands of the PRI leadership. So too were the means and organizational structures by which the delegates at each convention could be elected, creating an ambiguity that allowed the party leadership to decide who would be favored with a nomination (Langston 1996). This also eliminated independent battles between party members.

It was common practice that these conventions would prescribe that only candidates supported by one or more sectors of the PRI could be nominated as pre-candidates (Garrido 1993, 119). By 1987, those looking for a nomination were prohibited from campaigning before the call for nominations had been published. The National Executive Committee was charged with vetoing any pre-candidature or proposing another; they also had the power to refuse the ratification of decisions made at the convention (in the case of the elected nominee) and to nominate a new candidate in exceptional cases (Garrido 1993, 117–21). Although internal competition was not expressly prohibited, this structure effectively minimized the possibilities of intra-party struggles, which meant that extreme measures could be avoided. The system's effectiveness can be seen in the fact that between 1929 and 1981 the PRI managed to get a unanimous vote for the presidential pre-candidate as the sole contender in eight out of ten internal selection processes (Garrido 1993, 194).

Lastly, the electoral reform of 1946 concentrated the organization of electoral processes in the hands of the federal executive. Local political apparatuses no longer had access to this important resource to influence electoral outcomes.

The system of conventions led to the concentration of power over the nomination process in the hands of the party's national leadership. Yet, in reality, the executive power controlled all important aspects of the electoral processes. These included the law of no reelection in consecutive fashion to the legislature and the allocation of resources to favor the party's leadership. All of these measures, combined with the certainty that the PRI would maintain its continuous electoral predominance (Lujambio 2000a, 4), forced PRI members into a behavior of strong party discipline, which would be rewarded with the continuation of their political careers.

Party leaders' individual interests were also met in their relationships with various government sectors. The CNC became dependent on the bureaucracy charged with giving land donations and distributing credits and materials required for production. The leadership of the peasants sector was completely under the control of the federal and state governments (Langston 2002, 401–2). On some occasions, presidents such as Luis Echeverría tried to strengthen the peasants sector to dilute the power of the workers sector (Basáñez 1990, 202–3), albeit with little success. The CNOP, beyond the power of some of its unions, became the internal arm of the executive in his relations with the other two sectors. That function is illustrated by the fact that those aspiring to become deputies but whose political activities were not directly related to the unions (such as those allied with cabinet secretaries and governors) entered Congress as members of the CNOP (Langston 2002).

The subordination of the workers' unions and the strongest groups within the CNOP was achieved by guaranteeing its leaders a monopoly over labor representation and their permanence as heads of their respective unions. In contrast to the mobility found within the government, this could lead to decades of the same leadership.[14] Leaders additionally benefited by accumulating personal wealth through membership fees charged by unions and other sources of income, without the intervention of labor authorities. The continuity that existed in the protective social measures implemented by the revolutionary state, together with the economic expansion experienced during the era of "stabilizing development," provided union members with a sense of security that allowed union leaders to retain their positions without any questioning from the grassroots.

In summary, the executive power in Mexico controlled all mechanisms for the redistribution of resources and the political futures of party members, which created a dependable system of subordination of relevant actors. The personal interests of all involved were better served by abiding by presidential decisions and by a show of loyalty. The relationship between the president and party members consequently had clientelistic qualities as described previously, with the president sitting at the top of the political pyramid. During six years the president was the ultimate patron of the Mexican political system.

Despite the many formal restrictions on presidential power, the PRI presidents enjoyed informal powers that far exceeded their formal rights. Carpizo has called these "meta-constitutional" presidential powers (1978), which elevated the president to the position of (1) "grand voter," since he could intervene in the nomination of candidates to almost every position of electoral choice, including the presidential candidate, the members of the official party leadership, and, through his control over Congress, the members of the judiciary; and (2) "grand legislator," since he could count on the ratification, practically without modifications, of as many laws as he wished to propose, regardless if they changed conventional or constitutional laws, because Congress was subordinate and the judiciary was loyal to the president. The origin of this inordinate power came precisely from the fact that the president was the ultimate patron of the Mexican political pyramid.

Presidential Succession and Stability

The fact that political power was so concentrated in the president's hands led to another problem. Sartori states that authoritarian regimes, in which power is concentrated in the hands of an individual or a select group, present a "constitutional incapacity to submit themselves in a disciplined fashion to norms that regulate the succession of power" (Sartori 1999a, 91). It follows that rules regulating succession are not seen as binding by those aspiring to occupy the highest position of government, which places the regime in crisis each time there is a death or political weakness that requires a change. Successions without clear rules contain the danger of rupture: political adversaries in their battle over power can utilize any means to achieve their ends, and political losers may be excluded from ever again holding political positions with their concomitant benefits, since these are likely to be monopolized by the president and his/her inner circle. Situations like these make battles of succession into battles of life or death.

In Mexico, the structural problems faced by authoritarian regimes were not suppressed, but rather institutionalized and ritualized. The unwavering commitment to the constitutional prohibition for presidential reelection, within the context of a non-competitive regime and a clientelistic political culture, led to the creation of a series of informal rules (outstanding among which was the presidential designation of the PRI candidate, his de facto successor) that guaranteed the cohesion of political power groups.

The succession that took place every six years created movements in all the positions within the higher echelons of the government bureaucracy (the positions of "trust"). Nominations were made by each leader in favor of his/her action group respectively, which produced a circular, cyclical, and constant movement within the political elites. The certainty that these rules would also be upheld in the future provided professional politicians with reasonable expectations that they would rise within the bureaucratic hierarchy, even though it was not clear when and how these expectations would be met. Groups that had lost their political preeminence, due to their rivalry with or distance from the president, knew that they were not condemned eternally to this situation and that they had to bide their time for just six years for another opportunity for political ascension. In both cases, for future expectations to be realized, it was imperative that these rules of succession were accepted.

On the other hand, there were political exigencies that prevented presidents from relying exclusively on their own party as a base of power, which opened up political spaces to other groups and individuals. Even though every president designated important positions to trusted men and women, he also needed the support from PRI members to negotiate with groups distanced from the party and ensure their support, control important segments of the populations, and manage tasks that required specific technological and/or political skills. These "people of the system" functioned as communications channels between the president and those groups that did not belong to his inner circle or with the party bases. Since they were indispensable, these individuals were responsible for continuity beyond the six-year presidential term. It was generally expected that they would hold intermediary positions, in charge of implementing decisions made at the top.

The people in the president's trust constituted a vertical and horizontal network of subordinates and allies who rose within the bureaucracy together with their patron, made up the team in charge of the presidential campaign, and later held cabinet positions or took on leadership positions within government-owned industries. All of them became potential candidates to take over the presidential throne in the next election.[15]

Between the two groups, personnel could be interchanged. The "people of the system" could try to enter the future president's trust once his candidature was announced. The president often made the effort to convert his people of trust into "people of the system" as his presidential term was winding down.

The president's ability to distribute resources and political power, combined with the constitutional limits of his term, forced members of the dominant coalition to recognize him as the ultimate arbiter of the most important party decisions—such as nominating his successor. Candidates, as stated, were excluded from competing under other political groupings. This generated a nomination mechanism that forced those defeated to accept their loss. In early primary elections or semi-open conventions, groups who were not favored by the president felt they were participating in a game of "loaded dice" and ended up challenging the party from the outside. In such circumstances, the group close to the defeated potential presidential candidates could become subject to political ousting and/or persecution and even assassination. The designation of the presidential successor by the president was a clear rule, which guaranteed party unity and kept future expectations for political positioning alive among the losers. As stated by Weldon (1997, 252), the so-called *dedazo* (pointing out) was a key element in the party's submission to presidential power rather than a consequence thereof.

Since it was impossible for the president to extend his mandate beyond the six-year term, a balance was created between his ability to distribute resources and those within the party who had not been given a prominent governmental position. Any president who would have tried to perpetuate his power, and thus form a more personal dictatorship, would have annulled the future expectations of PRI members, and they would have withdrawn their obedience. The no-reelection clause is fundamental in understanding the stability of the Mexican political system in existence during PRI hegemony. The continuous circulation among political elites and the concomitant result that their expectations of future promotions within the system were kept alive, as well as the rule of no reelection, explain the temporary subordination of the party to the president and his decisions, even when some groups were opposed to him for a given period of time. Thanks to the no-reelection clause, PRI members had good reason to maintain their internal discipline and with that their internal unity.[16]

Succession problems during the hegemonic party system were solved according to two rules: (1) the periodic rotation of groups within government, which was guaranteed by the no-reelection clause for the presidency; and (2) the president's supreme power in determining who would be the presidential successor. The first rule served the interests of the Mexican political class, providing those groups outside of the presidential inner circle with future expectations of political promotion. The second rule prevented the open competition between factions for support from the electorate, powerful groups, and/or the military.

In this understanding between the president and the party, a relationship was established that guaranteed the continuity of the power structure, the party bureaucracy, and its revolutionary ideological components. Under its hegemonic umbrella, it unified a variety of groups and programs that did not compete against each another in elections.

Each presidency brought with it a change in personnel, styles, and government programs. During each administration, the PRI informally renounced its constitutional powers and control over its organizations to support the president's decisions. The president was accepted by the PRI as the ultimate arbiter in any internal battles and as the conciliator of heterogeneous interests contained within the party (Adler-Lomnitz and Gorbach 1998, 64–65).

The pact between the PRI and the president was highly clientelist in nature, since it institutionalized specific relationships of loyalty and subordination and led to the creation of an ultimate patron—the president of the republic. The quasi-monopoly of the PRI over representative spaces and over unionized organizations reduced the incentive for party members to be accountable for their actions vis-à-vis the electorate. On the contrary, all actors directed their behavior toward the person who had control over their careers and political futures. Citizens could not threaten to vote for other political groups should their demands and necessities not be met with satisfaction. In a context in which the political parties did not compete among each other for a majority of the citizens' votes, these parties end up competing against each other for favors from caciques, municipal presidents, or union leaders expressed in resources, employment, and public services proffered in return for political loyalty. As a result, all the members of the political pyramid directed their efforts from the bottom up, until they reached the president, who was not accountable toward anyone and who distributed resources as a function of subordinates' loyalty and their ability to control others.

The terms of the pact between the president and the party were revisited according to the political relational realities of Mexico over decades. Since the pact was based on an informal and implicit agreement without any legal sanction, it was always very important that each president honor the appropriate formalities: that he would not bypass Congress; that he would not personally announce the presidential candidate publicly; that state governors were allowed to claim that they were resigning for "personal" or "health" reasons. All of these acts were meant to ratify presidential wishes. However, a president who, for example, promulgated a law that had not previously been approved by the two congressional chambers was seen as disrespectful of the legislature and as disavowing one of the spaces of power reserved for the party. The party would clarify that its support and subordination was not for free, but rather implicit and based on certain conditions. This explains the high degree of formality that existed between the legislative and executive branches and the need for decisions that were based on mutual consent (even if nobody would dare challenge them), even if these were always approved by those entities assigned to do so by the constitution. This also explains why no PRI president, although they generally modified constitutional laws at their pleasure, ever changed the norms that governed the relations between the executive and the legislative powers in his favor—quite the contrary (Casar 1999).

It is thus shown that the respect for the formalities involved in democratic obligations was not a result of a response to horizontal structures of accountability, since such obligations suppose that these agencies operate independently and that they are willing to defend their autonomy (O'Donnell 1998). The president was not controlled in the constitutional sense of the word. Therefore, respect for rules (constitutional or party related) was a sign by the president that he would not extend his presidential term beyond the constitutional limit and that he recognized the party's capacity to impede such a move if there were any suggestion of it.

Over time, the treatment of the president involved extremely complex rules and codes and became a cultural manifestation of a factual phenomenon: for six years, the distribution of political and economic resources depended on his will. All actors knew that without presidential favor they had no prospects of realizing personal goals. The president allowed their careers to advance, either by direct promotion, or indirectly by not hindering the natural evolution of their political activities.

In a direct manner, the president rewarded loyal politicians with whom he dealt personally by mechanisms that were reproduced successively down the political pyramid, thus strengthening his own power. The reverential, fearful, and almost religious treatment the president received (at any rate the treatment that went beyond what the officeholder's position justified) stemmed from this reality. The immense inequality between those resources controlled by the president compared to those controlled by political actors who theoretically were on equal footing (such as the legislature and the judiciary) created a submissiveness that is characteristic of patron-client relationships.

In his role as the patron of the clientelistic structure, the president was responsible for the smooth functioning of the mechanisms that guaranteed that the interests of the party members were served, including honoring the no-reelection clause. He also had moral responsibilities toward his party—he owed the party loyalty and protection. This means that the president encountered limitations (diffuse in nature, if one wants to look at them in this way) to his rights as a patron vis-à-vis his clients—in this case, a network that went beyond his personal followers. The president had to take the role, the power, and the place of the party and its most important leaders into consideration. He had to avoid offending them by treating them as mere instruments, and he especially had to avoid acts that would force them to go against his interests.[17] This is the origin of the Mexican political system's dedication to "upholding formalities" and "respecting equilibriums." Violations to formalities implied deep, ongoing ruptures, disagreements, or the loss of power—at least that's how they were interpreted.

The Role of Campaigns in Non-competitive Elections

Apart from the no-reelection clause, the Mexican political system had another element in place that is a requirement for democracies: the party and its candidate would hold electoral campaigns throughout the country. This was implemented rigorously even in the 1975–1976 period, when no candidate from any opposition party ran against the PRI nominee.[18] Since the founding of the PNR in 1929 up until 1988, presidential campaigns launched by the revolutionary party were not in general terms campaigns as understood in established democracies. They did not represent the portion of an electoral process in which candidates from different parties participate in activities that are explicitly meant to convince the population to vote for them by diffusing their proposed government programs. In Mexico, the winner of the elections was known even before elections took place, and therefore, the candidate from the official party did not have to compete against others for the citizens' preference. The purpose of campaigns was not to gain votes.[19]

Consequently, a presidential campaign was classified by some independent press, academics, and intellectuals as a "ritual." The argument is only partially correct, since rituals are known to have no content. The campaign did serve to prepare all political actors for the changes that the arrival of a new group to power represented. It did so by utilizing symbolic mechanisms that were specific to the Mexican political culture and that ensured the continuity of rules and essential agreements. The inevitable crisis faced every six years by the Mexican political system was resolved without violence or ruptures since the shift in leadership was controlled through the campaign ritual.

Everything that was at stake throughout the campaign has been expressed in the following manner:

> The presidential succession has to be understood as an especially dangerous time for the system: it is a phase in which, firstly, the power of the outgoing president is at its peak (in his designation of a successor); then it is a period of a relative power vacuum, since the designation of a successor marks the decline of power for the outgoing president when the elected successor is not yet fully in control (a politically risky situation); additionally, the succession process creates a need to renegotiate positions within the PRI and the government, a process that needs to be successful to guarantee the continuity of the system. Lastly, succession processes within the PRI create risk, since . . . the internal decision of the party . . . can lead to the fragmentation of the party. (Adler-Lomnitz, Lomnitz, and Adler 1993, 230)

Under these circumstances, campaigns were

> a series of events that were highly ritualized and that represented a drama of power in the Mexican political system: campaign activities are a place where the drama of the president and the presidential power are expressed; the conflicts and alliances that upheld the old (and that will uphold the new) regime become manifest; the technical and mythical postures of the national political system are expressed

(the internal organization of the party, the government, the representation of these organizations and its myths); the new presidential persona is created; the forces that "move the country" are put into evidence. (Ibid.)

The presidential campaign followed a format by which power relations were reconstructed. This was the centerpiece of a process divided into regulated and limited phases that functioned within a precise framework of rules and specified times. It gave the political class an organized transition toward a change in government. The campaign represented a rite of passage in which political groups adjusted and adapted themselves to the new circumstances. The ritual represented an integrating process and repositioned relations of subordination and dominance between diverse groups united by personal, clientelistic, and hierarchical ties. During the campaign, the "revolutionary family" overcame internal divisions to join forces and finally regroup as a unified front in its pact with society (Adler-Lomnitz and Gorbach 1998, 62–63). The campaign was an instrument to reconstruct internal unity among the coalition in power, reaffirming the terms that provided the system with stability.

Several analysts and scholars have portrayed the elections during PRI hegemony as a device to legitimate the one-party rule (see Cornelius 1975, 79; Badie and Hermet 1993, 249; Centeno 1997, 33). Hermet (1982, 44) generalizes this legitimizing function to elections in all authoritarian regimes. If elections had this quality, then the electoral campaign should have been instrumental to the legitimation of the PRI regime.

The legitimacy approach exhibits problems of theoretical order, as well as inconsistency with the observed behavior of the actors involved in the succession process. First, if elections perform a legitimizing function anywhere, it is in democratic regimes. Thus, this approach is of little help when characterizing different types of political regimes.

More important, from a Weberian perspective, legitimacy is "the acceptance of the validity of an order of rules" (Lassman 2000, 87). If elections were a reason to accept the PRI rules' validity, we should expect the main actors involved in the campaign to erroneously believe that the office was at stake in elections. But if people were to hold that belief, we should observe them concerned about the election results, instead of making efforts to preserve their power when only one candidate takes office. In the following chapters, we show that the latter, not the former, was what occurred in the 1987–1988 succession process.

Moreover, the assumption of millions of people sharing a false belief is not only implausible but also inconsistent with facts. Thus, as an example, Cornelius himself presents survey data showing that "many Mexicans are not moved to vote by any belief that their action will somehow affect what the regime does, much less who will rule" (1975, 79).

The legitimacy approach, at least implicitly, does not take campaign events as problematic. They are just part of a big mockery aimed at disguising the regime as a democratic one. Instead, our approach takes the electoral campaign as a mechanism that reconstructs presidential power in times of change and uncertainty. Thus, while the legitimizing campaign is only a piece of information, the ritualized campaign is a fundamental piece in the political system's stability.

The sources of legitimacy of PRI rule are better conceived of as related to the substantive goals imputed to the state by the revolutionary ideology (Loza 2008) as well as to the nature of the patron-client relations explained in chapter 1. If clientelistic relations and ideology, not elections, are the sources of legitimacy, then the most important facts occur before Election Day and after the nomination. The political ritual approach focuses our attention on the facts occurring in that period.

Before entering into the succession process of 1987–1988, it is important to summarize the characteristics of the political context within which the process took place. The behavior of the political class during the succession process can be explained with three certainties that the members shared: (1) the PRI would gain access to the presidency of the republic and control over those entities that were constitutionally meant to limit presidential power (Congress, the Supreme Court, and the state governments); (2) the president would choose his successor from within his cabinet; and (3) the successor had ample freedom to incorporate his personal network of followers into his cabinet and practically into the entire apparatus of public administration, as well as to make crucial public policy decisions with the support of the constitutionally established branches of government. These rules, although of an informal nature, represented basic guidelines which politicians had to honor when calculating their future political options.

Formal rules prescribed by the constitution and other regulations created a series of institutions that in democratic regimes lead to electoral competition and place limits on political power. By following every minute detail of these rules, the Mexican politicians behaved as if they were functioning within a representative democracy; but at the same time, the norms that they took for granted (such as the electoral victory of the PRI) do not correspond to the characteristics of this type of government. This means that real politics took place within the informal terrain and beyond formal regulations. In this terrain, political struggles for resources and power were transferred from an inter-party electoral battle to an informal intra-party one. The most important political resource for everyone involved was the positioning of each person within the pyramid of political networks. Of particular importance was their degree of closeness to other important political actors within the same network and the size of the trusted following one could rely on. The intra-party battles were not legally regulated nor were they openly manifested, and party members always had to ensure that they took place within a framework that gave the appearance of internal unity. Therefore, they were expressed in an indirect manner by means of public announcements (events, constitutional proceedings, news, and newspaper inserts) that had to be interpreted by both the participants and observers. Over time, the Mexican political system as it moved between the formal rules of a democracy and the informal codes of authoritarianism developed a ritualized dynamic: the underlying significance of public events was immersed in interpretational codes largely shared by the political class and resulting in repetitive behaviors over time. This was particularly true for the process of succession, as demonstrated by the Mexican political system's ability to reproduce without interruption the rule of no reelection that generated a repetitive cyclical ritual (every six years) with known conditions that could be transmitted as "teachings from the past."

The written rules, although they lost their characteristic as processes that regulated decision making, did inform (by means of interpretation) the several relevant actors about the timeframe within which certain decisions had to be made; the manner by which certain pacts retained their validity and others were broken; in what way changes in the structure of opportunities could be taken advantage of to promote one's own political careers; and which path had to be followed so that these would be successful. In table 2.1, formal and informal rules of Mexico's political system are depicted. The first two dimensions—political regime and government type—are a part of this chapter's discussion, while the other dimensions will be clarified later.

During the succession process, the political class participated in a confrontation for an enormous prize: a presidency with inordinate decision-making power supported by a subordinate party. However,

Table 2.1   The relationship between formal and informal rules within the Mexican political system

Dimension	Formal rule	Informal rules
Political regime	Multiparty democracy	Pseudo-democracy (hegemonic party system)
Government type	Presidentialism: presidential rule constrained by separation of powers	Hyper-presidentialism: presidential control over other branches of government through control over the party
Competition for power	Inter-party; during campaign	Intra-party; between cabinet members; before the campaign; in ambiguous and indirect manner
Candidate nomination	Nomination of a pre-candidate by each sector; voting by delegates from the territorial structure	By the president, amongst his circle of trust; single pre-candidate
Campaign's functions	Obtaining a plurality of votes	Reconstructing internal unity; building a presidential image for the PRI's candidate; showing the party's and its leaders' strength to both the future president and society

this subordination should not be understood as a submission. The party controlled the instruments that forced the president to never act against the permanent interests of the organization and its internal power groups. Party expectations were that the presidency would be cloaked in the PRI. The presidency would ensure that members occupied public offices; resources (financial but also those used as an instrument of influence) flowed; clientelistic relationships and the power of leaders were fed; and, finally, he retired according to the timeframe established constitutionally. This in turn created a dynamic of elite circulation that guaranteed that those who were not favored would endure only relative losses, since these mechanisms planted the idea of future expectations firmly within all members of the party.

This relationship between the president and the party was always at risk every time the ritualistic cycle of presidential succession took place.

PART II

THE SUCCESSION PROCESS AND THE *DESTAPE*

The presidential succession during the hegemonic party's reign was bound to the schedule established by formal rules (the constitution and the statutes of the PRI). As has already been mentioned, the president had the informal obligation to name his successor. As a result, the successor was always chosen from within the president's inner circle, which by definition meant that he would be chosen from one of the people holding a cabinet position. From the first day of the new *sexenio* (six-year presidential term), all cabinet secretaries were considered *presidenciables* (presidential material), with a chance of becoming the next head of state. They would compete against each other to be in good standing with the "grand voter," forging alliances and breaking these according to their perception of their own possibilities and those of their competitors. This battle was based on informal, but very strict, rules, the most important of which was to remain "hidden" without mobilizing support openly or appealing to the public. The best way of annihilating one's own chances was to become too obvious about one's presidential aspirations. But it was also not possible to simply sit by and await a favorable decision.

As the official period for nominations approached, the competition became fiercer and the political networks became highly divided, until the party announced the name of the candidate. Note that at the beginning of the presidential period the cabinet formed a unified network that became ever more divided into separate ones. Over time, the cabinet secretaries created their own support groups—both professional, to fulfill specific functions, and political—to compete against other networks for the nomination.

This chapter focuses on the various phases of the presidential succession process. First, the general framework in which these phases took place over various six-year terms is discussed. Then, the particularities of the 1987–1988 succession process as related to these phases are analyzed. As stated, the 1987–1988 process represents the last one that operated according to the mechanisms of the hegemonic party system, and the first to actually have some electoral competition. The political class continued to behave as their experience and customs had taught them, following the cultural norms that had been valid for decades. However, and without contemplating the electoral cataclysm that this process represented, there were at least two events that diverged from traditional behaviors: (1) the formation of a splinter group out of the party that rejected the rules of succession and disputed the PRI's claim as heir to the revolutionary ideology; and (2) the public acceptance by the party of six cabinet members who competed against each other for the nomination, which largely came as a response to internal questioning from within the party.

3
The Structure of Presidential Succession in Mexico

The ritual of succession involved the fragmentation and then the reestablishment of unity within the party. The critical moment in the process, which clearly separated the "before" from the "after," occurred when the Institutional Revolutionary Party (Partido Revolucionario Institucional–PRI) selected its candidate to the presidency. The political dynamics were very different before and after this moment. While at first an atmosphere of competition prevailed, including rumors and uncertainties, in the second phase the future president was dedicated to reestablishing unity under his auspices and to offering guarantees of his commitment to the party's interests.

Phases of Presidential Succession

We divide the ritual of presidential succession into seven phases, which will be described in the general terms that tradition had assigned to them.

Prior to the *Destape*

This phase started approximately two years before the president would designate his successor, and it was understood that the competition for the nomination began after the fourth presidential state of the union address (*informe de gobierno del presidente*) was presented to Congress. Much has been written about Mexico's presidential succession process, and since its realities were only partially visible to the public eye, opinions about the process varied. There were generally two different interpretations related to the mechanisms by which a successor was chosen: on the one hand, there were those who argued that the president was omnipotent when it came to the final decision, and on the other hand, there were those who believed that his power was limited and that the designation came after intricate negotiations with different political and social forces. It was also argued that apart from loyalty, personal preferences, and considerations of ideological compatibility, the president had to bend to external pressures, power struggles from within the party, social conflicts, and the circumstantial needs of the country. Because of a dearth of public information with regard to the process, observers and participants felt justified in basing their assertions on heresy, suppositions, and rumors.

Over time, it became clear that those who made an argument for the president's omnipotence were right. The president designated his successor, but he did take into account his favorite's abilities in constructing some consensus among key political actors and groups represented in the national political arena. In his research, Castañeda (1998) refers to four former presidents who reaffirm the above, leaving no room for doubt.

This whole phase was marked by uncertainties about the identity of the PRI's presidential candidate and that candidate's circle of trust, which incorporated the people who would occupy the highest government positions. It was also unclear which people of the system the successor would find useful. Once the president designated a candidate, it was an absolute certainty that this candidate would be the next presidential successor, which meant that the political future of a large portion of the political class depended on this decision and that the whole administrative apparatus would go through a cascade of adjustments. As such, the nomination produced concrete winners and losers.

Custom had it that all those initially aspiring to become the next president were cabinet secretaries who were in no way limited by the constitution to run for the highest office. Eventually, a member of the party or of the cabinet would informally announce a more reduced list of candidates composed of four to seven names.[1] With the public airing of these names in the press, presidents tried to show the strengths and levels of acceptance of these candidates (Garrido 1987, 89). Of these, at the most only three or four pre-candidates were actually being considered. A source quoted in Castañeda (1998, 387–88) states that President Ruiz Cortines is supposed to have said the following:

> The president can neither have more than three candidates nor less than three. If there are two, and he is more favorable towards one than the other from the start, the pack-like attacks against him destroy him and he arrives at the presidency scarred. Furthermore, if the predestined candidate takes ill or is confronted by scandal, another one has to be supported, and he would then be seen as a second choice and

not as if he got to that point based on his own merits, and people will think that the president made a mistake. But there are never more than three: all others are just filler to dilute attacks among several people.

Even though candidates could be perceived as having certain ideological preferences or as being closer to one group or another, all true candidates shared a series of characteristics that could make them equally acceptable for the presidency: they were identified with the policies of the president; they were equally capable of forging alliances; and they were not likely to be substantially vetoed by the real power groups—Fidel Velázquez (leader of the Confederation of Mexican Workers), business leaders, the Catholic Church, and the United States (Castañeda 1998, 386–87).

The great danger that existed during this phase was in the degree to which different candidates together with the groups they controlled would be willing to take their battles to the level of rupture. Unlike what happens according to the formal rules of democracy, the competition never took place during campaigns, between candidates from different political parties, or for a majority of votes by the electorate. Instead, the battle took place prior to the official nomination, between cabinet members of the PRI and for presidential favor. The potential candidates and their respective groups fought among themselves for the nomination. Simultaneously, groups that were further removed from the presidential battle started to speculate which group would have more of a chance when the time came and tried to seek favorable alliances based on these speculations. The indirect nature of the competition for power affected aspects of social life without there being an explicit relationship. For example, a government functionary whom we interviewed pointed out that there was a correlation between the frequency of strikes and succession phases. Table 3.1 illustrates the number of strikes that took place between 1970 and 1989.

It can be seen that there is a greater tendency for strikes around electoral periods (1976, 1982, 1988). The data presented by González Casanova (1976, 233–34) for the period of 1920–1963 shows that the same pattern existed since the 1952 electoral process.[2] As with the press, the mobilization of unions was a controllable factor not only because of corporatism but also because strikes under Mexican law had to be declared legal by labor authorities. Therefore, each case was seen as a sign that

Table 3.1   Legal strikes in Mexico, 1970–1989

Year	Strikes	Year	Strikes
1970	4	1980	40
1971	20	1981	36
1972	48	1982	64
1973	60	1983	12
1974	64	1984	4
1975	94	1985	12
1976	100	1986	4
1977	92	1987	84
1978	44	1988	98
1979	48	1989	69

Source: de la Garza Toledo 1996, 425

"someone" was trying to send and never as a tactic used by workers to improve on their conditions.

It was the president's responsibility to keep the ruptures that arose between factions fighting for his favors within controllable limits. The potential for disintegration during this period was neutralized by party discipline. All activities that took place before the PRI's pre-candidate was officially announced were in essence meant to keep the political class calm and to submit them to party discipline. It was the only way in which the president could prevent the early decline of his political power and continue to control the traditional venues of the process. Because of discipline, nobody lost patience and nobody became violent; after all, the important thing was to demonstrate that everyone belonged to a united, peaceful, and revolutionary family.

Discipline was measured in terms of compliance with the political calendar, because obedience to the official schedule was a precondition for negotiations among power groups. In other words, if discipline was the unifying principle underlying the entire ceremony that allowed the political calendar to be met, the schedule, in turn, represented the mechanism that legitimized presidential authority to choose a successor. The real and the formal activities, both hidden and public, became articulated around a temporal sequence of phases. Once these were obeyed, everyone involved became convinced that the president retained his power and that unity and harmony among all PRI groups prevailed. In other words, phases defined in terms of key dates, like rest areas between floors of a long staircase, impelled those mechanisms that guaranteed party support vis-à-vis the new candidate and his team.

Exact timing was also crucial from the president's perspective. He would attempt to delay his decision as much as possible, since any early moves meant that he would start to lose power before it was necessary and even before it was desirable; but a prolonged delay gave any pre-candidates time, as a result of impatience, to be tempted into accumulating support and forcing a favorable decision toward one or the other (a *madruguete*). The nomination had to be carefully timed to avoid either one of these extreme scenarios, with presidents delaying the decision for as long as political pressures permitted. As one person interviewed stated, "It is easy to understand that this was the case and that the *destape* always took place when one least expected it. Otherwise, who would curb the *gallera* (cockfight)?" Honoring political times can also vaguely be defined as a show of loyalty for the president. Only if the political times and rules established by the top leadership of the PRI were obeyed was it possible to convince external groups that unity prevailed among everyone represented in the PRI. In this sense, a lack of discipline meant that the party had to acknowledge differences within it and that the stable, united, and strong party was becoming fragmented: "In my party there is discipline and order. There may be some different points of view, but these always are within the demarcations and the times established by the CEN [Comité Ejecutivo Nacional; National Executive Committee] of the PRI."[3]

The president of the CEN of the PRI defined the calendar and established a communications link between the party and the president that guided and contained the succession process. The president of CEN created the reference points: "One will act without any haste or pressure; one will continue to act with respect for the statutes and the times agreed upon by the highest organ of the party's decision-making body" (*Excélsior*, Sept. 23, 1987).

Among others, party discipline was upheld by continuously and explicitly reminding people that they had to obey the timelines set for the succession process. A series of implicit rules delineated what could and could not be said, who could say what, and, above all else, in which moment certain public announcements or proclamations could be made. For example, after declarations had been made by the upper echelons of the PRI hierarchy, others followed as if in response. These came from minor politicians as if everyone within this ritual of time and discipline played a specific role. In 1975, Jesús Reyes Heroles, secretary of the interior at the time, asked for patience: "We reiterate: neither before nor after, only at the right moment; neither will the impatient ones force us to make haste, nor will those inclined to mobility force us into delays. Everything in due time, colleagues."

If those aspiring to the presidency felt that it was in their own interest to uphold discipline, discipline was strengthened. For this to work, it was equally important that all potential candidates thought that they at least had a chance of becoming the chosen nominee, as well as for none of them to believe that they were most definitely going to be the winner of the internal competition for the nomination. This was the only way to prevent the formation of groups and attacks at too early a stage. The president made sure that he sent non-verbal contradictory signals to all of them that could be interpreted in one way or another. The president used ambiguity to keep all actors at a level of uncertainty that would guarantee him subordination and the general stability of the system.[4]

The president had to be conscious of the implications of all of his gestures and words and be able to control them, since they were all seen as signs. When Miguel de la Madrid finally named his candidate, he stated (2004, 737): "With the official announcement, a very trying emotional time ended for me. Towards the end, everything became very difficult. The relationships between the pre-candidates among themselves and towards me changed; the smallest gesture on my part was interpreted as if it were a sign, which frequently had an impact on the potential candidate's emotional well-being."

If a president was overly friendly with a favored pre-candidate, that person would become the center of attacks, which in turn would put his candidacy at risk; if all of a candidate's hopes were dashed, he would stop investing energy in forging internal alliances and take those government actions that could in the end make him a viable candidate. Castañeda (1998, 562) summarizes this part of the process: "The great disadvantage of a hasty succession is its undeniable ability to delude . . . it is important that various people participate in the competition. They, in turn, have to be convinced and encouraged in their abilities and endurance to continue in the race. The only way to achieve this is with support from the president, the implicit codes and explicit messages, all of which are meant to persuade each interested party of his permanence as a candidate. By definition, the vast majority of signals are false, but the recipient considers them authentic and acts accordingly."

This belief, widespread among potential candidates, was not merely based on illusion, even if those who ended up losing could argue that what they had experienced was an illusion. Each president could have a favorite from the very beginning whom he prepared, protected, and eventually chose to be his successor. However, by using manipulation throughout the six-year term, it was possible for one of the secretaries to convince the president that he was the only option and try to influence the president's decision accordingly. As Castañeda argues (1998, 386), this is how López Mateos, Luis Echeverría, and Miguel de la Madrid ascended to the presidency. On the other hand, since the president never acknowledged the list of potential candidates publicly, the level of uncertainty was heightened as potential candidates were neither certain that their own names were included in the list of favorites nor certain of the identity of their opponents.

Since the possibility existed that any of the potential candidates could be the chosen one, it was of utmost importance for each one to honor two informal rules. Both were upheld by the president, who was the only person who could sanction disobedience by eliminating the wrongdoer from the presidential list (the perpetrator would be *quemado* [burnt]). The two rules consisted of remaining loyal to the president (all were competing for his favors) and never making presidential aspirations known explicitly and publicly (which would create disunity). These rules applied not only to the potential presidential candidates but also to politicians of lower rank. Even if these politicians had made probability calculations for each candidate, it behooved them never to show any open support for any one of them, so that if they had miscalculated, they would not face later difficulties in making statements of support that showed their acceptance and unity. As long as these limitations were not bypassed, competitors could make every effort to demonstrate their ability to control social groups, make appropriate decisions, show that they were people capable of governing in the future publicly, and bring to light the deficiencies of their opponents.[5]

Ambiguity is a prerogative reserved for the most powerful person in his/her treatment of subordinates. While explicit statements lead to commitments, ambiguity leaves room for interpretation, and every ambiguous gesture and word can be denied. Loyalty and open support are two requisites for subordinates to remain within the political game. In contrast, to maintain his power, the president has to keep his subordinates' ambitions and certainty alive without making definite commitments.

This results in a highly unequal relationship, in which people became submissive to the president by having reasonable expectations of obtaining power-based benefits. But, the president always reserved the right to renege on these expectations.

The Destape

Once the actual candidate had been announced, the uncertainty of the previous phase was finally over and a process of ascension to power, not only of the nominee but also of his entire vertical and horizontal networks of subordinates and allies (the men and women in his trust), began. They were expected to hold the decision-making positions in his campaign team and to later take over the most important cabinet offices. Eventually, they would become frontrunners as potential future presidential candidates in the next succession cycle. After the destape, the positions that the different members and groups of the political class would occupy for the next six-year period would become known: finally it was understood who would be the new president's closest collaborators, which groups and politicians would definitely remain on the outside of political power, with whom positions would have to be negotiated, etc.

Ironically, and in the style of a Greek tragedy, once a president was at the height of his power, he had to make the decision that would mark the decline of his authority. The selection of the PRI's candidate led to a dual leadership within the country, with both the presidential candidate and the president sharing functions and decisions and even getting into conflicts, which could lead to a public rupture between the candidate and his mentor (Garrido 1987, 102–3). The official takeover of power took place approximately one year after the candidate had been announced, with the newly elected president initiating his term before Congress. Thus, the transference of power took place gradually, making this whole period one of marginal activities. On the one hand, the risk existed that any political crisis could have drastic consequences, since neither the president nor the candidate had the tools at their disposal to resolve them. On the other hand, it offered the overall political class a period of transition toward the new power relationship in an orderly and slow fashion. Thanks to this, the new president had already resolved a large portion of the problems associated with his ascension upon assuming power.

The way in which the destape took place varied somewhat from one election to another. Generally, the system of destape included a minister of a PRI sector announcing his support for one of the candidates. This was followed by other sectors, the unions, different PRI municipalities, etc., joining in with their support. In some instances, the three PRI sectors simultaneously announced their decision in favor of a candidate in a single event. In either scenario, the sectarian and party leaders presented their nomination as if the decision was based on a long process of consultation with the party bases. Once the sectors had communicated the name of the "pre-candidate" to the PRI leadership, he became the official presidential candidate in a party convention.[6]

Formally, this was the venue by which the PRI chose its candidate that functioned as a ratification process of the underlying and real process— a process in which the sitting president was the grand voter. The formal venue was a public process that took place within the domain of the party and reflected a decision that was supposed to have been reached through negotiations and consultations with the party bases and within the bounds of the statutes. The real process took place within the president's domain, and the decision was reached in silence. In a corollary to the process, each venue was accompanied by a speech. Party sectors tried to convince the people and public opinion that the presidential successor was chosen by party members and that the selection was therefore part of a democratic process. On the other hand, the declarations made by the president mirrored an authoritarian system more than a democracy, and they were accompanied by terms such as destape, *dedazo*, *futurismo* (futurism), and madruguete. Between these two venues—the formal and the informal—a special dynamic was created: the formal discourse, the democratic one, seemed to continuously cover up the real process or at least seemed to make every effort to distract the public's attention from it; it was common for the political class to deny that there even existed a predetermined candidate in political practice.

Just as with the calls to honor the official schedule of the process and to uphold party discipline, by its public reaffirmations that its statutes were valid and being upheld, the party in reality functioned as an auxiliary to the president in his enactment of his informal rights.

In interviews with Castañeda (1998), political protagonists confirmed that in the real and private venues the president sustained two key conversations: one with the designated successor to make him understand that he had been chosen by "the party," and one with the party to communicate his final decision. It is interesting that in both instances the president paid homage to the party's role of choosing the candidate, even though he was actually announcing his decision in both cases.

The Nomination

Once the PRI's candidate to the presidency was known publicly, all PRI members made every effort to show their approval of the decision. They also demonstratively showed their subordination and loyalty toward the future president. Here, the politicians' fervor to establish an allegiance and positive relocation vis-à-vis the new pre-candidate started. There were inordinate propagandistic displays of support by different groups toward the pre-candidate. This phase was also marked by a series of democratic rituals: the official vote that converted the pre-candidate into the official candidate, the simulations of spontaneous support expressed by sectors and people who in reality had secretively supported other potential candidates prior to the official destape, etc.

On the other hand, in this period, the pre-candidate forged the team of collaborators who would be closest to him and assigned them key positions for the organization of his campaign. These positions included those that were in reality the responsibility of the party, such as the coordination of the campaign; the leadership of the Institute for Political, Economic and Social Studies (Instituto de Estudios Políticos, Económicos y Sociales–IEPES) and the Ministry of Information and Propaganda; the administration of logistics; and the administrative presidency and the secretarial office of the PRI. In principle, those who received assignments were the "president's people": they would hold the most powerful positions within the following six-year presidential term (that is, if they complied with their campaign responsibilities effectively).

The Campaign

Once the candidacy was official and it had been ratified by the party, the campaign in search of votes formally began. The party's ability to gather a majority of votes did not worry anyone seriously, but this does not mean that the campaign served no purpose. Uncertainty centered around the new candidate, since it was not clear how far he would go in abusing the immense power he now controlled and using it against the party and its internal relationships of power. Any particular candidate and the team he formed had a history, a reputation, preferences vis-à-vis public policies, and a greater or lesser sense of identification with certain social groups and their interests. There was an expectation that the characteristics that were ascribed to the network that now would hold political power would make a personalized imprint on the new government. However, whatever the innovations they implemented, these had to be consistent with the survival of fundamental and historical pacts that were part of the official party in its relationship with the presidency. Therefore, once the candidate was officially announced, uncertainty went from focusing on the presidential nomination to centering on the new balance that would be established between continuity and change. With the announcement of the candidate's identity, assurances had to be issued to the party's permanent structures that the new government coalition would continue to benefit its interests and fulfill its expectations in exchange for its loyalty.

Even though the actual campaign will be covered in the next chapter, it should be mentioned that the campaign process served to resolve these sources of conflict. By honoring the obligation of holding elections (despite the fact that it did not serve as a method of choosing a government), the political system made use of formal processes that transformed the campaign into a rite of passage by which potentially destabilizing moments were replaced by the dramatization of conflicts and their resolution. Even if it was not meant to sway electoral votes, the campaign functioned as a means by which the political system could be reconstructed and stabilized through ritualistic and symbolic mechanisms.[7]

The campaign consisted of the following activities: meetings held in the regional Center of Political, Economic, and Social Studies (Centro de Estudios Políticos, Económicos y Sociales–CEPES) and in the IEPES; activities of party support; dialogues with the sectarian and other party segments at the national level; dialogues with special interest groups (ranchers, regional entrepreneurs, miners, indigenous groups, etc.); televised and radio-transmitted speeches (which were an innovation in the 1988 campaign); and popular celebrations and fiestas. By means of these different activities and events—usually organized around the candidate's tour of Mexican states—a series of agreements were reached between the state and various groups, classes, and regions of the country, which also revitalized the image of the country construed by the PRI.

This phase ended with an enormous event to mark the end of the campaign at the state level in the heart of Mexico City at the Zócalo and with a crusade to promote the vote. The phases that followed are not a part of this book, but will be briefly delineated below.

The Elections

This phase can be considered an additional official ratification of what was obvious to all and can be seen as one more of the "democratic" rituals that took place throughout the campaign. Once the PRI's candidate became the "president-elect" and before assuming his role as the constitutional president, he began to form his government plans and to discreetly organize his team of collaborators, while also beginning to influence policy decisions that were being made by the outgoing president.

The Takeover of Power

The new president officially took power in a ceremony before Congress, which marked the conclusion of a process that had informally begun with the announcement of the PRI's nominee to the presidency and the gradual transition of power from the outgoing president in favor of the newly elected president. However, the informal process was not completely over. The incoming president still had to take over certain spaces of power controlled by his predecessor's inner circle. These included at a minimum the governors who had been elected during the previous presidency even if their terms had not ended. Under normal circumstances, governors tried to show their good intentions toward the incoming president, and once their term was up, they were replaced by governors close to the new president. However, they could always receive a call from the secretary of the interior "inviting" them to submit their resignation. Depending on his own personal power, it was also common for the new president to accept a certain number of "suggestions" by the outgoing president on the people who should be a part of the cabinet or hold some important party or congressional position. Over time, and when the new president gained more power, he would make use of both his formal and informal rights to name people within his trust to these positions. As a result, approximately midway into his term he held control over all the most relevant power interactions.

The Succession Process of 1987–1988

This section focuses on the different phases of the succession process that took place during 1987–1988. From an ethnographic standpoint, its purpose is to talk about the actual events, highlight the specific details that surrounded this succession, and emphasize both the real and the formal venues that were implemented and coupled for this particular process.

In the first place, the events that took place during the selection process of the candidate by the president will be discussed. This refers to the movements that occurred within the political class as the president moved closer to announcing his decision. Afterward, in chronological order, both the real and the formal activities that preceded the most critical moment of the succession process, the destape, will be discussed. This will be followed by an analysis of the party activities that ended in the national party convention at which the presidential designee became the candidate chosen by the party. The purpose is to highlight how a series of events, more or less in tune with the political calendar's established timeframes and the rules of discipline, led the "people of the system" to define leadership positions and negotiate alliances with the president and his people, and how the group about to assume the presidency was consolidated. These activities, apart from establishing order among party members, forged the framework within which the different groups of the political class would eventually follow the party line determined by the president of the republic.

At this point, the members of the political class, in an enormous show of unity, recognized the unlimited power of the president and his capacity to negotiate and resolve conflicts. From the perspective of electoral strategy, the official party assumed the commitment to accept as its own the designation made by the president of the republic. In this sense, it should be noted that the 1987–1988 presidential succession was different from all previous ones. On the eve of the destape, the political class ruptured and a faction (the Democratic Current–la Corriente Democrática) formed a strong internal dissident movement. This group expected that power would continue in the hands of a group of technocrats whose candidates, they believed, would deviate from the doctrines and popular goals of revolutionary nationalism in favor of economic globalization and the neoliberal program known as the "Washington Consensus" (Williamson 1990). Reacting to these beliefs, the Democratic Current questioned the informal method by which the PRI's candidate was nominated and demanded an open and democratic nomination process.

The dissident group was expelled and became an opposition party, but its demands brought about some limited change in the succession ritual. The announcement of six potential candidates—the "six distinguished *priistas*"—insinuated that the PRI's presidential candidate would be nominated in a more transparent process. The purpose was to show that in political questions important qualitative changes had been made and that a wind of change was blowing within the PRI. But in reality, the change was seen as an aberration or as an irregularity. Many members of the political class saw the existence of six potential candidates as a meek response to the circumstantial threats arising over the normal process within the party. Therefore, the highest echelons of the PRI insisted that discipline, order, and the established schedule of events be upheld so that the need for ever greater modifications within the process could be avoided.

Structural Adjustment and Internal Dissidence

The succession process of 1987–1988 was marked by an alteration to prevalent internal political relationships. At the root was the exhaustion of the development model and of the mechanisms used by the groups in power in addressing this issue. The Mexican political system, within its fundamental structure based on pacts, included an economic management policy in which the state played the role of the primordial promoter of capitalist development. The state had implemented a strategy of "import substitution industrialization" (ISI). ISI was meant to satisfy national demand with the domestic production of durable consumer and intermediate manufactured goods, with domestic industries protected from foreign competition through state-governed tariffs and regulations. Initially, this model brought about an annual increase in the gross domestic product (GDP) of 6.5 percent between 1941 and 1981 and an improvement in the quality of life of the workers (Cook, Middlebrook, and Molinar Horcasitas 1996, 54–55). The 1982 economic crisis, a phenomenon that had an impact on several countries in the region, led people to rethink the model of growth and its relationship to the political structure.

Miguel de la Madrid started his presidency (1982–1988) with internal conflicts, severe corruption problems, empty national coffers, an angry private sector that was upset at the nationalization of the banks as one of his predecessor José López Portillo's last acts of government (1976–1982), and the state's inability to finance economic growth. To deal with the situation, especially after the fall of oil prices in 1985–1986, he implemented policies to reduce the public deficit and to open Mexico up commercially by progressively eliminating tariffs and other import regulations, privatizing government-owned enterprises, and deregulating economic activities (Heredia 1997b, 154–56). Between 1983 and 1988, total government expenditures decreased by 6.8 percent, with the exception of a 29.9 percent increase in debt-servicing payments, while social expenditures were reduced by 33.1 percent (Serrano 1998, 28n). A state that had traditionally controlled development and rewarded popular support with social benefits was being replaced by a state determined to reduce the government apparatus, support private initiatives, open up markets to foreign investments, and renegotiate the external debt.

All these measures reduced the benefits that the party—and state-based union bureaucracies—enjoyed and dried up the sources used to feed clientelistic ties. All of this took place within a context of decreasing salaries and standards of living, which in turn increased the demands made on the government by popular groups (Dresser 1996, 216–18). Decreases in public expenditures restricted the redistribution of wealth and the leadership's economic management abilities, consequently leading to a reduction in its power. Simultaneously, the drive to privatize meant that the number of employment opportunities available to politicians who had "lost" in the electoral process became very limited: "The sale, liquidation or disappearance of . . . state-owned entities left certain groups of PRI members without a piece of the political pie . . . when they did not find a place within central government or in Congress, they would occupy leadership positions with a bank, an airline, a television station, a mine, or a hotel chain. It seemed that only the economy was being trimmed by the privatization of the public sector, but at heart, the political elite was also being placed on a diet" (Delgado 2003, 12A).

The decreased flow of resources attacked the privileges of the party and its capacity to function vis-à-vis its party bases. Another aspect of the new economic policy was that it also went against the prospects of upward political mobility within the political elite. De la Madrid understood that his adjustment program required his insulation from the "rentier" pressures expressed by the groups that represented popular sectors. As a result, he formed a homogenous and cohesive team that shared his diagnosis of and approach to remedy the economic crisis.

Of the fourteen members of his cabinet, eleven were technocrats (Dresser 1996, 222–24). They had been recruited primarily from government agencies in charge of economic policies: the Ministry of Programming and Budgeting, the Internal Revenue Service (Hacienda), and the Bank of Mexico (Haber 1996, 343).

The profile of those representing the government's team was somewhat different from the one associated with more traditional politicians. "The Mexican technocrats are leaders with university degrees, with economic majors, studies abroad, an understanding of the United States's economic model, a career in the executive branch, and in general with professional experience limited to organizations dealing with economic matters" (Camp 1996, 294). In comparison to the traditional politician, technocrats had little experience with party politics since most had never held elected positions. "What these characteristics mean is that the technocrat-politician, even though highly qualified, does not have the same political negotiating skills as his/her colleagues who have followed a different path, and as a result of his/her experiences studying abroad could be more susceptible to political and economic strategies implemented in other cultures" (Camp 1995b, 145).[8] By its actions, it became evident that the Mexican technocracy did not have to be indoctrinated or pressured from governments or international financial organizations to embrace or impel changes related to the globalization phenomenon with conviction (Babb 1997).[9]

The cohesion and homogeneity of the elite in power generated concerns related to the possibility that its economic program would extend beyond the six-year presidential term. The network of traditional politicians tied together by ideological affinity and their left-of-center tendencies demanded the return of industrial protectionism, the import substitution model, and general education, social labor, health, and housing policies.

The dissident movement began to crystallize around the governor of Michoacán and son of former president Lázaro Cárdenas, Cuauhtémoc Cárdenas. In a speech given in August 1985, he suggested that the country's leadership had chosen an ideological path estranged from its original revolutionary purposes since 1940, leading to financial repercussions within the Ministry of Programming and Budgeting and to a campaign of disregard orchestrated by the secretary of the interior (Camacho Alfaro 1989, 45).[10] The speech contained a flow of ideas consistent with the nationalist revolutionary ideology that was contained in the constitution and represented the "national model" pursued by the ideals of the Mexican Revolution, specifically as related to articles 27, 123, and 3 (Cárdenas 1989, 207–8).

Cárdenas's position was supported by the former president of the PRI and one of the frontrunners on the list of potential presidential candidates in the 1975 elections, Porfirio Muñoz Ledo, as well as by the former general secretary of the PRI and ambassador to Spain at the time, Rodolfo González Guevara. All three had different views on how to reform the PRI; while Cárdenas emphasized the need to recuperate the revolutionary ideals, Muñoz Ledo had spent several years trying to update the PRI's ideology within social-democratic terms (Camacho Alfaro 1989, 44), and González Guevara focused on the benefits that formal participation of different currents would bring to the party's organizational and democratizing process (Garrido 1993).[11]

The existence of the Democratic Current of the PRI became known publicly on September 30, 1986, in Morelia, Michoacán, in front of a large peasant contingent. Members insisted that their actions did not imply disobedience or rebellion and that those promoting the movement's ideals had no intention of "going against the presidential system or the party's ideology." The dissident group considered that the creation of political spaces for popular participation and the implementation of several reforms that would open up internal processes were inevitable, especially in reference to the selection process of presidential candidates.

The Democratic Current arose in response to fears within the PRI that the president would ensure the continuity of his economic program by designating a technocrat as his successor, thus limiting opportunities for political mobility previously guaranteed by the "no-reelection clause." The continuity of the neo-liberal project was associated specifically with a young technocrat, Carlos Salinas de Gortari, who had been responsible for the design of the structural adjustment program implemented by de la Madrid. Known as the National Development Plan (Plan Nacional de Desarrollo), its principal economic policy goals were to decrease state expenditures, control public spending, modernize state-owned enterprises, and open up commercial activities (Avramow Gutiérrez 1989, 176).[12]

Those demanding internal democratization were certain that the traditional mechanisms of succession would favor the technocratic network. According to a PRI politician interviewed by Denise Dresser (1996, 225): "A group of marginalized politicians see the arrival of one of the candidates to a position of power . . . as an extension of their own marginalization for another six or even twelve years. The Democratic Current arises to impede the candidacy of Salinas. De la Madrid did not know the party. He did not realize how much discontent existed."

Another high-ranking politician confirmed the above in another interview. According to him, both Muñoz Ledo and Cárdenas had an understanding with the other pre-candidates. He said that the strategy was not to gain access to the presidency—this possibility was too remote—but that his intention was to put a candidate in the elections who could ensure that the group and its people would retain a position within the system. Initially, his plan was to launch a candidate who could strengthen the negotiating position of the group even though he would be sacrificed in the end (Garrido 1993, 22–23). The group within this network was transformed into a semi-official faction meant to pressure and influence the presidential succession in an effort to retain political permanence.

However, the discontent was also strongly ideologically motivated. The Democratic Current called for a reversal of those policies it believed responsible for the deterioration of the population's quality of life and saw as deviating from the revolutionary principles of the state. In his speeches of that time and afterward, Cárdenas expressed his desire to return to the Mexico in existence prior to adjustment policies and said that he favored state economic intervention, the defense of medium- and small-sized companies, a moratorium on external debt repayments, and the recuperation of privatized enterprises. His goal was to "renew the historic ideals of the Mexican Revolution and the real compliance with our constitution" (Dresser 1996, 226).

From its very first public statements onward, the Democratic Current combined its demand for a more open process of selecting presidential candidates with a nationalist critique of neo-liberal economic policies. In its first working document (September 30, 1986), its programmatic goals were expressed as "reaffirming national sovereignty vis-à-vis foreign intervention, correcting deviance, and blocking the path to those with attitudes of subjugation and defeat"; strengthening "the nationalist and popular orientation of our development"; and revitalizing the PRI "by means of a more direct and permanent participation of the bases in those decisions that have an impact on them, particularly with regard to the selection of candidates for positions of popular election at all levels" (Corriente Democrática 1989a, 211). On the last point, the dissident group felt that the informal rules posed a major obstacle to their demands. They claimed that political practices and political culture were primarily responsible for the fact that official party processes could not be implemented in a competitive fashion: "Our party should open up pre-electoral processes sufficiently in advance so that preferences can be expressed; personalities and programs discussed; candidates registered; and so that internal processes of selection can follow the rules established in the statutes" (Corriente Democrática 1989a, 214). Throughout the fourteen months that its confrontation with the PRI lasted, the Democratic Current claimed that its demands and actions fell under the internal rules established by the party. Its detractors responded by appealing to the political system's traditions and customs (Garrido 1993, 57).

The ideological disagreement between the Democratic Current and neo-liberal policies and its intent to restore the original characteristics of the party as delineated in its own proposal is fully illustrated in the September 1987 document it presented for inclusion in the PRI's electoral platform. It states that in the early 1980s "the country was moving ahead and upholding its struggle for independence" (Corriente Democrática 1989b, 218). However, the party had deviated from these objectives, which were also mandated by the constitution, as a consequence of the leadership in power since 1982: "The state envisioned by the 1917 constitution has to, as its primordial obligations, ensure the sovereignty, physical integrity, economy, and morale of the country, through the application of decidedly nationalist and redistributive policies.... Our economic vulnerability has increased and our productive capacity has been damaged by the inadequate management of our public debt and the adoption of a neo-colonial project, which has a tendency to tie us into the U.S. economy" (Corriente Democrática 1989b, 246).

For the dissidents, the policy of structural adjustment was doctrinally adverse to the revolutionary program not only because of its anti-nationalist character but also because of its social effects: "The neo-liberal doctrines and practices that are currently in vogue are contradictory to the revolutionary movement.... Fomenting inequality instead of fighting it and deepening social differences as a part of government policies is tantamount to destroying the validity of the constitutional order" (240). In light of this, they introduced an alternative economic and social program under the subtitle "The Rescue of the Nation," which established as its goals the "recuperation of our economic sovereignty," "slow foreign economic penetration," and the "strengthening of our identity" (231–32). All of this was based on the same premise: "Any decision that undermines the dignity of Mexicans internationally, goes against our fundamental rights, dilutes our national identity, or takes away our wealth, is in direct violation of our constitutional agreement" (230). Finally, the document makes an appeal "against authoritarianism, in favor of the recuperation of sovereignty and the reconstruction of the country" and "stopping the counterrevolution and the subjugation of the country's interests to those of foreigners" (252).

Members of the political class either supported or opposed the Democratic Current. Politicians initially sympathetic to the Democratic Current ended up disavowing its existence; others refused to be identified with it; and yet others saw it as a necessary movement. There were those who were surprised by its demands as, according to them, these had historically been addressed. This was confirmed by the governor of Jalisco: "The democratization of the PRI is constant and has always existed; and those who now talk about this and lead this [movement] did nothing in this regard previously; they talk about a democratization that has already taken place." On September 19, 1986, in a comment to the French newspaper *Le Monde*, the president of the republic said that democracy within the PRI was not a novelty, but that the party was constantly perfecting its methods in selecting candidates (Garrido 1993, 40–41).

There was a rumor about the Democratic Current that reflected the prevalent skepticism about the real danger that it posed and reflected the tendency in certain circles to see power as a force that controlled everything. It was claimed that the Democratic Current was a part of the PRI's plans to scare the "gringos" by showing a strengthening of the left, which would reduce the United States' support of PAN and allow Salinas to declare a moratorium on the external debt repayments as soon as he took over the presidency.[13] This is an extreme example of the many versions based on the belief that the dissident group was only another expression of presidential will.

At least up until December 1986, the Democratic Current and the party were negotiating. The PRI leadership tried to uphold an image of internal unity and stability vis-à-vis public opinion and those outside the party, which is why it was initially more intent on co-opting rather than provoking an open confrontation.[14]

One interpretation was that a personal rivalry existed between the leaders of the Democratic Current and the PRI. One of the people we interviewed, who was very involved in this matter, stated that the rupture was about old personal resentments, such as the one that existed between Muñoz Ledo and de la Madrid, who had been former colleagues in the Department of Law. Their animosity may have led to the president's refusal to do everything possible to resolve the conflict through negotiation—the preferred mechanism always used to resolve internal party conflicts.

On October 8, 1986, Adolfo Lugo Verduzco, who could not stop the Democratic Current from becoming a political reality, was replaced by Chiapas politician Jorge de la Vega as the head of the PRI. Upon assuming the party presidency, he focused on the party's basic principles: "There is no party without principles. There is no party without unity. There is no party without discipline." At first, it seemed that the party would take on a conciliatory approach, since de la Vega was considered a "man of the system" who had good relations with some of the members of the Democratic Current, such as Ifigenia Martínez and Muñoz Ledo. He immediately began to hold more frequent meetings with them and treated them more courteously (Garrido 1993, 46–48).[15] As of this point, however, in private the PRI would act in a more conciliatory fashion, while in public it would make reproving and discrediting remarks about the Democratic Current.

While the dissident group was visiting various states of the republic, the party launched the notice for the XIII General Assembly to be held on March 2–4, 1987. The assembly's purpose was to reaffirm the party's ideology, revise and reform its action program and its statutes, and prepare the party for the 1987–1988 electoral process.[16] In reality, its main purpose was to evaluate the positioning of people. Cárdenas insisted that the revolution was being betrayed by all the governments that had followed his father's presidency, and he insisted that candidates be selected by democratic means. Against all traditions, the proposal was submitted to a vote but was rejected, followed by a clamor for unity. At the event's closing, and to dispel any rumors that López Portillo was involved in the Democratic Current, Miguel de la Madrid sent a clear signal by being accompanied by former presidents Echeverría and López Portillo.[17] In his speech, de la Vega was firm: "This is a time to unite and close ranks with regard to our ideals, our action platform, and our national leader." He reminded everyone of the basics of discipline: "Freedom to criticize and open discussions should always honor the principles, the forms, and the times set by the superior organs according to their established statutes." He reiterated that the selection of a presidential candidate was an ascribed and unwritten prerogative assigned to the Mexican president, to whom he offered his loyalty, and finally he affirmed that a person's permanence within PRI ranks was based on his/her acceptance of its rules: "We will not tolerate that the democracy that we practice be used to derail our party's activities. From this great assembly we herewith manifest to all those who do not wish to honor the will of the vast majority of PRI members from here on to resign from our party and seek affiliation to other political institutions. . . . The PRI has no room for a fifth column or for Trojan horses" (Garrido 1993, 73–76).

The party's leader thus let everyone know that the presidential strategy toward the Democratic Current left no room for negotiation. In fact, there would never be a reversal in the tone used on this occasion. In an event that took place after the 1988 elections, de la Vega reminded everyone that the "most important virtue in the nation's existence is loyalty." He accused the dissidents of trying to "break us in an effort to foster a messianic electoral movement," and he compared them to a group of politicians who abandoned the party and challenged it in the past (José Escobar and José Vasconcelos in 1929, Saturnino Cedillo in 1938, Juan A. Almazán in 1940, Ezequiel Padilla in 1946, and Miguel Henríquez in 1952) whose actions, in the end, "strengthened our unity and our combativeness" (de la Vega Domínguez 1988).

The new instructions were followed by a series of events that caused public disdain. On June 23, 1987, the PRI's National Commission for Political Coordination stated in a paid insert: "Cárdenas Solórzano and Muñoz Ledo, far from obeying the decisions of the Supreme National Assembly to strengthen our unity and discipline that foster our militancy in a free manner, have insisted on the systematic use of external forums and the country to present ideas that are contrary to the volition expressed at the assembly. In our political organization we pointedly honor the right to criticize and discuss. What we do not tolerate is internal opposition to the party."

In August of that year, Muñoz Ledo was no longer invited to the Extraordinary Meeting of the CEN of the PRI. De la Vega, as well as other members of the PRI leadership, began to talk about expulsion from the party. The Democratic Current responded by increasing its pressure to make the nomination process competitive as established in the party's statutes, pressuring the CEN to issue the corresponding notice and present Cárdenas as its presidential pre-candidate as of July 1987. In September, Cárdenas stated that if his demands were not addressed, he would consider running for president under a party that was not the PRI.

The battle also took place on a symbolic level. Several of the declarations made by the PRI leadership and also by de la Madrid stated that the Democratic Current did not really exist. For the PRI, which was always so concerned with internal unity, to deny that there was any disunity, despite its obvious existence, was a way of handling the conflict and redirecting it from the public arena to a sphere of private negotiations. When the members of the Democratic Current organized a march on the CEN of the PRI to demand that the notice be issued, the party impeded this manifestation of internal fragmentation in a public manner. To prevent the march from taking place, the national leadership of the PRI organized a popular event in homage of Plutarco Elías Calles, the founder of the political system whose rules were being questioned and who had been Lázaro Cárdenas's opponent, even though there was no anniversary or anything else related to him that could be celebrated on that date. This maneuver was full of symbolic meanings. It showed the protest marchers that their demands would not be heeded and created conditions for only a small group to be received by middle-level leaders, who followed a different agenda (Garrido 1993, 152–53).[18]

The progressive ousting of the dissidents from the party was accompanied by an incorporation strategy that involved all the other groups that had taken advantage of the party's positioning. De la Madrid (2004, 665) comments that during 1987 he instructed de la Vega to incorporate all kinds of groups within the PRI's leadership positions, "since the time had come to give hope to all those that wanted it." By stimulating as many aspirations as possible, the president clearly was trying to deflect risks that could arise in the difficult phase that was approaching to avoid "any signs of rebellion," since, as he adds, "unemployed politicians are more dangerous than armed guerrillas."

The "Six Distinguished Priistas"

The selection of PRI's presidential candidate continued to follow the timeframes and the processes established by tradition with the national dissident movement running parallel to this process. The initial list of potential candidates included all the cabinet secretaries who were not constitutionally limited from participating. In this first list two names stood out: Jesús Silva Herzog, the finance minister, and Carlos Salinas, who headed the Ministry of Programming and Budgeting. Early on, both entered into a debate over the level and sources of public spending.

Salinas had technical and personal advantages over Silva Herzog (he was from the same generation and had similar viewpoints and administrative experience as the president), and the enormous public visibility enjoyed by Silva Herzog during his first years in public administration as well as Salinas's success in advancing his views on economic issues removed Silva Herzog from presidential favor and led to his cabinet resignation on June 17, 1986.[19]

On April 21, the governor of the state of Mexico, Alfredo del Mazo ("the brother that I never had" as he was called by the president), was appointed minister of energy, mines, and government-owned industries. Del Mazo was linked to Velázquez and the policies of López Portillo, as well as to industrial business circles. This made him a strong potential candidate, as he also had affective ties to the president and was somewhat less prone to be associated with the new economic policies than Salinas was (Castañeda 1998, 514–16). With Silva Herzog discarded, the cabinet secretaries mentioned as the most likely potential presidential candidates were Salinas, del Mazo, and Manuel Bartlett, the secretary of the interior.

As mandated by tradition, politicians of lesser rank were in charge of reducing the list of potential candidates. In this case, the president of the PRI's Administrative Committee of Mexico City, Jesús Salazar Toledano, named four potential candidates in front of a group of journalists on October 17, 1986. They included del Mazo, Salinas, Bartlett, and Miguel González Avelar, the minister of education.

This initial announcement led politicians to stake their positions, and several were faced with the unpleasant situation of allying themselves privately to one of the potential candidates without showing their support in public. Humberto Aranda (*Excélsior*, March 16, 1987) quotes Genaro Borrego, the governor of the state of Zacatecas at the time, in a discussion of who the possible candidate could be: "The candidate to the presidency of the republic may arise among the four mentioned potential candidates—Alfredo del Mazo, Manuel Bartlett, Carlos Salinas, and Miguel González Avelar—or from another twenty possibilities." Note that there is a purposeful play on possibilities as he first mentioned the most likely contenders specifically and then diluted the assertion by incorporating them within the context of a much larger and anonymous group. In this way, the speaker used the ambiguity contained in Mexican political language to avoid making any public commitments that could be seen as acceptance or denial.

The country's president hastily broadened the range of possibilities further, and when the Mexican Council of Businessmen (Consejo Mexicano de Hombres de Negocios) asked him to authorize a meeting with those mentioned as potential candidates by Salazar Toledano, he suggested that they also meet with Ramón Aguirre (mayor of Mexico City) and Sergio García Ramírez (attorney general). When asked whether they should also invite Ricardo García Sainz (head of the Mexican Social Security Institute) and Guillermo Soberón (minister of health), he agreed. Later, he stood up for all those who had been "mentioned," something he would be criticized for since he had given the impression that these people's candidacies were all viable (de la Madrid 2004, 747). De la Madrid's philosophy on a hasty destape is summarized in the following manner: "The equilibrium maintained among pre-candidates is deliberately upheld by the president by means of various demonstrative acts, such as the frequency of agreements made, the number of events that he asks to be accompanied to, and his participation at events that are offered by a given ministry or government entity. It related to a day-to-day mosaic in which the president acted according to his inclinations of that day, circumstances and public opinion" (ibid.).

Initially, the competition between the different pre-candidates was not that obvious. The battles that raged between Salinas, Bartlett, and del Mazo, the three main aspiring candidates of the PRI, were almost imperceptible. This does not mean that there were no low blows; for example, a rumor was spread that the massive mobilizations at the National Autonomous University of Mexico by the University Student Council (Consejo Estudiantil Universitario–CEU) throughout 1986 and 1987 were organized to discredit the university's president, who was associated with Salinas.

The pressure exerted by internal demands for a more democratic selection process led to the introduction of an important variation in the succession mechanism. On August 13, 1987, the president of the CEN of the PRI named "six distinguished priistas" as potential PRI candidates to the presidency. Ramón Aguirre, Manuel Bartlett, Alfredo del Mazo, Sergio García Ramírez, Miguel González Avelar, and Carlos Salinas were listed in alphabetic order to avert suspicions and precipitate speculations. The official version said that Jorge de la Vega had toured the entire country and interviewed party and opinion leaders as of March and that the six *presidenciables* resulted from this process (Castañeda 1998, 184). Each potential candidate had to appear before the 135 most important leaders of the PRI structure. They also had to make television appearances in which they explained their government program. In each case, the potential candidate started off by lauding the president and his government and then continued by discussing the content of his proposal in the vaguest of terms. Meanwhile, the PRI sectors discussed important campaign themes and made public insinuations about the men they believed to have the best possibilities of gaining the presidency.

Without a doubt, the explicit mention of six potential presidential candidates represented a symbolic concession to those who demanded greater openness in the selection process of pre-candidates. Between August 17 and 27, 1987, they made public appearances, which seemed to indicate that for the first time potential candidates would undergo public scrutiny and be selected in a process that took public opinion into consideration. For many, the new format represented a "positive change of the rules," an "act never previously in existence and without antecedents." A member of the political class affirmed that the appearance of the six "shows a contrary tendency to the dedazo that vanquishes the game of the destape."[20] For another person, the process diminished the president's leeway to act out of a "mere sentiment of friendship, personal sympathy, a specific interest, a momentary emotion, or a simple pet peeve."[21] Over time, the initial optimism evolved into straightforward skepticism. This was because the publicity surrounding the potential candidates was not accompanied by behavior that supported the existence of an open competition.

The CEN of the PRI polled the party bases and held dialogues with leaders in an effort to get to know the opinions of PRI members about the potential candidates to the presidency. The formal starting point of the presidential race came when the notice to the meeting of the National Extraordinary Council (Consejo Nacional Extraordinario) was published, at which the CEN of the PRI would state when it would submit the Basic Electoral Platform (Plataforma Electoral Básica). At this meeting, the CEN met with leadership groups of the state-based and Mexico City administrative committees and members of the party's three sectors. There were three rounds of talks. At the last one (September 23 and 24), the president of the CEN first met with thirty-two leaders from the thirty-two leagues of agrarian communities and peasant unions headed by the general secretary of the CNC. The following day, he met with the leaders of the Confederation of Mexican Workers (Confederación de Trabajadores de México–CTM) (9:00 a.m.), the National Federation of Popular Organizations (Confederación Nacional de Organizaciones Populares–CNOP) (12:00 noon), and finally, after delivering the homage to Plutarco Elías Calles given before old distinguished party members, he met with women's groups and young people (*Excélsior*, Sept. 25, 1987).

In the hallways and offices of the PRI headquarters, only one topic was being discussed: everyone wanted to know whether the PRI would register three pre-candidates or only one. The CEN called for calm and asked that the timetable of the established calendar be respected. The leader of the CNC declared: "It will be the sectarian groups who in a serene and meditated process will decide whether we have a unified decision that strengthens the party and the candidate or if it is more convenient to the internal process to choose different positions and people" (*Excélsior*, Sept. 24, 1987). Fidel Velásquez, the leader of the CTM who was rumored to have made discrete insinuations of support for del Mazo and/ or for vetoing Salinas, exhorted: "Nobody has a candidate until such a time when the party resolves the issue" (*El Sol de México*, Sept. 24, 1987).

In general, the PRI members were reticent to pronounce themselves in favor of any one of the potential candidates. Any time that a sectarian leader referred to a pre-candidate, he made certain that he would mention all of their names, listing them in alphabetical order. Even though the names of the potential candidates had been made public explicitly, "none of the sectors, groupings or so called 'political forces' dared to say, 'I support such-or-such candidate.'"[22]

Their reticence to support any one of the six potential candidates publicly showed that, more than the adoption of a new modality that became known as the *pasarela* (catwalk), the fundamental rule that the president would designate the candidate prevailed; the sectors would not make use of the prerogative that allowed each of them to present their own preferred candidate. They would wait for the presidential decision, from which each candidate hoped to benefit. The presidential innovation had no profound effect, as demonstrated by the responses of various participants, which proved that the substance of the informal rules of the selection process had in reality not been modified. Lorenzo Meyer's words reflect that continuity of the selection method prevailed over the new modalities that had been introduced:

The innovation that officially introduced six "distinguished priistas"— three who were already being discussed by everyone and three to give the matter a greater plurality—as potential presidential pre-candidates of the Great Party, was not followed by a true debate about the government alternatives for the next six-year term, but instead represented six expressions of homage to what had been done to date by the government of Miguel de la Madrid . . . nowhere can any of the members of the Great Party be seen taking an open stance of support toward one or the other of the six potential pre-candidates; even less have the six been seen discussing their alternative political programs. . . . Within the Great Party nobody takes sides since everyone knows that in the end the rules have not changed a bit: the president is the only one who decides and that is the end of it. (*Excélsior*, Oct. 1, 1987)

With a series of conventions, polls, public appearances, and presentation of documents, the decision would remain in the hands of the presidential figure, even if de la Vega assured that this was "the most vast, systematic and detailed process of democratic internal consultation that the PRI had ever had" (*Excélsior*, Oct. 13, 1987).

There was one instance, however, in which one of the sectors attempted to make use of its prerogative to present its own pre-candidate. Even though discipline was immediately reestablished, the incident resulted from the confusion caused by de la Madrid's decision to make the process more public without renouncing his role in handling the final decision. During the exploratory process, Héctor Hugo Olivares, leader of the CNC, "offered" a candidacy to the CEN, thus opening up the possibility that each sector present a different pre-candidate. The following day, Guillermo Fonseca, head of the CNOP, rushed to clarify that the PRI would present only one pre-candidate. Olivares ended up by saying that the candidate whom he referred to was none other than the PRI itself.[23]

Without a doubt, the exercise was still far removed from the exigencies of democratic electoral processes, and it is difficult to understand what de la Madrid hoped to achieve. His version is that by exposing the potential candidates to the press and the party he put them at risk: any one of them could end up disqualifying himself by performing poorly (Castañeda 1998, 185; de la Madrid 2004, 759). If one takes into account the role played by the communications media in the public's investigative processes of government functionaries as discussed in Part I, the pasarela had a more open character than the traditional selection methods. As a matter of fact, both del Mazo and Bartlett saw the decision as a sign that the final decision had not been made yet and that they were therefore still contenders in the struggle (Castañeda 1998, 525–27). The president probably intended precisely to send this message and thus to minimize any interpretations that he had already made up his mind to choose Salinas. However, Salinas himself points out that this was unnecessary. On the one hand, he states, the "innovation" convinced no one that the party was becoming more democratic; on the other hand, by naming the candidates explicitly, groups and support teams were formed that were also explicit, which created a higher degree of internal factionalism (Castañeda 1998, 305–7).

The dedazo method faced serious limitations by 1988, as it was no longer followed in a generalized manner within the party. It represented a method that was too rigid to be able to handle any variations of modalities, such as ambiguity and absolute hermetic silence.

The Preparation of the Political Platform

The PRI presidential campaign, apart from being an electoral task, also had another ideological purpose. The Institute for Political, Economic, and Social Studies (Instituto de Estudios Políticos, Económicos y Sociales–IEPES) was charged with carrying out the so-called national consultation among various sectors of the population to discuss the important national problems. For this purpose, it organized innumerable analysis meetings throughout the country to determine the problems that Mexico, its regions, and its social groups faced. This entity, among its duties, had the obligation to prepare the political platform for the PRI's candidate to the presidency of the republic.

Formed in 1929 at the same time that the party was created, the IEPES was its "ideological heart" and the entity designated for research and the diffusion of knowledge.[24] Its spokespeople were functionaries, politicians, and high-ranking technocrats with the additional participation of members from the political class, intellectuals, and scientists. Participants at the different IEPES preparation forums and final events represented the country's various institutions and regions. Thus, the IEPES offered a chance to form interregional and intersectarian networks.

While the IEPES was in charge of handling discussions on the "great national problems," its affiliates in the different federal states, such as the Center for Political, Economic, and Social Studies (Centro de Estudios Políticos, Económicos y Sociales–CEPES), handled the most pressing regional problems and looked at how national issues had a specific impact on the regions. There was a CEPES office in every municipality. These offices brought together information and performed socioeconomic studies on the area. The state-based CEPES collected and processed the information that was afterward handled by the IEPES. Through the CEPES, all sectarian organizations of the party participated at the state, municipal, and district levels.

The IEPES had an advisory council (*consejo consultivo*) composed of "imminent professionals, intellectuals, scientists, technicians and artists, active in diverse cultural areas" (Partido Revolucionario Institucional 1987, 253), and the most distinguished members of the PRI participated in their meetings. The president of the party, based on instructions from de la Madrid, named one of the people closely linked to one of the potential presidential candidates as the head of the council. He was charged with organizing a series of forums focused on preparing the electoral platform, not of the "man" but of the "party."

The council head's explicit goal was the "free and public debate of ideas in his effort of opening up spaces for political participation." The president was personally informed of the politicians who had been invited to participate in every one of the forums and was very cautious, as stated by one of the coordinators, in promoting the participation of all groups. By naming the head of the council, de la Madrid heightened the perceived strength of the potential candidate in question, while he simultaneously tried to provide explicit signals of the problems faced by the PRI and the country, so that these could be included in the party's proposal. The informal discussions about the problems that had arisen due to the PRI members of the Democratic Current were thus legitimized by the Advisory Council and formally incorporated into the party's platform.

Between July 25, 1986, and September 9, 1987, the Advisory Council organized twenty-four work sessions in different states of the republic. In each session, about twelve presentations were given to an audience of approximately three hundred people. All speakers were high ranking. It was common to find the party's state-based delegates, secretaries, undersecretaries, governors, high-ranking technocrats, politicians, and distinguished professionals, among others, at these meetings.

The explicit purpose of these activities was to prepare the party platform. Apart from their implicit purposes, which have already been mentioned—as a distraction to draw attention from the *tapado* (veiled candidate) and to incorporate the demands of the internal dissidents)—

these activities also served to circumvent and contain the effects of political activities related to the identity of the successor. As stated in the words of an individual close to one of the potential presidential candidates whom we interviewed:

> In the period close to the destape, the political animals become excited; it is common to see them in heat, and they are willing to act, be noticed and stand out. This is the ambiance and the emotional state that is produced. Since there is no sign of "who is the good guy" at the beginning and to protect the president, the organizations themselves launch the horse while the president launches the candidate. "The horse" is to put all organizations to work; put an oiled, exercised, warmed-up apparatus in place that is ready to go anywhere. These two items, the emotional state and the horse, produce these activities [hundreds of forums]. The president lets them do what they want and does not pay attention to them.

Before the destape, the same source continues:

> . . . the president puts all the people of the potential candidates to task to organize political ploys. You have everyone doing something . . . The purpose of all of this is to distract the political class. There is clear knowledge that at the highest level they will do any foolishness and will spend time with their own foolishness. It is a gigantic waste of energy and resources, since nothing that is said or written in the forums will be taken into account. Everything is thrown into the wastebasket and then everything starts over again. The forums that take place prior to the destape are simply meant to entertain; everything is thrown away, without even opening up and looking at the information.

As a first step, forums were organized. In two days, more than fifty work sessions were held, with approximately 150 people in attendance at each one. This means that approximately 7,500 technocrats and political leaders were mobilized. Every forum had a specific theme, and the institutions, professionals, and representatives of social groups in any way linked to the theme under discussion were invited to participate. The invitees belonged to the PRI, worked for the government, had good relations with it, or had some kind of relationship with the topic under discussion. An interviewee commented that in Tlaxcala, for example, the session for the agricultural sector was organized by an undersecretary, who was also a former secretary of agrarian reform, who was assigned to organizing the discussion sessions, inviting the participants, and selecting the speakers. Among those invited were peasant leaders renowned for their participation in the agrarian struggle and for their support of the party and the government, as well as heads of the CNC and the whole structural institutional leadership linked to agriculture. Even the governor of Michoacán, who was a member of the peasants sector, was present. Tlaxcala was chosen as the seat for this meeting because the governor of Tlaxcala came from CNC ranks.

In each forum, there were different work groups. Invitees gave their presentations to each group, and only the conclusions were read in front of a group of "important people"—the most select members of the political class. The role of reading the conclusions publicly was reserved for orators, who could consider themselves privileged. "From a total of 150 presentations," the same source states, "there were ten to twelve conclusions read. These, apart from supposedly contributing to the creation of a platform by the IEPES, forged a base of identifying the main national themes, and consequently, the following sessions of the IEPES were organized accordingly." Additionally, each meeting was preceded by several preparation meetings. For example, the presentation given on "Urban Development and Integrative Centers" (Desarrollo urbano y centros integradores) in February 1987 in Tabasco was based on 258 previous presentations that had led up to it.

The IEPES and its advisory council were not the only party entities dedicated to the creation of a platform that suddenly attained a priority status: every sector held national consultations to include specific concepts in their own platforms; the state sections of the PRI held their own forums within the federal entities. The PRI thus received sectarian, state, and IEPES contributions, which meant that people had to participate in forums, preparatory and synthesis meetings, national consultations, and congresses. Thousands of people had to be moved from one place to the other within the Mexican Republic.

On September 22, 1987, the IEPES director, in the presence of the leaders of the three PRI sectors, its state directors, legislative committee chairmen, and hundreds of PRI members, handed over the project for the Basic Electoral Platform to the head of the CEN. Officially, this document constituted a preliminary contribution that would be expanded on with the inclusion of statements by the party bases and final additions of comments by the PRI's candidate to the presidency. The IEPES had been in charge of gathering the proposals made by the members of the party and had organized and systematized these; the CEN of the PRI would make the final corrections to the document before handing it over to the future candidate.[25]

The Breakfast

On September 28, 1987, an event was organized with the explicit purpose of promoting PRI unity among its members. It came in response to the real divisions that existed within the party combined with the nervousness that arose from the challenge posed by the demand for the implementation of a more open nomination process. A breakfast dedicated to the president was held that all the main actors of the PRI's political class had to attend. This event, which we attended and which took place just prior to the destape of the PRI's presidential candidate, was geared toward upholding party unity. It will be discussed in detail since we believe it portrays the political class in its true colors and in many ways symbolically represents the Mexican power structure of the time.

The PRI employees were working at full steam. Lists of invitees were compiled, confirmations were received, name tags were sent out, and details were finalized to honor 1,500 PRI members. The governors would be present, as well as the party's congresspeople and senators, the sectarian leaders, the representatives of district committees, functionaries of the CEN, PRI members from every state, and political delegates from the Department of the Federal District. The only political figures missing would be the cabinet secretaries and the former presidents of the republic. The podium had to hold sixty PRI members; it was estimated that the event would take approximately an hour and a half, which included the placement of a commemorative plaque in recognition of the remodeling of the PRI facilities made with "the contributions of party members from all around the country" at the Benito Juárez Plaza next to the bust of Plutarco Elías Calles. During the breakfast, mango slices; grapefruit juice; ham and eggs; black beans; green, red, and mole tamales; coffee; and bread would be served.

The event took place on the esplanade of the party building, which was covered with awnings for the event. At 9:00 a.m. on the dot, the head of the PRI's executive committee arrived—dressed in a dark blue suit, a white shirt, and a red and blue tie—took his place at the center of the podium, and immediately officially inaugurated the event. While the waiters served the people sitting at the elegantly decorated tables, the mariachis played "Oro de América" with its melancholy lyric, "I have a love and I have it deeply inside me." Even though everything was going as planned, there was restlessness and there seemed to be insufficient places; everyone made every effort to be noticed, and they moved around in their seats, tripping over and elbowing each other. The organizer of the event assured the attendees that this was not a "traditional" breakfast, but that divisions within the party had forced them to reinforce rituals that promoted unity. Maybe that was at the root of the restlessness.

The spatial arrangements symbolically represented the power structure: at the front there was a podium with a long table where the president of the republic, the president and the general secretary of the CEN of the PRI, the leaders of the three sectors, the governors, and the former presidents of the party—with the exception of Porfirio Muñoz Ledo—were seated. Below, in nine rows of round tables, the party members were distributed according to their hierarchical positions. The first two rows held the union leaders, leaders of sub-sectors, governors, heads of decentralized enterprises, and some municipal presidents. In the third row, delegates from the PRI, members of the presidential entourage, deputies, and senators, as well as the heads of political groups and special guests invited by the president of the party were seated. PRI people from the states and former governors were placed in the fourth row, with the exception of Cuauhtémoc Cárdenas.

At 9:50 a.m., de la Vega took the microphone and gave a speech from five pages of notes, in which he reiterated his loyalty toward the president who, in turn, responded by thanking the party for its support. At 10:25 a.m., the president received his last public recognition, before a new political figure would start to gain preeminence.

The Destape

In the days just prior to the destape, the party leadership feared that someone would preempt the party by announcing the name of the candidate: the perpetual fear of a *madruguete*. The president of the CEN of the PRI, who was in charge of implementing the established timelines and of reminding the political class of these, insistently called for discipline and adherence to the established timelines; he publicly dismissed rumors of "surprises," "eventualities," "unforeseeable items," and "unusual occurrences" while also warning that "we have to act without hurries and pressures" and with adherence to the statutes and the agreed-upon time-frames set by the highest decision-making bodies of the party (*Excélsior*, Sept. 23, 1987). While supposedly pinpointing the exact moment in which those bodies would make their decisions, his statement had little informative value: "Without preemption or delays, neither before nor after."

The Democratic Current was cause for additional concern, especially since one of its specific strategies appeared precisely to be to exert pressure on the calendar through inappropriate declarations. Nevertheless, the highest-ranking labor leader, Fidel Velázquez, continued to assure: "There is neither nervousness nor anyone who is making hasty announcements within the ranks of the PRI. Never before have time-lines been respected this much, and I know this since I have been a part of several six-year [presidential] terms and have lived through various *destapes*" (*Excélsior*, Sept. 23, 1987).

However, in the same month that Velázquez made these statements, the CTM presented the demands it had for the next government, which included a change in de la Madrid's economic model (*Excélsior*, Sept. 1–15, 1987). Starting in January during the CTM's assembly, several workers' leaders had been demanding that the candidate should be someone who would defend salaries and employment (de la Madrid 2004, 667). Even if this sector's position may have been intended primarily to strengthen its negotiating capacity, in the immediate aftermath of these statements, people felt that they confirmed the interpretation that the CTM rejected Salinas, the potential candidate most associated with this economic model.

On September 29, de la Vega revealed that the Extraordinary National Council of the PRI would get together on Saturday, October 3, to authorize that the notice to the National Convention should be expedited—where the candidate of the PRI to the presidency would be selected. This announcement meant that this decision was about to be made. At three o'clock in the afternoon of October 3, propaganda was being placed at the esplanade of the PRI. In black letters on a yellow background on the wall of the Sanborns located immediately across from the main entrance to the PRI building, the CNOP placed an enormous banner that read: National Unity. Then, the red and white colors of the peasants sector appeared, stating: The CNC is present with its president. And, finally, the three-colored banners of the district committees were put into place. After a short time, the entire walls of the PRI and adjacent buildings on

Insurgentes Avenue were covered by propaganda. The party's trucks, Televisa and Route 100 buses, trucks from the cleaning brigades of the Department of the Federal District, ambulances from the national social security system, motorcycles, tow trucks, and patrol cars arrived at Aldama Street. A few minutes later, dozens of men appeared, using portable radios to communicate, while several large dark and recent-model black cars ominously entered the PRI's parking garage.

The Extraordinary National Council of the CEN of the PRI met at the Del Bosque Theater. If everything went according to plan, it meant that the PRI had, in the words of Jorge de la Vega, "complied in time and form with all the required phases preceding the internal selection process of our party's candidate to the presidency of the republic." A party functionary told us about some of the things that happened during the meeting.

Sixty delegates representing each sector, the leaders of the state committees of the thirty-two federal entities, the members of the CEN, and special guests were present. The purpose was to relate the party's activities throughout the last year, to agree on the norms that would govern the notice to the Seventh National Ordinary Convention that would determine the nomination of the PRI's pre-candidate to the presidency, to authorize the CEN to launch the notice for nominations of the official candidate, and to ask the Commission for Honor and Justice to select the PRI member who was deserving of the 1987 Revolutionary Merit Medal into consideration (*Excélsior*, Oct. 1, 1987). The leaders of the three sectors refuted that they had already selected a candidate and denied any "pressures, wrangling, or disagreements" within the sectors. In response to the question of whether there was any indiscipline within the party, one of the sectarian leaders reiterated: "No, sir! We are totally in unity, and we don't have any reason to talk about fissures because they don't exist" (ibid.). Velázquez denied the existence of any madruguetes and reiterated for the nth time that there would only be one single pre-candidate. "Nobody is ahead of him/herself. The three PRI sectors will make the nomination in unison."

As the meeting was being held within PRI headquarters, more and more people congregated outside of the building. The Union of Merchants from the First Quadrant (Unión de Comerciantes del Primer Cuadro) and the Civic Union of the Informal Sector of the Old Merced and the Seeing Impaired, Cuauhtémoc District (Unión Cívica de Ambulantes de la Antigua Merced e Invidentes, Delegación Cuauhtémoc) were present. The merchants and members of the informal sector, who according to their leaders were willing to spend the entire night there, set up food stands. Around two hundred petroleum workers arrived and, when gathered in front of the metal bars, took advantage of the situation to mention a union conflict. "Hernández Galicia, we want an interview! Petroleum workers . . . a solution. The right to vote . . . of the worker . . . in '34 . . . it was not honored." Everyone seemed to have taken their place. One could see from the outside how accredited journalists, politicians, and security personnel were being seated on the first floor inside of the building. Outside, everyone waited expectantly. Music became louder. One group was playing songs from Veracruz; another, northern tunes; and yet another, ranchera music.

Some flyers issued by underground critics were circulated, which exemplified the humor and the malice with which Mexicans viewed these processes and procedures:

Our President
Our President who art in the Pinos
Hallowed be thy six-year term
Give us your "finger that points out the next candidate"
May your will be done in the North
And in the South
As also in the Center
Give us our "atole" of every day
And forgive us our dissidence
As we forgive our
Former presidents
Don't allow us to fall in with the opposition
And free us from the PAN.
                    Amen

At 7:30 p.m., the meeting seemed to have ended as most of the press and the political class left the building. Information filtered out indicating that the president of the CEN had clamored for obedience and discipline vis-à-vis the established electoral schedule, warning that he was in charge of making the much-awaited announcement. It also became known that the sectors had not made any declarations or demands. Only then, and only because they were pushed, did the multitudes enter the esplanade as if they feared that the gates would close. As politicians passed, flags waved and rattles sounded. Various groups raised banners with the name of their affiliation. The informal sector, which represented a majority of the group, whistled and applauded; emotionally stimulated, they waved their red, yellow, and white pompons. Leaders yelled consignments, and the people answered them with "Tres por siete veintiuno, como el PRI, ninguno" (three times seven twenty-one, like the PRI no other one) or "Fresa, limón, y papaya, el PRI nunca falla" (strawberry, lemon, and papaya, the PRI never fails). The press took photos of the surrounding areas. The mariachis played "El Rey" (the King).

On the night of October 3, the notice for the Seventh National Ordinary Convention was finally issued. The registration of the pre-candidate had to be supported by at least one of the three sectors and a minimum of ten state committee leaders. The convention was scheduled for October 5–7 (Garrido 1993, 162–63). Immediately, the spread of rumors, gossip, anecdotes, and "information obtained from trustworthy sources" intensified throughout the city. Messages and return messages circulated. Communications rose like a dam that was about to burst.

Very early the following morning, rumors began to focus on one specific name. Radio messages announced that Sergio García Ramírez, PhD, would be the pre-candidate. Immediately, reporters and young PRI members arrived at his house. Everything started with a Ministry of Energy, Mines, and Government-Owned Industries press release that stated that Alfredo del Mazo had congratulated the attorney general for his nomination. Afterward, in a radio interview, del Mazo himself said: "I believe it is a positive sign that our party has focused on the many qualities of a public servant who is clean and brilliant, and as talented as in the case of Dr. Sergio García Ramírez. I am convinced that it is a fantastic decision of our party and that he will be successful and represent our party and the electoral process with dignity." As soon as del Mazo announced his support of García Ramírez, everyone descended on the latter's house on Hidalgo No. 18, in San Jerónimo Lídice, which was instantaneously full of reporters and politicians. A mobile station of a commercial television was set up; two banners of the Revolutionary Youth Front in support of Mr. García were quickly raised.

Pedro Ojeda Paullada, the minister of fishing and a potential pre-candidate himself during the López Portillo administration, also became a victim of this news. In his rush to show support for the pre-candidate, he arrived at the supposed favorite's house at 7:55 a.m. "to be received by García Ramírez' wife, who said that he was in the shower." He left the house and told reporters that he was García Ramírez' longtime friend, a "man of the system," and an institutional character (*Excélsior*, Oct. 11, 1987). Another politician who acted with haste was the architect and former governor of the state of Hidalgo, Guillermo Rosell de la Lama. However, he did wait until 9:15 a.m. to act since the president of the CEN had called for a conference at that time. Without anyone really knowing why, the conference was delayed by an hour. A reporter speculated: "It is difficult to believe that the functionaries let themselves be influenced by radio announcements, since they are supposed to be better informed. . . . Is the conference delayed as a result of disagreement?" (*Excélsior*, Oct. 10, 1987).

The information was wrong and the madruguete as well as the statements by Alfredo del Mazo and others made in haste to show their discipline and acceptance became famous.[26] In retrospect, it can be seen that the announcement was part of a series of flaws, starting with the internal dissidence of several prestigious PRI members, which culminated in the "failure of the system" on the day of the elections. These incidents, taken jointly, illustrate the PRI's loss of control over the succession process. Even for those who were more prudent and who resisted their natural impulses to openly support the chosen candidate, the formal rules had a significant impact: according to tradition, the destape had to be confirmed by one of the party entities charged with the statutory obligation to present the pre-candidate.[27]

While all of this was going on, the podium had been set up at the Benito Juárez Plaza, which was surrounded by strong walls, similar to those of the atria of colonial churches. Our research team was present. An enormous photograph of President de la Madrid was hung up, and in the background, a banner read For a United Mexico. Then there were three bands of color: Agrarian, Workers, and Popular. A long line of merchants received their portions of tacos and tostadas at the improvised food stands. Approximately one hundred thousand people were expected to show up. Walking along every avenue that led to the plaza, people were arriving to squeeze into the main entrance of the PRI. By 8:00 a.m., the plaza was practically full. "Where is the CNC? Here we are in support of you!" On the other side, announcing their presence with huge banners, were the merchants, the members of the National Union of Workers in Education (Sindicato Nacional de Trabajadores de la Educación–SNTE) and the Mexican Association of Engineers, the contingents from the Cuauhtémoc District and from the Union Federation of Workers of the Federal District, the women, the petroleum workers, the sugar mill workers, and the informal garbage collectors from Ciudad Nezahualcóyotl, among many others.

At 8:50 a.m., an incident took place: it seems that one group's banner blocked another group's view. Fistfighting ensued and bystanders shouted: "Take them down!" The official spokesperson of the PRI asked people to calm down. There was a sense of disorganization, both at the podium and the esplanade. People tried to form a human wall that was to open up from the fence to the podium, which was barely finished before important politicians began to arrive. The voice of the emcee was heard as he welcomed the different contingents: "Your vigorous presence is welcome! Viva Mexico!" He welcomed the different unions and made special reference to the presence of the union leaders: "May they show themselves with revolutionary vigor and conviction. This is an act of political unity."[28]

Fifteen minutes before 10:00 a.m., an official spokesperson made the first comment: "We expect that the announcement of who will represent the revolution will be made." As of that moment, a new phase began. There was really no need to prepare the audience for the official announcement of the candidate. With this in mind, the spokesperson, after reiterating a call for unity, made reference to the innovations that had been made in the selection process of the pre-candidate, specifically that the names of potential candidates had been announced publicly in a "democratic election process."

Throughout the morning of October 4, the upper echelons of PRI leadership were nervous.[29] This date had been set by Jorge de la Vega and Miguel de la Madrid for the members of the National Commission of Political Coordination to let the president know the results they had obtained from their national consultation with various party leaders after the pasarela.[30] Initially the date was October 5, but upon the insistence of Fidel Velázquez, the date had been moved up by one day, since he was concerned that there was a risk of information being leaked to the press that could provoke erroneous and hasty announcements—a fear that was confirmed by events. Two days before, on October 2, de la Madrid had told Salinas that he saw a "current that was very favorable towards his candidacy" within the party, that Salinas should continue to be discreet, and that he, de la Madrid, could not give him "any guarantees." Salinas immediately prepared a speech.

The president instructed de la Vega to state at the breakfast held at the presidential residence of Los Pinos that the pre-candidates who had been mentioned most included Manuel Bartlett, Alfredo del Mazo, and Carlos Salinas. He further instructed that immediately following this statement he should ask de la Madrid whom he thought of as the natural leader of the PRI. De la Vega followed these instructions. The president expounded that the most appropriate person, in his opinion, was Salinas, and he invited those present to give their feedback. Everyone ended up supporting the then secretary of programming and budgeting unanimously. After the meeting, de la Madrid talked to Salinas by telephone to let him know that he would be the pre-candidate for all three sectors. De la Vega went to his office to inform the six potential candidates of the decision that had been made.

At 10:00 a.m. sharp, with only a few seconds left before the name of the person who would rule the country would be announced, a few politicians continued to run to greet Dr. Sergio García Ramírez, mentioning his merits and attributes in erroneous adulation. In the meantime, the president of the CEN of the PRI passed through the human wall, accompanied by security personnel. He was in charge of providing the press with the name of the chosen one: "The three sectors of the party and its territorial leadership have decided, unanimously and categorically, in favor of the pre-candidacy to the presidency of the republic of our comrade [shouting] Carlos Salinas de Gortari!" Once the announcement was made, accolades, shouts, and applause were heard. Later, some people said that both La Quina, the leader of the petroleum workers, and Fidel Velázquez had made sure that the people's ovations were kept short.[31] At 10:15 a.m. at the house of Sergio García Ramírez on Hidalgo 18, a portable television announced the identity of the "true candidate," and the hangers-on left for the new location (*Excélsior*, Oct. 5, 1987).

Upon de la Vega's request, the commission in charge of inviting Carlos Salinas to the esplanade was formed so that Salinas could "personally hear the proclamations of support for his pre-candidacy." As the unveiled candidate made his way to the esplanade, the official spokesperson retook the microphone and emphasized the qualities of the chosen pre-candidate and the basic principles of his political thinking: "He is the best man for the Institutional Party." He outlined Salinas's curriculum and ensured that those witnessing the event would show enthusiasm. Cheers were rehearsed, with drums and trumpets in the background. From the top of the building, a banner was displayed with the initialism CNC and, in small letters that had been hastily written, the words "With Carlos Salinas de Gortari."[32]

Governors and some of the union leaders entered with great difficulty through the throng of people to take their seats at the podium. Velázquez showed up, accompanied by the secretary of agriculture. The "chosen one" was about to arrive; the contingent that accompanied him was moving forward with great difficulty since so many hands and bodies were in their way as people tried to ensure that their presence was noted. At 11:12 a.m., Salinas arrived, surrounded by security personnel. He was dressed in a dark blue suit, a white shirt, and a red tie. Trying to keep a straight face and a smile, the pre-candidate was pushed through the human throng. He was accompanied by the leaders of the CNC and the CNOP. As soon as he sat down at the podium, the banners from the various contingents were readjusted so that they would hang right in front of him. By this time, placards with Salinas's photograph appeared by the dozens. His father was seated in the first row, and his wife and children looked on from the balcony of PRI headquarters.

Jorge de la Vega, who was at Salinas's left, made the first statement. Afterward, Héctor Hugo Olivares, who seemingly supported the candidate fully and who did not stop nodding his head as a sign of paying special attention, spoke. They were followed by the representative of the Labor Congress[33] and then the leader of the popular sector who reaffirmed: "He is the best man with his lucid vision to confront our challenges and demands" (*Excélsior*, Oct. 5, 1987). The candidate used this moment to greet the storekeepers who were right below the podium in a privileged location. Lastly, the president of the Federal District PRI talked. All speakers referred to de la Madrid and emphasized that the candidate would surely continue with his predecessor's innovative work. When the president's name was mentioned, Salinas applauded effusively. After each speech, the candidate embraced the speaker heartily.

Finally Salinas spoke. He read a speech of "thirty paragraphs and ten proposals" (*Excélsior*, Oct. 5, 1987). Drums and applause interrupted him on several occasions. "The revolution has not stopped" (applause); "we are the party of the people" (first cheer). Salinas made reference to de la Madrid, whom he defined as a "democratic leader," who "recovered dignity and republican sobriety"; he mentioned what he had learned from him and he stopped speaking during the ovation. He spoke of the party leaders—Jorge de la Vega, Fidel Velázquez, Guillermo Fonseca, and Héctor Olivares—as "distinguished party members, whose leadership is able to bring about consensus, reconcile differences, and generate unity." He referred to the other distinguished priistas as being "five

Mexicans who had brought true benefits to the revolution's political system." He dedicated words of respect and recognition to each one of them: "Ramón Aguirre, with deep popular roots"; "Manuel Bartlett, a formidable politician and institutional man"; "Alfredo del Mazo, with a vision for change and the ability to transform"; "Sergio García Ramírez, of exceptional talent"; and "Miguel González Avelar, a cultured and conciliatory man." Of Jorge de la Vega and Humberto Lugo Gil (general secretary of the party), he said, "Leaders who are greatly politically efficient, loyal and dedicated to transformational activities." He lauded the method of destape that had been chosen: "This new way of electing the presidential pre-candidate allowed for positions to be presented, theses to be debated, and preferences to be expressed; this is democracy."

The speech ended at 12:32 p.m. with the cheer of "Viva PRI! Viva Miguel de la Madrid!" The pre-candidate walked two steps forward, smiled, raised his left arm in greeting, and thanked people for their enthusiastic ovations. Afterward, he hugged a leader of the downtown area storekeepers, who had climbed onto the podium. At 12:35 p.m., he left the plaza and went inside PRI headquarters, where he received all those who were waiting for him in an enormously long line.

The *Salutaciones*

The pre-candidate received expressions of support from the secretaries, the other contenders to the nomination, deputies and senators, friends, and colleagues for two hours, while various contingents began to leave and the banners were removed from the buildings at the Benito Juárez Plaza esplanade; even the political class began to leave the PRI facilities. Some peasants from the state of Guerrero who had arrived the previous night were asking for money to return to their village since their bus had left them behind; they insisted that they had come to the capital city to "vote for the PRI."

Around two hundred reporters, functionaries, politicians, and curious bystanders, all dressed in suits and ties, awaited the pre-candidate's departure, forming a human wall that went from the auditorium to the gate at Insurgentes Avenue. Others had gone to the parking lot where a bus, a blue Grand Marquis, several patrol cars, and police on motorcycles were waiting. Since for some strange reason the bus kept moving from one place to the other, the followers, running behind it, had to follow suit.

The salutaciones (salutations) to the new candidate began with the delegation headed by Alfredo del Mazo, who was accompanied by approximately sixty people. Humiliated by his earlier mistake, both de la Madrid and de la Vega had insisted that he would have to express his support to the chosen one personally, for the second time that day (Castañeda 1998, 250–51, 531–32). The pre-candidate received the group in the PRI's multipurpose room, a large and ugly reception area. Later, he received other secretaries in the Presidential Salon, a much better-equipped room. The best space was without a doubt the Salon of Honor, which was reserved for the pre-candidate's reception of the director of the government-owned oil company PEMEX, former comptroller, and one of the pre-candidate's closest friends, Francisco Rojas, who arrived with approximately five hundred people in tow.[34]

Ten minutes later, the radios of the security agents acted up, which meant that the pre-candidate was about to leave. People tried to form a human wall, and Salinas took advantage of the momentary confusion to leave by another door and, accompanied by Alfredo del Mazo, went to his car. Everyone ran. Both smiled while they protected themselves against the shoving of the crowd. This public expression of camaraderie represented the party's unity and harmony, as well as the attitude of a "good loser" in sports events. After a few seconds, they hurried to the blue Grand Marquis car. A policeman on motorcycle and two cars with bodyguards preceded them; behind them the bus and other vehicles followed. The pre-candidate went to his house, where he received many more groups of people.

In the following days, the salutaciones continued or, as they are also known, the *cargada de los búfalos* (the charging of the buffaloes) and the *besamanos* (hand kissing). The same ritual was replicated on a smaller scale in each one of the federal states as numerous groups passed by the offices of the party to celebrate the pre-candidacy. For example, in Querétaro, the radio stations provided live coverage of more than three hundred groups passing through the PRI's Directive State Committee offices. The groups consisted of municipal committees, unions, and groupings from the three sectors in that locality that showed their support; at night a commission went to the governor's office (*Excélsior*, Oct. 8, 1987).

The "Right" Candidate

Two days after the destape, and after Salinas had resigned from his government position, the registration of the pre-candidate took place. With a massive concentration of people in the esplanade of PRI headquarters,

Salinas received the official document confirming his candidacy, and he took advantage of the moment to ratify the positions of the president and the secretary of the CEN of the PRI. However, he named several new people to leadership positions within the party—several of them close collaborators from his Ministry of Programming and Budgeting team.[35] Otto Granados was named secretary of information and propaganda; Dionisio Pérez Jácome as head of the Coordination of National Associations; Patricio Chirinos as head of Electoral Action; Luis Donaldo Colosio as the campaign coordinator and head of the presidential campaign; the governor of Tabasco, Enrique González Pedrero, as the general director of the IEPES; and José Córdoba Montoya as the candidate's advisor on special issues. The idea was that the team of trusted collaborators would be formed within a week, before the Days of Proselytizing (Jornadas de Proselitismo) began, which are the first acts of any campaign. Actually, in May 1988, Salinas asked de la Madrid to replace de la Vega with his close collaborator Camacho Solís as the president of the PRI. President de la Madrid declined, since he believed that de la Vega would be a good link between Salinas and the party and said: "One has to respect the outgoing president and let him get to the end of his term with his political team, among which the presidency of the party is included" (Castañeda 1998, 256). During the campaign, the candidate tried once again to incorporate his friend within the general secretariat of the party, and was again dissuaded by the president (de la Madrid 2004, 824). Camacho Solís would not hold the position until August 1988 once the elections had taken place.[36]

While the pre-candidate was forming his team, advertisements of all sizes appeared in the main newspapers of the country stating that there was "complete and unlimited" support for the candidate. Groups of all kinds joined in (sugar producers, the National Federation of Lawyers in the State's Service, the Mexican Society of Sanitation and Environmental Engineers, etc.), who not only showed their support and adhesion to the candidate[37] but also offered their "vote" and stated their willingness to participate in the electoral campaign.

Statements were also made by the governors and state-level PRI members, who told the CEN of the PRI that they stood behind Carlos Salinas and that they supported his pre-candidacy fully. Within the PRI structure, a double vote of confidence was displayed both toward the president and the party, in congratulations for the excellent choice made in designating the pre-candidate. From these it seemed as if this was the best decision and the best succession process that had ever taken place. The statements congratulated both the "person in charge of the nation's destiny"[38] and the party entities that had juggled to combine informal mechanisms with the process, while upholding the statutes—as they insisted. The National Institute of Statistics and Geography's (Instituto Nacional de Estadística y Geografía–INEGI) display thanked de la Madrid "for the constant support received" and joined the general sentiment by reiterating "the positive decision [made] by the three sectors of the PRI." Any recognition of the role played by the PRI in the designation was, in reality, a show of loyalty toward the president, since he himself insisted on presenting the nomination in these terms. An editorial in *Excélsior* (Oct. 5, 1987) commented: "If anything can be said about the mechanisms in place for the selection process of the pre-candidate on this occasion, it is that the party reevaluated its positioning, returned to its roots, fully respected the statutes, and acted with democratic calling."

It appeared as if Carlos Salinas was the right man; among all the potential candidates he was the right age and had the appropriate professional know-how, the right personality, the exact amount of militancy, and the expected conceptual framework. The governors, the sectarian leaders of the PRI, the cabinet secretaries, the deputies, and the senators all agreed in pointing out that Salinas was the best candidate. According to the governor of Querétaro, Salinas "has the ideological commitment, the academic preparation and the social emotion [*sic*] to become a great president of Mexico" (*Excélsior*, Oct. 8, 1987). Fidel Velázquez, the highest-ranking leader of the workers, despite the fact that he had balked at the impact of Salinas's salary policies throughout the foregoing six-year presidential term (Camacho Alfaro 1989, 49), affirmed: "I am certain that the best person was selected . . he meets the needs of the current demands of the country; he is a man of very clear intelligence, completely dedicated to the revolutionary cause and a person who knows the problems of the country and who certainly will know how to resolve these" (*Excélsior*, Oct. 6, 1987). The PRI congress of state legislations assured: "He is the man who guarantees the historic continuity of our national project, which has been defended and outlined with true passion and patriotism by MMH [Miguel de la Madrid Hurtado], president of the United States of Mexico" (*Excélsior*, Oct. 7, 1987). The governor of the state of Guanajuato said: "The election of CSG demonstrates the force of a new generation of politicians who have, however, inherited the experience of the Mexican Revolution." The governor of the state of Oaxaca stated: "He is a modern, young person who understands the internal workings of the party, and who does not have to improvise." The positive quality of the choice was so obvious that all assured, especially the press, that they had foreseen this choice since, of course, all of them knew that only Salinas brought together all the necessary qualities. Finally, as stated by the IEPES director: "The party always finds the right man who can measure up to the problems, as is the case now."

Some people even compiled a compendium of all of the pre-candidate's qualities: he is part of "a generation of politicians who were formed in the revolutionary school"; "he has worked for the government of the revolution"; he has shown "knowledge of the historic process of our homeland"; "he adheres to the doctrinal platform of the Mexican Revolution and of the PRI"; he is a PRI member with "firm convictions and complete revolutionary congruence"; "he has in-depth knowledge of our constitution"; "he proposes the continuation of the revolutionary process"; and "he has found a formula to preserve unity among PRI members and revolutionary forces." Without a doubt, these comments strongly contributed to the creation of the pre-candidate's presidential image. Salinas appeared as a "young Mexican, with experience and talent, formed in public service, with a profound knowledge of national problems, and a loyal and true interpreter of the president's politics."[39]

Even if the candidate's selection had been entirely in the hands of the president, the party immediately appropriated his persona in compliance with the first part of its fundamental chore, which was to manage and organize the campaign that would make him president. The candidate had to be made fully aware of the fact that it was thanks to the party that he would become president.

The Days of Proselytizing

In the phases preceding the destape, there had been some indications that the workers sector would support some other pre-candidate. After all, a continuation of the neo-liberal policies that Salinas seemed to believe in was against its interests. Salinas, however, used the formal processes of the party to produce the desired results. For five weeks, he had an opportunity to sway people in his favor during the Days of Proselytizing—which in principle existed for pre-candidates to compete among each other for support from various party sectors. When there was only one pre-candidate, however, he had the luxury to plan activities that could make him more acceptable to the sectors and vice versa. As a result, Salinas's first meeting was with the workers' leadership.

On October 6, 1987, Salinas met with the mayor of Mexico City and members and leaders of the Union Federation of Workers of the Federal District in Mexico City. The meeting took place in the auditorium of the old PRI building, which was filled with delegates, directors, department bosses, and office workers. Thereafter, and in full dress, he met with the Workers' Congress in session. On this occasion, "just during his intervention in the Auditorium of the Workers' Congress, he was interrupted seven times by applause from the representatives of the different unions" (*Excélsior*, Oct. 8, 1987). With that, "CSG had stood up to those who speculated about a supposed distancing between Carlos Salinas and the workers sector" (*Excélsior*, Oct. 9, 1987).[40] Fidel Velázquez offered his support to the candidate and handed Salinas a document prepared by the CTM to be taken into consideration for his electoral platform.

Two days later Salinas was at the CNC building for more than seven hours. There, the festive tone, set by the CTM, continued: "Along the entire street of Mariano Azuela, a colorful Tlaxcalan-style mosaic [made from flower petals] marked the path to the CNC's headquarters. Young people, indigenous people, Mazahuas, and Otomíes provided a human wall and traditional groups sang. There was lamb prepared Greek style, fruit, guacamole, small nopales, machaca with eggs, Sarazen-style meat, goat, consommé, and Mexican *barbacoa* (barbecue), Mexican-style rice and Mexican sweets for dessert, as well as toffee with nuts. . . . Some three hundred people were eating their tacos" (*Excélsior*, Oct. 9, 1987).

Salinas listened, talked, joked, and greeted every one of the more than 1,140 members of the different CNC organizations personally; he also stood guard in front of the Emiliano Zapata bust and met in private with the former secretaries of the CNC whose leaders used the occasion to provide him with a document that contained their demands. A little later, more than a thousand leaders of the country's urban middle class expounded the urgent need to remedy the national economic problems and to revitalize the political participation of the popular sector to the pre-candidate (ibid.).

The pre-candidate immediately began his campaign in the country's interior. He was determined to visit several state capitals. In each one, he was scheduled to receive *salutaciones* from each one of the sectors, which meant that there was an attempt to coordinate his visits to coincide with their respective state assemblies. In each city, he met with PRI leadership, members of Congress, senators, and representatives from all of the social and economic sectors of the region, as well as the governors. He began with the peasants in Veracruz (October 16) and ended with the teachers of Puebla (October 31). The last campaign activity was coordinated by the Workers' Congress and took place at the Monument of the Revolution. In between Veracruz and Mexico City, he visited Hermosillo, where he inaugurated the National Assembly of the CNOP; in Mérida, he met with women; and in Zacatecas, he met with young people.

On the night of October 7, which marked the deadline for the registration of pre-candidates, it was announced that only Salinas had been registered with the support of the totality of all the sectors and of the various state-based leadership committees (Garrido 1993, 172). On October 12, Cuauhtémoc Cárdenas finally accepted PARM's invitation to be its presidential candidate, which led to his formal expulsion from the ranks of the PRI. He would also run as the candidate for the PPS and the Party of the Cardenist Front of National Reconstruction (Partido del Frente Cardenista de Reconstrucción Nacional–PFCRN, formerly the Socialist Workers' Party). The three parties that traditionally made up the National Democratic Front were allies of the hegemonic party. When Cárdenas's candidacy was announced, they too expressed discontent with the increased technocracy, a discontent that was based on some ideological motives and the perception of a decrease in their opportunities to keep the privileges they had enjoyed within the system.[41]

The other candidates who ran in opposition to Salinas included Manuel de Jesús Clouthier, the former leader of the Council for the Coordination of Business, for PAN; Gumersindo Magaña Negrete for the Mexican Democratic Party (Partido Demócrata Mexicano–PDM); and Rosario Ibarra de Piedra, a human rights promoter, for the Trotskyite Revolutionary Workers' Party (Partido Revolucionario de los Trabajadores–PRT). Heberto Castillo stood as the candidate of the Mexican Socialist Party (Partido Mexicano Socialista–PMS), but declined to run in favor of Cuauhtémoc Cárdenas a month prior to the elections.[42]

The Workers' Pre-Candidate

One day before the National Convention on November 6, 1987, the workers sector held its national assembly in which it declared Salinas its pre-candidate to the presidency. Our research team attended the event. The Palacio de los Deportes was the venue for the event, and it was completely full. Almost thirty thousand leaders and workers from the thirty-three groups that constituted the Workers' Congress, as well as the PRI and workers' leadership, had come together to welcome the pre-candidate. A table of honor for sixty people was set up at the front of the room. Next to the enormous banner that read "National Assembly of the Workers Sector," there were forty-four red flags hanging from the roof with white lettering. They displayed the acronyms of all of the sectors' organizations. Joaquín Gamboa Pascoe, the head of the Union Federation of Workers of the Federal District, stated that it was "the feast of the proletariat" (*Excélsior*, Nov. 7, 1987).

Salinas walked through a 95-meter-long hallway. "Thousands of members from the Workers Federation of the Federal District made the largest human wall ever. They were dressed in brick-red jackets, beige pants, and ties. Many looked uncomfortable in those clothes" (*El Nacional*, Nov. 7, 1987). First, Salazar Toledano spoke; he was interrupted by the shout "Give him my veil remover!" which was followed by laughter. Emilio M. González, the secretary of political action of the CTM, took the microphone while thirty thousand voices shouted, applauded, and then booed when there was a problem with the sound system. The shouts of the petroleum workers overpowered the others. People at the podium seemed to be getting upset. "And, the truth be told, why would they not be upset and worried, especially the representatives of the workers' old guard who had previously announced with pride: 'Here nothing will go wrong, here Salinas will feel the warmth and the force of the workers sector of the PRI'" (*Excélsior*, Nov. 7, 1987). The four minutes that the sound system problem lasted seemed like an eternity. The speeches continued, but the multitudes could not be quieted by any means, especially not the petroleum workers. At one moment, Velázquez got up from his seat "and, forgetting his patriarchal demeanor of the beginning of the assembly, he gestured for them to calm down" (*El Nacional*, Nov. 7, 1987).

Despite these inconveniences, at 11:00 a.m., Velázquez got up and between shouts managed to say, "In the name of the workers sector, I declare Carlos Salinas de Gortari candidate of the national proletariat to the presidency of the republic." Workers responded with shouts and the noise of rattles; the banners were raised and everyone rose, with their hands raised to show their approval. The Palacio de los Deportes shook. Salinas stood up, humbly thanked everyone, eulogized don Fidel openly, and said, "I understand that it was the workers, who in the voice of Fidel Velázquez were the first sector to announce their support of my pre-candidacy." Immediately following, a long human wall with hundreds of Goodrich-Euzkadi workers, all with wine-red jackets, looked on as the candidate walked by on his way from the podium to the exit.

The National Convention

Everything was ready for the PRI's Seventh National Ordinary Convention which would take place on November 7 and 8, 1987. The events that had started before the destape and that included formal activities and informal negotiations would conclude with this enormous democratic ritual during which the pre-candidate put in place by his colleagues was transformed into the official candidate of the PRI to the presidency of the republic through the vote of four thousand party representatives, who had made this decision in 2,378 plenary sessions of municipal committees.[43] At the National Convention and through a formal and direct vote, the delegates representing all of the federal states officially chose their candidate to the presidency.

At 9:30 a.m. on November 7, people began to arrive at the National Auditorium. Under enormous banners that covered the large facade of the building, women with shawls, young people in leather jackets, and workers in their Sunday best were all carrying placards of the different unions or federations. Ocassionally, members of the political class dressed in a suit and tie showed up, as did representatives from different industrial sectors and delegates from different states of the republic who were carrying placards with their accreditation. Outside of the building, vendors set up their food stands selling hot dogs, soft drinks, and sandwiches; they put the stands close to the buses that awaited the departure of the delegates to take them back to their places of origin. The orchestras and bands played jarocho and norteño music, and the mariachis stood on the wooden platforms while entertainers with enormous loudspeakers encouraged the people to dance. Even if the time of day did not make the invitation particularly attractive, some young couples accepted the invitation.

Inside, the seven thousand political party members, among them governors, cabinet secretaries, members of Congress, senators, and municipal presidents, began to take their assigned seats. They had arrived early to avoid problems and traffic jams. Five hundred delegates of the three sectors made up of 250 representatives of the Young People's Revolutionary Front and 250 of the Council for the Integration of Women were present. Similarly, there were also leaders of the state-based directive committees with ten members from the district or municipal committees and twenty from sectional districts, members of the CEN, the party's senators and members of Congress, and the specially invited guests—the latter without a vote (*El Nacional*, Nov. 7, 1987). There was music inside the auditorium too: a band played "La Adelita" while pompoms and rattles were shaken. There were placards, some with the image of the Virgin of Guadalupe and others referring to surprising groups, such as "The Revolutionary Union of Mechanical Toys." The whole place was similar to a bullfighting ring or a football match where national teams were playing, and everyone seemed happy to be alive in a wonderful country thanks to the caretaker role of the PRI.

At around 10:00 a.m., everyone was in their place: the upper echelons at the podium, the PRI bases in the auditorium, the people in the street. Every group could be identified and differentiated by their clothing and their physical characteristics. In front of a long table covered by a red tablecloth with sixty chairs, reserved for the leadership, there were another seven hundred chairs lined up in seven rows. The workers' highest leader sat at the center of the table; those already at the table on the podium got up to greet him. Little by little, the members of the elite began to arrive, embracing one another before sitting down. Below, the state delegations sat in alphabetical order. "Friends and colleagues of the party . . . welcome to this transcendental event of the party!" the emcee said before listing the names of the different groups represented. When the president of the party entered, the entertainer asked the audience to applaud, while announcing that the convention's purpose was to "approve in a democratic manner the nomination of the party's candidate Carlos Salinas de Gortari."

For two hours, between the shaking of placards, pompoms, rattles, and flags and the music played by the bands, cheers, and whistles, the entertainers never stopped lauding the candidate, the party, its sectors, the delegates, the states, and the PRI leadership at the podium.

At 11:45 a.m., the session was called to order. The secretary of the CEN of the PRI took attendance of the states represented in strict alphabetical order. Once done, everyone rose and shouted the names of their states while wielding flags and banners. Then the entertainer announced: "We have a quorum!" and asked the highest-ranking leader of the workers to

officially declare the convention open. The first speech was by the coordinator of the IEPES, who introduced the candidate, gave a summarized
version of his background, and talked about his project and the party's
ideology. The speech was so long that after thirty-five minutes the people
began to whistle. In between the noise, one could hear mention of the
terms associated with the PRI's program: "social justice," "nationalism,"
"revolution," "freedom," "democratic challenge," "perfecting the institutions," as well as more ambiguous phrases such as "change with continuity" and "the audacious prudence of the party."

Suddenly, Velázquez announced that he was leaving to attend the
closing ceremony of the petroleum workers' convention, which was taking place at the same time. Murmurs and gossip ensued as this was seen
as a discourtesy of the workers sector vis-à-vis the pre-candidate.

The voting began. Each delegation was called to make its will known.
"Aguascalientes!" "Yes!" "Baja California!" "Yes!" In this manner and
after each "Yes!" the platform of the party and the candidacy of Carlos
Salinas were approved in a few minutes.

Once the process of voting had concluded, those items that had been
agreed to were read. The system by which delegates had been named was
explained, highlighting the voting procedure's legality. After a few discourses were given that received ever smaller applauses, the event ended.
People began leaving, and some groups waited outside, resting on the
ground between the garbage and paper trash.

The following day, November 8, the closing event of the convention
took place on the esplanade outside of PRI headquarters. In front of
150,000 party members, Salinas was sworn in as the presidential candidate according to the mandates of the statutes, and he gave his first
speech in this role. Parts of the parking lot of the party's headquarters
had been adapted with bleachers and an enormous platform that could
seat one hundred thousand people in five rows: the first two with tables
and the following three with chairs only. There were place cards at the
tables for the important people who were to be seated at them. There
were no specific seating assignments for the chair section, except that
people had to be clearly identified as being a part of those seated at the
podium. Basically, this included national political leaders and important
government functionaries. There were also lateral bleachers and chairs
on the esplanade: to the right of the podium and in the front rows, seats
were reserved for the cheerleaders, and to the left, another part was
reserved for the press and for television equipment. In the center, lines

in different colors had been painted (yellow, red, blue, and grey) so that the different delegations could easily be seated. In this way, each group, no matter how small, had to leave behind testimony of its presence and its loyalty toward the party. This event was of great jubilation, and the spatial distribution of the different social sectors and the party, the colors, the banners, photos, and speeches were meant to reaffirm the event's democratic nature, the cosmology of the nation, the unanimous approval of the party, and the people's loyalty.

We had the opportunity to speak with a group of people in attendance who exemplified what is popularly known as *acarreados* (carried people). They were peasants from the state of Coahuila who had been expressly brought to attend this event. They claimed that they used to come to Mexico City as young people accompanied by their parents to attend events and that, in reality, they came to have fun and to sightsee. One of them was a commissionaire of a communal landholding in Coahuila and the other an advisor to security guards. They commented that their expenses were covered by the "governor of the state," that they received the bus tickets at their house, and that they had instructions to report to the central office in Mexico City, where they would have an assembly and receive money for their expenses. They were housed at a hotel near the PRI facilities. They also stated that in the past when they came to the events in Mexico City, they were taken to Banrural (the rural bank), where they were served coffee and given checks and were taken in buses to places like Xochimilco and Veracruz; they remembered that it was the first time that they had seen the ocean. But that was before. Now, they said, "It is not the same anymore; the bus passes through the states and is full of people from all municipalities." Nobody takes them around anymore; they are taken to the offices only to handle communal landholding business. After all, this is what happens in times of economic recession and austerity.

At 9:30 a.m., the Benito Juárez Plaza was full of people. Everyone had arrived in buses assigned to their respective organizations. The entire space, on three of its sides, was covered by banners in support of Salinas. On one side of the podium, there was a large photo of de la Madrid and next to it a photo of Salinas. The people in the esplanade were members of union groups and delegations from different states, but above all else, they were young workers. Each group had some distinctive piece of attire: hats, rattles, or uniforms. Of course, there was also a band that provided music. On the side bleachers sat groups of public employees, men dressed in suits and ties and women wearing make-up dressed in silk dresses or dresses made of shiny material wearing high heels and jewelry. The ambiance was festive. Other sectors occupied other sections of the bleachers. They could be distinguished from the peasants who wore their "sombreros" and other workers who wore their characteristic caps and jackets. Three-colored confetti fell from nearby rooftops. Beyond the plaza, the voices of the entertainers were heard who were shouting: "Dance! Dance! ... What is the matter with you today that you don't want to dance!"

At the pre-established time, 10:00 a.m. sharp, the candidate arrived. People arose; the bands played. Salinas, who was dressed in a dark blue suit, white shirt, and a dark tie, was very formal despite the tone of the event, which was that of a popular feast. He went to the platform in front of the podium. At that point, the president of the CEN of the PRI asked Salinas to take his oath and Salinas responded by saying: "Yes! I accept!" Confetti, rattles and drums. . . . He gave a speech talking about the virtues of Miguel de la Madrid, referred to the economic crisis, and restated what he had discussed during the Days of Proselytizing. He talked about the four big challenges that would be recurring themes throughout his campaign: sovereignty, democracy, social issues (eradicating poverty), and economic problems, which included curbing inflation (one of the important neo-liberal issues).

At no time did the drums stop playing nor did the feeling of popular jubilation subside when the outgoing president was mentioned and when reference was made to the Mexican Revolution and the need to preserve it. However, it seemed that it took the public a few moments to understand when they were supposed to express contentment, since the speeches paused and a few moments elapsed before applause could be heard. People began to leave even before he was finished; they were hoping that the buses that were parked along nearby streets would arrive as soon as possible to take them back to their homes.

Thus, the nomination of the PRI's presidential candidate ended, despite the fact that the validity of the process had been questioned and despite the variations that had been introduced into the process. These had been adjusted to the basic established norm that concentrated the final decision in the hands of the president, therefore simply ending up as adaptations of traditional mechanisms to new conditions. A political analyst commented: "The election of Carlos Salinas was handled and became a reality within the most traditional ways of the *tapadismo*, a context that in many ways is anachronistic and a source of illegitimacy. When the process began, there appeared to be a desire to overcome the past, but in the end it turned out that the PRI made a great leap backwards and returned to a time of a more pure destape: the one of President Ruiz Cortines" (*Excélsior*, Oct. 7, 1987).

4

The Press Prior to the *Destape*

As discussed in chapter 2, the selection phase of the Institutional Revolutionary Party's (Partido Revolucionario Institucional–PRI) potential candidate was characterized by an almost absolute dedication to *futurismo* (futurism), and the whole nation lived obsessed with the *dedazo* (pointing out) and the *destape* (unveiling). Public and private discussions focused on issues regarding the succession, the problems of the country, the challenges that the chosen candidate would have to overcome, and the characteristics the "right" candidate needed in order to face these problems. These statements were meant as suggestions or as expressions to somehow influence the selection of a successor. As in no other moment throughout the succession process, the role played by the print media in this phase was essential. It was not only a place for a good dose of participation (by means of statements made) but also a venue for the members of the political class to gain information on what had taken place at events where support was shown or suggestions made, such as in the discussion forums organized by the Institute for Political, Economic, and Social Studies (Instituto de Estudios Políticos, Económicos y Sociales–IEPES) and in the meetings with pressure groups—for example, when a potential candidate met with business leaders.

The press reflected all the political rituals that symbolically represented the battle for power. In the period preceding the destape, these consisted mainly of events related to the presidential succession and those political pressures launched in an effort to influence its evolution.

Press Presence

Potential candidates for the presidency could not survive without extensive press coverage. Given the formal prohibition for anyone to state that he/she wanted to be the PRI's candidate, these desires had to be communicated by other means. The press played an essential role in diffusing information and reporting on a potential presidential candidate's persona. This was achieved by maintaining a constant and exemplary presence (even if not too exemplary, as we will see) in the press and by ensuring one's mention in the news. Activities geared toward achieving media presence started at the very beginning of the six-year presidential term and increased as the moment of the destape came closer. In his study of the media and bureaucracy, Adler (1986) found that those in charge of managing press relations for any "important" politician (such as the cabinet secretaries) ultimately aspired that he/she would become the candidate, regardless of whether such a goal was realistic or not. The head of an unimportant ministry wanted to stand out and be promoted to an office that made him *presidenciable* (presidential material). These ambitions were supported by historic antecedents as seen in the cases of José López Portillo and Miguel de la Madrid, who became the PRI's presidential candidates at the end of six-year terms in which they initially occupied lower tiers of importance.[1]

Politicians who received constant press coverage could have their political virtues publicized, making their political power more obvious. The ultimate goal was that press reports would influence the president's decision even, and this is important to reiterate, if there was never any certainty about how much these efforts could change the president's preferences regarding potential candidates. Press appearances could also be risky for politicians with presidential ambitions: they could be *quemados* (burnt) in the press. Although there was no clear definition of when someone had received excessive coverage, there was a danger that more coverage provided more chances for a potential candidate to end up discussing a controversial issue. Another possibility was that if the potential candidate was benefiting from a particularly positive coverage, then he/she would steal the limelight from the president. According to different interpretations, the latter is said to have happened to Jesús Silva Herzog, for example. Throughout the six-year term of Miguel de la Madrid, he gained national and international fame, and was quemado for his premature actions.[2]

There are various media indicators that illustrate the importance and political power of potential candidates to the presidency. One measure is the frequency and volume of news items and comments related to one person. Other measures are the frequency with which a potential candidate is mentioned in front-page coverage (a show of political power) or the frequency with which the potential candidate is shown accompanying the president on trips or at public events, or acting as a representative of the president (demonstrating a close relationship of

Table 4.1   Coverage of potential PRI presidential candidates in
Excélsior, January–August 1987

Candidate	Total news items	Front page news items	With Miguel de la Madrid	Rep. Miguel de la Madrid	Editorials
Salinas	55	24	13	3	42
Bartlett	41	16	8	1	52
Del Mazo	47	17	8	3	34
Aguirre	45	10	3	0	9
García Ramírez	24	6	3	3	16
González Avelar	45	17	12	1	32
Soberón	5	3	2	0	5
Petricioli	5	3	2	0	5

Criteria: Any mention even if not related to the succession process; everything related to the "unveiling" as "candidate," "successor," etc.

Total amount of news items/commentaries: 420.

trust). Statements made and the divisions that existed between potential presidential candidates were reported and discussed in the press. As a result, all potential candidates made every effort to receive coverage and to ensure that it was favorable.

In table 4.1, data corresponding to the frequency of coverage of potential presidential candidates of the Institutional Revolutionary Party (Partido Revolucionario Institucional–PRI) in the newspaper *Excélsior* in January through August 1987 are shown. This newspaper was chosen since, at the time, it was considered the most important one politically— more for its long trajectory in providing broad coverage than for its journalistic qualities. In all the news items covered, the person playing a central role in each was recorded. When news items covered various topics and several key figures, a determination was made on the most important central figure in the article by using the following criteria: (1) the person mentioned first, and (2) the person receiving the most coverage (measured by the number of paragraphs).

The table includes the names of six official pre-candidates. The names of Guillermo Soberón (minister of health) and Gustavo Petricioli (minister of finance and public credit) have been added for comparative purposes. As members of the cabinet, they were by definition part of the long list of potential presidential candidates.

The following items were recorded: the total number of news items; the total number of items on the front page; the total number of times the person was mentioned in conjunction with the president; the total number of times the person was reported as representing the president in appearances; and the total number of times the person was mentioned by regular newspaper columnists. These indicators measure what has been called the "press presence" of each of the potential pre-candidates.

The coverage received by de la Vega owes to the fact that he had been assigned to handle the entire process by the president. It is in this role that his activities and statements received special attention. Anything he did provided information on the advances of the process and compliance with established phases, and offered indications of the president's intentions and the position he was taking.

Based on the aforementioned criteria, the potential presidential candidate who received the most mention was Carlos Salinas in almost all categories. The names of Manuel Bartlett, Alfredo del Mazo, and Miguel González Avelar came in second place and were also mentioned often. Candidates considered as "filler" (Ramón Aguirre or Sergio García Ramírez) received less press attention. Albeit not in an explicit manner, these results illustrate how the press mirrored the distribution of political power.

Of particular interest is the frequency with which the potential candidate was mentioned in association with or at the side of the president, since this was generally interpreted as a manipulated move by the president (the president made the decision of who accompanied him or who represented him). Such coverage was thus generally seen as a favorable political "sign": any physical closeness was generally interpreted as a positive political disposition toward the potential candidate. During the campaign, the same values were attributed to physical closeness to the candidate. A photographer of a nationally circulated newspaper told us, for example, that one way of supplementing his income was by selling photos to people who had greeted the candidate or who during the six-year term were with the president when he visited the federal states. "A local leader," he commented, "will give us anything we ask for in exchange for a photo in which he/she is seen next to the president."

Talking about the Pre-candidate

Given the characteristics of the press coverage of the potential candidate's unveiling process, any person who took the time to carefully read the written press found all the arguments and information necessary to make educated guesses about the presidential succession. This represents one of the most interesting phenomena of the traditional political process in Mexico: all (even those members and followers of other parties) talked and speculated about the "good one" (in other words, the pre-candidate who would be unveiled) in a discourse geared more toward an attempt to impress the interlocutor than to exchange information.

Politicians tried to decipher who the pre-candidate would be, since this could be a determining factor in their behavior—for example, they could forge certain alliances. For the vast majority of those who were or who felt that they were members of the political class, however, there was little they could do with this information, nor could they influence the designation of a candidate.

What seems to have taken place is a social ritual by which people tried to become a part of the process by involving themselves in almost obsessive conversations about the destape. The members of the political class presented themselves as "experts," and as people close to power. In this context, people eagerly tried to gain a reputation of "degrees of excellence," showing themselves as knowledgeable and astute in political matters. A heightened reputation "of excellence" could open up many doors and economic opportunities, such as political consultancy positions.

This communications ritual has been detailed in the study by Adler (1986) in which innumerable examples have been recorded of politicians and other members of the political class (especially those working within the federal bureaucracy) who repeated versions of the same press coverage as if this coverage originated through their personal contacts and as a consequence of their access to privileged information. In this way, the discourse surrounding the question preoccupying the entire nation (who will be the pre-candidate?) did not come from a public source (the press); rather, the news was transformed to make it valid on an individual basis. In this way, rather than saying that according to "so-and-so as mentioned in the newspaper X, the pre-candidate will be Z," the preferred statement was something like "according to my cousin who works with Minister Y, the pre-candidate seems to be Z." As part of an experiment, Adler (1986) chronicled the different reactions of the interlocutor if the press was mentioned as a source or if a personal relationship was quoted. Adler found that if the recipient believed him/herself also to be an expert he/she tended to discredit the public source ("one should not believe what that columnist has to say . . . he/she has been bought").

In contrast, the same interpretation quoted as supposedly coming from a confidential and personal source generated more respect, even among those who were potentially in disagreement ("Look, it could be that your cousin knows more about these things, but I was told by my brother-in-law who works in V, that the candidate is going to be W").

To simply be known as someone with a good eye for politics had considerable value among members of the political class, even if their real power within the political process was small. At the same time, their participation in this national discussion was a ritual that allowed their integration in the process by means of communicative-social mechanisms. To be seen as a participant with a degree of "excellence" was as important to the PRI members as it was to opposition party activists, businesspeople, university professors, and union leaders.

The Public and the Private

The ritual that converted public information into private information represented one of the dominant features of Mexican political culture: the private side overshadowed the public side, and personal information revealed much more than any public document. It was easier for people who wanted to feel like participants to do so in the private realm (for example, not everyone sees their ideas published). It was also within the private realm that a process of such inordinate magnitude as the presidential succession could become a personal and intimate experience.

The relationship between the private and the public could be seen throughout the entire process. Public information (for example, the information that shows up in the press) had to be interpreted, an action that took place primarily in the private realm. If those people who attempted to demonstrate that they were knowledgeable managed to feel that they were part of the process, then a process that was primarily highly authoritarian (the dedazo) became—through this communications ritual—a shared and integrating experience of the political community.

The Problems of the Nation

In the period prior to the destape, there were only a few politicians who risked giving their support to a potential candidate openly. It was considered extremely risky and, more important, an act of disloyalty toward the president, since his final decision had to be accepted and celebrated by all PRI members. However, different factions tried to influence the results of the succession (including, of course, influencing the potential candidates) by making statements on the major problems currently faced by the country and the problems of greatest importance for the next president to deal with. In many cases, the themes that were propounded were related to the positions that were held by those making the statements—for example, the entrepreneur obviously talked about the economy, whereas a union leader talked about the important issues faced by workers. However, the topics under discussion tended to be appropriate for any sector. The economy is a relevant theme for everyone, as are the themes of security and politics. Thus, a person's statements on any subject were interpreted as an indication of his/her favorable disposition toward a certain pre-candidate. In 1987, the names of Salinas and del Mazo were more associated with economic questions than those of Bartlett or García Ramírez. Again, what was important was how the main problems the nation had to confront were interpreted and defined, which in turn led to their association with the qualifications of each of the potential candidates to the presidency.

Table 4.2 illustrates how the "problems of the country" were defined in the period from January through June 1987. It lists the "current" problems and the problems of the "next administration." In both cases, economic issues dominated political and social security ones. Within the economic topics, the issue of scarcity/inflation received the most mention.

Public discussions were far and away the norm as defined by the liberal model of informed and pluralistic discussion in which diverse participants provide something to the joint and qualitatively superior determination of which path to follow (Sunstein 1993, chap. 1). Matters were seen as "problems," and the relevance of every problem represented its relationship to "the man" called on to resolve it: that is to say, every mention of a public issue insinuated the tacit support of a specific potential candidate.

Relying on this information, people reached conclusions regarding the person with greater or lesser possibilities of becoming the actual pre-candidate. Similarly, press presence was seen as a sign of political strength, and the preponderance of certain themes—as these were seen as relating to a specific candidate or candidates—in the press were also interpreted as indicators of advantages with regard to the potential presidential successors. In 1987, for example, the view of inflation as one of the central problems of the country greatly favored the political aspirations

Table 4.2 Current and future national problems reported in the print media, January–August 1987

Topics	Current	Future (next administration)	Total
Economy	29	53	82
Scarcity/inflation	8	13	21
Crisis/instability	11	6	17
External debt	2	6	8
Recuperation	3		3
Nationalist economy		3	3
Development		2	2
Production		2	2
Distribution		2	2
Modernization		2	2
Economic freedom/ private investment		2	2
Efficiency		2	2
Price guarantees	1		1
Scarcity	1		1
Corruption	1		1
Deficit	1		1
Finances	1		1
Planning		1	1
Speculation		1	1
Fiscal reform		1	1
Industrialization		1	1
Exports		1	1
Diversification		1	1
Reorganization		1	1
Social market economy		1	1
Continuity		1	1
Globalization		1	1
Integration		1	1
Commerce		1	1
Costs		1	1
Politics	13	43	56
Democracy	4	14	18
Sovereignty	3	8	11
Nationalism	1	2	3

(*Continued*)

Table 4.2 (*Continued*)

Topics	Current	Future (next administration)	Total
Succession	2		2
Decentralization	1	1	2
Modernity		2	2
Latin America		2	2
Internal order		2	2
Cooperation and regional unity	1		1
Migration	1		1
Consolidation		1	1
Continuity		1	1
Structure		1	1
Exchange/ presidentialism		1	1
Political confidence		1	1
Populism		1	1
Freedom		1	1
Separation of church and state		1	1
Foreign relations		1	1
Strengthening of state		1	1
Civil society		1	1
Political culture		1	1
Social justice	14	14	28
Employment/ unemployment	6	5	11
Rural areas	1	4	5
Housing	1	2	3
Education	1	2	3
Security	1		1
Use of justice	1		1
Salaries	1		1
Nutrition	1		1
Suffering	1		1
Health		1	1

of Salinas, since his work as the minister for programming and budgeting was closely tied to the government's anti-inflationary program.

The Right Candidate

Prior to the destape, the political community also participated in the selection of the presidential candidate by expressing their opinions on what they considered to be the characteristics of the "right candidate," a supposedly abstract person without a name. These opinions could be descriptive of a person ("knowledgeable about the problems of the country," "nationalist," "honest") or could refer to his political and intellectual abilities ("someone who understands the management of the country's economy"). Because of the interpretative schemes that existed, these qualities in reality pointed toward one specific person, or sometimes were meant to discredit the possibilities of one of the potential candidates mentioned.

An example of the typical way in which certain specific comments were interpreted with regard to the right candidate is discussed below:

"He should be a member of the cabinet." This excludes Muñoz Ledo, Cárdenas, and, in a narrow interpretation of the term, Aguirre. "He should be a politician" was probably a reference to del Mazo, the only one among all other potential candidates who had held a publicly elected position (governor of the state of Mexico), or to Bartlett who as the secretary of the interior obviously was a politician and had also been the general secretary of his party from 1981 to 1982. It excludes Salinas, a "technocrat." The comment "he should be knowledgeable about the economy" refers mainly to Salinas.

In table 4.3, descriptive statements and comments made about the presidential candidates appearing in *Excélsior* from January through April 1987 are listed.

It is noteworthy that great importance was given to the fact that the successor be a person of the "system." This idea was based on the belief that only someone from the inside could fulfill the job effectively. Even though each one of the candidates promised that things would improve during his six-year term, and every six-year term started with national euphoria and ended with a preponderant pessimism within the collective psyche, the traditional political culture asserted that only a man of the system could make the necessary changes. This contrasts with the political tradition of other countries such as the United States, where

Table 4.3   Characteristics of the "right" candidate
listed in *Excélsior*, January–August 1987

Characteristic	Times mentioned
Knowledgeable about politics/honest/other	271
Will follow Miguel de la Madrid's policies	169
Knows about economics and confronts problems	108
Man of the system	95
Committed to social issues	102
Member of the cabinet	26
Scarcity	22

the candidates present themselves as outsiders whose mission is to fight against the dominant political elites, even when referring to people who are completely integrated into the system such as presidents campaigning for reelection. While in the United States people eventually turn to an outsider like Ross Perot to fix the nation's problems, in Mexico people turned to the astute and knowledgeable candidate familiar with the system, who had the experience to take over the reins of the country. Terms such as "familiar with politics" and a "member of the cabinet" can be placed within the same context.

Newspaper columns referring to "economic knowledge," "follows the programs of Miguel de la Madrid," and "scarcity," despite their apparent abstract nature, called attention in the minds of the readers to the secretary responsible for handling the country's economic matters—Carlos Salinas.

The Columnists

The role played by columnists in the political life of the country largely involved providing interpretations that were considered insightful in political terms. For the period of January through August 1987, the content of the following *Excélsior* newspaper columns were submitted to analyses: Ocho Columnas, Foro, Los Intocables, Al Margen, Gabinete, and Frentes Políticos, as well as other commentaries by intellectuals and occasional commentators to this newspaper.

Political columns generally occupied several pages, and often, important comments were not mentioned in an obvious fashion at the beginning

Table 4.4   References in *Excélsior* political columns to the possible candidate to be unveiled, January–August 1987

Politician mentioned	As potential candidate	As favorite or strong candidate	Total
Salinas	12	11*	23
Bartlett	13	9	22
del Mazo	12	9	21
González Avelar	11	2	13
Aguirre	9		9
García Ramírez	5		5
Others	5		5

* This figure includes three mentions of Salinas as a potential frontrunner candidate. He was the only one who received this type of mention. There were several references to del Mazo as the "second favorite."

of the article. Through these spaces, interested parties gleaned information and interpretations, and consequently, columnists enjoyed a privileged journalistic position. On the other hand, the columns also provided "confidential" information submitted by politicians (generally anonymously, which led to speculations about their identity and their agendas) to which the authors of the columns had access. In indirect form, this type of information could be indicative of the positioning and intentions of informants, once the information had been submitted to interpretation. Politicians, and especially the potential candidates to the presidency, were delighted when columnists dedicated articles to them, even if these were critical, as long as their presidential potential and image were projected.

Prior to the destape, the importance of columnists as certified interpreters was especially significant. The primordial role of columnists in this political phase was to (1) reduce the uncertainty surrounding the presidential succession by defining the "strong" candidates, and (2) offer rational interpretations (the grammar of the political succession) of factors that defined candidates as strong or weak. The political class did not only need to "know" who would be the successor but also needed arguments that they could use in exchanging their impressions with others on this topic.

In table 4.4, future outlooks regarding the presidential succession mentioned by select columnists are shown. The data includes the number of times that a candidate was mentioned as a "possible successor" and as "a strong or favorite candidate to the succession." Clearly, there were three names that came up as strong potential candidates to the presidency: Salinas, Bartlett, and del Mazo. These three received the most mentions, with only a very small difference between one another, but with many more mentions than any of the other potential contenders. These three people were also referred to as those preferred by everyone according to the national consultations that de la Vega supposedly held on behalf of the National Executive Committee (Comité Ejecutivo Nacional–CEN) of the PRI and as the names he mentioned to de la Madrid. Finally, Salinas—the chosen one—was the potential candidate with the highest number of mentions and the only one that received coverage as a "frontrunner."

Several examples can be quoted about how columnists offered their "wise" interpretations about the succession, even when these were speculations about a certain potential candidate considered to have low or remote possibilities. Adrián Lajous (*Excélsior*, Feb. 6, 1987) wrote about the then minister of public education's, Miguel González Avelar, possibilities. It includes three references to Salinas as a potential "frontrunner," the only one receiving any comments of this nature. There were various mentions of del Mazo as the "second favorite."

> In the political race to the candidacy of the PRI for the presidency of the republic there is a foursome made up of three. Why should one speak of a foursome if there is such a distance between the possibilities of the first three and the fourth? . . . Imagine the worst possible scenario for next September: uncontrollable hyperinflation; labor uprisings; universal rejection of the PRI; and an opposition candidate who has accumulated general support. In this case, it is logical to look for a candidate of the system who could not be made responsible directly or in any other way for the situation. . . . One would have to go for an emerging batter. I am uncertain that even in such a case the dubious prize would go to González Avelar. Despite this, I continue to consider him within the foursome because he was put there by professional politicians.

The same commentator, speaking of those who were unlikely to become the pre-candidate, believed that "Guillermo Soberón is in the battle with breakfasts and lunches for 2,500 people but he does not have the least bit of presidential strength. . . . Sergio [García] Ramírez does not have the personality to be president" (*Excélsior*, Feb. 13, 1987). Another commentator, Edmundo González Llaca, disagreed with his colleague's reasons for disqualifying one of the potential candidates: "One of the arguments made bothered me ... Adrián Lajous discredited the presidential possibilities of Sergio García Ramírez by saying that the attorney general had written a book that he did not understand" (*Excélsior*, Feb. 19, 1987).

The columnists defined who the frontrunners were and the logic that underlay their reasoning and analyzed political groups surrounding potential candidates, offering their predictions of cabinet members. Adrián Lajous wrote: "I believe that once he is campaigning, Salinas will transmit all the positive qualities of his personality to the electorate. His main defect is that he is an economist. The principal members of Salinas's large team include Manuel Camacho, secretary of SEDUE; Pedro Aspe, undersecretary of the Ministry of Programming and Budgeting; Francisco Rojas, secretary of the comptroller's office; and Emilio Gamboa Patrón [personal] secretary of the president. Until recently Ramón Aguirre also belonged to this group, but in the last months his insane ambition to become president has grown" (*Excélsior*, Jan. 16, 1987).

As could be expected, any physical closeness—affective or political—with the president was interpreted in detail. That was the case, for example, when Carlos Medina noted that on the one hand del Mazo accompanied the president on his visit to Colima, while on the other hand, García Ramírez went with him to Tabasco (*Excélsior*, Aug. 16, 1987). Columnists highlighted the importance of who accompanied the president to the state address given by the governor of Colima—its significance greater still since Colima was the state in which Miguel de la Madrid was born. Similarly, many commentators placed the potential candidates in a relationship of "familial" closeness to the president. Del Mazo was "the younger brother that he would have liked to have," but Carlos Salinas was even closer: "Carlos Salinas de Gortari, secretary of programming and budgeting, is the frontrunner because he is his [Miguel de la Madrid's] political creation; in other words, speaking metaphorically, he is his son" (Marco Antonio Aguilar, *Excélsior*, Jan. 23, 1987).

Trips made on behalf of the president met with a great deal of interpretation also. The person who was sent to lead independence celebrations in another city or abroad in the year that the destape was to take place had been discarded as a potential candidate (by being outside of Mexico City). The position of anyone who accompanied the president on any trip was strengthened. Important relationships of support were valued highly—whether these were public or "simply known." In other words, columnists were experts on the political dictionary of the PRI and were also actors in the decision-making process.

In this critical period of time preceding the destape, the press mirrored the existing distribution of political power within the party and simultaneously interpreted or reported on wise interpretations made about potential candidates' strengths or lack thereof. The press significantly reduced the degree of uncertainty experienced by the whole nation by restricting and defining the list of the potential candidates with the greatest possibilities (for example, after March 1987, no columnist mentioned García Ramírez or Aguirre as strong potential candidates, even though they were among the "distinguished *priistas*"). At the same time, they were constructing a possible political figure of one of the three most frequently mentioned potential candidates. For example, they already had a very detailed political profile written up for each one of them.

There is no doubt that the political class used the press as a source of codified information for their own interpretations, and that they had good reason to do so. In this sense, a politician who observed the frequency of mentions and references to problems in the press during these times was able to evaluate a candidate's probability for success. This was done not only by noting the number of times that names and problems were mentioned but also by interpreting the comments made by the authoring journalist, as well as within the context of his/her relationship to the pre-candidates, the personal agenda of the owners and editors of the newspapers, which candidate had greater "freedom" to mobilize his contacts in the media, and who would handle the president's information office and for what reason.

The selection process surrounding Salinas's candidacy signaled a continuation of the neo-liberal project beyond the six-year presidential term. One of the problems with this particular process was that its results were anticipated. The basic characteristic of the president making the final decision and the party's collaboration in giving the selection process the appearance of complying with the statutes and of counting on broad participation by the party bases meant that a small group of select members of the PRI who were relatively certain of de la Madrid's preferences felt that they had no option other than to promote a change in the informal rules guiding the selection process to prevent the perpetuation of the technocracy and to restore the revolutionary state. The demands made by the Democratic Current went against PRI unity by disavowing presidential arbitration, and they could therefore not be handled by traditional negotiating mechanisms.

The questioning of the rules of succession ran parallel to the battle for power concentrated within the cabinet. De la Madrid sought to give the appearance of an "open game" with the explicit mention of six names; however, the cultural norms of political competition still had such a force that in public appearances (the *pasarela*), none of the potential candidates competed to be favored by the PRI rank and file or appealed to the public in search of its support. On the contrary, the six limited themselves to presenting their programs in a neutral tone and coincided in their willingness to continue with the president's work. This demonstrated that the true nature of competition was to gain the president's favor. After all, in the end he held the deciding vote. In return, none of the party-based organizations that rightfully could determine the nomination pronounced themselves in favor of any one of the potential candidates publicly. So, even though there was a remarkable and unusual precision as to the number and identity of contenders, the real competition continued to take place in an indirect manner and behind curtains. It was all in the press, but to make its evolution intelligible, one needed to understand the codes or have access to an interpreter.

The caution and discretion of all political actors involved in the process became transformed into an explosion of public manifestations of support as soon as the candidate was unveiled. A ritual of accepting and abiding by the president's wishes took place between the destape—which was equivalent to the election of the next ruler—and the implementation of the president's decision by formally proclaiming Salinas the PRI's candidate. In their celebration of the decision, all PRI members, from the defeated potential candidates to those belonging to local committees, signaled that they were at the service of the person who without a doubt would become the "ruler of the nation's destiny." The demonstration of public and explicit support that had been risky and in violation of formal rules prior to the destape became indispensable once the identity of the candidate was known. Once the political class had complied with its obligation to hail the decision (regardless of personal opinions on the matter), the candidate had the foundation that allowed him to continue to the next phases of his ascension to power.

In the process analyzed here, the first of these phases was to cement the relationships with those who had accepted the traditional rules of the selection process but who were clearly displeased with its results. In the phase used by candidates to formally promote themselves, Salinas sent (negotiated) public signals indicating that popular groups represented by the sectors happily accepted his candidacy. The most urgent conflict that needed to be addressed was with the workers sector. Here, an event was organized that allowed workers to claim Salinas's triumph as their own, as if he had been their own chosen pre-candidate, thus signaling this sector's particular closeness to the candidate.

If the convention was not decisive in defining the candidacy, it did signal the climax and the culmination of the ritual of acceptance. With the unanimous vote of the entire PRI structure supporting his candidacy, Salinas initiated the process of constructing his presidential persona. At the same time, diverse groups within the party that had already put their loyalty in evidence prepared themselves to test the candidate's strength and political usefulness. This tone would persist throughout the entire campaign.

Part III discusses the PRI's presidential candidate and his activities during the electoral campaign. A large portion of these activities were geared toward the reconstruction of the party's unity, which was often confused with that of national unity. The manner in which the candidate began to take over presidential control was noticeable, even before he formally held the position. It also appeared that his image became a symbolic reference, in which all the elements of the system—defined as components of the whole nation—converged in an effort to create identity. The relevance of the political ritual in communicating the validity of the fundamental pacts of the government, and in renegotiating and reestablishing the relative power of its groups, will be discussed here. Additionally, we will observe how the campaign was used by various actors to promote their political careers. The diffusion of the PRI candidate's activities (and only those of the PRI's candidate) by communications media allowed the political class unable to witness events personally to be informed of the degree of power that each group enjoyed as a function of their closeness or distance to the candidate. This process encouraged the general public to form an appropriate mental image of the future president of the country.

Our analysis is based partially on bibliographic materials and journalistic coverage, although it relies mainly on hundreds of personal interviews and direct observations of events that took place during the presidential campaign in Chihuahua, Coahuila, Hidalgo, Jalisco, Puebla, San Luis Potosí, Tabasco, Veracruz, Yucatán, and the Federal District (Mexico City).

Following the convention, the candidate initiated his electoral campaign in Querétaro, the place where the 1917 Mexican Constitution was signed. His first stop was Agualeguas, Nuevo León, where his father was born. The candidate had declared himself the "son" of the state of Nuevo León. It symbolized his place within a large extended family (with grandparents and uncles and aunts included). Simultaneously, the trip to Nuevo León alluded to the revolutionary North and private initiative, as its capital city of Monterrey was the symbolic seat of business enterprise. As a result, many believed that the decision to start the campaign in Nuevo León was indicative of future preferential treatment of this area where, it should be emphasized, an anti-centralist climate had prevailed the previous few years. This attitude had been expressed in electoral terms during Miguel de la Madrid's six-year presidency when the greatest electoral challenges launched in opposition to the PRI and in favor of PAN had taken place in local state elections of the North as in the cases of Baja California, Nuevo León, Sonora, Sinaloa, and, most notably, Durango and Chihuahua (Molinar Horcasitas 1991, 123–33 and 204–5).

The candidate arrived in Monterrey by train, accompanied by the leader of the workers sector. The presidential candidate's arrival by train in this city was meant to remind people of Pancho Villa's revolution and to give Salinas an opportunity to greet groups of peasants while slowly passing by. In Monterrey, Salinas held twenty-two private meetings, a dinner with local businesspeople, and a meeting with the IEPES, and he participated in three public acts. In Agualeguas, "eight thousand countrymen received him fraternally." The following morning, he went jogging and spent time with his family. In the evening, the people had prepared a popular slogan for him: CSG: Pride of Agualeguas. He also traveled to the General Terán municipality to visit with the family of Plutarco Elias Calles, who was credited with forging the post-revolutionary political system. He traveled by bus to the communal landholding "Emiliano Zapata," named after the revolutionary leader who represented the interests of the peasants in the 1910–1917 Mexican Revolution and who continued to be a symbol of peasants, their participation in the revolution, and of land redistribution, as well as the hero of the National Confederation of Peasants (Confederación Nacional Campesina–CNC). Salinas chose this historic figure associated with the ideals of noble actions, justice, and benevolence toward the underprivileged as his own emblem to such an extent that on several occasions he affirmed that the name of his son honored this caudillo.

After participating in other activities in the northern part of the state, on November 12, he returned to Agualeguas to spend the night.

This first phase of the campaign was characterized by a squandering of symbolism: the candidate showed everyone that he was part of the revolutionary tradition: Querétaro and the constitution, the train of the North, Plutarco Elías Calles and the restructuring of the Mexican political system, Mexican-ness expressed in the extended family, and the concept of the "small homeland" represented by Emiliano Zapata.

Before the political campaign started officially (in December), the candidate continued to travel throughout the country's interior. He visited Tamaulipas, Michoacán, and other places, where he participated in events that congregated multitudes of people.

Campaign activities included the following types of events: meetings with the Center for Political, Economic, and Social Studies (Centro de Estudios Politícos, Económicos y Sociales–CEPES) and the Institute for Political, Economic, and Social Studies (Instituto de Estudios Políticos, Económicos y Sociales–IEPES); party support rallies; dialogues with the sectors and national fronts of the party; dialogues held with special groups (ranchers, regional entrepreneurs, miners, indigenous groups, etc.); appearances on television and radio programs; shows and popular festivals. These events were generally organized around the candidate's visit to a state and led to the creation of a series of agreements between the federal states and different groups, classes, and regions of the country. Simultaneously, the image of the country itself as construed by the system was being revitalized.

One could say that the campaign presented two basic axes: the state visits and the meetings with the IEPES. Participants in the former were primarily regional even though the whole country had access to these events through the media; the participants at IEPES meetings, on the other hand, represented political and technical elites whose purpose was to discuss the major national problems.

The following chapters deal with these two axes of the campaign, starting with the visits to the federal states.

5
Touring the Federal States

The visits to the federal states provide an excellent picture of the political campaign. On a general level, they allowed the candidate to construct his political persona and reinforce reciprocal federal and sector pacts. The series of agreements that the candidate initiated with various regions, classes, and groups of the country made him the link between the central and the state governments, the incarnation of the federation, and the representative of conciliation between the classes. One of the functions of the state campaigns was to guarantee each entity its specific place within the overall federal structure. Each state was seen as indispensable to the formation of a national whole. The visits also defined the exact position that each political group occupied within the general framework of the country. The workers, peasants, and popular sectors, together with women and young people, were fundamental components of the regional political scene and also essential elements that forged the political universe.

The state-based campaigns were at the same time a manifestation of local forces and an expression of the totality of "the forces that move the country." Visits to places with economic, political, or historic importance to the state reinforced or realigned those attributes that made up their specific characteristics. In this way, the nation was reproduced in the states, which consequently were converted into a complete universe in and of themselves. At the same time, the message that the states were not self-reliant was conveyed. Even when the state reproduced in its entirety the institutional framework of the country with its power structures, negotiations, and political culture, the identity of a "nation" pertained to it only in fragmented form. The state by itself was an incomplete image of nationality. One can not understand Benito Juárez if he is studied solely from the perspective of Oaxaca. Within the context of an incomplete reality, interdependence becomes indispensable. During the visits, the specific identity of each state was highlighted as was its importance to the country, while at the same time the importance of the country to the states was demonstrated. Thus, the states were only "a partial expression of the whole Mexican being." Only the federation could inculcate and provide each with nationality.

The interplay of totality and fragmentation was seen in campaign activities. On the one hand, activities were the same in every state. The same organizational structure was implemented throughout the country. The way the ambiance was set up followed a standardized design. All actors in this play were basically the same, as were their places on stage: the candidate on a platform approximately thirty centimeters in height; the invited special guests in the first rows or on the stage behind the candidate; the press to one side of the platform; and the public below, gathered on immense earthen or wooden esplanades.

The speeches by orators and the candidate were similar. Invariably, they began by mentioning the greatness of the state and by lauding its natural marvels, economic advances, historic events of relevance, and the people who had achieved grandiose trajectories. A line-up of national heroes who had passed through the state followed. "Welcome to this northern state, to this land that witnessed Don Miguel Hidalgo's pilgrimage in his inexhaustible battle to attain the nation's independence." "Welcome to this capital city that offered support and shelter to Benito Juárez during hard times experienced in his titanic battle to defend the republic's sovereignty and to save the nation's archives." "The teachers of the land of Miguel Ramos Arizpe, of Madero and Carranza, receive you with optimism, with jubilation, and with the hope of better times to come. Licenciado Salinas de Gortari, welcome to Coahuila. Welcome to Saltillo."

Frequently, the candidate was "made" into a person "belonging to the place" or one of its "own" by people referring back to some biographical reference that tied him to a certain state of the federation or to a specific sector. In Tlaxcala, it was said that Salinas was an honorary Tlaxcalteco (person from Tlaxcala) because he had done some fieldwork in that state; he was considered to be from Puebla because he had worked in that state at some point; because his mother had been a teacher in the state of Veracruz, in one event he was considered to be from that state and at another as being sensitive to the problems of the teachers; on the Day of the Agronomist, the Agronomists' College named him an honorary member since he had written his thesis on Mexico's agrarian problems; in a meeting with scientists, they referred to him repeatedly as "doctor Salinas de Gortari" (substituting the traditional term of "licenciado" used among the political class with one more appreciated within academic circles), claiming a special affinity between the candidate and their sector. In Xochimilco where the twenty-fourth electoral district was located, people argued that he was part of them since he owned property there—which was true.

The candidate actively promoted this process of appropriation by wearing specific attires. He either tried to make his appearance similar to that of the members of the sector he was meeting with or wore the clothing used in the region he was visiting. This meant that he often had to change clothes several times in one day. One interviewee compared this to a film in which Doris Day played a movie actress whose films were seen by her own children:

> The mother comes out suddenly, dressed as a cowgirl, shoots a few bullets, and goes with a man; another harasses her and the former defends her. Thereafter, she appears dressed as a Roman with chariots; she goes with a man, another harasses her, and the former defends her. Afterward, in a similar scene, one of the children says, "Look, this is the third time that my mother comes out and does the same thing—the only thing is that she dresses differently." This stayed with me very much. The regional differences consisted in that [the candidate] does exactly the same thing, but he simply dresses differently.

Commemorations were never complete until the candidate had responded to the local PRI members' remembrances of heroes and the state's history. Salinas's speeches always began by recognizing the importance, beauty, or strength of the state in question or by highlighting the events and the people of the state that had played an important role in national history (national heroes, key political and social events, relevant artists or writers). Mention of these individuals was intended to affirm the region's importance to the country and vice versa: this region gives its "best children" to the nation, finding its reason to exist in the recognition it receives by the country. In his final act in his tour of Puebla, Salinas said: "Puebla has contributed a lot to the nation's causes: during the independence and reform movements, with Gabino Barreda, and on May 5th—one of the historic dates that gives the majority of Mexicans their greatest pride. During the revolution there were the Serdáns, as well as many other people from Puebla, who participated in the reform and independence movements." Guanajuato was the birthplace of independence: the Tabasco-born Carlos Pellicer, the Veracruz-born Salvador

Díaz Mirón, and the Jalisco-born Juan Rulfo and José Clemente Orozco had transformed regional values into Mexican values and were now recognized by the entire world.

Simultaneously, new heroes and historic periods were selected that provided the state with transcendence. In a televised broadcast, the candidate stated:

> I rejoice in the fact that you are deserving descendants of this tradition of Juan Sarabía or of Ponciano Arriaga or of other renowned citizens of San Luis Potosí of this century, such as the teacher Jesús Silva Herzog [senior], and Don Paco Ramírez de la Vega, and also, such a distinguished person from San Luis Potosí as the engineer Manuel Moreno Torres, who was from Matehuala and who performed an extraordinary job in the Federal Electricity Commission. These, just to mention a few of the renowned children of San Luis Potosí, have not only served their state but also their homeland.

Specific details disappear within a homogenizing context; the states exist thanks to the nation and they disappear without it. However, the standardization process was never complete. Between one state and another, there were important variations. These variations defined the specificity of each case. In each state and in each location, there was in fact a conscious interest in highlighting these differences. Specifically, the decorations used made each scenario different. The wardrobe worn by different ethnic groups always provided a distinctive touch to each location and event: from the embroidered white materials worn by the women of Yucatán to the broad flowered skirts of the Tarahumaras. Music and its interpretation had its own style in each region. It is not quite the same to receive the candidate to the rhythms of "Zacazonapan" as it is to greet him with the traditional mellow music from Yucatán known as the trova.

The characteristics of those in attendance also varied from place to place. The participants in a state-based campaign, from the general public to the special guests, were natives from that state, or maintained political or economic ties in matters that were of concern to the region. The local heroes who achieved national exposure—those who had always been a part of the history and those who had never been fully recognized—were proof of the specific realities of the state.

Local specificities were further highlighted in the candidate's references to thematic or partial national programs. Salinas made ad hoc references to his four main national topics in his speeches: to the challenges of sovereignty in Cuatrociénagas, Coahuila (February 9, 1988); to issues of democracy in Puebla, Puebla (April 3); to social concerns in Chalco, state of Mexico (May 12); and to economic questions in Monterrey, Nuevo León (May 31). Respectively, these references were made in a border-state manufacturing city, the seat of the first revolutionary uprising, a municipality characterized by its poverty, and the cradle of tremendous national private capital.[1]

Two strategies stood out as generating a dialogue on the concept of nationality during campaign activities. On the one hand, events allowed party sectors, which were the same in each state, to demonstrate their positions and establish and reinforce alliances with diverse groups and with the different interests that they represented. These events were an appeal to the nation in the present. On the other hand, some events directly represented, one could say almost without the intervention of the states, the nation's past with a discussion of the myths of origin of the Mexican people and the organization of the nation's historical realities. One strategy reconstructs the territory at a political and institutional level, and the other traces the mythological map of the country.

The Campaign Slogan and the Candidate's Conflicts with the Party

Specific messages presented during presidential campaigns in Mexico were provided by slogans that gave a preview of the national program (or rhetoric) that the future government would implement. It had become a custom that the campaign slogan, instead of emphasizing a comparative advantage of the PRI's candidate vis-à-vis competitors, would make a veiled reference to the outgoing government. In a hidden fashion, it could refer to rectifying that which presumably had been handled poorly, or it could be a message of open rupture.[2] Salinas's initial slogan, however, was a message of continuity. Modern Politics were the means by which the four great national challenges pointed out by him would be resolved (Avramow Gutiérrez 1989, 178). He also made negative comments about certain aspects of the party's organizational force, such as the statements made against *caciquismo* (domination of local political bosses) in a speech given to petroleum workers (*Excélsior*, Nov. 6, 1987).

In the first few weeks, there was some concern about Salinas's willingness to strengthen the "new political culture" that he promised.[3]

In a conversation with a close collaborator of Salinas in January 1988, the clash between the modernizing concepts of the candidate's team and the customary rules of the PRI were obvious. According to this source, in events "the same words, presentations, ways of seating were always used within a formal ritualism that never led anywhere"; in events organized by the party bases without the presence of the PRI sectors, "people were more content" and showed interest in "the importance of symbols and how they could be changed."[4]

Whether it was because Salinas was associated with the permanence in power of a single group or because some sectors of the party felt aggravated by his reference to modernization, the candidate eventually had to give in and change the slogan to Let Mexico Speak.

The campaign was organized as a series of dialogues between the candidate and the citizens and representatives of the various sectors and regions. In each state, the slogan was adapted to give it a more local feel: Let Puebla Speak! or Let Yucatán Speak!

The slogan was supposed to show sensitivity and the candidate's intention to return to the country and get to know its needs after six years of crisis. However, there was no intention to break away from the past. For the first few months, Salinas continuously insisted on honoring the presidency, and he was hesitant in offering support to his party colleagues (as a form of rejecting the clientelistic methods). However, on February 8, 1988, during a meeting with members of the Regional Confederation of Mexican Workers (Confederación Regional Obrera Mexicana–CROM) in Tlaxcala, he declared: "I am in no way committed to any continuity" (*Excélsior*, Jan. 9, 1987). In the following days, political commentators in the print media began to speculate on the differences between Salinas's and Miguel de la Madrid's policies. Simultaneously, the campaign's strategy shifted, and Salinas ended up making concrete commitments in the talks he held throughout the country. These commitments showed PRI members that the candidate understood the specific problems he would face and that he had decided to resolve them. In the same way, his initial condemnation of "bought" support, after the experience he had in the Comarca Lagunera, which will be discussed later in this chapter, was replaced by vindicating the role played by massive public events as a way for the PRI to express its strength (Cándano Fierro 1989, 56–57).[5] Salinas combined this more or less explicit rupture with symbolic distancing that reinforced the growth of his own strength at the expense of the president's power. At the beginning of the campaign, there were similarly sized photos of the candidate and the president; however, the photos of the candidate became ever larger in comparison to those of the president as time passed.

Although Salinas had conceded to modifying the slogan on the party's behest, modernization continued as a constant theme that Salinas managed to insert in each summary of the historic formation of Mexico and its immersion in the revolutionary nationalist ideology. In his speech at the end of the campaign (July 2, 1988), he said: "As was the case in the independence movement, the reform movement, and during the revolution, today, the people's just struggle arises in their efforts to modernize in the construction of a country that is more just, stronger, and more sovereign. We will modernize the nation. Our proposal has its roots in the past and is profoundly revolutionary" (Salinas 1989a, 310).

Toward the end of the campaign, concrete commitments made by the candidate at different stops of his tour were added to the slogan written on walls, fences, and billboards. In each state, and even in the municipalities, the commitments that had been announced were different and were tied to local problems. In the nation's capital, for example, one could read: "My commitment is with the Federal District. [I will] foster a more equitable distribution of the tortilla bonuses (*tortibonos*)."[6]

The PRI's undersecretary of information and propaganda analyzed Salinas's campaign speeches, taking out the promises made and transforming them into a form of propaganda of "acquired commitments." The propaganda office inserted these commitments as if they had arisen from the population's demands, even though the commitments in reality represented the candidate's adherence to party ideology ("My commitment is to Mexico. I will defend the principles of non-intervention and the free determination of its peoples") or the assimilation of the candidate's program to demands with social content ("My commitment is with the popular classes. [I will] stop the excessive increase in prices"). Congressional candidates of PRI used the same design in their propaganda.

The sense of an apparent direct popular participation that was meant to be transmitted in the campaign was provided through radio announcements in which the "citizen" stated a demand ("The inhabitants of Mexico City want to live in a clean and healthy environment") so that afterward an answer/commitment could be described ("The commitment: to end the Ruta 100's pollution,[7] expand and improve collective transportation, apply the pollution laws rigorously, to decentralize"), ending with another voice on behalf of the candidate ("My commitment is to Carlos Salinas de Gortari").

The Organization of Events

The campaign events, that is to say the public events in which the candidate was present, required enormous logistical and political mobilization. Each visit by the presidential candidate to one of the states required a previous negotiation among at least three actors: the candidate, via his campaign boss and the regional coordinators who were chosen by him; the governor of the state; and the National Executive Committee (Comité Ejecutivo Nacional–CEN) of the PRI via its state representatives. The municipal governments were also involved, as well as the state-based, district, and municipal committees of the party and the sub-departments for information and propaganda and for logistics of the central PRI. The representatives of the CEN determined the general characteristics, the formal rules, and the profound issues that the tour should cover. The governor and the state-based PRI, on the other hand, had the responsibility for the event's actual organization—raising funds and coordinating with local leaders to ensure the event's success and large attendance. The presence of a large number of people in the meetings was considered of great importance, since the party's legitimacy and strength were measured by headcounts. A PRI functionary commented that in one of the visits to a state, "one can no longer say that PRI does not have support in this state: Salinas has filled all the spaces in all of the cities he has visited."

In this way, the organization of each visit to a state represented an opportunity for the candidate to forge alliances with various sectors and local groups. Each event also constituted proof of loyalty, power, and the governor's and regional leaders' political efficiency. If there were any failures in their organization, the CEN of the PRI intervened directly with people and resources from the capital city. Since the personnel involved were members of the candidate's team, he would immediately find out the state of affairs of his alliances with the governors.

The route that the candidate followed was covered by propaganda (placards, flags, banners, painted billboards, etc.) that also had to cover the roads that the contingents of followers used, as well as the main avenues of the city. After the candidate's visit, the movable propaganda was taken to popular or residential areas of the city or was sent to other locations for future visits. Besides the propaganda, events offered those attending useful and personal objects, such as balls, caps, pencils, T-shirts, pins, or stickers with the logo and the slogan of the campaign.

According to the testimony of a team member of a regional coordinating office and a member of the candidate's team, the first part of organizing the campaign consisted of gathering relevant information about the state that was to be visited:

> In [the state of X] I went to do a political analysis. I went to see who the friends or enemies of the governor were, who the political leaders of the region were, the "live forces," etc. I interviewed people in the style of anthropological fieldwork. I talked to almost everyone and handed in my report. . . . They stopped elaborating on these types of reports that demonstrated tendencies. And when we returned, the people we had interviewed recognized us.

> We produced the basic folder with economic, political, and demographic information for each electoral district. The folder was handed over to Robledo; he and Colosio read it, and if they liked it, they made their summaries, which they then passed on to Salinas, who, in turn, had information provided by the INEGI[8] and his own people.

> Information flows vertically and never horizontally. I would tell Robledo [the situation in the state], Robledo would tell Colosio, Colosio Salinas, etc. The delegation of the federal CEN is the one that would give Robledo the "between the lines" information. . . . The president of the state-based PRI is chosen by the governor; the governor by way of the president of the state-based PRI proposes; the delegate releases the information and the negotiation starts. Sometimes, the delegate turns out to be quite mediocre or bought by the governor . . . in this case we would have to do the fieldwork.

Once information was available, depending on the pulse of the state, different groups entered into negotiations about the route that the candidate should take. For everyone, it was important that the chosen route would have many people standing by in a festive mood and that there would be no negative incidents. In negotiating details, each person's own interests were being promoted:

> First, Colosio would speak with the governor of the state, and they would plan out the possible campaign route. Then, the president of the state-based PRI and the federal CEN delegate would arrive and

meet with Colosio and Robledo to negotiate the candidate's route; the president of the PRI or the CEN delegate would continue to negotiate with the governor. For example, the people of the state suggest that Salinas visit the university, and the group from Mexico says no, that the students are very rebellious, but then it turns out that the president of the university is a friend of the governor and insists on the visit.

Each group also pressured the governor. For example, the governor would like that meeting X take place in the industrial park since he constructed it and the people who are there are his . . . in contrast, if Salinas was taken to a popular area, surely people would complain that they did not have water, electricity, that there was corruption, and finally, they would talk badly about the governor [of the state].

The degree of success or failure of each visit was seen as directly related to the governor, who not only was ultimately responsible for state politics but also was responsible for accepting the candidate wholeheartedly:

The governors who were not with Salinas did not care. In [the state of X] we had a bad time. The events turned out badly: there was a confrontation between the delegate and the president of the PRI. The delegate was bought. . . . There were only a few people present and the event was cold. The largest event had twelve thousand people.

In [state Y] it was very good: the governor is very good even though he was a "man of Bartlett"; he had run-ins with Otto Granados and with the delegate of PRI who had just been changed; the president of the state-based PRI really was very good. . . . In this way, the campaign was highly successful with meetings of forty thousand people . . . each one of them very good.

Those on the candidate's team charged with negotiating operations in the field had to do so in a conciliatory manner, taking the interests of local party structures into consideration while assuming responsibility toward their hierarchical superiors:

We arrived and introduced ourselves to the state-based president of PRI and the municipal president wherever we went. They provided you with a hotel, food, and car. You arrived and introduced yourself, "Sir, I am so and so" . . . and the other would answer, "Yes, what do you want?" "I am going to work in such and such municipality."

The difficulty of the situation was that we went in support of the state-based PRI. That is to say, the programs and the events are theirs and their responsibility. But, if anything goes wrong I am the one who gets fired. Before the state, we were the people of Carlos Salinas de Gortari. They would say to you, "Of course, sir, anything you say," and suddenly the music fails, the carpenters needed are unavailable, and they give you hell. . . . I never carried money or covered expenses. They [the state-based PRI] provided everything, but if anything was lacking it was your responsibility.

It starts with vagueness: we want to have peasant events, an event with young people, one with women and one with indigenous people, the middle class, etc. You start arguing, and they tell you: "The one with peasants is not going to happen and you had better add an event with fishermen that is really good because the [union] delegate is a congressperson and a really good leader. Think about it."

These arrangements, which specified or introduced slight variations to the negotiated plan, were never final since they had to be discussed with the higher-ups and as a result were subject to continuous new changes until the plan got to the candidate, who had the last word. Therefore, information on programmed activities was treated with an enormous degree of caution:

This is going to be discussed [a particular event] with the governor: he says no to this and says that another event should be held instead . . . and you start discussing with the delegate all over again. There are many circles—coming and going. The delegate will pass the gossip along to Robledo and information filters out.

We negotiated, but de la Vega also negotiated with the governor. The delegates had the obligation to report all movements to the president of the PRI [de la Vega], not to Colosio [the head of the campaign].

Once a project had come together, Colosio took it to Salinas, and he would either accept or reject it or suggest changes. . . . Colosio took it to him and made the pertinent changes.

We could not say anything, until a week before; nothing was said because everything was being negotiated [in case] something did not turn out right. The people start having expectations and then they become disillusioned. Each village wants to have its own event, and people put up a substantial fight to get it.

Once the political part and negotiations about events were finalized, another logistical phase followed that was no less complex given that in each one of the events specific groups and individuals had to show the candidate and his followers the political group that they represented:

> The people are brought in. . . . The meeting involves around twenty steps, with complicated logistics.
> We talked to the president of the party and the delegate. We coordinated with the municipal president. He told us whom we should talk to, and we also—without him knowing it—talked to others. We started to develop the event, to identify the local leaders. If you knew which events were going to take place, you talked and chose those leaders. As the time of the event gets closer, the pressure is on. The most important thing was how many people would attend, to ensure that people would be there, and you ask the person from the municipality, "How many people are you going to gather?" "Some five thousand." And you talk to an old man, and he tells you, "Here no more than one thousand people have ever been brought together." And you have to get together with the municipal president, and in order not to offend him, you suggest a smaller-scale event to be held at a smaller place (so that it is not as noticeable that so few people are in attendance), and you continue negotiating: the ones that are responsible for filling up the trucks with people, the ones that are to come from the productive sector, etc.
> The second problem arises: who is going to speak—the negotiation about the orators. . . . He proposes [someone], and you investigate if the person is a drug trafficker, if he beats his wife, etc. You decide who will speak and who won't, but the one you decide will not speak you put on the podium, or you have him be the moderator or the one who hands over some document to Salinas, all of this just so he won't be offended. In each place, there is a person responsible for the event, but usually he/she knows nothing about the event, and you have to make all the decisions, even the color of the photo of the candidate and whether a photo or an oil painting should be hung, and make sure that he does not look awful! If this is the case, you have to tell the responsible person: "I don't believe that this is a good idea, we should better use a photo in which he appears with some corncobs, since this is going to be a peasant event." If you don't do these things with tact, they get upset, and they don't bring in people

and they tell you: "You just go and have lunch; we have experience since the people of de la Madrid were here before. You will see the event that we will organize for you!" And you say, "What do I do?" because you don't want to offend them, but sometimes they don't pay attention to you.

Another person interviewed, who at the time was a functionary of the party in one of the states, elaborated on the importance of the decisions about who would be invited and who would speak in public. With regard to the first point, she said, "It was very important that invitations were made without leaving anyone out, unless the political intention was to purposefully leave someone out." Speeches represented an opportunity for promotion for those who spoke: "You always let a person you wish to promote speak at events. When someone spoke at an event, you always knew that they were being given a space so that they could shine in front of the candidate, that they were being *placeado*, that he/she would be taken to the balcony so that the people could see them and so that they would get to know them. [They could be] local leaders or candidates to the federal congress, or it could be a person wanting to become a candidate to a federal or local congressional position or the person wanting to become mayor."

As soon as the candidate issued a signal, the promotional mechanism was automatically activated. In an event in the Santa Anita colony of the Federal District, the speaker Rosita discussed the conditions of poverty, and Salinas in his speech noted that "Rosita was the type of leader who was needed in the Federal District," since she upheld ties between the leader and the party bases. Immediately, someone in the audience said to another person, "One has to support Rosita's son," and both joined in the cheers organized at the start of the event.

Finally, the order in which the speakers were introduced was also significant, since it corresponded to hierarchies not necessarily based on rank within the formal power structure but rather moral issues. Therefore, determinations regarding the order of speeches were based on an informal "protocol," as stated by the previous interviewee.

Continuing with the version presented by the person who was a member of the campaign team and charged with organizing events, once the speakers had been selected came

the third phase: the place of the event. How many chairs, what type of podium, the separations, how many people at the podium, who would they be, and who should speak. Here the logistics come into play of those [of the presidential office] in charge of security, sound, lighting, and they make two or three prior recommendations. . . . Robledo oversees logistical matters and negotiates with the presidential office.

Afterward, one has to get the carpenters, painters, etc. I coordinated, but you can only make suggestions to the people of the municipality: "Sir, time is upon us."

[At some moment] you call Mexico City quarters because propaganda is missing and you don't have enough photos. At this stage, we could already envision the event.

The fourth stage was made up of preparatory meetings with those who would participate—a kind of rehearsal—who will meet the candidate Salinas, where he will enter, what people will be at the podium once Salinas arrives, and there are not allowed to be any empty seats.

Once everything has been rehearsed, the speeches are checked. They should be short, at most five pages long. I used to cut down the speakers' presentations. I censured them, "Don't say this; say that there are substantial problems with corruption; say the same thing, but in a different tone; if not, everything is going to go downhill." Then the speeches would be given to Robledo.

Finally, I would make the "no. 3 card" that had the name of the event, the place where it was taking place, the time at which it was scheduled to start and end, who would be speaking and what they would say, how many people would talk, etc.

I would give this card to Colosio, and then one could only wait for the event. That wait is terrible: people don't arrive, what happened with the buses, what happened with the human wall, they were not given any money for gas, and "Remember, sir, I told you" that a speaker will not show up, the sound or lighting system fails. Sometimes Salinas arrived, and they would just be setting up the platform that they had not had time enough to finish.

Colosio in his capacity as the campaign coordinator personally headed the advance team that would check the conditions of the event before the candidate arrived. He asked for additional information that could be useful to the candidate so that Salinas could improvise during his speech and present himself as if he were a local resident, such as "when the cathedral was built" or "who built it."

"The event passes. If things go well, Colosio calls and congratulates you. Thirty-five days of work are put at risk in an hour; if the electricity goes out, if not enough people showed up, everything is your fault." If the event turns out extremely well, the explicit congratulations by Colosio were replaced by a pat on the back or some other subtle gesture by the candidate. As another person we interviewed stated, the importance in this case was not the gesture in and of itself, but that all those present would see it.

Events could go wrong because of logistical errors, but also because of political reasons since they also represented an opportunity to sow seeds of internal discord:

> I had two bad events: one with parents that was boycotted by the union, and they sent me a group of high school provocateurs. It was because of a conflict between the union and the PRI. I did not have enough experience and know-how.
>
> In [the municipality of Z], I had to organize a lunch for the productive sectors, and everything went well. Salinas was happy. I also had a bad event in Ciudad Cuauhtémoc: another lunch. It was a stupid mistake—the meeting and thereafter the lunch. People went to the meeting first, but Salinas got there before them, and he arrived before the guests and found empty tables.

The campaign represented a test for middle-level organizers. Specifically, if the candidate noticed any flaws in the organization, those responsible could see their political careers hampered. Unofficially, it became a selection and recruitment process of leaders, as those who showed efficiency in political and logistical chores in their implementation of the candidate's various events could become future administrators.

Those charged with handling these types of activities were generally young PRI members with university degrees. Their campaign participation was a type of political training where they were tested. Because of their age and educational background, they could fulfill their tasks without generating suspicions since they were not associated with any specific network of loyalties.

The mechanisms used by diverse PRI groups to mobilize contingents of followers at these events were a function of the relationship between the different leaders, their personal power, and their social bases or subordinates. These structures were part of the overall negotiations of leaders with the candidate and eventually of followers and their leaders.

Mobilization—popularly called the *acarreo*—happened in three ways. The simplest form was an exchange of money for attendance at meetings. This type of mobilization does not create personal relationships and represents only a simple market exchange.[9] As stated by Etzioni (1975), this brings a kind of audience that is passive or indifferent to the comings and goings of party politics. In another form of mobilization, personal relationships were created, but with a coercive component. It was based on the bureaucratic control exercised over subordinates' sources of employment: typically, a union leader cross-checked the attendance list at events with the names of employees on the payroll in a factory or a public office, issuing threats that they would be sanctioned in economic terms, such as by having a work day discounted if they did not attend the event. This modality lacks an element present in the third type of mobilization: a long-term relationship of loyalty between the mobilizer and the mobilized. In this third case, mobilization is in relation to a leader's ability to obtain resources (money, support, services) and relies on a personal and reciprocal commitment to his/her followers who would provide active support for the PRI through the leader. This form of mobilization reflected the vigor of social relationships which lasted for years. As an added benefit, it constituted a "live" test of the strength and social reach of the PRI.

Groups of followers that had been brought together in one way or another demonstrated the mobilizing capabilities of leaders attending an event. The leader's (and the leader of the leaders') strength was measured by the number of people he/she had mobilized, which meant that different attires and banners of support were a means of determining who should be credited with people's attendance. For example, in just one event in the Iztacalco area, we observed placards of the Confederation of Mexican Workers (Confederación de Trabajadores de México–CTM); the Union Federation of Workers of the Federal District; the Council for the Integration of Women; the Federation of the Educational Leagues of Parents; the Federation of Popular Organizations; and the association of merchants in street fairs, public roads, and the free zones of the Federal District.

Campaign Activities and Events

Almost every tour of a state lasted for three days, during which time the candidate participated in what became called "dialogues with social groups" in different parts of the country. All tours included an event in the capital city or in one of the most important cities of the state, an event with each one of the three sectors, personal visits, meetings with businesspeople and with the communications media, as well as some meetings with the Center for Political, Economic, and Social Studies (Centro de Estudios Políticos, Económicos y Sociales–CEPES) and the Institute for Political, Economic, and Social Studies (Instituto de Estudios Políticos, Económicos y Sociales–IEPES). In the multipurpose events, a "mailbox for the candidate" would be set up.

The following agenda from a tour of Puebla in February 1988 is an example of the activities that took place in the states during the campaign:

Thursday, 18

10:30 Meeting with the three sectors of the PRI in Atlixco

11:50 Meeting with the agrarian sector in Tehuacán

17:25 Evaluation meeting with the PRI at the headquarters of the state directive committee

Friday, 19

10:00 Meeting with the agricultural sector in Teziutlán

12:00 Celebration of the 50th anniversary of the CNOP in Cuetzalán, with three awards of recognition to be given to distinguished PRI members

17:00 Meeting with electricians in Necaxa

19:00 IEPES meeting in the Puebla area

Saturday, 20

9:00 Television program

10:00 Meeting with agronomists of the National Confederation of Peasants (Confederación Nacional Campesina–CNC) at the Main Theater

11:00 Meeting with the National Union of Education Workers (Sindicato Nacional de Trabajadores de la Educación–SNTE)

12:00 Closing event with the participation of the entire town at the zocalo of the city

RECEPTION

The Reception of the Candidate

It was common to welcome the candidate in airports and bus or train stations, on dusty sports fields, or in football and baseball stadiums that also functioned as helipads. Hundreds of people gathered in these places to celebrate his arrival. The banners of workers, peasants, teachers, the popular sectors, market merchants, taxi drivers, public accountants in the service to the state, and other groups, organizations, and unions filled the place.

Some receptions were more successful than others, with success being measured by the number of people in attendance and by the emotional component of the event. One example of a successful reception at an event, according to the organizers if not the attendees, took place at the San Luis Potosí airport, which marked the initiation of the PRI candidate's campaign in this state.

At 10 a.m., thousands of PRI members had gathered at the airport. It was extremely cold: everyone was covered up, and some women even wore fur coats. To warm up, everyone was given coffee and tamales. Even though there was little time left before the candidate was to arrive, a party-like atmosphere was created. A woman who always participated in PRI events began to sing regional and mariachi songs while the Trio Alma Llanera interpreted other types of music. A man took the microphone and began rehearsing cheers for when the candidate arrived: "Salinas to the presidential residence [Los Pinos] with the votes of the people of Potosí"; "With the people present, Salinas will be president"; "Yes, yes, yes, Salinas is here."

At 11 a.m., the airplane arrived. Cheering intensified. At this point there were around ten thousand people at the airport. A group of people hurried out to the waiting area. It seems that the candidate was walking in their midst, surrounded by a large number of people. Within seconds and without anyone noticing, he got on his bus and left. After him, the buses holding his contingent left as well as the cars of leading Potosí PRI members.

Even though the candidate's time at the airport was minimal, people who had come to welcome Salinas continued to stay at the airport for several hours. The buses of the contingents had left; the vehicles of the various sectors had returned to PRI offices in the city. Many buses that had brought people to the airport returned empty. For many, there was no other solution than to walk back and to be furious. Five kilometers separated them from the nearest highway. As they were walking, they began making comments. They said that "it was unheard of" that the PRI would simply leave the people stranded at the airport. A very indignant man commented: "And we did not even see the 'bald' one." Another remembered the time when Carlos Jonguitud, the leader of the Revolutionary Vanguard of the SNTE, was the governor of the state: then they would not have closed off the waiting area of the airport just for a select few, as they did now; on the contrary, everyone would have been able to get in. There were of course also those who associated this abandonment with the lack of political participation: "There is no one anymore who wants to participate in the events; we work ourselves to the bone, and there is no one to give us anything in exchange, not even respect." They said that the important thing was not to co-opt people, but to know how to keep them on one's side.

At PRI offices, the state delegate was a little bit worried because a woman had just demanded an explanation as to why three thousand people had been left stranded at the airport. He dialed a number and reported the various complaints. But the truth is that for the organizers the welcome had been successful, since the candidate had seen an enthusiastic multitude of people, and everything else (such as the level of satisfaction or discontent of this multitude) had much lesser importance.

Acts of Collaboration and Party Support

The candidate's tour of the state of Tabasco started with a massive event at the Plaza of the Revolution. The three PRI sectors from the state and the seventeen municipalities were present. Early on, the "mailbox of the candidate" was installed. It literally was a box in which anyone could present his/her views in writing to the candidate as they pleased.[10] A voice came from a loudspeaker saying:

> Carlos Salinas asks you to submit your petitions, that you denounce abnormalities and irregular practices in your community, that you make suggestions. Mister, missus, and young person, fill out the form if you want something; whatever it is you want, only by filling out the form will you have a solution. Give us your solution. If you have a problem in your community, fill out the form! If you want there to be an expansion of some sporting facility, a tank, fill out the form! If you have any problems with some local authority, any problems with the costs of guarantees, if your community needs a highway, a bridge, or a communal landholding. . . . Rest assured that you will receive a response. . . . Whatever you need, some special permit that exists, fill out the form! Any abnormality, any solution to so many problems

that exist, write to the candidate. If you have any idea how to solve the country's problems, say so! If you need anything, this is the time to tell the candidate. If you, lady, want to petition the candidate, if you need to hospitalize someone, or send someone to the country's capital, do it!

There were about thirty people gathered around the mailbox listening or willing to sit down at a small portable table and write to the candidate. "Take advantage of this opportunity to express what you are thinking and how you think. If you don't state your problem, nobody will know about it. Tell him the problem that you have, who is extorting you, who is denying you credit, if you have any problems with your representative . . . a price guarantee that has not been pointed out to you. . . . Rest assured that you will receive a response. If you don't point out [your problems], if you don't state them, nobody will know about them. . . . Now is the moment, remember that after July 6 it will no longer work."

The plaza, as is customary in these events, was decorated with the propaganda of the various party sectors and of each of the municipalities. The banners seemed to be talking to one another. On the one side was No More Scarcity, and Enforce Judicial Laws in the rural areas; on the other side was Let Tabasco Speak!, I Am Committed to Listening to All Mexicans. CSG.

At the end of the plaza there was the official photo of a smiling Carlos Salinas with a look of understanding and at his side Miguel de la Madrid, dry and somber, preoccupied with the moral renovation of the country.

The public had been asked to arrive at 10:30 a.m.; of course, they had to arrive much earlier. Some commented that from Paraíso the buses left at 7:30 a.m. and that they had arrived in Villahermosa at 9:30 a.m., a time at which the plaza had been taken over by fruit, ice, sweets, and cookie vendors.

An hour before the event was scheduled to begin, there were approximately ten thousand people at the plaza. The region of Jalpa alone had sent nine buses filled with people. The seventeen municipalities were organized in columns and in alphabetical order. Once in a while, the professional entertainer took attendance. At the mention of the municipality's name, the respective contingent had to shout "Present." "Paraiso"; "Present"; "Nacajuca"; "Present"; "Jalpa"; "Present" and so forth in this manner. "This is perfect, but you have to shout louder: Shout! Shout! And when you shout, raise your placards."

The wait for the candidate served as a time to rehearse cheers, songs, and slogans. The entertainer, with a strong and vigorous voice, transmitted his enthusiasm to those present. The purpose of the entertainer was to make this long wait into an orderly and festive event; his responsibility was to keep the public calm, avoid at all costs people leaving, and to ensure that the candidate would not be received by people with long and tired faces. Thus, the "warming-up exercises took place": "Those adolescent cheers! May they be heard as if they were a political symphony!" And, since they still were not heard: "They should have had some chocolate milk this morning!"

An exercise that had been organized substantially ahead of time was put to the test. "Let us show the candidate that we are convinced, that we are committed, that we are PRI members! Let us renew the practice of making demands!" This exercise involved the exchange of questions and answers between the entertainer and the public. Attendees received a written form with basic instructions. On it was written:

> Proposal for consignments for the working meeting of the candidate
>   with the sectarian committees of the PRI in Tabasco:
> What comes before everything and everyone?
> THE NATION
> Who in Mexico is in charge of sovereignty?
> THE PEOPLE
> What is our form of life like?
> DEMOCRATIC
> How do we speak in Mexico?
> WITH ACTIONS
> Which is the party of the people?
> THE PRI
> Who is the candidate of revolutionary unity?
> CARLOS SALINAS DE GORTARI
> Whom are we going to vote for?
> FOR CARLOS SALINAS
> Who will win?
> CARLOS SALINAS

"Very good, but you also have to raise your fists!" The exercise was repeated innumerable times. The entertainer urged people to shout out loud and to demonstrate to the candidate, once the moment had come, how much they were convinced of and committed to the PRI and its candidate. Generally, Salinas arrived when least expected, as if each event were a type of test for all those interested in "being on the good side" of the future president of the republic.

The event was scheduled for 11:00 a.m., and at 11:55 a.m. Dart-K cars arrived with security agents, the contingent of Federal District politicians, three ADO buses carrying special guests, and two buses with members of the press. The total number of people was around one hundred. Most of them were dressed in guayaberas (a formal shirt worn by men in Mexico) or short-sleeved shirts, appropriate for the heat of the time, although an absentminded woman dressed in a woolen suit could also be found. The well-uniformed aides were already at their designated positions. The special guests and the press occupied their places on the bleachers. For a few minutes, a helicopter flew over the area.

At the forum, a musical group and a band entertained those present. Among the multitudes, some had written the acronym of opposition parties over the PRI logo on their caps with red pens. They were against the PRI, but were present at the meeting and thus complying with their obligations.

At 12:05 p.m., the candidate finally arrived, suddenly as always. He raised his right arm in greeting. By this time, there were over fifteen thousand people in attendance. The candidate, dressed in one of his characteristic light green suits, was accompanied by his wife and Enrique González Pedrero, general director of the IEPES, and preceded by security agents who could be distinguished by their walkie-talkies. His arrival led to upheaval. The entertainer regained his enthusiasm, sirens sounded, the rattles and cheers could be heard, and the peasants raised their sombreros. In the middle, a human wall formed to allow the candidate to reach the podium. The shoves and pushes began: "We ask our colleagues to be so kind as to let everyone see the event since we are all of the same party."

The candidate crossed the plaza while the multitudes closed the path behind him. At the center of the plaza, he walked up to the podium and sat down next to the governor of Tabasco; the speakers sat to the right of the podium. While they were settling down, the entertainer continued: "Banners up, banners down so that our candidate can appreciate this act of cohesion and party support." Applause, cheers, and noise could be heard. "Before you, comrades, you have the presence of our candidate to the presidency of the republic—Carlos Salinas de Gortari!"

The leader of the state-based PRI spoke first, followed immediately by Salinas. While this took place, the ice cream vendors were making a windfall. At the beginning of the event, flavored ice in a bag cost around 200 pesos, but in the midst of the candidate's speech, it reached a price of 250 pesos. Someone who was enjoying a bag of flavored ice proposed that the vendor be denounced in the candidate's mailbox, and others said, "Yes, man, you are not a participant in this act of solidarity."

The speech ended with an exchange of questions and answers. Salinas asked whether the people were willing to vote for him in the next election, to which the multitudes replied, "Yes!" But amidst the affirmative chorus, some Nos could be heard.

These types of events took place in the capital and main cities of the states. In all of them, the PRI sectors and the municipalities that made up the area participated. They were both sectoral and territorial acts, even though in some cases the organization was based on a municipality and in others on a specific sector. When municipalities were the focus, people formed into columns and each carried a placard with the name of their place of origin. When it was the sectors, the entertainer was charged with taking attendance of the different sectors from the regional structure. "May the workers sector show its presence!"; "May the popular sector show its presence!"; "Present!" Each group was dressed in outfits that were distinctive of their sector. The peasants, for example, wore palm sombreros, and their traditional greeting throughout the country consisted of shaking their sombreros with raised arms.

The acts of cohesion and party support were always similar. Generally, there were three speeches, apart from the candidate's. The speakers were the presidents of the sectoral and municipal committees of the state-based party. Frequently, one of the speakers was a woman.

The speeches given were traditionally PRI-like. The same structure was repeated over and over again. First, the speeches opened with a magical charm and with the phrase: "Citizen Carlos Salinas de Gortari, candidate to the presidency of the republic, party comrade." Secondly, everyone referred to the blessings enjoyed by the region: "Before this beautiful panorama of this northern corner of the coast of Jalisco, land that has given birth to a number of illustrious men and talented women." Thirdly, the political sectors or groups that were included were mentioned (workers, peasants, popular sectors, and women). Fourthly, the president and the governor received recognition and assurances that the state was "eminently in favor of the PRI." Lastly, the economic crisis that tore through the country was recognized, and with this, complaints and demands, always to the point, began: the peasants demanded the adjustment to guaranteed prices of agrarian products; the workers required an increase in the general minimum salary; the popular sectors asked for support for housing and public services.

It should be noted that the complaints and demands were always within the publicly tolerated margins, even if at times they were truly heartfelt. In San Pablo Oxtotepec, Milpa Alta, the peasants angrily demanded a solution to their water and transportation problems, also requesting that a property be expropriated. Salinas offered facts and not promises—which in the end is a way of not offering anything.

The speeches usually closed with a guarantee that the solution lay within the party, in the candidate to the presidency and his modern politics, and with the confirmation of unlimited support for the candidate and a renewed regional pride.

The candidate, on his part, took the demands of the sectors and promised to return to meet these demands with actions "if the people on July 6 take me to the presidency of the republic." Salinas's commitment in this sense was continuously expressed. In general terms, it was made in similar fashion in all the events, as stated in a district of the capital city: "I did not come here to make promises, but to make a commitment, and if I get to the presidency, tomorrow I will return to Iztacalco and with actions fulfill what today I am promising. Mexicans don't want promises, they want actions, and I will come back to act."

If the acts of cohesion and party support were similar, they were never completely the same, and in some cases there were notable differences. In particular, the characteristics of those in attendance varied substantially from place to place. Even though the three sectors of the party were always present, in some cases one of them dominated over the others. Additionally, in the interior of the country, within a sector such as the workers, there would be events geared toward mining or train workers' segments, for example. In every instance, details made each event unique in its character. The regional touch was always present in the form of music, in the content of certain speeches, and in the small surprises among those invited and the speakers. For example, in Saltillo, Coahuila, a television actress was present who was introduced as a woman "one hundred percent of the PRI." Amidst cheers and applause, Mrs. Carmen Salinas, who was a part of the group of special guests, went to the podium and took the microphone: "Thank you, thank you so much and good evening dear fellow country people. I join you in celebrating the reception of Carlos Salinas de Gortari. Let all of us support him because I believe him to be the right man to lead this country, and also he is a tremendously straightforward person, a person with a great sense of humor. Is this because he is a Salinas? I am very pleased to be here with all of you, sharing in this moment, and above all else because I feel very proud to be from here, from Coahuila."

In Monclova, an "artistic festival" was organized with the participation of Ángeles Robirosa and the northern musical group Los Rítmicos. Even the noise level varied. In some places, trumpets ruled, while in others there were rattles or sirens; sometimes what was heard the most were the whistles of a train.

The time spent waiting also varied from place to place. In Tabasco, people had to wait for the candidate for almost two hours; in Puerto Vallarta, Jalisco, the wait was as long as five hours, which was a true challenge to the entertainer's abilities. Three hours after the contingents had arrived, he announced: "And now, music Mexicans! Yes, sir! The moment has arrived." But nothing happened, and there were no signs of the candidate. "The moment has arrived . . . for the municipal band to entertain us with jubilation." And he intoned the song "Guadalajara, Guadalajara."

In some places, the organization of the event was impeccable; in other places the organization was lacking. In an event in the northern part of the country, the candidate arrived while people were still handing out placards, the sound system cables were being installed, and last-minute arrangements were being made. In the same region of the country, an event that took place in the evening was poorly attended. The entertainer had to perform a miracle to convince those in attendance to keep their placards raised so that the candidate would not notice that only a few people were present.

In this campaign, there were events that went beyond anything projected by the organizers and even by the candidate himself. This was the case in the party events organized in San Pedro de las Colonias and in Francisco I. Madero, Coahuila. The region of the Lake District (Comarca Lagunera) was a Cárdenas area that awaited the arrival of their leader on the following day.

In San Pedro de las Colonias, a place where Lázaro Cárdenas started agrarian land redistribution and where Francisco I. Madero wrote the book that would light the fire of revolution, tensions could be felt long before the event actually started. There were no banners listing demands or requests: there was only PRI propaganda. Salinas arrived, accompanied by Enrique González Pedrero, Héctor Hugo Olivares, Otto Granados, and Guillermo Fonseca. As they got closer to the podium, the shouting started: "People who have been bought, people who have been bought." The young people were shouting that they had been paid five thousand pesos to be there and they were there waiting for the candidate. The candidate had to leave through a back exit.

In Madero, the situation became even more difficult. It was around 8:00 p.m., and it was getting cold. There were about three thousand people congregated along a street that had only one exit. When the candidate arrived, they began jeering and pushing and shoving. When the candidate moved toward the podium, "a woman came close and threw a glass of water on his face" (*Excélsior*, Feb. 11, 1988). When the candidate actually arrived at the podium, support slogans for Cárdenas could be heard. Salinas decided to change the schedule of events and took the microphone: "Here in Madero the peasants want the truth, and they want to discuss the problems that exist with the handing over of credits and insurance payments. . . . Here in Madero the peasants rather than those who come offering illusions would work the hard soil, just like the peasants do. Here in Madero they no longer want promises: they want the offers that have been made fulfilled."

Salinas tried to turn the situation around by blaming Cárdenas supporters and by acting as if he represented the opposition. When the event finished, the candidate decided to walk to the bus among the multitudes. He seemed to want to show his valor. People closed in on him, renewing their insulting chants and their slogans supporting Cárdenas until, about thirty meters away from the bus, a group of young people began to throw the sticks that had held up PRI propaganda. Surrounded by the presidential security forces, Salinas got to the bus. He received no blow, but once inside the bus, and while the people continued throwing bits of wood and stones, he kept silent and somber.

The newspaper *Excélsior* reported the event in the following manner:

It seemed that the world was coming down on him. The human wall closed around him with every one of the candidate's steps, pushes, blows, shouts of the multitudes, "Cárdenas, Cárdenas!" intense jeering, and once again people were coming toward the candidate, until at the end, there in Madero, a group of the Cárdenista Front ended up throwing sticks at the base of the bus. Salinas left for Batopilas. Slowly, he recuperated his good mood. And there everything seemed

to change. The smile returned, he partook in the *barbacoa* [barbe-
cue], received hugs, and the insults and the blows appeared to be a
thing of the past.

The following day, the official newspaper *El Nacional* (Feb. 2, 1988)
quoted the words of two legislators. One of them saw the acts committed by the people as irresponsible and as representative of a minority
within the great masses that supported the PRI candidate. The other one
assured that when at a meeting sympathy toward various candidates is
expressed, this was nothing other than a clear sign of the "ambiance of
freedom in which all Mexicans live."

An Event with Women

These statements were written on banners carried by PRI supporters:

The housewives will transform the country through our children.
CSG
CSG. The women's vote will take you to the presidency.
The peasant and indigenous women will vote for hope. CSG
CSG. Women are life, women are votes, women are transformation.
Mrs. Cecilia Ocelli de Salinas de Gortari: the female teachers give you
our demonstration of support and our vote.

For the first time, it seemed that the presidential campaign of Carlos
Salinas included the active participation of women. The organization of
women represented an additional category to those of the industrial sectors and specific professions. In any event, a meeting dedicated to women
was organized in all states and in all the capitals and main cities.

"We are in party mode. It is an honor and a pride that for the first
time in the history of our state there has been a meeting and an open
dialogue with our candidate to the presidency of the republic," said a
female candidate for a congressional position in the state of San Luis
Potosí. A female senator from the same state commented: "These types
of events constituted an opportunity to discuss those issues that in the
past could never be discussed as much in depth . . . because of that little
bit of prudery, that little problem that existed, which luckily we have discarded from our mentality . . . because we women will not be gagged."

Every event organized with women had its own tone: it depended on
the place and the characteristics of the participants. Usually, the events

took place in closed areas that were well furnished. They could range from the very elegant, like the ones that took place in the main theater of Mérida or in luxury salons of the Hilton Hotel in Guadalajara, to those organized in party halls converted to auditoriums for the occasion. They could be crowded events similar to those of the acts of cohesion and party support or like the "meeting and open dialogue" sessions: working tables with a podium and a moderator, usually the female coordinator of the Council for the Integration of Women (Consejo para la Integración de la Mujer–CIM), the PRI party division that was responsible for coordinating the participation of women in the three party sectors. While in the multitudinous events, the decorations were the same as in any other event of this kind; in the "meeting and open dialogue" events, they were rather somber. Except for the banner that hung on the back wall that indicated the name of the event and the date, there were no other banners or propaganda.

The events were attended by women from all walks of life: young and old, middle class, married women from high society, wives of the powerful people of the area, and peasant indigenous women from the community and the communal landholdings that had been asked to come. Everyone always dressed up in gala outfits for these occasions, according to their styles and abilities, ranging from the traditional regional style of the indigenous woman to the pearl necklace of a female workers' leader.

Through the CIM, the representatives of all party sectors participated. The candidate attended these events dressed in an elegant dark suit, with a serious attitude on some occasions and a flirtatious nature on others. In fact, he was seen as having a certain "charm." In a radio program in Orizaba, Veracruz, the host asked Susy, the leader of the CIM, the following question:

> Does the personality of Carlos Salinas have anything to do with the fact that he attracts women? I remember that in Veracruz when we were together, he turned around and gave women that were in the so beautifully organized event at the plaza a smile, and they were overwhelmed with a sense of extraordinary happiness.
>
> Susy: I will give you my personal point of view since it happened to me. . . . In reality he is more straightforward in his dealings and I believe that you won't let me lie, Pepe, we were together, and he is easygoing, so simple, and the truth is that yes, yes, he is very attractive, sensitive to talking about women. He was an angel.

The national and state-based coordinators were a part of the podium of the CIM, as well as female senators and deputies, and of course, the candidate, his committee, and the special guests. There were cases in which the podium primarily included men. In Ciudad Valles, San Luis Potosí, the entire audience consisted of women, while the podium included all the representatives of the different sectors, the coordinator of the campaign, the president, the leader of the party, the substitute representative candidate, and only two women—the municipal president's wife (doña Emilia) and the head of the CIM.

If the events with women had anything in common that differentiated them from the other campaign events, it was the apparent cordiality, the extreme respect, the displays of caring and affection, and the concern for details specifically associated with women.

We attended the meeting of the CIM in Ciudad Valles, San Luis Potosí. While waiting for the candidate to arrive, there was a festive, buoyant ambiance; the women seemed to be much more enthusiastic and participatory than men at other events. The moment the candidate arrived and started walking toward the platform to take his place at the center of the podium, the cheering started: "The women represent strength, valor, tenderness, courage, and millions of votes for you, Carlos Salinas de Gortari . . . an applause for our candidate."

When a "meeting and open dialogue" event was involved, the speeches covered specific themes such as "the current situation of housewives" and "support to indigenous women." Each speech started off with a greeting sent to the wife of the candidate. During one of the speeches, a woman got up from her chair at the podium and launched a *bomba* (improvised rhyme): "Las mujeres potosinas somos de convicción, y para apoyar al PRI tenemos puesto el corazón" (The women of Potosí are of strong convictions and we have our heart supporting PRI).

Speeches emphasized affective ties, caring, love, and those virtues "associated with femininity," sometimes exaggeratedly: "A lightening flash of love, justice, and peace reign at the end of this six-year term so that you may change the situation of our Mexico. May there be a state of peace and love for all Mexicans, a love that all of us who are alike and live in this wonderful and beloved Mexico need."

Women's complaints referred to different issues. First of all, the hard labor performed by women in their double shifts was mentioned: "We, the women of Potosí, have many problems since as housewives we have to comply with our obligations and because our society demands additionally that we meet our daily duties day in and day out." Thereafter, they requested that the rights given to them by the revolution be granted, and they called for an end to paternalism: "Women no longer need paternalistic attitudes. We have shown over time that with the support of our governments, women have responded to problems that have arisen in stellar fashion, whichever their nature."

The problem of scarcity was brought out frequently: "In this area the mother, as well as the father and the family in general, is passing through precisely such difficulties as a result of the high prices, scarcity. In general terms, it is a crisis which we can not get away from, we see it on a daily basis in our classrooms, we feel it on a daily basis when as housewives, as heads of a household or as sisters, we frequently can not give children their required food supply for them to receive their intellectual bread, and less so the materials that can nourish them."

Common themes included the lack of water, prostitution of young girls, and drug addiction among children. When a speaker ended her talk with a discussion of this problem, saying, "I was meditating whether I should say this since you are doing us the favor of listening, but at this stage, if I were to keep silent, the stones would talk," the candidate leaned over to the state-based coordinator of the CIM who was sitting next to him and asked her quietly if there was any truth to this, upon which he was told that in this state drug trafficking and drug addiction were serious problems.

In similar fashion, women asked for employment opportunities, schools, roads, electrification, bridges, and health clinics and, finally, a commitment with an eye toward the day of elections: "And before all else, and to end, you, Mr. Candidate, can count on our vote and on our work. We will be there for you in your exercise because we hope in time to be able to call you president of the republic! Thank you very much!"

The indigenous women's speeches usually were a lot simpler and more emotional and gained higher levels of applause. Angela B. from the Nahua community of Tamazunchale spoke. She was dressed in an embroidered blouse and a black skirt with an indigenous apron. She took the microphone to speak in the type of Spanish common to these communities of the dual discrimination faced by indigenous women:

Mr. Candidate to the presidency of the republic, father Carlos Salinas de Gortari, I come in the name of all the indigenous peasant women to tell you about the necessities that we have in our rural communities. The women in the fields are the ones most bogged down by work because we have to get up at 3:00 a.m. to crush the corn flour in the metate, to provide our families, our children, our husbands with food, and also to feed the few animals that we have, and not only that, we have to carry water from distant places. Also, the peasant woman moves away from us. We are not recognized as what we are, people like everyone else; we are also not allowed to participate, to demonstrate that we too, the indigenous women, have the mentality and desire to work our lands.

We need, Mr. Candidate, all of your support; we need schools, clinics, roads, bridges, electricity in our rural communities. . . . We really need to be taken into account; we really need not to be cornered, as we are made to feel, Mr. Candidate. We are treated as if we were cornered animals that the peasant woman only knows how to have children and to work.

We believe in you because [you are] a young man who will really support us, and I assure you that all, all of us will go to the urns to deposit our votes and as a Nahua woman I will say a few words in my language: Tata Carlos Salinas de Gortari, chi ka jucu van mu yulu, le ton juati pechto jua—keep in your heart what hurts us. Thank you very much.

In that moment, an anticlimactic bomba was heard: "Todas las mujeres, sea indito o sea obsidian, les dijeron que don Carlitos nos ayudará mañana" (All women, whether a little Indian or made of obsidian, were told that little Mr. Carlos will help us tomorrow).

Ángela went toward the candidate to give him a cloth bag from the Huastec indigenous people and a traditional water holder. Salinas gave her a big hug. Speaking, he was relaxed and in a good mood. The woman who had launched the verbal bomb kept interrupting him constantly. The candidate was forced to ask her on various occasions whether she had anything to say. He preferred interrupting himself rather than being interrupted by bombas: "En el estado de Nuevo León, echaron un president y el próximo año ya lo tendremos al frente" (In the state of Nuevo León, they threw out a president, and next year we will have him in at the top).

He thanked everyone for such an enthusiastic reception. He recognized the courage, the intelligence, and the struggle that the women of that state faced:

In reality, our female comrades have been participating in a long battle throughout the entire republic to demand true equality, because even if equality is accepted between men and women, in reality the facts show that there is a high degree of discrimination against women [applause], and it exists because when a position with a high level of responsibility is being filled, when the communal landholding commissioner is being chosen, when in the rural area a decision is being made about who will run the country store, when in the factory a possibility exists for promotion, when a decision is being made on who will hold a position of real responsibility, those who decide assume that women don't have the abilities and the talent to take on positions of responsibility, and they are very wrong [applause].

Because of this, I have taken on the national commitment to join in the struggle of all of you women in San Luis Potosí and the women of all of Mexico that in action we give you the treatment that you deserve as dignified human beings [applause]. We have to make all of our comrades and all Mexicans understand that the strength of women is the strength of Mexico . . . that the strength of children, of adults, of Mexicans, the strength of all of us is what gives us strength as a nation and if we leave more than half of the population out from the great national effort, we will only have half of the vitality of our great republic [applause].

The candidate's speech ended as follows:

Let us take on the so simple but so profound demands that a peasant woman, a Nahuatl woman, from the state of San Luis Potosí has made to all of us and to all Mexicans. She has asked for little, but it is worth so much that we should commit ourselves to make it into a reality. She has demanded, and we have to comply with her demands, that indigenous women in Mexico enjoy social justice and respect that are implemented in actions.

I want to tell her yes. I want to assure Ángela that I will take with me always the words that she said at the end, in my heart that which most hurts her. Thank you very much.

With all the speeches concluded, the entertainer took the microphone, asked for applause for Salinas, and in chorus with all of the women intoned: "For whom will we vote?" "For Carlos Salinas de Gortari!" "For whom will we vote?" "For Carlos Salinas de Gortari!"

Events with Indigenous People

Some of the events at which indigenous people were present were in reality events for peasants in which indigenous identity did not play a relevant role. When indigenous people were protagonists, a stereotypical pattern could be seen as well as one in which the indigenous identity overshadowed the party role. In the first case, everything indigenous is, before all else, a great folkloric show of Indians with their outfits and ways of talking and of suffering: in two words, representing themselves. In the second case, we have events with a true symbolic value whose purpose was to express myths of the national origin of the Mexican peoples. The common characteristics of all events were, on the one hand, the majority presence of ethnic groups, and on the other, the familiar attitude of the candidate, who was humble and modest, combined with the commonly accepted belief that the indigenous people are sincere, honest, and that when they talk they do so with their hearts.

We start with the events portraying the indigenous in a folkloric fashion. In the Huasteca region of San Luis Potosí, an event took place with ethnic groups. According to information from the representative of indigenous women, this was the first time that all the ethnic groups of San Luis Potosí had come together. It was a market day, which meant that all the special guests, the candidate's contingent, the press members, the public who had come specifically for the event, the functionaries of the National Indigenist Institute (Instituto Nacional Indigenista–INI), and the Indians from Aquismón who had come down from the mountain to make their purchases were all in one place at the same time. Some of the guests took advantage of the occasion to go to the market and buy "items that are typical of the region."

The meeting was held in the municipal center, where dances and fiestas traditionally took place. There were groups of dancers from all over: Nahua and Huastec groups, three groups of jaranero dancers, a Chocantón dancer, a trio from Aquismón, a group of dancers from Tanute, and a Huastec trio from Cerro de San Pedro, among others. The place was so colorful and spectacular that there were those who asked whether the Indians dressed this way in their communities or if they had worn these outfits to celebrate the visit of the candidate. There was some truth to this, since on that day the Nahuas were dressed in embroidered blouses with linen undergarments and shirts which they did not wear on a daily basis.

At one end of the plaza was the forum. Below the shade of a banner that read "The Nahua, Pame and Huastec indigenous groups support your candidacy, the National Indigenous Confederation has risen and is fighting. PRI. Mr. CSG," the platform was being raised with twenty chairs reserved for the candidate and indigenous representatives. None of the local politicians who arrived with the candidate were seated on the platform. Below, approximately three thousand people stood. The chairs were reserved for the special guests and the president's contingent.

Two entertainers worked interchangeably for a significant period of time—in Spanish and in Pame, Huastec, and Nahuatl languages—and made a series of comments and gave instructions in an effort to cheer people up and to make the wait for the candidate less tedious:

Entertainer 1: Let us have a rehearsal. Huastec, Nahua, and Pame people, all of you, this way in Spanish, when our candidate arrives here, we will stand up. Please, let us do it, let us rehearse it, let us take off our sombreros. Come on, come on, pretend that he is arriving. Come on all of you, over there, stand up, stand up, with jubilation, with energy, let your enthusiasm show, that the peasants of San Luis Potosí receive our candidate with affection.

Entertainer 2: This day is so important because the candidate to the presidency of the republic is coming here to get your opinions, or our opinions, peasants, artisans, farmers, professionals, bilingual indigenous people. We are present here because we want to tell him what our worries are, so that these can be incorporated into his work plan and so that our candidate will make a commitment to us when he gets to the presidency of the republic. And we the indigenous want to show him today not only our problems but also our greetings, our fraternal greetings, greetings of brotherhood, a greeting from the Huastec people, and from us the indigenous considered as ethnic groups. Because of this, we ask all of you to be here, that you come closer; we know that you are uncomfortable, but this is our obligation as citizens and Mexicans.

We still . . . have not adopted hypocrisies because we are sincere, and we will show this to our candidate today with our presence and the human warmth of all the ethnic groups of our state. Because of this, you will see that the women have kept their traditional Huastec dresses . . . this is a cultural legacy and a cultural heritage of our indigenous people. . . . We are making this invitation because we have the presence here of the municipality of Aquismón, as well as the Huasteca as a region, San Luis as an entity, and Mexico as a country.

With the gestures of the last entertainer, it appeared as if he were inviting the indigenous to get up on the platform and to sit down next to the candidate, who by now was about to arrive. He asked that preferably the women dressed in traditional outfits get on the stage.

At last the candidate arrived. The "three ethnic groups of the state" gave him "a strong fraternal applause." First, the representative of the Pame indigenous people spoke: "I want to tell you about the survival worries of our group. We are few and highly dispersed; we are no more than ten thousand, and each day we lose more of our language and our customs. The migration of our brothers, due to the lack of water and bad soils, has meant a rapid advance in the loss of our culture and in our uprooting."

He asked that lands given to them in 1922 be handed over to them, for a "water work" to be constructed that still had not been authorized, "because it is not fair that in other parts more than four hundred million pesos are spent to take care of crocodiles and that nothing should be spent on the Pame people." At the end, he assured the candidate that he could count on the votes of the Pame people on July 6: "Surely we will lead you to victory, simply give us a hand, Mr. Candidate."

While the entertainer, who was a young man from the Tancanhuítz community, said: "This is how the Huastec people talk, this is how the indigenous people talk, and above all else our Pame people. This is how they talk: frankly and with sincerity." The Pame representative went to greet the candidate.

The emcee then introduced the representative of the Nahua people who "with human warmth and with his heart in his hand would greet the candidate in the Nahua indigenous language." The representative, who originally came from the Tanlajás community and was a former surrogate deputy, ended his speech as follows:

We remain loyal to the revolution and to our country, but we don't want to be forgotten . . . we too should have a commitment from the government, because history speaks for us. Or do we have to wait for another Juárez to implement and defend the interests of the weak peasants? We are aware and believe that Salinas de Gortari, our candidate, will also know how to respond to our lamentations for support, at least with those things that are most urgent, which is where to best sell our products. . . . We ask for support because the indigenous peasants from Potosí don't have sufficient guarantees that are given by our constitution to all Mexicans. . . . In consequence of all of this, we hope that the voice of the indigenous people of Potosí has been heard by our candidate, and we await, as we await daily when the sun rises, Carlos Salinas de Gortari's response.

A woman spoke in the name of the women of all three ethnic groups. After making a greeting in Tenek, she offered her sincere support to the candidate. She was followed by the leader of the agrarian communities of "our glorious CNC," who gave the candidate rugs, together with a document that listed the priority needs of the communities.

Thereafter, the three presidents of the supreme councils of the Pame, Huastec, and Nahua people of the state of San Luis Potosí handed over the ceremonial wand of rule to the candidate: "Heritage and cultural legacy of our indigenous peoples that represents authority, respect, trust, faith, and wisdom in applying and distributing justice in an equitable manner." The ceremonial ruler's wand was made of a strong tree branch decorated with multicolored ribbons that the candidate had to keep in his hand throughout the rest of the ceremony.

With the wand and the documents in hand, the candidate spoke:

Indigenous comrades of the Huasteca of Potosí, I want to tell you that a few years ago I lived here in the Huasteca of Potosí with a group of indigenous people and witnessed their work personally. I understood then the meaning of the essential question that you raise and that today in the document of the Nahua people is stated in all clarity: "Why?" The Nahua document asks, "Why?" We don't understand why in this area that is so rich, we are so poor. And that is the fundamental question and the one that all of us have to give an answer of commitment to, one of solidarity and of understanding the enormous work done here in the Huasteca area of Potosí by the diverse indigenous groups: the Nahua, Pame, Tének people, not the Huastec ones since this is the name of the region and not of the indigenous people.

I have listened carefully to what the three groups have stated. I have done so because I am convinced that it is precisely with the indigenous groups of Mexico that our essential roots reside that make up the base and the foundation of our culture and consequently of our nation. Here, among the indigenous of the Huasteca Potosí region, as

I have also done with the indigenous peoples of other regions of our great nation, I have emphasized that it is our unwavering commitment to turn our eyes back, turn our attention back, and once again make a commitment to all those who represent our origin, and in many ways the reason for our existence as a nation.

Incited by Salinas, the head of the Supreme Nahua Council translated his words. Without letting go of the ceremonial wand, and after picking up the demands of each of the indigenous peoples, the candidate concluded with: "Indigenous people of the Huasteca region of Potosí, I want to tell you that I will always remember the words that were spoken when you handed over the ceremonial wand to me. You said with clarity, with simplicity, but with exactitude: Candidate, this wand should not be used to hurt us but to support us, but for those of your collaborators who do not do their job vis-à-vis their commitments towards the indigenous people of the Huasteca Potosí region, use it with energy and firmness."

Before leaving the platform, the candidate received regional artisan products: a bag made of petate, flowers, a wooden arch, etc. While the candidate was leaving, the Huastec trio intoned a song that had been specifically composed for him.

At some events, there was a real closeness between the candidate and the indigenous people. This was the case in the meeting held between the candidate and the Mazahua people of San Pedro del Progreso in the state of Mexico. In the case of one of the Mazahua representatives, the candidate was humble, modest, and grateful; he exuded closeness and familiarity.

Sitting in the earthen patio of Jesús Rosas's house, which was surrounded by several corn silos and corncobs from the recent harvest, the candidate listened to the Indians. The men were sitting next to the candidate, while the women, dressed in traditional regional clothes, remained standing. All presented problems and sought possible solutions. Electrification projects, migration, and issues of commercializing artisan products were discussed. When the Mazahua representative asked, "What will happen over the next six years?" the candidate answered: "I have to answer you with the truth, because that is what you have asked me to do and because you want words transformed into actions . . . that I not make promises but implement realities. . . . I would be lying if I said that in six years we will resolve all of the problems that have accumulated over centuries, but what I will aim for, is that the program of commitments that we will jointly integrate will be met and fulfilled. Within six years you will have more justice in the Mazahua area."

A symbolic act took place at the archeological site of Uxmal. Around thirty buses, the majority filled with Maya peasants, arrived in Uxmal at around 10:30 a.m. It appeared that this event had been organized by the INI, an institution that a few months before the presidential campaign started to collaborate to integrate the Maya Council, made up of thirty-nine representatives of the Maya communities. There, the council people presented their needs, and they proposed that the governor organize a "direct" event with the candidate. The representatives made the commitment to bring the people and take care of transportation, as stated by one of the people interviewed.

Inside the Quadrant of the Nuns of the archeological site, thousands of Maya people beautified the area with their impeccable white outfits, their sombreros, and flowers. There was no sign of any party propaganda, no placards or banners, no bands or podium. The archeological site displayed its silence and nostalgia.

Salinas arrived shortly thereafter with his wife and the governor of the state, who for the first time participated in the campaign tour. They sat down toward the top of the main staircase. Behind them and also seated on stairs were special guests. Below, on one of the staircases in front of the candidate, a Mayan priest was preparing an offering to the "five winds." One person interviewed stated that never before had a ceremony like this been organized during a political campaign.

The entertainer welcomed the candidate in Mayan, and his words were translated into Spanish: "Today, the Mayan people retake their place; the Mayan people are pleased to be here with you and to speak with you." He asked that the protocol be broken, since this was a religious and not a political ceremony.

A group of girls dressed in regional clothing formed a chorus of cheers while releasing some doves. A few men handed over enormous papayas; a large watermelon; zucchini with honey; bags of corncobs, peanuts, and hot peppers; and lemons and avocados to the candidate. The candidate bent over to receive them and to express his thanks.

The priest, an old man, dressed in a guayabera and white pants just like everyone else present, brought oil and totumas to drink; simultaneously, copal was being burnt in adobe receptacles. At the microphone, the priest invoked the gods, who were the providers of rain and of good harvests. A jug of balché, a drink made from tree bark and the honey from bees that live in the trunks of the trees, contributed—it was believed—to the fact that the five winds would come closer to the place and preside over the event. For a few minutes, Mayan songs were intoned.

Many of those attending were familiar with the meaning of the ceremony. According to one of them, the Maya made offerings to invoke their gods. This ritual is similar to the one used to sanctify ground and used to avoid "evil winds" from appearing.

The priest looked through a small crystal, awaiting a sign of the arrival of the winds. In the esplanade, there was only silence; after all, this was the visit by the future president. However, some were impatient; they could no longer wait for the winds to arrive.[11]

The speeches began and were simultaneously translated. Each speaker was respectfully listened to with a great deal of attention. All those who spoke were Mayan, and their presentations served a concrete purpose. Gaspar Xin, a local deputy, who was the son of Agapito Xin, a descendant of the last Mayan ruler, spoke:

> Mr. Carlos Salinas de Gortari, Mr. [Governor of Yucatán] Manzanilla Schaffer: I apologize for the heat. . . . This pre-Hispanic city of Uxmal is not a political center; we have come here to speak without any intermediaries and so that you can hear the voice of the Maya in the presence of these temples. Here we have reunited a humble and hardworking people. We want you to hear of our situation and how you can help us. In the indigenous villages, there is a lack of water, food, housing, and clothing. We feel marginalized when the price of corn is bartered down. We are forced to produce at high costs and sell at low prices. The indigenous people seek justice.

And he warned him: "Be very aware that some day our human resistance may get tired, and nothing leads more easily to the military prison than an excessive desire for justice. And that is what the indigenous person is looking for: justice!" The Maya representative asked for help in rebuilding the Mayan buildings that were falling to pieces and for agricultural equipment, supplies, and farming credit. In conclusion, he gave the candidate some advice: "Continue to go at it alone, without intermediaries to communicate with the peasant communities. You are young and strong; we saw you walk up the stairs of the temple. . . . Don't forget this moment in which you are communicating with Uxmal, with the descendants of this people who made this civilization." At that moment, Salinas broke his silence and applauded, obviously affected emotionally.

Afterward, a special council person, Kuhn-Kal, spoke:

Mr. Carlos Salinas de Gortari and Mr. Manzanilla Schaffer: We are descendants from the Maya. When the Mexican people were born, they brought people to this region to learn from it. In this manner, we bring the words and the advice from all the Mayan peoples. Everyone has considered us as inferior. We have come to ask for the necessary infrastructure to work farmlands. Now we are here to bring the words and the thoughts of the Mayan people [to you]. We ask for credits and that the children who know how to read participate in their management and administration to avoid current corruption. With regard to the guarantee, we ask that the expenses involved in the management of these accounts by the peasant be taken into consideration [applause].

Another councilperson spoke—this time a young woman with a red armband that read "Member of the Mayan Council." Passionately, she said:

In the name of the Mayan Council and of the Mayan peoples, we want you, Mr. Candidate, to read a pact to see if you would sign it: "Pact between Carlos Salinas de Gortari, Manzanilla Schaffer, and the Mayan people, whose descendants remember that their ancestors made a pact of peace between Chichén Itza and Uxmal. This pact is now being repeated with a commitment to develop the peoples by guaranteeing their minimum rights, to honor their identity and culture, grant fair guaranteed prices, to construct health centers, promote research and the restoration of the [archeological] ruins, and give the Indians an opportunity to promote their handicrafts, impel bilingual education, and cultural diffusion. The Mayan peoples commit themselves to defending the revolution, the economy, and to continue to develop the Mayan culture with dignity. Lastly, we ask that you lead a crusade to declare the Mayan culture a World Heritage [Site]."

The councilwoman handed a piece of bark paper to the candidate that listed the points of the pact. In silence, the candidate signed the pact, and afterward spoke solemnly:

As always, those that have the least are the most generous. I am grateful for these fruits and vegetables. I accepted the invitation from the

Supreme Mayan Council to have an event in Uxmal because I wanted today's Maya to be present and to take possession of that which their ancestors built. I asked for it to be an event of complete respect, without set-ups, a podium, not even banners with propaganda, respecting this site which is a glory of humanity. I am willing to take on the demands of the Maya. We are here to speak of the present, to suffer what the Mayan peasant is living today. . . . Because of this, I was willing to sign the document that commits me as the candidate to the presidency of the republic, but I have signed it so that if I can count on your vote and that of the majority of Mexicans and I become the president of the republic, tomorrow I will meet these commitments and make them a reality for the benefit of the Mayan peasants of Yucatán.

He announced a drastic reduction in the interest rates of farming loans, and he committed himself to giving peasant children scholarships so that they would not leave school, to constructing and maintaining roads, to beefing up the health clinics, and to supporting bilingual education and cultural promotion.

While the event lasted, the exterior world ceased to exist. Far removed from local politics and the noise produced by two simultaneously organized presidential campaigns (the PRI and PAN), in Uxmal silence ruled. In contrast to the events that took place with other social groups, in Uxmal, instead of fiestas and ebullience, there was silence and sobriety. Not a single banner; not a single musical band. Silence is a sign of respect and humility.

Time seemed to stand still; the ceremony went far beyond this. It was an almost religious act: the archeological site, without any intermediaries, brought the present into communication with its origins. It was an imperial act: only the candidate, sitting on the platform of the pyramid that served as a stage, could bring the community into communication with the gods. He, with his head lowered and his voice lower than usual, was in charge of returning a heritage that had been expropriated a long time ago from its legitimate owners.

Events with Workers

The events with workers tended to have their own characteristics depending on the activities of the specific sectors of workers that had been called in, characteristics that were adopted by the candidate when transmitting his messages. We will show an example of this last point with a description of an event that took place involving railroad workers. Afterward, we will discuss an event dedicated to workers in general that was held in a working-class neighborhood. It should be noted that this sector was more demanding than those that have been discussed previously.

The candidate traveled to San Luis Potosí by train; he spent the night in a sleeper wagon. At 9:30 a.m., he was supposed to leave the station to participate in a railroad workers' event and inaugurate his campaign tour of the state.

In front of the entrance to the old train station, the forum was being set up. The platform was carpeted. The railroad workers, who were all men, had blue caps on. The mariachi music could barely be heard over the noise made by rattles and the whistle of a train. On the podium, a railroad worker with his blue cap and his rattle led the cheers of his colleagues. There were approximately seven thousand people present at the meeting, and all of them were preparing for the candidate's and his contingent's arrival. A railroad worker's banner read "Let us go to the station of triumph with Carlos Salinas de Gortari."

At 9:30 a.m., the train whistle was heard, announcing Salinas's arrival at the train station. From the railing of the last wagon, the candidate greeted those present with his hand raised. The scene seemed to depict events of the Mexican Revolution. Salinas was dressed in brown and wearing a leather jacket. Through a human wall, the candidate walked from the entrance of the station to the platform. He was accompanied by the governor of the state, the leader of the Revolutionary Vanguard of the SNTE, the director of the National Railroad Company of Mexico, and the secretary of the National Confederation of Peasants (Confederación Nacional Campesina–CNC).

The emcee welcomed the candidate, and Salinas hurriedly pointed out the importance of the train for his presidential campaign. Thereafter, three speakers spoke: the general secretary of station repair of the Union of Railroad Workers of the Mexican Republic spoke of the necessity to modernize the railroads; the president of the National Commission of Security of the same union referred to the technological advances that had been implemented for the sake of comfort and efficiency; the general secretary of the union stated the entire sector was loyal to the PRI and that they supported the candidacy of Salinas.

Finally, the candidate read his speech. He began by recounting the history of the railroad and the participation of railroads in the revolution "because the revolution took place on horseback and on trains." At this moment, the railroad workers, motivated by their representative at the podium, shook their rattles. The candidate abruptly yelled, "Wait a minute!" and silence was restored. When he finished reading the paragraph, in an attempt to apologize and with a smile, he said, "You are the ones who deserve the cheers!" With this, everyone could once again give their noisy cheers and shake their rattles.

From the role played by the train in the revolution, the candidate went on to relate its importance in the history of San Luis Potosí. He pointed out that currently the most important facilities were located in this state because it was where the largest number of railroad workers lived and where most train wagons were repaired. He also promised to fill all employment vacancies, support the workers, stimulate decentralization, prevent the emigration of workers to Mexico City, and provide dignified salaries to retired workers.

The event ended at 10:15 a.m. Despite the fact that it was a special event, it lasted the strictly programmed forty-five minutes.

Another event involved workers of the National Workers' Housing Fund Institute (Instituto del Fondo Nacional de la Vivienda para los Trabajadores–Infonavit)[12] in the district of Miravalle, Jalisco. There was no need to create a complicated logistical structure to mobilize the contingents, since the workers lived in this place. To welcome the candidate, workers from the Revolutionary Confederation of Workers and Peasants (Confederación Revolucionaria de Obreros y Campesinos–CROC) and the CTM were gathered, as well as women, many children, and in general, "all the beautiful people of Miravalle" (entertainer).

The event was conceived of as a dialogue between the candidate and the workers of that area. From the very beginning, the entertainer announced, in terms that were reminiscent of those used by the entertainer who promoted use of the "candidate's mailbox": "We are making a cordial invitation so that you can present any question, any doubt, and proposal you have to our candidate Carlos Salinas de Gortari. Of course, this will give an overview of the problems that Miravalle has, what the uncertainties of Miravalle are, and what Miravalle wants Carlos Salinas de Gortari to consider within his program. . . . So, if there are some small ones, if there are some children that are having problems in their school, problems with desks, chairs, teachers, problems in construction, these children also have a right for their voice to be heard."

The candidate's arrival was announced. Microphones were tested: "21, 35, 42, 11." At the front, in what was to be the podium, the candidate placed himself at the center, with the representatives of the CTM at his right and those of the CROC at his left.

Cheers were heard as the voice of the entertainer continued: "The workers of Jalisco and their families are united here on this occasion as a single person surrounding the candidate Carlos Salinas de Gortari. This, Mr. Candidate, is the second most populated district in the country. At this time, we have 160,000 inhabitants. The workers and their families are present . . . and this afternoon we are here to tell you that our ideal continues to be Juárez, our guide Miguel de la Madrid, and the Knight of Hope for the workers, and for Mexico, Carlos Salinas de Gortari [applause]."

The first speech was given by a senator. He spoke on behalf of the whole district; he thanked the party in power for "making it possible that the workers have a comfortable house as established within the political constitution of our country."

Then, the emcee handed the microphone over to the president of the Second District Committee of the PRI who, after welcoming Salinas to "this house of the workers," took advantage of the opportunity to submit a question-petition to the candidate: "We want to know, sir, if once you get into government you will act energetically against the large-scale merchants, the great hoarders, the great intermediaries who are making products more expensive and have an impact on our working-class families; if you are going to act against those buzzards that spread hunger over the people of Mexico . . . if the Mexican government can close down those businesses definitively and decommission their goods to take these to the people and the popular classes by means of its own institutions. Thank you very much [applause]."

The general secretary of the Dough and Tortilla Industry Workers (Trabajadores de la Industria de la Masa y la Tortilla) uttered another concern along similar lines:

Sir: In this time that should be of unity of all Mexicans, it has been noted that the large commercial monopolies have become dictators of prices, which are always going up because they hoard all goods and products, demonstrating that they are not interested in the well-being of the Mexicans. . . . Added to this incomprehensible behavior is the complacency of the authorities that are in charge of regulating the market. Don't you think that with these precedents that go back a long time that the Commercial Code should be reformed [as well as] its complementary laws, to regulate the enormous profits that these merchants make, sums that make things more expensive and that have decreased the purchasing power of the workers? [applause]

The director of the Institute for Workers' Education of the Workers' Federation of Jalisco asked for greater punishment against drug traffickers. A worker, after highlighting the results of the housing policies followed by the revolutionary governments and, specifically, the 1980 creation of Miravalle, "the first great housing center of the Jalisco working class," warned that Infonavit's housing programs were limited: "We request that once you are our president and as a priority you act in response to the urgent national need of greater housing concentrations."

The complaints and questions for the candidate continued. A worker from the Mexican Petrochemical Industry and a model-maker from the Lubricant Industry spoke.

Both the spokesperson and the speakers insisted that this event constituted a dialogue between the workers and the candidate, which was not very common during the campaign. But it was a peculiar dialogue since it appeared to be previously planned. First, the questions and demands were formulated, and afterward, the candidate responded to all of them in one single speech. When the candidate was finished with his discourse, no new questions were raised. In the end, the young children did not mention any of the problems they had in school.

Events with Peasants

The events with peasants were characterized by their diversity. All of them had their own tone. As the campaign distanced itself from the cities and moved closer to the small settlements, most with limited communication with the external world, the events stopped being so homogenous and took on a local nuance. Next, we will present the different events that took place with peasants in different parts of the country.

The Old Guard. The meeting with the Old Agrarian Guard took place in San Luis Potosí in the municipality of Graciano Sánchez, the site of the founding and first general secretariat of the CNC. At the entrance to the town, on the road, the buses for communal landholders' transportation of the CNC gathered. The peasants yelled "Viva!" and cheered and honked their horns at the same time. This is how Carlos Salinas was welcomed. There were not that many people present at the meeting, only approximately three thousand, all of whom were listening to the music played by the band. Apparently, before people went down to the meeting, they preferred looking out their doors and windows. In the meeting place, approximately two thousand people were present, including the candidate's contingent, local politicians, and special guests who were all awaiting the candidate's arrival. Those who did not fit into the auditorium and those who preferred to avoid the suffocating heat went out to the patio and, by means of loudspeakers, listened to the speeches.

The representatives of the Old Agrarian Guard were present from almost all the states: Zacatecas, Puebla, Campeche, Sinaloa, Tabasco, Aguascalientes, Baja California Norte, Veracruz, Morelos, Guanajuato, Oaxaca, Querétaro, Colima, and the state of Mexico. All the representatives, all elderly, wanted to speak. And all of them did speak. They gave discourses reminiscent of a previous time that were read with difficulty and parsimony.

The first speaker was the national president of the Old Agrarian Guard. He finished by saying, "We don't want tutelage; we want to work with the state." This speech set the tone for the rest of the speeches. Every speaker highlighted the fact that they had fought in the revolution and that they had participated in their respective states in the redistribution of land. The representative from Querétaro assured the listeners that the communal landholders paid a much higher price for the land than money—they paid with blood. The Puebla representative remembered Saturnino Cedillo, "caudillo who fought for the Potosí peasants." With the simple mention of that name, some applauded timidly and others pretended to be coughing.[13] For his part, the representative of Veracruz noted that his father was one of the founders of the CNC in that state.

The candidate took the microphone and continued along the same lines. He also recounted history. He highlighted the participation of heroes such as Graciano Sánchez, Emiliano Zapata, and Lázaro Cárdenas. With regard to Cedillo, he said that he could not be considered a hero, since he had stopped half-way: only half of his life was dedicated to working for others and thereafter he deviated from that path. At the end of the event, the candidate stood guard at the house of Ponciano Arriaga, one of the main authors of the liberal 1857 constitution who was born in this state.

Tour of Tlaxcala. A lunch. The peasant community of Tetla, with the support of the Tlaxcala state government, offered a luncheon to the candidate. Tetla provided the necessary labor, and the government provided the rice, mole, chicken, pots, and all other primary products (almost a rehearsal of what later on would become the government program Solidaridad–Solidarity). In this place Salinas was seen as a friend. According to a radio program, fourteen years earlier, the person who was now the candidate to the presidency of the republic had shared a house with a peasant in the region for almost a year while he was performing research for his doctoral thesis. He established a close relationship with the García family and once in a while he went back to visit with them.

With the candidate's visit, Tetla was in fiesta mode. Along the cobblestone road that covered parts of the zocalo, the great banquet was organized in honor of the candidate. Tables and chairs were set up for the people of the region, as well as a table on a platform approximately thirty centimeters high that was the chosen place for the special guest. Each table had two small clay pots on it, one with mole and one with rice. On the sidewalks, women prepared tortillas and mixiotes in their wood-fired stoves. The men were in charge of cooking maguey worms, which was the special plate of the day.

Because the wait for the candidate ended up being lengthy, people began to eat. Then there was an announcement that the Carmen Serdán bus was arriving at the building housing the municipal presidency. The candidate was about to arrive. The press positioned itself strategically along the place and installed television cameras. The inscriptions on banners referred to the special relationship that the candidate had with this community:

Salinas, friend, Tetla is with you.
Carlos, friend, the people are with you.
Friend Salinas support us with an irrigation system.

The candidate and his wife got off the bus and went toward the table of honor where Salinas took the microphone. The enthusiastic people got out of their chairs. The entertainer asked for a demonstration of how much Salinas was liked in Tetla, and a cheer and prolonged applause could be heard: "Tetla is your second home!" "Tetla is the PRI!" "Long live Carlos Salinas de Gortari!" "Long live the PRI!" "Long live Tetla!"

The president of the municipal committee of the PRI spoke. Nervous and in a broken voice he said:

> Friend Salinas: Once again as fourteen years ago, we receive a young man who has come to work. We receive him today as the candidate in charge of everyone's wishes. When he left, he left with our affection and respect. He has come today as brothers come to our houses, your house, the town of Tetla. We receive you like a brother who has been absent but has not abandoned us. . . . We ask that you don't forget to support education and a drainage system for Tetla. . . . We commit ourselves to making Tetla the first place where the electoral urns are closed and, proportionately, where you will have the majority of votes. Welcome home!

Thereafter, the candidate was given two landscape paintings: one of them given by roadmen from his time spent in that town.

The wife of the municipal president, who was the hostess of the event, also spoke. Nerves prevented her from finding the right words in naming the candidate. She ended up referring to him as "Mr. Salinas de Cortés." Thereafter, Salinas spoke:

> Between 1974 and 1976, I lived for ten months in Tetla. I spent time with rural people, whose friendship and affection I have kept to this day. Because of this experience, I am aware of the realities of the Mexican countryside: not through photos or books but from its soil, its housing, its labor, and its daily oppressiveness . . . the fact that with their labor they make the dry soil flourish. I did not get to know poverty in stories but shared it at the table. . . . The solutions to your problems are not found in an office but only after one has worked your plot of land with you. . . . I got to see your sense of friendship when the peasant hand was stretched out [to me]. I got to know the house of a peasant as I lived with the García family and worked with the community. In Tepeyanco, I also lived with peasants who have been engraved in my memory and in my heart [applause]. In Tetla I came to understand that a proposal for transformation has to have popular content. We can not call on the Mexicans if we have not lived together with those who have the least. One has to work side-by-side

with those who have the least. One has to share in the pride of the most humble people of Mexico [applause]. I am certain that with the vote I will be the next president of Mexico . . . And today I assure you . . . that tomorrow I will return to Tetla to make it into the pride of the entire state of Tlaxcala [applause].

During lunch, he served himself mole and rice, lemon and tamarind water, as well as mixiotes and maguey worms. Salinas shared the table with local people and not with functionaries. The female governor of the state was not present. They dedicated the songs "El Rey (the King)" and especially "Canción del alma (Song of the Soul)" to the candidate.

A Walk. Twenty-two municipalities of the state of Tlaxcala participated in an event where farmers and communal landholders were expected to attend. At 11:17 a.m., the presidential contingent arrived in Huamantla. Salinas got off the bus and walked through the narrow main street. The street, seven city blocks long, was covered with copper sand and adorned with palm flowers. On the sidewalks, forming a wall, were strings of pines that were tied from pillar to pillar; at the base of each pillar, there were maguey and palm decorations. At the end of each block and at the beginning of the next, there was an arch made of flowers that had been woven together to spell the name of the municipality and the candidate: "Welcome to Huamantla, Carlos Salinas de Gortari."

Members of the Charro[14] Association Emiliano Zapata came out as he walked along. As the candidate passed by, they took off their sombreros as a sign of greeting. Nobody wanted to miss the show. Some placed themselves on the sidewalks to see him pass, while others with the same purpose looked out of their windows or down from their rooftops. Some peasants walked silently by his side or behind him toward the place where the event was to take place.

The candidate arrived at the House of the Peasant, where approximately seven thousand people were expecting him. All those present had flags, placards, and sombreros with the CNC acronym. Banners were hung in a semi-circle.

The peasants of Tlaxcala will not take one step back with regard to agrarian reform.
The SARH Union is with Salinas de Gortari.
We are a current reality, not a future hope. Youth Agrarian Vanguard

Huamantla CNC: not one step back on communal landholding
The one who has no time to listen has nothing to do.

Salinas headed the event; he was accompanied by the leaders of the national and state-based CNC. There were no cheers or applause; people did not seem to be very enthusiastic. The same silence that had been there during his walk continued.

The event ended at 12:00 noon. Outside of the building, comments were made that the auditorium had been too big a place for the event. The lack of enthusiasm at the event was explained as being due to the empty spaces and absences.

An Event in Rio Verde, San Luis Potosí. On a street at the center of the city, eight thousand people settled down on chairs and on bleachers. On the platform, the same photos and banners that were always present were placed. One of the banners stated the electoral commitment that existed toward the candidate: "Mr. Salinas. The peasants of Potosí are committed with 293,500 votes in your favor. We are organized to sow, and we are organized to vote."

The leaders of the Executive State Committee of the League of Agrarian Communities were present, as were the members of the fifty-five municipal peasant committees, the communal landholding commissaries of the majority of the 1,462 communal landholdings within the entity, and "all those of us who are loyal and determined activists in our glorious National Peasant Confederation and proud members of the Revolutionary Institutional Party" (secretary of the Peasant Committee of the Huasteca Area).

The candidate arrived, accompanied by the leader of the Revolutionary Vanguard of the SNTE. The speeches started. First, the secretary of the Municipal Peasant Committee of the Middle Area spoke, complaining about the credit institutions and the legal disputes over land that were never resolved; he pleaded for the modernization of agrarian reform and asked for subsidies to purchase technology. He ended by saying that the peasants had faith in the system and in Salinas.

Next, the secretary of the Technical Peasant Council spoke, followed by the secretary of the Peasant Committee of the Huasteca Area:

With the honor of representing my fellow peasants of the CNC, I extend a friendly and frank hand that we, the peasants of Potosí, know how to offer. Welcome, comrade Carlos Salinas to this the land of the man who, jointly with Lázaro Cárdenas, organized peasants in Mexico, to the land of the person who would become the first general secretary of our organization, to the land of Professor Graciano Sánchez.

We the peasants continue to be the loyal soldiers of the revolution as were our fathers. With their battles and their blood, they formed the institutions that gave us peace and social justice; the battle that bore fruit in the permanent alliance between the state and the peasants. This alliance has made us responsible for defending it and working in the benefit of the homeland.

Woe to him who wants to destroy what cost our fathers' blood. We are willing to give our lives on this point. But I also wanted to tell you that many functionaries have mistreated us, have cheated us, thinking that according to them we are minors. You know us and you know us well; you know that when we have a problem we understand that we have to know if it has a solution or not. . . . That is why we ask you to look hard at whom you will put in charge of serving us. We want that person to speak in simple terms, that he understand us, that he listen to us and not only that he hears us, that he feels that we are human beings and that even if we did not go to school we never go around saying that this country—as if it were just anything—as if it did not have its own importance, and they don't realize that they are speaking about Mexico that to us means everything.

Comrade Salinas, you know, and you know it well, and there is no need to say this, not to repeat it but I am going to do so, that we are loyal soldiers who will not fail you or our party. On July 6, we will go to deposit our votes in favor of our Revolutionary Party and of Carlos Salinas de Gortari. We will move forward.

Immediately following, the general secretary of the Municipal Peasant Committee of Real de Catorce spoke. After expressing his gratitude for this "undeserved honor" of speaking, he reminded everyone of the ideal of the homeland (justice and land distribution) and reaffirmed the need to make current agricultural areas into cattle-raising plots, construct health clinics, and repair the water wells controlled by the SARH. He concluded by saying: "When you are president, don't go back on your commitment to us, renouncing the rural area that listens to you so much."

The female president of the San Luis Potosí state-level Union of Coffee Growers and a candidate to a federal congressional position of the party followed. She insisted on the need to improve the commercialization of coffee and to battle against plagues that had an impact on the second-highest product of Mexican exports and, on behalf of the women of the CNC, made this assurance: "The women of this sector are pleased to witness that the person chosen by our party is a man with sensitivity and political emotions, but above all else, with a deep understanding of the agrarian problems and their origins. Because of this, when hearing about his decision to eliminate old paternalistic practices, he reaffirms that these were not the authentic demands made by the peasants of Mexico. Therefore, our commitment today is reflected in our willingness to work together with the only goal of achieving social justice for which our fathers fought."

After the director of the Municipal Peasant Committee of the Huasteca Area had concluded, the candidate gave his speech. He thanked everyone for their presence and offered an apology for the involuntary delay in the start of the event:

> I have said that it is indispensable to modernize Mexican agrarian reform. Modernization does not mean going against the best traditions or against family living that is so appreciated by the peasants of Potosí, as also by all Mexican peasants, but instead means to precisely strengthen these traditions. . . . Therefore, I have stated that as ordained by the constitution and as exacted by the traditional struggle in the Mexican countryside for communal landholdings, we will not take any step back, not in the communal landholding nor in communal properties, nor in the small properties, but recognizing the conditions established in the constitution. . . . I have also said that to modernize and make headway in the Mexican agrarian reform, we need to leave behind paternalism, which for a long time has allowed minor authorities to pretend to know more about the needs of rural areas than the peasants who demand that their emancipation be recognized . . . it must be accepted that they know what needs to be done and that the authorities must be willing to join peasant efforts and not to aspire to a tutelage that we have to leave behind. That means that we have to accept co-responsibility and the new forms of organization that the peasants themselves have demanded.

This speech is odd, when seen in retrospective, especially because of its ambiguity. The candidate commits himself to defending the communal landholdings and communal properties, while simultaneously speaking of "modernization" and the end of "paternalism." Of course, there is nothing in these words that suggested the later reforms made to Article 27 of the Mexican Constitution. The speech even included such statements as "not one step back," which could be interpreted as a negation of the reform. At the same time, allowing the peasants to sell their land is a way of "leaving behind tutelage," just as "the peasants themselves demand."

Events with the Popular Sector

In the National Federation of Popular Organizations (Confederación Nacional de Organizaciones Populares–CNOP), many heterogeneous groups participated—from street cleaners to university-trained professionals. Despite this, their events were very similar. Almost all took place in popular city districts throughout the country, although there were also events involving street vendors, state employees, and, especially, the union of teachers. Generally, urban groups participated.

Tetecala, Morelos, one of the popular areas where people live on top of a hilltop, was chosen as the site of an event during the PRI campaign. This area, in which workers, state employees, and small merchants lived, had recently been urbanized.

For the event, one thousand chairs had been set up for about three thousand people. The majority of men, women, and children who held placards and rattles had to stand while waiting for the special guest to arrive. Not everyone was aware of the arrival of the candidate. According to one person interviewed who attended this event, a few days earlier, children who were students at the secondary school had brought home something that looked like an invitation. Others had coincidentally heard the loudspeakers on trucks inviting them to participate in the event that same day. At any rate, at the scheduled time, everyone was there, standing behind the ropes that separated them from the chairs that were reserved for "the PRI comrades who will have a dialogue with the candidate."

A white Lincoln car arrived. The enormous car was received with cheers, rattles, and the sound of jugs filled with coins. From it emerged the gubernatorial candidate of the state, who was also conducting his political campaign. He went toward the platform to the rhythm of the musical band, which had been playing for a while. In the meantime, more buses with women, the elderly, and children were arriving from the neighboring areas.

Everywhere, the presence of the workers from the social security system, the National Banking Federation (Federación Nacional de Sindicatos Bancarios), the popular committees of the milling and tortilla production programs, the Neighbors Social Movement, the Federation of Working Class Neighborhoods (Federación de Colonias Populares) of the state of Morelos, the Union of Pemanent and Semi-permanent Street Vendors (Unión de Comerciantes de Puestos Fijos y Semi-fijos), and the telegraph and collective transport unions were announced. Some of the banners read: "CSG. The engineers together with you constructed a more political, just and participative society: National Association of Revolutionary Engineers," "Dialogue of the CNOP with Salinas de Gortari," and "We are with our candidate and we want support so that this program can continue to benefit popular classes in our popular districts: Committee of the Corn and Tortilla Program." Among these, one enormous green banner stood out, reading "The Force of Hope."

At the platform, the municipal president of Cuernavaca sat down with some professionals, local PRI leaders dressed in "popular outfits," and women adorned with long braids. The audience standing on the esplanade wore yellow caps made of cartons with the letters CNOP and carried round fans with PRI written on them.

Everyone was already in their place. The entertainer began by inviting the audience to initiate a dialogue with the candidate once he arrived: "After the event, you can make suggestions and tell the candidate what you want." In a more effusive manner, he continued: "Let us prepare ourselves to receive the candidate of our party to the presidency of the republic! Let us give him a warm round of applause!"

The candidate arrived, walking through the crowd, surrounded by journalists, young people, security agents, and hundreds of CNOP placards. He was accompanied by the president of the IEPES, the governor of the state, and the head of the CNOP of Morelos. In the instant, the figure of the "grand guest" was seen, the audience rose, sounded their rattles, and raised their placards.

The municipal president of Tetecala, Morelos, spoke first. Following the rigorous greetings, he talked about the problems faced by the municipality. Salinas took out pen and paper and began taking notes. The speaker talked about the irregularities that existed in human settlements in his municipality, of the demographic explosion, and of inflation. "We need investment projects, regularizing of land titles to urban and rural properties, the creation of new businesses, distribution to the popular sectors of the middle class, and to get the high school going that was constructed two years ago."

Another speaker of the CNOP asked for low-price housing, employment generation, support to the medium- and small-sized national industries, lower credit charges for the small stores, and continuation of the program for the distribution of LINCONSA milk.[15] The next speaker handed over a computerized list to the candidate with information on the 140,000 members of the CNOP in the state, offering it to the candidate in case he could use it during his campaign.

The candidate began talking while remaining seated, with paper and pen in hand, and said: "I have listened to the main problems and requests that concern the families and their living conditions. The party takes these seriously and is not indifferent to them." He referred to the demographic problem that had made it difficult to fulfill popular demands; he acknowledged the problems related to land ownership that created conflicts between communities and towns; he spoke about migration to Morelos from the states of Guerrero and Oaxaca; he promised that the PRI would achieve regularization in land ownership; he proposed that the social housing and LINCONSA programs be continued and strengthened; and, in response to the reiterated complaints about inflation, he assured that he was committed to combating it. He also promised that he would think about the demands made by Tetecala, especially in reference to the high school, because Benito Juárez spent the night there. Lastly, he asked for a vote in favor of the PRI, the only way in which the popular demands would be met.

All the speeches were short, clear, and direct. The candidate left by car, while the people stayed behind cheering a little while longer. The music got louder. Now the party could really begin.[16]

Taking the Oath of the Promoters of the Vote of the Teachers

> Let us Salinas supporters go to the fields
> To sow the seed of PRI-ism
> Let us go without envy and egotism
> to fulfill this historic mission
> With Salinas as the president, better education!
> With Salinas as the president, better education!
> 　　　　(To be sung to the music of the
> 　　　　"Agrarian Hymn")

Of all the events, those involving the SNTE seemed to be the best organized and the most enthusiastic. Generally, they took place in stadiums
and auditoriums set up for the occasion. In Guadalajara, for example,
the event was organized in the sporting facilities of the National Council
of Resources for Youth Support, a public entity, which were impressive
because of the enormous dome that covered the entire space.

Teachers came not only from the state hosting the event but also from
all over the country. Their mobilization required enormous logistical
organization. The teachers from Veracruz participated in the event in
Puebla, while in Guadalajara the shouts of "Michoacán!" "Michoacán!"
could be heard.

These events involved multitudes of people. There were approximately fifteen thousand people at each one, and control over those
attending was especially rigorous. One person interviewed stated that
teachers who did not attend an event had their credentials taken away,
or in other cases, they had to hand over their credentials at the entrance
to an event to have them returned to them once the event was over.

These events also became truly popular fiestas, not quite in the same
way as in the acts of cohesion and party support where sombreros and
rattles were everywhere, but more reminiscent of school parties. There
were enormous banners; green, white, and red tassels; music bands;
folkloric dance groups made up of students from the teaching colleges;
and songs referring to the campaign that were intoned by everyone.

The participants at SNTE events were very homogenous, as were the
characteristics of the staging, the tone of the speeches, and the details
of the protocol. It is true that at each event there was always some
distinctive touch related to regional differences or the faculty, through
the presence of some families or in some organizational aspects. For
example, in Atlacomulco in the state of Mexico, the special characteristic was its shortness and the absence of many people. The event took
no more than fifteen minutes. The candidate arrived at 3:45 p.m. and
came out at 4:00 p.m., got on his bus, The Regiomontano, and from
its window smiled and waved. His contingent never entered the place.
There were no musical bands, and there had not even been enough
time to hang up banners. In the case of San Luis Potosí, the "birthplace" of the national leader of teachers, the special touch came from
the spectacular ovations that he received. In Guadalajara, the special
note came at the moment that everyone—the teachers, leaders, and
even the candidate—sang the song "Jalisco no te rajes" together. One

of the organizers who was moved by this stated, "Wasn't this exciting? Even the candidate sang."

At any rate, there were no significant variations. The participation of teachers from all over the country provided for distinctive regional touches. The speakers always talked about the nation; they discussed the ideal teacher and referred to education as one of the great national challenges. Schools were seen as national institutions that breached all regional differences. All speeches had a sentimental and sugary tone.

The following descriptions of events involving teachers are based on materials and research gathered from events in San Luis Potosí, Jalisco, Coahuila, and Yucatán.

In Agualeguas, under the shade provided by the photos of Miguel de la Madrid and Carlos Salinas, the podium was being set up. A number of well-known people were sitting at it. Apart from the candidate and his contingent, the different sections of the unions were represented by their national leaders and, in this case, the candidates for congressional and senatorial positions of the state. The president of SNTE, Professor Carlos Jonguitud Barrios, was also there. Emiliano, the candidate's son, went up to the podium and stayed at his father's side throughout the event.

Salinas was welcomed with song and dance: "Like this, singing as we do everyday in the classrooms, we receive the candidate of the Institutional Revolutionary Party to the presidency of the republic, Mr. Carlos Salinas de Gortari. Feel at home here in Agualeguas." The enthusiasm seemed to overflow: "Listen to how this auditorium rings with joy from teacher to teacher, which is motivated by only one thing: your presence, Carlos Salinas de Gortari."

There were many long speeches. The speakers represented union sections and national leaders. The tone of each speech was very similar. "Modern politics" was defined as the condition required for "Mexico to advance on the path of the revolution." And the teachers were above all else revolutionaries who were proud to fulfill an ideological function:

We the teachers are revolutionaries because our union accepts its historic responsibility in upholding the ideals of the Mexican Revolution, the fundamental reason for the education of children. . . . We are at the vanguard of the civilian army that watches over the preservation of values, traditions, and the cultural wealth of our people. We are revolutionaries because we are worried about the direction of national education and its quality. We will continue to revolutionize the country through education, because we participate in making into reality one of the most-felt demands of the Mexican Revolution, education for all, because we the teachers have known throughout how to infuse in our students love for Mexico, love for our homeland, respect for our heroes, and respect for the institutions that arose from the revolution.

Teachers were seen as "natural leaders": "The faculty is restless and the restlessness that moves us may be the reason for our natural social leadership." The history of Mexico that is taught by teachers is not a cold summary of facts, dates, and names, "but an analytical history of reflection and criticism that serves as a living lesson for the present and the future, related to the realities we live in, if you wish, a cordial history."

The speeches provided an opportunity to express complaints and demands:

We must make an additional effort to improve the quality of education. We ask you to allow us, once you get to the presidency, to get authorization for our participation in the analysis of study plans and programs.... We don't aspire to becoming usurpers of positions, but we have a desire to become main actors in education planning, and quite frankly, we do want to hold the highest positions of responsibility in the area of our competencies.

Mr. Salinas, we the teachers also get sick. How many times have you heard in meetings with teachers what we are presenting to you today: foster the medical services provided by the ISSSTE [Instituto de Seguridad y Servicios Sociales de los Trabajadores del Estado; Institute of Social Security Serving the Workers of the State] so that they are sufficient, human, and adequate.

Our restlessness has been condensed in a demand for a national pedagogical university that acts as a national instrument in the formation and continued education of teachers. Unfortunately, due to factors beyond the control and the will of its organization and the teachers, this project has become deformed, but all of the teachers in the country are willing to rescue it at any cost. Let us dedicate our efforts and our caring, our party militancy, and our purpose on the transformation of the national pedagogical university into the only instrument that forms and further educates the education workers.

We demand the creation of workshops that elaborate the didactic materials for all educational levels in the country.... On several occasions, we have seen how teaching methods are improvised that have been brought from abroad. We have also had to accept systems that don't function within the context of the idiosyncrasies of this country. Because of this, we need pedagogical laboratories. . . . Never has a teacher had the opportunity to get to a classroom abroad to study towards a specialization. We ask for this opportunity.

How much could we the teachers do, how much could parents do in an organized fashion to collaborate with our state, to participate with the authorities so that the textbook becomes available throughout the national middle teaching section . . . and the teachers, Mr. Candidate, we want to be present in the development of the free texts because therein the thoughts of thousands and thousands of prepared teachers who are fully aware of their duties will be contained.

All speakers specifically made mention of the "ideologue of our union and permanent advisor to our union organization, because thanks to the actions implemented by Carlos Jonguitud, who started the Revolutionary Vanguard, we the teachers can fulfill our lofty mission that falls upon us during this critical phase of our country." The simple mention of Barrios's name gave way to prolonged applause.

All speeches ended with the reiteration of the teachers' support of the candidate on July 6, the day of the elections: "Mr. Candidate, Carlos Salinas de Gortari, we the teachers see you as the candidate of hope. If you so wish and we wish to do so, we will give more. If we have to make further sacrifices, we will sacrifice ourselves, but when advances are made or in times of adjustment, absolutely everyone will participate proportionately to our understandings and knowledge. Go ahead! On July 6 you will have our vote."

Salinas de Gortari can count on certain victory,
because all of us want him as the primary leader,
the teachers, the teacher will take Salinas
to the presidency, to the presidency in the National Palace.
                (To be sung to music from "La Cucaracha")

The events involving the SNTE served a specific purpose. In each one of them, the candidate was handed the charters of each one of the so-called political education and social promotion squads: "The goal of this crusade is to fight against absenteeism . . . our political squads are not made of paper, they are not made of cardboard, they are effective, real, and composed of convinced PRI members who have their electoral credentials. This is serious political work that guides the Jonguitud union with responsibility and passion."

The thick folders that contained the names of the members of the squads constituted true factual evidence of the vote-raising efforts that the teachers had made, "because participation should not be proclaimed only with the soft comings and goings of words. It has to be substantiated by the potency of numbers, with the potency of the voters."

In the moment at which the constitutional documents were handed over, the festive atmosphere became solemn. While the candidate received the folders, the gathered teachers kept their arms raised in a kind of strange salute. A great deal of work by teachers for many months had gone into getting to this point.

In reality, a person interviewed told us, quite some time before the presidential campaign started, each teacher committed him/herself to guaranteeing a certain number of votes for the party. Each one received a piece of paper on which he/she had to write down ten names of people with their respective addresses so that on July 6, the teachers could check that these people went and voted.

> The teaching faculty, sir, has a political culture. It has maturity in its dealings with the union. Today, you give us the honor of receiving an oath of compliance from our squads, but we have spent time working with them, and we have a minimal program that we have to comply with on July 6. In a previously established place, the teachers, our families, our children that are of voting age, our friends, our relatives, and the workers and the peasants that form part of our squads will depart at 11:00 a.m. to deposit our vote for the Mexican Revolution, for Carlos Salinas de Gortari.

The campaign to raise votes had been successful. In the case of San Luis Potosí, 15,200 squads to promote the vote had been formed, each one of them with ten teachers. On the Yucatán peninsula, 9,000 squads had approximately 90,000 people subscribed, "only a third of what we have established as our goal."

> I am the son of a schoolteacher,
> therefore I understand your problems.
> (CSG)
> (banner)

Before the candidate gave his message, the organizers of the event had planned a surprise for him. After rounds of speeches and after the documents related to the promotion of the vote had been handed over, silence ensued. The entertainer announced the presence at the event of the teacher María Angélica. From the masses' whispers, one could hear that she had been the candidate's teacher in third grade. She went to the podium and emotionally embraced Salinas. For the remainder of the event, she did not let go of his arm.

Then Salinas spoke. As did all the other speakers, he thanked the leader of the Revolutionary Vanguard for his presence. "Respected female schoolteachers and dear male schoolteachers, I thank you very much for your presence in this event which makes me even more committed to the teachers from our entire republic. I also thank my friend and candidate for a senatorial position of the state of San Luis Potosí, Carlos Jonguitud Barrios, for his presence."

Thereafter, he referred to the role the teachers played in the modernization and transformation of the country. He promised to firmly and substantially increase the resources available to education in Mexico. He spoke of the necessity of improving the quality of the educational system to increase the standard of life of Mexican teachers, make available indispensable didactic materials to teachers in a reliable fashion, raise the salaries of professors, and emphasize the history of the country and the pride of children in being Mexicans.

The candidate returned to the demands of the teachers because, he said, he understood their needs and feelings. He said that he had been moved by his reencounter with his teacher who had taught him to read and write, and by his responsibility as the father of a family, at which point he gave his son at his side a light pat, and also remembered his mother, who was a self-effacing teacher and graduate from the teaching college: "These demands that you have made, respected female teachers and dear male teachers, I rationally understand and I take them on with feeling since what you have presented I have known in the midst of my family. The experience I lived with my family and my understanding of the true vocation of the teacher with the double task that he/she has in educating the children of others and their own children I experienced by being, and I say this with pride, the son of a schoolteacher [applause]."

Finally, the speaker turned to Salinas and said: "You who are the son of a schoolteacher and who values his mission vis-à-vis society . . . we know that you will work toward improving the salaries of the teachers [lots of applause]."

At the end of the meeting, and after the candidate requested the teachers' votes on July 6, they handed him a carved wooden arch and a shawl inside a carved wooden box for his wife.

Events with Young People

The vital element in the youth's causes
is to have a young leader
 —Banner in the airport of San Luis Potosí

Even though in 1988 the National Executive Committee of the PRI had an assistant secretariat of policies for youth, young people did not comprise a specific sector of the party. As a partisan group, the category of age was subsumed under the sectoral structure. In this way, the so-called Revolutionary Youth Front was composed of the youth section of the CNOP, the Agrarian Youth Vanguard, and the Federation of Youth Workers' Organization. These three organizations, together with the state-based leadership of the party, were the ones that participated in the organization of events that involved young people.

These events were a result of a particular national criterion. References to specific locations were rare. Speeches were not characterized by recounting complaints and demands or by the concrete requests. However, they focused on the general problems faced by young people, and on the need to integrate adolescents into the productive system of the country and to promote their political participation; all of this was geared toward ensuring the vote of young people in the next elections. The contents of speeches were also determined by the sector the speaker belonged to.

We will use the event organized for young people in Orizaba, Veracruz, as an example. There were high expectations with regard to the event. The sectarian committees of the party had spent quite some time in organizing the meeting. Everyone agreed that there was a substantial degree of euphoria among the young people of Orizaba in welcoming

our candidate, since after all what great surprise it was for us young people to discover that the candidate was also young, only thirty-nine years old, who was leading our party and occupying the position of responsibility as the president of all Mexicans through the PRI. The event of the young people will be one of the biggest receptions that has given tribute to our candidate at the level of youth anywhere within the Mexican Republic; the biggest one and without precedent.[17]

Approximately fifteen thousand young people who were members of the three sectors of the Revolutionary Youth Front of the state were expected to participate. Also present were the leader of the CEN of the Revolutionary Youth Front and the most important members of the state Leadership Committee of the party.

Also, the "young distinguished people of Veracruz" were participating. The emcee was René Casados, a young man from Veracruz well known for his role in the television medium. "We are inviting [the singer] Yuri and several artists who identify themselves with the party and who will join us in this event for the young people from Veracruz and the young candidate to the presidency of the republic."

The event was planned in the following manner: "A child from the Orizaba region will welcome the candidate in the name of the children and adolescents of Veracruz. Thereafter, the state leaders of young people of the agrarian, workers, and popular sectors will speak; this will be followed by me, and afterwards, we are looking into the possibility that a space for dialogue will be opened up with Salinas de Gortari so that any young person who wants to make a brief comment to the candidate can speak spontaneously . . . and he can respond in the same manner."

The young people had been asked to be at the Orizaba Cinema at 10:30 a.m., and the event started an hour later. The place was packed; there were young people who had come from all over the state. They were wearing T-shirts and caps and held placards that referred to the event and indicated where they came from. All were given a sheet that contained a short biography of the candidate and his photo. When the candidate arrived, the entertainer switched between stating the importance that the young people had for Salinas and mentioning the cities and municipalities that were present at the event.

The candidate, who was coming from Córdoba, entered the Orizaba Cinema from Sur 18 Street, surrounded by a human wall formed by young people. He walked toward the forum and took his place at the center of a semicircle with leaders from the Revolutionary Youth Front representing different districts of Orizaba next to him. Behind him, in chairs that had also been set up in a semicircle, special guests and the candidate's contingent were seated.

An eight-year-old boy, Rosendo Ochitlanihua Sánchez, a fourth-year student in the bilingual hostel in the Zongolica mountains, welcomed the candidate. Then, the speakers had their turn. There were five of them in total: the leaders of the young people of each of the three sectors that made up the Revolutionary Youth Front, the leader of the front, and finally, the candidate. Even though in each case young people were discussed, each speaker spoke as the representative of his specific sector.

The first speaker represented the Agrarian Youth Vanguard:

> Here, Mr. Carlos Salinas de Gortari, the young people who represent the rural areas of Veracruz, the peasants who will continue to be the support and path of the Mexican Republic as stated by Héctor Hugo Olivares Ventura are present. We are not only a title, we are not only a memory, we are not only a class that is in bankruptcy, we are a real force and a source of power. They have asked me to be the spokesperson for their questions and demands, and they recommend that I speak to you with the truth, clearly and directly, since you are convinced of Mexican agrarianism . . . we ask that your government program contemplate the provision of a greater stimulus to agro-industry to incorporate more young peasants in the productive process of the country and to stop them from expanding the lines of the unemployed.

The leader of the young people of the popular middle classes continued: "As the young people of Veracruz, we are concerned with having a candidate who is firm in his convictions, committed to the Mexican Revolution ideology, consistent in his ideas and theses, open to criticisms and without fears, young, with an understanding of the exigencies of young people, who is proud to be Mexican and who is willing to heighten the principles and bases of the Mexican Revolution with serenity and balance."

The general secretary of the State Leadership Committee of the Federation of the Juvenile Workers' Organizations assured the candidate that "the young people of the small, medium, and large industries will go as a single person to deposit their vote in favor of the party that has guaranteed us the continuance of freedom and social justice and the full respect of democracy in the hands of our rulers. The doctrine and political teachings that have been given to us by the visionary and patriotic man Fidel Velázquez have taught us to be at the vanguard of the principles of the Mexican Revolution, as well as jealous guardians of national sovereignty in the case of attacks from enemies from internal or external sources."

Lastly, the leader of the state-based Revolutionary Youth Front spoke, focusing on the numerical strength of his organization.

It is not possible, Mr. Candidate, that there are still some regressive people within our party who consider young people simply as inept servants and trainees, that there are still some stubborn members of the gerontocracy who think that youth is synonymous to ostracism, immaturity, or the color green. It is not possible that we continue to be blocked from access by the pseudo-policy of the complacent look or the pat on the back, or with sterile and inane phrases of "you are running ahead of yourself, you have your whole life ahead of you." . . . This, comrade Carlos Salinas de Gortari, is not being said by resentful young people . . . this is being said by a powerful, vigorous, state-based organization of young people that currently holds two federal congressional positions and five substitute federal positions, with one local congressperson who heads one of our youth sectors and three substitute positions with fourteen municipal presidents that have come out of our ranks and files, with twenty-six union members and forty-three regional leaders.

Before the candidate could speak and reiterate the importance of young people as "outstanding intermediaries in the great debate about the national problems," and before he could respond to the petitions and demands made by the youth sectors, the speaker intervened: "Mr. Carlos Salinas de Gortari, we want to hand a list of three hundred thousand votes over to you, representing the commitment of the young members of the PRI in Veracruz that contains their name and the number of their voter registrations."

The event ended at 12:50 p.m. The planned program was pretty much followed in its entirety. The only thing missing was the dialogue the leadership of the young people had hoped to establish with the candidate. He left in a hurry, as usual, from the Orizaba Cinema through a human wall, walking to the Main Plaza to participate in an act of party cohesion.

Reunion with Intellectuals in Cuernavaca, Morelos

After meeting with students at Morelos University and attending an event with women in the elegant municipal auditorium, the candidate arrived at 12:00 noon for a programmed dialogue with intellectuals from Morelos at the Borda Gardens, which had recently been inaugurated as a cultural center.

Approximately one hundred people awaited his arrival. All had entered with an identifying tag and an invitation. All of them also had high expectations since, as was rumored, it was a good sign that for the first time the candidate was talking with artists and intellectuals of the states. One of the women attending commented that when she received the invitation she was very surprised, since in reality she sympathized with the left. She attended the event, because apart from the fact that there are few social events in Morelos that are appropriate for public relations, she was interested in hearing what "the man had to say."

Already at 11:00 a.m., the writers, painters, and bureaucrats of the Cuernavaca cultural scene were gathered. There were female writers, painters, and local cartoonists. The city writer, the director of the orchestra of Morelos and its organizer, three famous intellectuals from Mexico City, and the director of the Fine Arts Institute of Morelos were also present. All of Cuernavaca dressed appropriately for the occasion: the men in impeccable guayaberas or light-colored suits with well-groomed beards, and the women in regional outfits.

While awaiting the candidate's arrival, the folkloric ballet of Veracruz was preparing to come out on stage, a chamber orchestra played in the gardens accompanied by two popular musical groups, and a woman was collecting signatures against the Laguna Verde project (*comme il faut*). Those in attendance had sufficient time to visit the exhibit, listen to the concerts, talk, do business, and even get to know people and establish new friendships. It was already 1:00 p.m., and the candidate still had not arrived.

A few minutes before 1:30 p.m., a whole troop of people came in: two hundred people including people from the IEPES, reporters, and above all else security agents; in the midst of all of them was the candidate. At a hasty pace, and followed by his contingent, the press, the security agents, and the participants at the event, he went up to the choir and listened to it for a bit. He went down to the gardens and stopped at the lake and, from the staircase that leads to the stage, he watched the ballet performance from Veracruz for a few moments. Then, with a multitude of people in tow who were trying not to lose sight of him, he returned to the building to look at the exhibit and listen to the explanations of the delighted sculptor.

The wait ended up being over two hours long, and the actual event took only twenty minutes. There were no speeches. Salinas left the building, and once inside his bus, he attended to the groups that approached him with some verbal or written request, or simply to shake his hand. From there, Salinas went to the market to talk with the merchants and to eat with the leaders of the state at the restaurant Las Mañanitas.

The intellectuals interpreted what had happened as a bad sign: the candidate was not interested in culture. The same person who at the beginning had said that she wanted to hear what he had to say ended up convinced that she had been invited solely to pad the number of people present. She confirmed, and this was her solace, that the people who were at the event had no hopes of Salinas changing anything. A journalist of *El Día* evaluated the event as an empty ritual: people are mobilized and when everything is over, they are left with nothing. In the end, he concluded that one does not talk with intellectuals because they are too contentious.

The disdain experienced by the artists of Cuernavaca was not to be taken lightly. The political importance ascribed to each group determined the care that the candidate took in dealing with them, so that his behavior would not be interpreted as a political distancing; whenever possible, he avoided irritating the unions, certain business sectors, or the intellectuals of Mexico City, while in certain towns, support groups could be left waiting for hours or a visit might actually be cancelled.

In any case, the intellectuals in Cuernavaca for the weekend—the poetesses and painters and their cultural functionaries—had more than two hours to get to know each other and spend time with one another. As at all parties, who had been invited, what they wore, who had talked to whom, and what the fashionable subjects were became public knowledge. Contacts were renewed and new relations established, and it became known that many would most definitely not vote for the PRI.

Summary

The campaign events that took place in the states had a more political character: at these, the candidate asked for the vote, and the party handled the mobilization of its bases. These events had two fundamental axes: the territorial one and the sectarian one, in strict correspondence to the dual structure of the PRI. The campaign covered all of the states of the country (including the capital city). Municipalities were selected for visits according to their economic, political, and historic importance. The ability to essentially cover the entire national territory during the presidential campaign confirms the opinion of a politician who was interviewed: "In any corner of the country, you will always find the presence of the PRI, the [Catholic] Church, and of Coca Cola."

For campaign events, negotiations had to take place between the CEN of the PRI, the three sectors, the governor of each state, and the candidate's team. During the campaign, these groups had to deal with the dialectic between continuity and change: the events that were wholly party based in an effort to uphold the image of the party, the internal structures of power, and the ideological percepts of the revolution. All were associated with the permanence of the party as a long-term hegemonic party, while the candidate's team fought to gain greater power and introduce new ideas and styles that would make an imprint of innovation for the incoming government. Both goals were in direct conflict with each other, but were necessary for the stability of the system, and therefore, a delicate balance had to prevail. The candidate interacted directly with the real elements of political power he would have to face during his government in these negotiations. At the same time, relevant political actors became reoriented in their loyalty and subordination toward the person who without a doubt would be the president of Mexico. The candidate, in turn, learned throughout the campaign what the limits to his power were and how he had to behave in order to use it.

The campaign was characterized by a totally endogenous orientation. It had no competitive purpose, such as attracting new voters or of convincing opposition citizens to change their preferences. In this sense, the campaign satisfied internal necessities, highlighting and reaffirming two fundamental pacts: the federal and the sectorial. In his travels throughout the country, the candidate was exposed to local particularities of each state. Although the candidate had to recognize these particularities and give them their place in the construction of a national image, he also had to make sure that they were seen as indefinable without their interaction with the whole. On the other hand, the constant presence of all the sectors in all of the events throughout the country was seen as the consolidation and renewal of the pact that had given birth to more than a national "being"—more specifically, to the revolutionary political regime.

Before ending this chapter, it should be noted that Salinas dedicated a large portion of his campaign time to meetings with businesspeople.

These meetings were completely different from all others because they were held behind closed doors: they did not "send" messages nor did they contribute to the strengthening of internal party relations. They involved dinners in which the candidate was questioned about his economic and political policy projects (Portilla 1992, 324–27). It is possible that the candidate had to provide more details at these meetings about the specific content of his modernizing project than what he was willing to discuss at public events.

6

The Role Played by the Institute for Political, Economic, and Social Studies

The Institute for Political, Economic, and Social Studies (Instituto de Estudios Políticos, Económicos y Sociales–IEPES) operated as a permanent information and research center. Every six years, the work performed by IEPES was viewed as an opportunity to study national and regional issues in depth. It was not unusual, however, for it to change the direction of its research during the campaign. Once PRI's candidate had been unveiled, a person in his/her trust took over as the director of the IEPES. The director named all sub-directors and all others who held positions of responsibility. At this point, the IEPES's activities became more clearly defined.

The structure of this political institution was entirely based on meetings. There were many different types of meetings: forums, preparatory sessions, meetings with sectorial groups and those of the Center for Political, Economic, and Social Studies (Centro de Estudios Políticos Económicos y Sociales–CEPES), as well as the national meetings held to summarize and discuss the results of previous meetings. Meetings, even when they covered the same topics, varied depending on the interests and the style of the coordinator in charge of their organization, the participating public institutions, the topic, and the specific objectives. The IEPES's tasks required involvement from all levels of the party structure, including district, state, municipal, and sectorial committees in the organization of these meetings. The three sectors, as well as the Revolutionary Youth Front and women's groups, also participated.

According to a person knowledgeable about the activities of the IEPES and the CEPES who was interviewed, their activities made no major contributions once the candidate had been unveiled, but represented an opportunity for people to get to know the candidate and to interact with one another. "The candidate spent hours listening to nonsense and taking notes and on extremely few occasions did someone say something intelligent. . . . The Global Development Plan does not serve any purpose either; it is not even taken into consideration for anything, except to use it to make speeches. The one who has been asked to give a speech focuses on the plan and from there quotes something that he is certain is in line with Salinas. The speech given by Salinas when the plan was presented is referred to, but never the plan itself."

As part of its functional mechanisms, the IEPES operated from top to bottom when it came to asking for people's participation in discussions on certain topics. According to an interviewee, national sectors addressed their respective state-based sectors, and these in turn addressed the municipal sectors. The national head office requested the participation of central offices that operated at the margins of the Confederation of Mexican Workers (Confederación de Trabajadores de México–CTM) and the National Confederation of Peasants (Confederación Nacional Campesina–CNC)—such as the Regional Confederation of Mexican Workers (Confederación Regional Obrera Mexicana–CROM) and the Revolutionary Confederation of Workers and Peasants (Confederación Revolucionaria de Obreros y Campesinos–CROC); "this is how everybody is involved." Information, however, flowed from the bottom up, and social demands were received from all the affiliated and non-affiliated groups gathered at municipal and state assemblies. The IEPES was in charge of collating information obtained at the different meetings to summarize it and select those items that would eventually be received by the candidate.

Meetings held by IEPES were not organized by the ministry linked to a specific theme, as one might think; these meetings were reserved for the new teams, the "new values." The secretaries acted only as invited guests and consultants. Two main people in charge of organizing IEPES meetings were named: one in charge of the topic or substance, the other in charge of the organization and logistics.[1] A coordinator, generally a specialist on a specific subject, was named to help organize meetings on chosen topics. The general coordinator in turn named the regional coordinators who were specifically in charge of organizing the preparatory meetings. People in the country's capital and in the states had to collaborate for a meeting to be held. For several weeks, they dedicated themselves to putting together the list of speakers and deciding on facilities where the event would take place. Each event required weeks of arduous work, from sending out invitations, interviewing the speakers, and reading and correcting their discourses to identifying a place suitable for the meeting's theme, creating a schedule, and determining the number of people who were expected to attend. Any event also had to be coordinated with the agenda of the candidate.

The sectors not only participated in the meetings called for by the IEPES but also formally understood that they would contribute directly to the platform of the party and of the candidate. Therefore, the leadership of the sectors organized their national congresses and the preparatory meetings preceding them while campaigns took place. To the latter, the sectors invited professionals, technocrats, and entrepreneurs. Table 6.1 lists IEPES meetings, called "national dialogues," that took place during Carlos Salinas's campaign.

Many people had to be mobilized for these events to take place. As an example, in Mexico City, there were fifteen summary meetings of the CEPES with six speakers at each one. These were preceded by thirty-five preparatory meetings with twenty speakers at each. This gave a total of almost eight hundred people who presented problems and solutions. There were between eight hundred and one thousand people invited to each meeting, out of which approximately four hundred showed up. For summary meetings alone, thirty thousand invitations were delivered personally.

In the meetings organized by the CEPES of Mexico City, the participation of "spontaneous people" was especially promoted—in other words, the intervention of people who had come to the meeting through public notice. It was common for citizens to arrive with written work in hand. In these meetings, the speakers—both experts and "urban voices"—were identified. If a spontaneous voice was deemed outstanding, his/her name was noted, and he/she was invited to present the same topic in front of the candidate. Everyone always received advice on the elaboration of their discourses.

The political class in its broadest terms and a high percentage of professionals were mobilized throughout the campaign. As stated by a person we interviewed:

Everyone is asked for a paper and everyone is involved, all the way to the last political entity. For example, in the five hundred important municipalities of the country, you have people spinning around, preparing speeches, meetings. . . . If you calculate some five hundred municipalities with twenty-five meetings in each, this adds up to some twenty thousand meetings that produce about one hundred thousand papers that are said to help gain an understanding of how the country is doing [and that can not be processed]. A simple forum of some sixty people costs about two hundred thousand dollars.

Table 6.1   IEPES meetings during Carlos Salinas's campaign,
November 1987–July 1988

Topic	Place	Date
November 1987		
Population: future challenges	Monterrey, N.L.	10
Security and social prevention	Matamoros, Tamps.	12
Use of justice	Colima, Col.	17
Ecology	Morelia, Mich.	19
Nutrition	Tuxtla G., Chis.	24
Rural society in national development	Oaxaca, Oax.	30
December 1987		
Water as a vital resource	Acapulco, Gro.	2
Young people and the modernization of the country	Cuernavaca, Mor.	7
Education	Tepic, Nay.	8
Tourism	Mazatlán, Sin.	10
Integration of women into development	Tijuana, B.C.	15
Communications and transportation	La Paz, B.C.	18
Metropolitan areas	Toluca, Mex.	21
January 1988		
Health and social security	Tlaxcala, Tlax.	8
Sources of energy	Guanajuato, Gto.	11
Social welfare	San Juan del Río, Qro.	16
Federalism and decentralization	Aguascalientes, Ags.	19
February 1988		
Culture and national identity	Villahermosa, Tab.	1
Housing	Campeche, Camp.	4
Export commerce	Saltillo, Coah.	9
Domestic trade and supplies	Durango, Dgo.	12
Financial modernization	Zapopan, Jal.	16
Science and technology	Puebla, Pue.	19
Modernization of the public sector	Mérida, Yuc.	28
March 1988		
Southern border	Chetumal, Q.R.	2
Fishing industry	Tuxpan, Ver.	9
Integrative rural development	Zacatecas, Zac.	12
Northern border	Chihuahua, Chih.	25

(*Continued*)

Table 6.1 *(Continued)*

Topic	Place	Date
April 1988		
Industrial modernization	San Luis Potosí, S.L.P.	14
Higher education	Ciudad Obregón, Son.	26
Scientific research	Hermosillo, Son.	27
May 1988		
Regional development and municipal strengthening	Tlalnepantla, Mex.	13
Sports	Mexico City	24
Indigenous peoples	Ixmiquilpan, Hgo.	29
July 1988		
Submission of the government's program outline for 1988—1994	Mexico City	1

Source: Portilla 1992, 380.

Half the world is invited to the forums also, so that everyone feels as though they are involved.

Every one of the meetings of the IEPES took place in a different city. The choice of a location was by no means arbitrary. There was always a symbolic link between the topic under discussion and the geographic place where the meeting took place. For each area of the republic, a particularly important theme for that region was chosen. The meeting discussing decentralization, for example, took place in Aguascalientes, where the National Institute of Statistics and Geography (Instituto Nacional de Estadística y Geografía–INEGI) offices had been transferred from Mexico City together with its twenty thousand employees. Based on the topics, society was divided into sectors and groups, and within these divisions the ideal people were selected who were experts on the topic and able to represent businesspeople, young people, professionals, university students, women, workers, etc. These processes eventually meant that you "had the entire world involved."

During the campaign, there were thirty-four topics that were classified as being of national interest. Each theme was organized into one of several meetings and organized with political, party-based groups of the country, with technocrats, entrepreneurs, and academics. The long sequence of forums and meetings ended with the summary or national meetings. These were organized as a part of the national campaign program.

The candidate, accompanied by the director of the IEPES, attended the national meetings. At these, all the communications media were present. To attend the national meetings, people had to be previously invited since they were much more closed events than the preparatory meetings and forums. Supposedly, each discourse that was presented at these meetings contained the essential points of the papers presented at preparatory meetings, which in turn occasionally included the topics discussed at the forums. The Meeting on the Modernization of the Financial System was held in Jalisco, for example, after six preparatory meetings, while the Meeting on Export Trade took place in Coahuila where work from other preparatory meetings that had taken place in "Veracruz, Hermosillo, Ciudad Juárez and Mexico City with business-people, workers, functionaries and experts on the topic" was summarized (speech by the candidate in Coahuila).

The operational mechanism was as follows: when the time came, the director of the IEPES assigned the coordinators of the meetings, who supposedly were experts on the topic; these in turn named additional people to coordinate the preparatory meetings. A summary was written up after each preparatory meeting of all the important topics, with a selection of the papers presented. The meeting's coordinator was in charge of inviting speakers for the summary meeting.

Supporting the coordinators there was a team of individuals. The coordinator of one of the CEPES told us that she relied on two personal secretaries; one assistant and his/her secretaries; five sub-coordinators in charge of press, analyses and surveys, and transportation and logistics; two individuals in charge of elaborating documents and working papers; and one individual in charge of political operations. Additionally, an individual took care of identifying the "spontaneous" participants in the audience and then following up on them with a visit to a particular area of the city, a review of the problem, and the location of people interested in speaking to the candidate. There was also an administrative group that handled accounts and the distribution of invitations. An area dedicated to documentation and filing composed of fifty people and support staff ensured that a written record was kept of everything that took place. There, information was collated on a daily basis, and stenographic versions of speeches were written up to be analyzed at a later date.

In the summary meetings, a selection of points that had been discussed in previous meetings was presented. Formally, the purpose of these presentations was to motivate the candidate to give his position on different topics that afterward were summarized by the IEPES to form the groundwork for his government plan, which the candidate had to present within the first six months of his administration. The organization thus started with the activities that took place prior to the *destape* (unveiling), after which the platform of the IEPES had to be created from which the candidate's doctrine was extracted and which formed the basis of his government plan.

The dynamics of the summary meetings were as follows: ten to twelve people—including speakers, the candidate, the director of the IEPES, and very special guests—sat at a hexagonal table that had been specifically designed for this purpose, so that all participants could look at one another. Once seated, the director raised the general issues that would be covered in the meeting, followed by a reading of papers by their respective authors. Once all the papers had been heard, the candidate revisited some main points and put them within the overall context of potential administrative actions. The candidate never ceased taking notes, and at the end of a second round of discussion, he questioned certain guests according to their area of expertise.

Even though the coordinators proposed who should speak and some of those who should be invited as guests, they did not have the last say. In the same way that these issues were handled in the case of the state visits, those who would speak before the candidate were decided on after negotiations among the governor, the campaign team, and the candidate took place. For example, in four preparatory meetings for the meeting entitled "Urban Soil and Housing," functionaries of the IEPES and the director of the Mexico City CEPES found a balance within a large group of speakers that included intellectuals, public functionaries, representatives from private enterprise, left-leaning participants, etc.

Summary meetings were officially meant to identify the most important problems of the country, beginning from their appearance at the municipal level during which the most important points were extracted so that at the end "the essence" of national problems reached the candidate. One can therefore say, following the tone of the official discourse, that the candidate in the end heard what could be considered a summary of national problems, a type of national exploration at IEPES meetings that took place throughout his state visits. This type of exploration so characteristic of the PRI system functioned somewhat like a plebiscite that served to replace those mechanisms associated with a formal democracy.

The Style, the Actors, and Other Objectives

There were substantial differences in the objectives, the tone, and the political actors participating in the electoral versus the ideological campaigns. Although the formal purpose of the IEPES was to organize analytical meetings to discuss large national problems, it also had important additional functions that were evident, but did not form a part of the formal objectives. In their meetings, whether these were forums, preparatory meetings, or summary meetings, people knew one another, exchanged information, and shared experiences. People from Mexico City and from the states met at these meetings. In the summary meetings that were part of the state-based campaign, people from the Mexico City committees met with locals and people from other parts of the country. Many times, people participated who were originally from the locality but who lived in Mexico City. Their attendance at meetings organized by the IEPES provided an opportunity for networking, and for the reestablishment and creation of relationships.

In this way, the IEPES offered an opportunity for the local, regional, and national political classes as well as technocrats and specialists from different entities to get to know each other and to exchange and meld different points of view. The fundamental purpose of the IEPES, according to many, was to give the impression to those invited to the meetings that they were taken into consideration when decisions were made. Inviting so many people had the goal of making them feel part of national politics.

As far as the style was concerned, the majority were serious, solemn meetings. Their character was primarily informative, in contrast to the festive atmosphere in the events attended by a multitude of people. Here there were no placards or banners, and no cheers, rattles, or slogans could be heard. Meetings took place in modern facilities that were set up specifically for these occasions. Generally, unlike other events, these meetings started on time. There were fewer people, with no more than fifteen at the podium, with the candidate in the middle and approximately three hundred people in the audience. Men wore suits. The support staff were always elegantly dressed. There was not a single sombrero made of straw or a cap in the room. At the wall at the end of the room behind the table where the speakers, some guests, and the candidate were seated, there was always a sign stating Let Mexico Speak and the name of the meeting with the logo of CSG and photos of the president on the left and the PRI candidate on the right, both dressed in suit and tie.

When the candidate entered the room, people got up and applauded. Thereafter, in a formal manner, they handed over the papers collected at the preparatory meetings. The members of the podium, one by one, presented their papers. They spoke quietly and read as clearly as possible. At the end of each reading, people applauded enthusiastically. Salinas took notes on what the speakers said. The candidate was the last to speak; his tone was calm and serious. It seemed as though he participated in the meeting to become informed and to learn. He listened, took notes, and asked questions.

In these meetings, the speakers informed the candidate about a specific problem, which gave him the right to raise whatever questions he wanted and to ask whomever he wanted. Even though these appeared to be informational meetings, the candidate in the end formulated the basic postulates of his government plan in a series of proposals, listed as key points.

There was a clear intention to show that the national problems would have to be discussed further. And sometimes, discussions went beyond the peaceful sequential presentation of papers. There were some meetings where harmony was ruptured. In some ways and within certain limits, discussion and even confrontation was promoted. This was the case in the meeting on export business that took place in Saltillo, Coahuila. A representative of the Workers' Congress, in a tone reminiscent of left-leaning students from a university philosophy department, denounced businesspeople and the protectionism of the state, and an important businessperson ended up arguing with him.

The candidate always took notes, and when he addressed the public, he did so "with an innovation in informality." It seemed as though this was a new way of working: invite some people from the audience to give their opinions apart from the official speakers. The questions raised by the candidate had an informal tone because discussions were not possible if there was no spontaneity. Even when there was a tendency for discussion or a simulation thereof, in reality, the candidate appeared as a professor asking his students many questions.

With regard to spontaneity among those invited, there were different options. Sometimes those guests who were asked a question outside of

the program had been warned previously, which allowed them to prepare their responses; some guests would prepare their comments, but
in the end were not requested to speak. Some of those invited who were
not official speakers did not know whether they would be invited to give
an opinion. In one version, Salinas was said to be more open to listening
than any other candidate; a person interviewed even stated that "Salinas
promotes the intervention of people who, since they don't have anything prepared, don't really know what to say."

As far as the speeches went, and in contrast to those that were held in
the meetings with multitudes of people, the emphasis here was on reaching a concrete conclusion. The candidate was particularly fond of ending a meeting by enumerating the "basic points." This provided a venue
for him to start to diffuse his political principles. Interested audiences
seemed to listen to these concluding summaries with special attention.

Reports by journalists about IEPES meetings were also written in a
solemn style. Generally, these articles focused on the candidate's speech,
which was reproduced almost in its entirety, and not as much on the
participation of those present. The final summarizing points that covered the candidate's synthesized future action plan were always there.

An exceptional case was the meeting held on national culture and
identity in Villahermosa, Tabasco. The topic, the prominence of those
invited, and the disposition to argue went beyond the usual parameters.
"Some thought that they would rest pleasantly in the meeting of the
IEPES about national culture and identity. The midday heat made people's eyes heavy. Additionally, the topic made one think of the tedium of
an almost incomprehensible verboseness and some sterile contributions
by intellectuals. This was not what happened. On the contrary, it was
the most plural forum of the entire political campaign of CSG. Indeed,
culture was discussed, but in an argumentative manner and confron-
tational style between the people presenting the topic" (*El Nacional*,
Feb. 2, 1988).

Before the event was over, the candidate caused a debate that lasted
for several hours (and in some respects for years) between two renowned
intellectuals—Enrique Krauze and Héctor Aguilar Camín:

CSG invited them to talk, so that this debate would be created. The
structure of other meetings was broken in the sense that normally
topics were discussed in a cool manner based on the corresponding
papers and that was it. Today was different. Today, PRI's candidate

gave another meaning to these national meetings about the great themes that are of interest to the country. "Let Aguilar Camín speak. And now let Krauze do so. Again Héctor. Now Enrique . . ." and in this way, the candidate promoted a plural forum so that this national meeting on "national culture and identity" ended up being highly successful. (Ibid.)

One of the main differences between the events of the IEPES and of those organized during visits to the states had to do with the participating actors. In the IEPES events, the people of the PRI and the IEPES who had a direct link to the candidate and the campaign were present, followed by the representatives from the public sector familiar with the theme. If the meeting discussed transportation issues, then the people who worked in transportation were invited, including functionaries, truck and taxi drivers, and experts who studied the topic in the engineering depart-ment of the National Autonomous University of Mexico. The meeting on supply was attended by directors of companies such as Bimbo and Herdez, as well as government functionaries from the CONASUPO and Ministry of Commerce and Industry. Environmental issues had SEDUE functionaries, employees from the Ministry of Health and the Mexican Petroleum Company, directors of polluting industries, environmental-ists, and specialized academics on the topic as invited guests.

The list of those invited always started with the public sector, which included those who currently held or had held an important position; this was followed by researchers, specialized academics and artists, busi-nesspeople, and finally, the sectorial leadership of the party. An inter-viewee affirmed that priority was given to those who made up the "first circle of people loyal to the candidate" and who were certain to hold the most important cabinet positions—the "people of the president." A second group of invitees was composed of those who formed the foun-dation of the political class, which included on the one hand the "tradi-tional politicians" (the people of the system) who were elected officials or who had risen within the party, and on the other hand, the "modern politicians" who had been formed by the federal public administrative hierarchy and who were called that because they favored new types of political operation based on scientific and technical knowledge. A third group was made up of intellectuals and academics, whose role, accord-ing to an informant, was "to give the event the legitimacy that in olden times was provided by priests: the opinion of science. Since there is no

Church that can approve, a few scientists and intellectuals are brought in to use their knowledge to legitimize what the politicians propose."

At the actual events, it was possible to determine the hierarchies according to the place that each group occupied within the space. In an IEPES meeting, for example, the audience was seated in three sections: one for special guests, one for the people invited by the IEPES who arrived from Mexico City that day, and one reserved for local guests.

Noting the sequence in which the papers were presented at an IEPES meeting was another way of understanding better the composition of the political class. In Saltillo, Coahuila, in the aforementioned meeting on export business, the director of the Mexican National Bank, the vice President of the Workers' Congress, the director of the INEGI, who previously had been the undersecretary of programming and budgeting, and the minister of foreign relations, among others, were present. The meeting's coordinator referred back to what had been analyzed in the five preparatory meetings. Afterward, the director of the IEPES spoke, introducing the topic; he was followed by an economist, the director of the Multimex bank who discussed "operational modernization." Next came a businessperson, the advisor to Salinas on economic matters, who referred to issues related to financial instruments used to consolidate [exchange rates]; the head of fiscal affairs from the Ministry of Finance and Public Credit; the president of the maquila industry; the president of the National Chamber of the Clothing Industry; a representative of the Workers' Congress; and finally, the candidate, who gave his conclusions on a list of points that let the audience know what his economic policies would be once he was elected.

An IEPES Meeting on Technology and Science

The meeting described below can be considered a typical event in its organization and functioning. However, it was also an atypical meeting since at certain moments serious organizational problems arose, which were highly unusual. This example is discussed extensively since we had the opportunity to follow it closely from its beginning to its end.

The Coordination of the Event

Among the meetings organized by the IEPES was one on science and technology. The person in charge of organizing this meeting was the director of a department of the National Science and Technology Council (Consejo Nacional de Ciencia y Tecnología–CONACYT).[2] It was rumored that he had been given this responsibility because he was a close friend of the candidate, both of them having been students at Harvard at the same time. Because he was named the coordinator, many believed that he would shortly be promoted to head of the institution. As coordinator, his job was to organize the final meeting on science and technology in Puebla with the participation of the candidate, as well as to handle the preparatory meetings that had to precede that meeting. The coordinator determined the place of the event, named the coordinators for each one of the meetings, and developed the topics.

Seven preparatory meetings were held in different cities of the country. Those responsible for coordinating these meetings were all important scientists from those areas. In Sonora, the director of the Nutritional Center of the state became the coordinator; in Morelos, the director of the Institute for Electrical Research located in Cuernavaca was the coordinator; and in Nuevo León, the president of a local university was the coordinator.

The function of the regional coordinators was primarily to invite or recommend local people to attend, while the general coordinator was in charge of inviting those who lived in Mexico City. In the preparatory meetings, approximately 320 papers were presented, which were heard by an audience of approximately six hundred people coming from different regions of the country who supposedly had some connection to science and technology. In Cuernavaca alone, there were forty speakers and commentators and between two hundred and three hundred guests plus the regional audience. In Nuevo León, forty people presented their papers to an audience of approximately four hundred people.

It was common for the same person to be invited to participate in several meetings. One of the guests commented that the coordinator "sent me a list of preparatory meetings, and he invited me to participate in all of the ones I wanted to, and in the role that I wanted to. Of the seven preparatory meetings that were held in various cities, I participated in those in Hermosillo, Monterrey, and Cuernavaca; in one as a speaker, in another as a commentator, and in the third one as a guest." Therefore, it was also common for the same people to be found at various meetings of the IEPES.

Invariably, the general coordinator gave meetings his/her own conceptual imprint. In this case, according to several of the participants, the coordinator invited speakers who represented the peasant, workers, and industrial sectors, and the institutions, researchers, and government in an effort to discuss the topic of science as it applied to national problems. In the words of a regional coordinator, these were meant to support certain projects with the ultimate goal that the research would be considered part of development planning. This was the general coordinator's assignment given to regional organizers. In fact, according to one person in attendance, the speakers invited by him to the preparatory meetings denounced basic science and, ironically, called the scientists "Little Mister Nobel Prizes."

Puebla: The Summary Meeting

All the preparatory meetings that were organized and all the papers that were presented were meant to serve as input to the science and technology meeting that was to take place in Puebla. There, the discussion was going to focus on the role of science in the development of the country. For this purpose, the general coordinator believed that it would be good for peasants, workers, and businesspeople to provide scientists with insights on the problems they faced.

In this way, the esplanade of the Puebla Cultural Center had representatives of the peasant, workers, and business sectors, as well as government functionaries, directors of centers and institutes of science and technology, the president of the Scientific Research Academy, and, to a lesser extent, politicians present. The majority of speakers were local. It was a meeting on science where there were few scientists invited to present papers. It seemed obvious that the people who were invited to the meeting were those the coordinator thought the candidate would like to find—those who make use of science and not the scientists themselves.

As usual, at the podium around a hexagonal table, the president of the Science Academy, the director of Banamex, the minister of communications and transportation, the former director of the CONACYT, the general coordinator of the meeting, and the speakers were seated. The audience was made up of university students, scientists, and those holding scientific positions.

The speakers began. The director of the IEPES introduced the speakers and spoke of the strategic importance that science and technology had. The first presenter, the head of the Agricultural Cooperative Atenayuca complained that "technical assistance is lacking and year after year we try to produce grain and fail, and without corn the life of the community loses its reason for existence and falls apart." Afterward, the director of the National Institute for Research in Forestry, Agriculture and Fishing and the director of the Scientific Research Center of Ensenada, Baja California, spoke, stating that he was in favor of decentralized research in the areas of science and technology. The next presenter, the director of the Scientific Research Academy, spoke of the crisis faced by the sector and requested increased funding. A businessperson said that the state, within its guiding principles, should promote scientific and technological advances. Finally, the candidate spoke (*Excélsior*, Feb. 20, 1988).

Once all the papers had been presented, the usual questions asked by the candidate to the audience were raised. Each one of them was directed to an expert on the topic. The director of Banamex was asked about the relationship that existed among research, technological development, and the educational system; the director of the Institute for Didactic Materials of some university was asked how to improve the quality of basic research; a director of a computer center was asked what the link between science, technology, and production was; and the director of the CONACYT was asked how technological research geared toward production could be stimulated.

The candidate's speech followed the questions and contained seven points: first, giving technological and scientific development the prioritized position that its strategic importance deserved as "we need to keep our technicians and scientists working and doing research in Mexico"; second, strengthening the link between applied research and technological development; third, making better use of technological resources by the national productive apparatus; fourth, upholding and stimulating the innovative and adaptive capacity of the National System of Science and Technology; fifth, strengthening the research and development performed by private and public enterprises so it is considered a strategic part of their obligations; sixth, forming basic principles in scientific areas and in engineering; and seventh, strengthening the decentralization policy in the sciences and technology (*El Nacional*, Feb. 20, 1988).

These statements seemed to reflect more what the candidate expected from this meeting than what really took place. Even though everything had turned out as planned by the coordinator, among the scientific community there was a sense of discontent. Even the candidate seemed to be dissatisfied and said in his last comments: "Finally, I consider this topic of such importance that I have asked the general director of the IEPES to call together the members of the scientific and technological community to extend the dialogue that has taken place in this meeting; above all else to recognize the changes that are taking place all over the world today and their impact on our country. We can not distance ourselves from these changes. I know we have the available talent to realistically place us within the innovative world currents in the areas of science and technology, while maintaining a great sense of nationalism and efficiency."

He asked the director of the IEPES to call on the members of the scientific and technological community to organize another meeting. The request was seen by many as a direct reflection of the coordinator's failure—who, by the way, would not be in charge of the next meeting—as well as of the director of the IEPES who had chosen such an inappropriate collaborator.

The meeting ended, and the interpretations spread throughout the people in the hallways. It was said that the meeting had not gone well; that in Puebla "everyone had ended up unpleasantly surprised." The meeting was more like a popular event appropriate for a campaign state visit than for a IEPES meeting and was therefore demagogical, since it was "demagogical to bring in peasants" to a meeting on science. One of the people invited expressed this opinion: "The peasants and the workers played the role of contrarians; they knew that they would not be influential nor would they play a part in scientific policies, but they could make the scientific community feel that they were not meeting the needs of these sectors." It was an insult to the scientific community to have to listen to the complaints peasants and workers issued against them.

Others stated that people had begun to feel displeased starting with the preparatory meetings. There was little discussion at them, and the quality of the papers presented was varied and even poor. In the end, the meetings were "of little usefulness": "I got the impression that everything said was said to the wind. I imagine that the same was felt by everyone else."

In some of the meetings, the papers were three to five pages long, too brief to discuss significant ideas. In others, the opposite was the case: the papers were long and useless. The last one, given by the general coordinator, was too long: "In a speech that was half an hour long, the Eagle Knights and the historic antecedents of Mexican culture were discussed. The general comment was: where does this *tlatoani*[3] want to take us?"

The coordinator of one of the preparatory meetings was convinced that the discontent was due to the rigidity in the purposes established by the general coordinator: "There was a dissonance between my guests and those invited by the general coordinator. . . . The meeting in Puebla followed his designs and his ideas. The scientific community was not pleased, but they never are. . . . At any rate, the coordinator did not handle things well; he did everything for the PRI and not for the community, and he focused on political interests of applying and linking science and technology to society, the topic the coordinator believed to be of the candidate's interest."

And why did the people not show signs of resentment from the very beginning? There were various opinions, but it seems that many believed that it was not in their interest: "The audience was furious, but no one showed their discontent in front of an individual who could become the head of the CONACYT, or even a secretary of some new ministry . . . and the people do not want to fight with a person whom they may have to deal with in the future. No one wants to become an enemy, and in that way, people continue to behave as if there was some value to what they are doing."

In summary, it seemed that the general coordinator had not guessed the real interests of the candidate and that he was confused about the purposes and the functions of the IEPES. From an official point of view, the meetings of the IEPES left a sense that the candidate was still missing a clear political platform in the science and technology realm. In Puebla, where the 280 papers presented previously were supposedly presented again, there was no line that could be followed to provide coherence for the establishment of scientific policy. From another perspective, rumors and interpretations abounded. In the same way that the coordinator tried to interpret what Salinas wanted with regard to scientific policy, other people were trying to interpret the process by which the candidate would choose cabinet members. In reality, independently of whether these interpretations were accurate or not, it was clear that everyone doubted that the coordinator would become the new director of the CONACYT: "I believe that the director of the IEPES ended up like the rest of the scientific community, that the coordinator had designated himself as the future director of the CONACYT, and that the director himself was unclear about the validity of this speculation, because of which he had no choice but to let him be."

All eyes were now on the coordinator and the invitees for the next meeting on science and technology.

Sonora: The Meeting on Higher Education

Just a few days following the Puebla meeting, there were talks about where and how to organize the next meeting. The person in charge of coordinating it would be, it seemed, a friend of the IEPES's director. The topic would cover higher education in addition to science and technology (because he wanted to avoid humiliating the previous organizer).

In two meetings held in Ciudad Obregón and in Hermosillo, the scientists of the country gathered. On this occasion, everyone could more or less express his/her viewpoints as members of the scientific community.

Two weeks before the meetings took place, the general coordinator invited all participants to a kind of general rehearsal. At FLACSO headquarters in Mexico City, the coordinator asked the speakers and the director of the IEPES to attend. The rehearsal lasted for three hours, and the papers were read while people criticized each other: whether the paper was too long or too dense to be read out loud. They were asked to formulate questions within their areas of expertise so that the candidate could ask these questions in the forum. They were also asked to recommend two people who could answer the questions. Everything seemed much better planned than in the Puebla meeting.

In Hermosillo, the speakers and the guests were asked to be at the Casa de la Cultura at 4:00 p.m. The candidate was scheduled to arrive at 5:00 p.m., but he actually arrived at 6:30 p.m. Even though people had to wait for two and a half hours, they used the time to get to know one another and to talk with acquaintances. One of the speakers said that "such a long wait had helped them relax, and if there had been any nervousness, the wait had diluted it."

The invitees arrived and sat down at their places on the podium. However, either name cards were missing or there were too many chairs. The person in charge of protocol said that some places were purposefully kept empty up to the last minute so a private secretary of the candidate could tell him which of the special guests would be seated at them.

Ten minutes before the candidate arrived, new name cards appeared on the podium. Two candidates to senatorial positions for the state of Sonora, the coordinator of the meeting and the speakers, the president of the polytechnic university, an engineer and industry person of the region, the undersecretary of health, and the director of architecture, among others, ended up joining the director of the IEPES at the podium.

The candidate finally arrived. On this occasion, he showed up accompanied by a contingent of women, among them his wife, his sister, the governor of Colima, and eight young women who sat down in the first rows.

With this the session started. Except for one, all those who spoke were renowned researchers in the natural and social sciences. The first speaker talked about how the social sciences had been forgotten. Thereafter, teaching and the education of scientists was discussed, and finally, the last specialist to speak gave a political speech in conventional terms. Even though many had prepared their answers, there was no time for the candidate to raise questions in this session.

The meeting in Hermosillo was, for some, almost perfect because it had met all of its objectives, and especially because it had been an "academic" meeting. Comments were made that the director of the IEPES had stated that the most interesting meeting and the meeting of the highest caliber was the one on identity and culture in Tabasco, but that the most academic meeting of all was this one. It was also stated that Salinas's speech had been good, well articulated, and delivered in the right tone. An invitee said: "I am convinced of one thing: of all the times that I have seen Salinas, and I have seen him twice in two different scenarios, in another meeting similar to this . . . and at a political rally. . . . Salinas is infinitely better in this type of setting."

As a result, the meeting on science and technology held in Sonora had an official purpose. Even though it was considered to be an atypical meeting since there were no previous preparatory meetings and it was not scheduled, it was organized to fulfill two purposes: "To somewhat erase the image in the minds of people on the inside and the outside left by the one held in Puebla and to allow the group that . . . will be a part of the Ministry of Public Education, to work in the area . . . of scientific research."

But the truth is that a meeting of this nature also had other purposes that were generally not very explicit. One of them was for people to get to know one another and for them to exchange ideas and projects. In this case, research, education, and policies were discussed until there was almost nothing left to say.

However, there were always questions regarding the real usefulness of these meetings, and in this specific case, the possibilities of influencing scientific and cultural policies. This concern was greater since one of the meeting's purposes was, even if not publicly stated, to open up the possibility for participants to show off in front of the candidate and in front of his/her colleagues. One of the speakers confirmed this in an interview:

> Then I spoke. I felt very good because my discussion was well-prepared. . . . I was interested in seeing two things. One, if while I was speaking Salinas was taking notes . . . that seemed to be important since even though he has his own comments written on cards that he will give at the end (one can see that he has a script), obviously he incorporates things there that seem interesting to him, and therefore it was important to me to see if he took notes. The other thing that interested me was to see how much of what I had said would be reiterated by him in his final comments. So, I read slowly, partially to be able to turn around and look at him and to see if he was writing something down. . . . I did see that he was taking notes. I saw that he was paying close attention. . . . At the end, when [the candidate] said his good-byes, he shook everyone's hand, and the truth is that with me he hesitated for a moment and said, "Listen, I liked your presentation very much, I congratulate you, I hope you will continue to develop these points so we can get a good document out of them."

Without a doubt, several intellectuals participated gladly in the IEPES meetings and were full of expectations. Additionally, they thought they knew how to behave in them. An "academic" behavior in a political meeting raises the level of the meeting. In the words of one of the participants:

> Only one of the speakers fell into the usual party-speak of "Mr. Candidate of our party to the presidency." All others were quite somber. I believe—even if this is a result of my narcissism—that I added an interesting tone to the meeting. I was very somber and talked with deliberation: "Mr. Salinas de Gortari, ladies and gentlemen . . . ," straightforward and nothing more . . . not even "candidate" and I never mentioned the party. . . . And apart from that one person, the others were equally somber as I was, they may have felt the tone that I set, which really imbued the meeting with great dignity, honestly. There was not even one eulogy of those that everybody makes.

Generally, the meetings raised inordinate expectations among the participants, at least at the beginning. However, it was also common that once the meetings were over and once the "follow-up meetings" took place, skepticism set in. A particularly enthusiastic participant at the beginning told us: "I did come in with the hope that there would be a change; by the fifth meeting, I was skeptical with regard to what all of this meant. . . . Tomorrow is the third follow-up meeting. The battles and struggles for power, to be chosen, to demonstrate that one has the support of such-and-such groups and people continue." After some time spent trying to elaborate a working plan,

> you realize that you are just a part of a farce. . . . Nobody is really looking for ideas on how to improve the educational system because their only interest is in politics and not educational policy nor science nor technology. In the end, no one is interested in what happens in the community, nor are they interested in attending to the needs of their constituencies, their area; they are only interested in presenting themselves in a positive light to those above. They don't seem obligated toward the community because, in reality, they have not been chosen for their position by the community, but have been assigned to it by those above, not by those of the community. . . . I feel as if everyone was working for the candidate personally and what was of least importance to them is the impression they left on the community. [The candidate] was only interested that the event be well organized, but he was not interested in structuring a platform of research for Mexico. He lectured but did not listen. What this is all about in the end is for them [the speakers] to sell themselves to the candidate.

The same person was convinced that people attended these meetings for three reasons:

> (1) to have the opportunity of being close to the candidate in case it occurs to him to invite you to work with him, (2) to get closer to those who will be making decisions, and (3) to provide ideas that are useful for the topic under discussion. I would discard the first and last reasons. The candidate can not remember everything that is said, the thousands of speeches that he hears during the campaign, nor can he remember the people who attended them. To try to convince him of one's ideas is also not operationally feasible because in these meetings the idea is not to establish a dialogue; nobody listens. The reason people actually go is to be near those who supposedly are the closest to the candidate, but I believe this to be a long shot, a very silly bet. The meeting was useless from the perspective of formulating a government program since it is generated by designated individuals so

this whole show is to get closer to people who will possibly have these responsibilities, and in the end Salinas de Gortari will not choose people whom he heard speak there.

The Purpose of the IEPES Meetings

The majority of those interviewed agreed that the IEPES meetings functioned for people to get to know one another, to forge relationships, and to exchange opinions. However, they were skeptical about the fulfillment of these meetings' official purposes.

Certainly, for the politicians, functionaries, and academics interviewed, the materials that came out of the forums and meetings were of little use. It was evident to everyone that although an attempt was made to give discussions an overriding political line, there was an inevitable rupture between the meetings that were held prior to the *destape* and those that took place thereafter. According to this opinion, the results of the meetings in the first phase were essentially thrown out since these were held with a specific potential candidate in mind. In this manner, the president of the advisory council who had been appointed by Miguel de la Madrid really worked for the "wrong" pre-candidate; after the destape, all of his work lost all meaning. One of our interviewees was more radical in his beliefs and thought that none of the phases of these meetings served any purposes. "Before the destape, hundreds of forums are organized for everyone to become privy to the possible candidates. In the second phase, after the destape, the meetings take place so that people meet other people and become known by the candidate. If the materials produced in the first phase are not even read, the ones from the second phase at least serve to elaborate speeches. Beyond the speeches, the political platform of the party is not taken into consideration in the least."

Other skeptics did not believe that the IEPES meetings could lead to positions in the next six-year presidential term. "In the hundreds of forums that the IEPES and the PRI are organizing, everybody looks to be there and to be invited and 'to be seen.' But, in reality, every candidate already has his own team, and each member of the team has his own people."

In all of the IEPES events, rumors and interpretations were abundant. Every person present, every person absent, and anything that was said with or without any significance was susceptible to interpretation.

At many levels, everyone conveyed messages to one another, and these could only be understood by the political class because they were directed to this class. Everyone interpreted everything according to his/her position within the system. Those who were not invited to certain events felt excluded, and those who were invited were convinced that they had possibilities of holding a great future position. There were those, upon not being invited, that consoled themselves by saying that "the candidate is taking care of him/her."

One can affirm that the majority of participants at the meetings did not doubt their usefulness. Some kept up hope that the materials produced in these meetings would be used in political decision making. Additionally, a great number of participants were convinced that they were becoming an integral part of the country's political life by attending. And lastly, they knew that the meetings of the IEPES served to keep the political class entertained during moments of change and uncertainty.

The presentation of papers and other materials followed a hierarchical structure, with the official discourse going from the lowest to the top. None of those who participated in the first stages of the sequence knew, in reality, what would happen with his/her work, especially in reference to the papers; however, it seems that everyone hoped that their work at forums and preparatory meetings would reach the top of the pyramid. To reach the top to some meant the possibility of forming a part of the future team of the candidate (the so-called *hueso* [bone] as this is called in Mexico); for others it meant influencing future policies directly; and for all, it meant the creation and strengthening of contacts, as well as the opportunity to be seen, at different levels, as an expert in the field. Therefore, the participants limited themselves to complying with their duties and trying to make a good impression on the audience.

The uncertainty about the final destination of their work and the future implications of participating in some event created an ambiguous attitude among those attending. There was confidence and skepticism at the same time. The many interpretations that could be made about the success or failure of an event, about the presence or absence of important persons, about the topic discussed, and about the attitude and the gestures of the candidate allowed people to have some confidence. Conversely, the absence of total certainty was cause for hesitation. Everything seemed to depend on the place that each person occupied and how confident he/she felt in occupying that place.

In the analytical meeting on national, regional, and local problems, the entire political class was involved from the municipal level through the party structure and at the regional and national levels through to the political elite. This included the workers, peasants, and popular sectors through to the high-level political functionaries, passing through intellectuals, scientists, technicians, and businesspeople. At the very least, participating in an IEPES meeting meant that one would be seen by the country's political class; it was as if one were invited to an important party. It could mean that one would not only be seen by the members of the candidate's team and the higher party echelons but also be called upon and taken into account in the development of policies in one's area. Herein lay the essential function of these meetings, particularly the summary meetings: to rub shoulders with the members of the political class and to be heard by the members of the candidate's team or to be seen and greeted by the candidate, all raised the possibility (not the certainty) for a hueso or important government position during the next administration. Even if one did not receive greater attention, discipline was upheld: at least one stayed on good terms with those who had made the invitation. In the last instance, the meetings organized by the IEPES served to foment the creation and the extension of the contact and friendship networks that were always an absolute must. In this way, those who participated in these meetings did so because they were convinced that they were a part of the right team with the right political line.

Additionally, there is no doubt that the IEPES meetings served to choose future leaders for specific areas from among the organizers: the meetings were a test. Even though there were no rules to follow, it was possible to follow some general guidelines. The fact that a summary meeting had been especially successful did not guarantee the person responsible for its organization that he/she would be a part of the candidate's team nor that he/she would gain access to a good government position. However, what became clear was who definitely did not pass the test; that is to say, those who were *quemados* [burnt].

Finally, the IEPES meetings were informative, the candidate listened and took notes, and those invited ended up listening to the candidate. The candidate got to know local, regional, and national problems by means of updated facts, while the participants got to know the basic principles of his program. The candidate made use of these meetings to provide advance notice of his government policies.

7
The Press and the Presidential Campaign

Once the electoral campaign started and the names of all of the potential candidates were known, the press abandoned the role it had played prior to the *destape* (unveiling) as described in chapter 4.[1] Formally, the communications media were instruments by which various candidates presented their proposals on a massive scale, providing the public with the information they required to cast a more or less informed vote. Naturally, this democratic-liberal function required an independent press that was at least somewhat impartial vis-à-vis the various political options. As discussed in chapter 1, the press did not meet this requirement during the period analyzed in this book. Even though the majority of the print media were privately owned, they were usually closely linked to political figures or financial interests that used the media to forge alliances with powerful groups (Mahan 1985).

Television and radio, as is the case in many other countries, were subject to a more direct and formalized regulatory structure than the written press because of their licensing agreements. At the same time, a certain number of radio and television stations were run directly by the government. Only one public television station, Channel 13, was transmitted nationally, but many regional radio and television stations were operated by state governments and, given the hegemonic power of the Institutional Revolutionary Party (Partido Revolucionario Institucional–PRI), showed few indications of independence in reference to government or party policies. Some of the government-owned radio and television stations were run by higher education institutions, such as Channel 11, which was managed by the National Polytechnic Institute.

Many electronic media were privately owned, but there were no limits on the number of stations that could be owned by one company. As a result, the Televisa conglomerate enjoyed a virtual monopoly in this realm, creating a communications empire that extended from radio to the written press, films, sports, cable television, the record industry, publishing houses, and other spheres.

Even though under Mexican law all political parties had access to airtime, such time was highly limited in proportion to the overall time allocated to electoral issues by the electronic media. Political parties could buy airtime, but stations could refuse to accept these ads, and most important, stations had no obligation equivalent to the so-called fairness doctrine.[2] There were no legal grounds to challenge an information program and demand equal treatment.

This chapter analyzes the role played by the media during the electoral campaign by examining the content of a random sample of articles on the elections published by the *Excélsior* newspaper, along with select coverage by *La Jornada* newspaper, the weekly magazines *Proceso* and *Siempre!*, Televisa's nightly news program *24 Horas*, and several radio interviews. These media were considered the most important at the time in terms of audience and political impact.[3] During interviews, journalists representing various media who worked on the elections provided additional materials on journalistic practices common at the time and their opinions on innovations that arose during the period under study.

The Coverage

For each type of media, it is possible to identify a distinctive pattern within the universally provided large-scale coverage of the PRI's presidential candidate.

Campaign Coverage in the Print Media

We analyzed a sample of articles published by *Excélsior* on twenty-four days chosen at random between January and May 1988. For each of these days, the average space dedicated to each candidate's campaign was measured in terms of the average length of columns discussing the campaign, the average number of articles on each of the candidates, and the number of op-ed pieces on the back page. The results of this study are shown in table 7.1.[4]

The PRI's campaign received more coverage from *Excélsior* than all other campaigns combined, with more than 50 percent of the total reports on the presidential campaign process dedicated to the PRI. Such a volume can not readily be explained simply by the pure journalistic merit of each campaign. The opposition parties acquired a degree of political power that could be seen as unusual, which meant that their

Table 7.1   Average daily coverage of the presidential candidates in *Excélsior* in a 24-day sample taken between January and May 1988

Candidate	Length of columns of newspaper articles (cm)	Number of newspaper articles	Number of op-ed pieces
Salinas	250.2	4.0	2.3
Cárdenas	76.5	1.1	0.4
Clouthier	77.0	1.2	0.2
Castillo	72.1	0.9	0.3
Others	12.7	0.3	0.1

Note: Election coverage by political columnists (all candidates): 89.4 percent. The format used by political columnists makes it difficult to create a category referring exclusively to the campaign. However, in a limited sample and by going through each paragraph, the PRI's campaign was the main topic in 75 percent of the cases.

campaigns were particularly newsworthy, just as in the United States the presidential candidacy of John Anderson in 1980 received an impressive level of coverage by both the electronic and print media, which gained him approximately 5 percent of the votes (Robinson and Sheehan 1983).

It should be noted that *Excélsior* does not represent a typical example of the country's journalistic coverage. At the time, *Excélsior* and other newspapers and magazines were seeking to keep a large group of loyal readers by covering important events even at the cost of offending the ruling party. *Excélsior*'s prestige provided it with sufficient journalistic muscle to allow it to be open and critical. But this was an exception. If the analysis had included other, more representative newspapers, the hegemonic presence of the PRI would have been even greater.

The only newspapers that extensively and regularly covered the campaigns of parties other than the PRI, especially those of Cuauhtémoc Cárdenas and Manuel de Jesús Clouthier, were *El Universal, La Jornada,* and *Unomásuno.* Nevertheless, *Excélsior* provided a broader coverage of opposition campaigns than in previous years. *Proceso,* a weekly magazine that played a significant role in the evolution of Mexican journalism as a forum for critical coverage of political issues, published interviews with opposition candidates. The latter agreed that, in comparison to electronic media, the written press provided significant space for their campaigns. Cárdenas described the press's coverage of his campaign as "objective and truthful, but sparse." In an interview published by *Proceso* on March 7, 1988, he stated: "While the press may publish a daily news item about the opposition candidates, the official candidate [Salinas] receives several pages of coverage."

The print media opened up a new area by publishing criticisms of the official candidate. For example, on October 14, 1987, just after the announcement of Salinas's nomination, the political weekly *Siempre!*, one of the most important magazines in the country, published this statement: "The nomination has fallen to Carlos Salinas de Gortari who until now had been the secretary for programming and budgeting. The irony is that we have reached such extremes [in Mexico] that we no longer need for him [the candidate] to have a solid preparation or any great knowledge of the issues."

The publication of strong criticism of the person who would become the next president of Mexico was considered a break with tradition by journalists and observers alike. As a journalist who was interviewed stated: "The tradition in Mexico has been that there are three 'sacred' subjects that journalists don't dare to criticize: the Virgin of Guadalupe, the military, and the presidency. Obviously, we have now broken one of the taboos."

Of the print media analyzed in this study, *Proceso* was the most implacable in its critical coverage of the PRI's campaign and the presidency of Miguel de la Madrid. It was also the only national print medium that reported on the campaign's media coverage as a topic on its own merit, dedicating several articles to detailing PRI methods, some of which were corrupt, to ensure the media's support of its campaign.

The Coverage of the Campaign by *24 Horas*

The televised news program *24 Horas*, anchored by Jacobo Zabludovsky, the most renowned television reporter in Mexico at the time, long enjoyed the highest rating among television audiences for news programs. It was seen everywhere in Mexico; in the United States, it was presented by television stations that had programming in Spanish. Ideologically, Televisa followed the lines of big business; it was strongly pro–United States and anti-left, as extensively documented by Gutiérrez Espíndola (1989). Its conservative inclinations became particularly evident in its coverage of international news, and it frequently swayed from the official position of the government on these topics. Perhaps the large audience that watched its news programs—especially *24 Horas*—can be attributed to its independence in this area.

Table 7.2   Distribution of coverage by *24 Horas* of presidential candidates in the 1988 campaign, April 4–June 24

Candidate	Number of segments	Average length of segment	Total Time
Salinas	74	1 min., 55 sec.	141 min., 40 sec.
Cárdenas	10	55 sec.	8 min., 51 sec.
Clouthier	7*	31 sec.	4 min., 9 sec.
Castillo	9	50 sec.	7 min., 30 sec.
Ibarra	7	38 sec.	4 min., 23 sec.
Magaña Negrete	3	48 sec.	2 min., 23 sec.

Note: This table includes only news directly related to the campaign. General articles about elections (technical explanations, etc.) and political articles that are not linked to the campaign are excluded.

*This figure does not include one news item that lasted for 7.5 minutes, which is discussed later.

In the first phases of the campaign in 1988, Emilio Azcárraga Milmo, president of Televisa, stated that the company was a "soldier of the PRI," surprising journalists and intellectuals with this statement of explicit support. Discussions on the extent to which this statement may have harmed Salinas's candidacy led to speculation on the reciprocal favors that the company would receive from the PRI. The statement was also interpreted by some as evidence that the PRI had lost touch with its traditional popular bases and was now more closely identified with big business interests. However, until the campaign started, *24 Horas* was considered a source of more independent information than that provided by public television.

Table 7.2 shows the number and average length of segments covering the candidates that were transmitted by the evening edition of *24 Horas* between April 4 and June 24, 1988. More than 80 percent of the airtime given to the campaigns focused on the PRI's candidate. Coverage of opposition candidates was sparse, and the occasional segment on them was short. The difference between the airtime provided to the PRI's candidate and that provided to all other opposition candidates was so large that all opposition candidates appeared to be of equal (un)importance.

What is especially interesting is the limited coverage received by Clouthier, which was even less than that received by Heberto Castillo, even though Clouthier was the candidate of the opposition party that traditionally had been the strongest and could therefore have been considered a more attractive topic from a journalistic standpoint. This extremely limited coverage of Clouthier was, however, not accidental.

An effective analysis of television news coverage includes examination of its visual and auditory elements, since the message that is transmitted and received contains both of these elements (Graber 1989). The news coverage on the PRI usually included long audio extracts from Salinas himself, while the voice on the segments that covered opposition candidates generally was the anchorman's or the reporter's. Only in two news segments on Cárdenas could his voice be heard. The tone used for candidates differed greatly. The news coverage on Salinas was read with great enthusiasm and always referred to him with reverential language befitting a president. The news coverage on opposition candidates was usually read in a neutral voice, and the only references to the candidates were simply as "another candidate."

Sometimes the sarcasm in dealing with opposition candidates became extremely evident, especially toward Cárdenas. On one occasion, news coverage included a speech that Cárdenas had given in which he had stated: "My government will be plural and there will be space for representatives from all parties . . . except for those from the PRI." The next image was the anchorperson, who raised his eyebrows and commented: "Not that plural."

There were also notable differences in the images used to cover the PRI's campaign and those of the opposition candidates. In the majority of cases, the images of Salinas showed large groups of enthusiastic people, with the candidate in control of the crowd. In contrast, the images of opposition candidates showed few followers, and in the case of Cárdenas, they focused on students to give the impression that his candidacy was attractive only to "young and educated people." Few images reflected peasants or workers at Cárdenas rallies, although it was well known that he enjoyed large-scale support among these groups in some parts of the country.

24 Horas became a topic of discussion in the campaign as opposition parties criticized its exaggerated bias toward the PRI. These criticisms were difficult to ignore since the majority were made by the candidate of the National Action Party (Partido Acción Nacional–PAN), which followed a free-market ideology and which enjoyed the support of various groups that believed in the same economic philosophy as Televisa did.

Clouthier, who was frustrated by the disdain that his candidacy received from radio and television news coverage, denounced the airtime the media assigned to his campaign. With the support of other opposition parties, PAN organized Civil Resistance, a formal boycott of

Televisa. A sticker placed on various cars read: "Don't watch 24 *Horas* because it does not tell the truth." Clouthier was seen throughout the country with his mouth covered by adhesive tape to symbolize the media censorship that was, according to him, aimed at his party and him.

The opposition's insistence on denouncing electronic media in their campaigns (which was reported in some print media, including *La Jornada*, *Proceso*, and *Excélsior*) led to a response by Televisa. In his program, Zabludovsky read the entire text of a paid insert published in several newspapers and signed by Netzahualcóyotl de la Vega, the secretary of the Radio and Television Industry's Workers' Union (Sindicato de Trabajadores de la Industria de la Radio y la Televisión–STIRT). It took Zabludovsky 7.5 minutes to read the text, giving the impression that the opinions expressed in the paid insert were part of a factual journalistic article. The last words of the text, read in a slow and emphatic manner, were "Mr. Clouthier does not deceive anyone" and ended abruptly with "This is how the public statement ends."

In another program, Zabludovsky explained and defended the journalistic criteria used by Televisa in determining opposition coverage: "We studied the procedures used in other countries. In Italy, the four most important [television] channels have different political orientations and function accordingly, supporting their preferred party. . . . In the United States, political parties can purchase as much airtime as they want. In Televisa, we believe that political parties should receive airtime proportionate to the number of votes they received in prior elections." In the same editorial, Televisa claimed that Cárdenas had received greater coverage than he deserved according to this formula. Zabludovsky concluded by saying that Televisa's respect for the audience impeded it from dealing with the demands made by the opposition candidates. It was as if the credibility of 24 *Horas* had unjustifiably been damaged by the controversy.

Radio Coverage

We did not have a chance to tape radio news programs of the campaign in a systematic manner. Instead, we interviewed radio reporters who covered the campaign and taped radio coverage of select stations in Veracruz and the Federal District.

Since control over the radio industry was less monopolistic than it was for other media, in some cases opposition candidates were interviewed freely or could buy airtime. Some programs dedicated a significant amount of airtime to them; however, even this coverage was minimal in comparison to the airtime that focused on Salinas's campaign. In Veracruz, for example, each candidate was interviewed, but all the events that the official candidate participated in also received coverage.

The opposition parties, especially PAN, protested the limited radio coverage, but both Clouthier and Cárdenas placed great importance on those opportunities offered by this medium. In Veracruz, where he was interviewed by the program *Ocho en Punto*, Cárdenas compared the realities found in the different media that had the greatest reach: "I should say that I have had the opportunity to campaign through radio transmissions. There have been many stations in different parts of the nation that, in my opinion, have opened their doors to us and have allowed us to reach their audiences, as is the case here [with *Ocho en Punto*]. On the other hand, if we look at what the official television has done, it almost does not mention anything about what we are doing on a daily basis. With us, at times all they say is that 'candidate "X" was in such town' and that is all."

While the radio programmers and reporters could not deviate too far from "official" party lines, the general public could, by means of telephone calls, express their criticisms of or their support for opposition candidates on the air. A radio reporter provided us with an explanation: "Basically, when the official candidate is in a specific location, you have to be careful. But as soon as he leaves, they [the PRI] don't look closely at what we do. Things happen very quickly in radio."

The radio was the first medium to transmit the name of the PRI candidate, and it played a critical role in his unveiling. In the hours preceding the announcement of Salinas as the nominee, a radio station wrongly announced that Sergio García Ramírez was the PRI candidate, which has become known as the "erroneous unveiling." This error, committed by such an important politician as Alfredo del Mazo, as well as its meaning within a political culture whose rules, even if informal, were very rigid, was the subject of many discussions even after the elections. Several reporters gave substantial importance to this matter since it gave radio the status of an actor and not simply a transmitter of Mexican politics.

The importance of radio grew during the campaign since it occasionally became a venue for public expression through conversations and interviews with the opposition candidates, as well as a means for the population to express itself.

The Purpose of the Media in the Electoral Campaign

During the PRI's presidential campaign, the candidate took the time to ratify the importance that alliances and negotiations had, thus forcing the members of the political class into constant interpretative activities. In parallel fashion, he became transformed into a symbol of the nation and its component parts, with attributes similar to those of an emperor. We found that the print media was the tool for transmitting the negotiation activities, while television was used primarily to transform the negotiating candidate into the president-emperor of the republic.

Reporters who were interviewed during the campaign said that the PRI's coverage was ensured by a very costly[5] system of co-optation in which reporters, editors, printers, photographers, and all others comprising the media received ample compensation for dedicating time and space to the PRI candidate. These compensations generally provided the financial sustenance of newspapers and magazines, according to those interviewed. In return, the press was expected to not only provide ample coverage of the PRI's campaign but also accept photographs and informative bulletins produced directly by the PRI as if they were their own. Very few publications could boast non-compliance with this system of co-optation. *La Jornada*, for example, which was often hard to obtain in Mexico City because of its extensive coverage of Cárdenas's campaign, also published these bulletins. Many of its journalists were opposed to this practice, and editors conceded to publishing the bulletins in distinctive typeset (in italics) so that at least the journalistic community would notice the difference.

The PRI's campaign, including how it used the media, was more than a series of strategies to attract votes. The style and size of the 1988 campaign were very similar to those of previous campaigns. For example, José López Portillo, the only presidential candidate in 1976, received greater coverage in *Excélsior* than did Luis Echeverría in 1970, and more or less the same level as Miguel de la Madrid in 1982 (Secanella 1984). The PRI acknowledged the importance of newspapers and magazines, and the majority of reporters who followed the campaign in 1988 represented the print media. With this in mind, the question is what underlying logic existed behind the PRI's expensive and time-consuming concern with the media, especially the printed press, since it was not geared toward producing votes.[6]

As shown in chapter 5, the PRI candidate traveled to every region of the country where a series of events, ceremonies, and political rituals were organized that were particularly important in moments of ambiguity and potential disruption of the social order. In the political campaigns, the Mexican media provided an arena for political rituals that could be shared by a larger audience.

Reporters assigned to cover the PRI's campaign usually were in charge of providing their readers with interpretations on political battles that were acted out through rituals. As one reporter who was interviewed emphasized: "Frankly, the newspapers don't have to send reporters to cover the events [of the campaign]. We receive all of the information, including photos, directly from the PRI, so that the only important thing I have to do in this campaign is to report on the subtle symbols that can be used to reveal who will be what in the new government."

This role allowed members of the political class who for one reason or another could not be present at campaign events to gain insights into the evolution of the political game. For this reason, the political columnists, especially those chronicling political life and the campaign, were considered an elite force among members of the press. The majority of the reporters who covered the PRI's campaign were invited by the party, and the PRI covered their expenses and complemented their salaries. Political columnists were considered to be invited participants of a special rank. They stayed in the best rooms at hotels, had ample access to the candidate, and received more favors. These columnists were renowned and their columns were generally read by the political class (Adler 1986).

A similar role was played by some reporters who were not invited and apparently were not supported financially by the PRI. They followed the campaign and interpreted the events, as did the reporters who worked for the weekly magazine *Proceso*.

This status was reserved for the press and not for the electronic media, since the vast majority of the information required by the political class could be found exclusively in the print media. For example, a photograph of the candidate offering his hand to a well-known person automatically became a journalistic comment on the state of negotiations between the groups that appeared on the photograph, or it could be seen as a signal of the relative power of the person appearing to be "close" to the candidate. Photos that showed the extent of a public manifestation, the "special guests" (people of political importance) at these events, and all others present contained important and valuable pieces of information.

Our analysis of the political columns published in *Excélsior* shows that the topics that received the greatest attention were the following:

> The presence or absence of national or regional leaders in the campaign, with particular focus on those considered to have a certain degree of political power.
>
> Who spoke to whom—special significance was assigned to the simple fact that two politicians were seen together or greeted one another.
>
> Dissidence within the party. Although not a common topic, this issue was raised on several occasions in the case of La Quina, the leader of the Petroleum Workers Union, whose supposed "secret" support of Cárdenas garnered much speculation.
>
> The candidacies to Congress were discussed the most and generally interpreted in terms of who was a close ally or follower of Salinas and who the members of the system were. Much of this discussion was based on the candidate's power and that of his inner circle, as well as of some key PRI leaders in placing people in these positions. These references were interpreted, as were the results of negotiations in terms of the relative power that they reflected. Much attention was given to the workers sector of the PRI, which was considered to have favored the selection of Salinas.

In interviews, some reporters underscored the "contradictions" (the ambiguity) contained in the candidate's speeches. For example, sometimes Salinas said "with complete candor" that the system of a single party was a thing of the past, while on other occasions he highlighted his support of the "goals of the revolution." The latter statement was sometimes seen as a warning against a reformist and hasty interpretation of his modernizing program.

Contradictory messages kept politicians in a state of uncertainty and presumably made them unable to act, especially those who could be negatively affected by the candidate's ideology. The press acted as a fundamental instrument in diffusing these messages of uncertainty. For example, in one of the speeches the candidate gave in Puebla on February 19, 1988, Salinas said that "in politics, alliances have a price. Those who forge them against my party will have to live with the consequences."

This statement was made in an event organized for the Mexican Union of Electricians and the Petroleum Workers Union.

In the following days, columnists as well as politicians interpreted the candidate's statement. He was criticized because his speech seemed to contradict the new democratic spirit that he apparently identified with, and some questioned whether he would reliably honor the slogan of his campaign. Was this a message directed at the opposition or at PRI members, singled out by the candidate for their lukewarm support? Those who stood up for him said that it was common practice for candidates to reward their followers. A reporter who was interviewed stated that she was able to stay in the limelight as a result of Salinas's statement: "It really does not matter what he meant to say. At that moment, the country was busy unraveling the potential impact that the candidacy of Cárdenas could have on the traditional support bases of the PRI, especially among organized labor. As soon as he [Salinas] uttered these words, everyone started to talk about what he meant to say. It kept everyone quite busy for some days."

The press publicized campaign rituals among a larger audience, served as an arena in which messages could generate uncertainty, and interpreted campaign events. Ambiguity was supported by a journalistic style that required that the reader have a deep knowledge of who was who to be able to understand the events and the interpretations that could be found in the press.

As discussed in chapter 1, experiences had an impact on the manner in which politicians interpreted newspaper information, while others found it so hard to decode that they asked for help from "experts." A former reporter with a specialization in political issues worked for a state ministry of the Mexican government where she translated journalistic articles into "concrete facts" for a North American audience. She often found that articles were obscured by so much uncertainty that the information ended up being wrong:

I believe that the journalists themselves displayed a lot of caution when they interpreted or reported on facts in an erroneous manner. Their articles were written with so much ambiguity that if erroneous information was printed, they could always easily say that the reader had interpreted the information incorrectly. This made it difficult to extract actual information from articles, but provided reporters with an "escape" when a furious politician accused them of reporting what he/she had said incorrectly. The only way that I could be sure that facts were correct was if something was repeated at least five times in different articles.

The PRI's campaign also served to create the persona of the president of the republic. The candidate traveled throughout the country during his campaign to receive support, listening to complaints, accepting petitions, and talking with diverse people and groups that demanded a privileged negotiating position. While listening to regional complaints, the candidate gained an understanding of all parts of the country. Simultaneously, based on his willingness to listen, he became identified with the solutions to regional problems.

The candidate's link to each of the regions became symbolically represented in ritualized acts where he listened to local concerns and affirmed his commitment to resolving the problems. The PRI made use of radio and television as forums for these acts. The candidate's slogan Let Mexico Speak was used each time he appeared answering questions from the general public in either one of the media. These ceremonies, which were carefully staged, were used to transmit the candidate's desire to "listen to the people" and to make an endless list of commitments.

Apart from regular transmissions in which the candidate answered questions by phone, local radio and television stations often dedicated an entire day to covering all the local campaign events. Popular programmers were recruited to give the coverage a festive spirit (emulating the entertainers at campaign events), while local politicians and personalities from the entertainment world acknowledged the importance of the candidate's visit. The image was clear: this was not so much about a visit by a presidential candidate as it was about the visit of a president-emperor stopping to meet with his people and offering himself as a solution to their problems.

The television images of these stops were carefully staged to show the divine qualities of the candidate and to demonstrate the support given to him by the general population. His words were reported as if they came from a demigod and were almost always followed by shots of multitudes of followers. The way in which he was presented giving his speeches, the angles of the photos, the presentation of the candidate as someone who could be identified with all the regions of the country—all of this was a part of his transformation into a national symbol.

Many of those we interviewed believed that they were exploited by the campaign in an effort to gain votes, since radio and television were the most extensive information media. It may be that this was the intention, but if this was the case it could also have had an adverse effect. The PRI, it seems, did not take seriously the need for a certain degree of press credibility for it to be effective as a persuasive tool. The open and uncritical support that the PRI received from Televisa and Televisa's sidelining of opposition candidates are examples of the lack of credibility found in the media. But, as one expert on government-media relations told us: "It does not matter, or does it? They [the electronic media] ingratiated themselves with the person [Salinas] that they had to please."

The media, it is clear, are an integral part of the political system, with their own political and economic interests that in turn are also part of a process of negotiations. For many newspapers and magazines, the campaign represented their greatest source of revenue, not only during the campaign but also for the future since the relationship of the media with the next government was established in this time period. Many publications offered the candidate their unconditional support from the very beginning, thus creating a system of rigid self-imposed censorship. Without the resources they received from the campaign and from the future administration, they were unable to survive. Reporters and media administrators knew that the president could order other governmental institutions to favor or not favor a particular radio station, television channel, or publication with public funds.[7]

The most important newspapers and magazines, such as *Excélsior* and *Siempre!*, published some hard-hitting criticisms of the candidate, especially at the beginning of the campaign. For example, many politicians believed that the criticisms against the PRI's candidate issued by *Siempre!* represented a negotiation strategy to guarantee greater resources for its owner and personnel. Other interpretations suggested that the editor, who was mortally ill at the time, was mentally unstable, or wanted to leave behind a mark in journalism, or had a personal issue with Salinas. Whatever the reason may have been, the reactions to the criticisms again illustrated the dominant role played by interpretations in Mexico. In similar fashion, the appearances of television stars at campaign events for the PRI's candidate were interpreted as a general show of support by Televisa toward the candidate, not as personal support from the stars.

In light of the importance that the media had in giving form to "facts" and in constructing the image of the president, their products were seen as important instruments of power. The importance that members of the political class assigned to the media could be found in their symbolic representation of power. From the moment of the destape, the candidate was expected to ensure favorable coverage by the media and to successfully shape the style and content of the media's coverage of his campaign. It was further expected that the candidate would dominate all news coverage.

During the first few weeks following the announcement of Salinas as the candidate, President de la Madrid still enjoyed a domineering presence in front page newspaper coverage and in the first news item given by radio and television news programs. Specialists on radio-media relations saw this as a sign of the candidate's weakness. One of them told us: "If he [Salinas] can not get his name to appear in eight columns, he will not be able to do many things [during his administration]." Lastly, the political class interpreted control over the press not so much in terms of the media's effectiveness in persuading the general public, but as a symbol of the future president and his team in exercising power.

From the perspective of the traditional political system, the media fulfilled an important function, which explains why the PRI allocated so many resources and paid so much attention to them, even though gaining votes was not a part of its principal goals. On the one hand, the media played an important role in campaign rituals, which helped to interpret the drama of negotiations and political alliances. The press was also an arena for the members of the political class participating in and/or affected by the formation of the new power structure. In this way, the press made it possible for these rituals to be extended to political personages who could not participate directly in campaign events. On the other hand, electronic media, especially television, were related to the campaign rituals that forged the presidential image. The hyperpresidentialism of the traditional Mexican political system demanded that the candidate take on this image: he had to be presented as wise, concerned, and above all else, powerful so that he could be transformed into a symbol of unity for all Mexicans.

PART IV

CONTINUITY AND CHANGE IN PRESIDENTIAL POLITICS

The following chapters present the main results of our research, as well as an effort to evaluate the degree to which its implications shed light on events that occurred after those that were analyzed in this book. Chapter 8 consists of the main conclusions inductively derived from the facts and events put forth throughout this book. During the campaign, the presidential candidate acquired, as well as projected, the features of a man situated at the apex and at the center of the social pyramid. The hierarchic and holistic political culture provided the framework in which the future president was able to allocate material and symbolic resources between PRI militants and the entire population.

Two elements were displayed as the campaign went by that ended up consolidating the candidate's power by the time he was sworn in as president. First, the candidate's ability to govern over several political issues was recognized, including any singular political career and the population's day-to-day concerns. Second, the candidate was shown as a symbol of the nation as a whole, and of its functional and regional parts as well. In both cases, the codes, the order phase of the ritual, and the rules of interpretation turned the formal act of attracting votes into the gradual acceptance of the leadership of the candidate seen with certainty as the future president.

Chapters 9 and 10 deal with presidential successions that occurred after the succession process of 1987–1988. Both have a conjectural nature, since we didn't study directly the facts related to these campaigns. Nevertheless, we think they represent an opportunity to evaluate the degree to which the social structure and the cultural features present during the late 1980s changed or resisted change as the political regime moved toward a competitive democracy.

The subject of chapter 9 is the events that occurred from Salinas's presidency to the first years of Vicente Fox's administration—the first president coming from a party other than the PRI. This period was marked by change, led by the growing electoral competitiveness. The uncertainty regarding the identity of the winner undermined the foundations on which party discipline was built, which affected the presidential ability to nominate his successor. Furthermore, concerns over electoral efficacy pressed the campaigns to abandon the endogenous character that we stressed in these pages, in order to send a message that emphasized the candidate's strengths in comparison with his/her adversaries. Thus, current campaigns are a means to obtain votes—more than to produce internal cohesion.

In chapter 10, we argue that the 2006 campaign showed signs indicating that the traditional political culture is adapting to the new competitive conditions. We contend that the nationalistic discourse and the clientelistic methods were close to making their way back to the presidency, this time with electoral support. Nevertheless, this new version of the culture we associated with the PRI regime was not displayed by this party, but by the group displaced in 1988 by the technocratic clique and restructured during the 1990s as an opposition party.

8
Conclusions
Ritual and Stability in the Presidential Succession

The factors discussed in this study allow us to conceptualize the presidential succession as a cyclical ritual that began with uncertainty, continued with a period of liminality (rites of passage), and culminated in renewed stability of the political system. Changes in personnel within the executive power represent a critical moment for all authoritarian regimes; in the Institutional Revolutionary Party's (Partido Revolucionario Institucional–PRI) case, it subjected the crisis to ritualistic times and guidelines in an effort to reproduce its domination. In this chapter, we will present some conclusions on the presidential succession of 1987–1988 based on the ethnographic materials discussed previously.[1]

The presidential elections of 1988 already contained a breach in regards to the certainty of an electoral triumph the PRI elite could reasonably expect. This is seen in the electoral growth of the National Action Party (Partido Acción Nacional–PAN), the existing discontent brought on by the inflationary crisis, the internal factionalism, and the social tendencies that were linked to the "modernization" of the electorate. However, the scale of the electoral crash that actually took place in the end was not expected at a time when Miguel de la Madrid had implemented the legal reforms necessary to give the government ample room for maneuvering in the event that electoral "surprises" should occur. Despite changes in social conditions, the behaviors that we have highlighted during the succession process were predominantly in line with patterns established by tradition and custom. This means that the process took place with an assumption that the PRI's triumph was a certainty. In contrast, the tensions that were caused by the economic crisis and the rise of a group of technocrats raised doubts about the disciplined conduct of the PRI regarding the president's decisions.

The Management of Ambiguity Prior to the *Destape*

Miguel de la Madrid was firmly convinced of the necessity of his structural adjustment policies and the resulting subordination of the government's political needs to the economic objectives of his program. His program attacked the ideological foundations of his party and the clientelistic operational mechanisms by which the party and union leadership linked itself with the party bases. For the PRI, a period of sacrifice was reasonable, as long as it was followed by the restoration of the previous status quo. The president was responsible for ensuring that the succession process take place without any ruptures, but he either did not know how to or did not want to hide his preferences in order to feed this expectation. This means that the phases preceding the *destape* (unveiling) were not sufficiently ambiguous to preserve the system's stability.

A group of traditional PRI members felt that the rules of succession would definitely exclude them from the political scene, since signs indicated that there would be continuity of the same network of people beyond the six-year term—the continuity of the neo-liberal technocracy. The harshness with which he confronted the dissidents only showed the president's intentions to continue with his program at all costs. Similarly, the attempt to democratize the process of unveiling launched by de la Madrid with an explicit list of six presidential hopefuls, of which everyone understood that only three were viable, generated more divisions than usual. It provided a greater degree of certainty among the potential candidates, as well as within diverse groups that were looking for a favorable alliance. In both cases, because of reduced uncertainty, political tensions increased, as did threats to the political system's stability.

It is important to note that a great part of the battle between the PRI and its dissidents took place in reference to the rules of selecting a successor: to hinder the neo-liberal continuity, the Democratic Current appealed to the formal legality of the party that permitted competition for the nomination, while the party leadership in actions and speeches defended informal rules that concentrated the decision in the president's hands. Cuauhtémoc Cárdenas and Porfirio Muñoz Ledo's group, whose political motivations were conservative in nature (the restoration of policies associated with revolutionary nationalism), followed a strategy that if successful would have led to the establishment of radical changes in the conditions of the PRI's stability.

There were, however, efforts to create suspense with regard to the nomination. Among these, the use of the Institute for Political, Economic, and Social Studies (Instituto de Estudios Políticos, Económicos y Sociales–IEPES) stood out: it was charged with elaborating a party platform, concentrating on and implementing future activities of the potential candidates, and in so doing, creating an image of strength for one of these hopefuls by making one of his collaborators responsible for these activities. This was meant to balance this person's apparent possibilities in relation to those of Salinas before the eyes of the public. The press was supposedly an instrument meant to create greater uncertainty, but it was biased toward the technocratic candidate: even if political columnists gave the impression that the three real potential candidates were equally strong, the relative frequency with which their names were mentioned in news stories and the issues highlighted in them made it clear that Salinas held an advantage in the battle for the nomination (see chap. 4).

Despite all of this, the system's traditional mechanisms continued to operate under difficult conditions. The president relied on the collaboration of the party's leadership throughout, not only to isolate the dissidents but also to reiterate the legitimacy of the informal mechanisms of the nomination process by constantly calling for discipline. In the end, de la Madrid was able to enforce his decision and confirm the conflictive continuity of the technocracy, albeit with the acceptance by the vanquished candidates and an overall celebration by the political class, as demonstrated by several examples throughout this study. The cost was the ouster of the Democratic Current, which took place immediately following the formalization of the candidacy of Salinas and led to the return of a political instrument that had not presented itself in many decades.

The Campaign Ritual and the Restoration of Party Unity

The expulsion of the Democratic Current did not mean that all those who were discontent with the nomination left the party. After initial hesitation, Salinas in his campaign showed that he was fully aware of the situation and also showed a tremendous capacity to take advantage of traditional methods and call for unity within the party under conditions that transformed him into the undisputed leader of the country for the next six-year period. In the last instance, to impel his modernizing program, he needed to get to the presidency, and the path to this end was clearly indicated by custom within the political culture. If de la Madrid responded to discontent with cosmetic innovations (the *pasarela* [catwalk] of the "six distinguished *priistas*"), Salinas confronted it by adhering to the discourse of the past on conduct during the presidential campaign.

The conflicts between the candidate and the party became evident through signals that were relatively easy to interpret and through his negotiations and resolutions. Examples of signals that confirmed the existence of conflicts included the delayed congratulations given by Fidel Velázquez, leader of the Confederation of Mexican Workers (Confederación de Trabajadores de México–CTM), to the candidate after his unveiling, his early departure to participate in the closing of the Petroleum Workers' Union Congress from the party event that formalized Salinas's nomination, as well as leader of the Petroleum Workers Union La Quina's demands to support Salinas that were seen as "aggressive." Conciliatory signals included Salinas's recognition of the workers sector as the first to have nominated him, the active presence of petroleum workers during the campaign in Veracruz, and the pro-Salinas statements made by Velázquez. These gestures communicated the continuity and validity of the fundamental pacts of political power equally to spectators trained in the reading of signals of political actors involved in the process.

Actors were never totally certain whether they were completely excluded or in a good position in the candidate's eyes since, as was the case prior to the destape, uncertainty induced actors to show obedience. Salinas used ambiguity with greater precision than his predecessor: one and the same actor could receive, without it ever being mentioned directly, guarantees and hidden threats. The candidate made intentional use of the press to diffuse these ambiguous messages. Ambiguity once again became a tool exclusively for the most powerful level. We return, as an example, to the nomination of Salinas made by the workers sector as "their" precandidate. This event, and its explicit mention by Salinas, made the support by the workers' leadership an issue that could not "be taken back"; the candidate, however, could still at a later date launch warnings to its members about the consequences they would suffer for other alliances forged, as he did during his speech in Puebla mentioned in chapter 7.

There are many other things that can be said about the content of the speeches given by the candidate during his campaign. They show his efforts to introduce innovations in upcoming public policies within the framework of a national revolutionary discourse. The economic proposals made by Salinas were unwavering. He declared, "My first commitment is to eradicate inflation," and he explicitly spoke in-depth about redefining the public sector and greatly opening it up to international commerce, as well as funding economic growth through private investments.

On the other hand, he adhered to a traditional foreign policy approach when talking about challenges to sovereignty, using expressions such as "nationalism," "independence," and "national identity." He rejected the idea of creating a North American common market and instead said that he favored regional Latin American integration and closer relations with the countries of the Pacific Rim. He equated modernizing rural areas with a defense of the ejido system; introduced the battle against inflation as part of the workers' demands; stated that reducing the state apparatus would not only be a question of economic rationality but also one of social justice; and painted the opening up of borders as a retribution by the international community for Mexico's adjustment program.[2] He spoke of democratic reforms of political institutions, of community participation without corporatist mediation, and of reforming the PRI at an inter-party level, calling the latter "the party of the majorities" and others the parties of "minority opposition," while he simultaneously defined "national unity" as "the essence of democracy."[3] Finally, modernization was presented as a part of the revolutionary program and the historic evolution of the country.

All of these messages in the end tried to signal that the candidate's policy preferences were all an integral part of the PRI's ideology—despite the discontent that existed within the official party with neo-liberal policies starting with the most orthodox believers in the postulates of the revolution. This leniency in bringing together contradictory concepts in an attempt to legitimize a government program that was without a doubt innovative created a state of "symbolic confusion" (Adler-Lomnitz 2003) among those who felt that they would be affected by the actions of the future president. In the end, this led to greater difficulties in organizing these groups to work toward the proposed program.

Building the Presidential Image of the Candidate

One part of reestablishing internal party unity within the dominant coalition consisted of making it known that the future president would not abuse his power and go against the interests of the party. Another aspect of equal importance was the creation of the presidential persona of the candidate. The candidate was transformed into the "highest leader" of the political pyramid during the campaign. Acknowledging his position was a pre-condition for political stability throughout the following six-year term. In the creation of the figure of the candidate, a mixture of selective and collective incentives were used[4]—both within the realm of those elements that defined national political culture as discussed in chapter 1—and all of which were disbursed by the candidate.

Selective Resources and the Vertical Orientation of the Campaign

The selective incentives existed in the organizational aspects of campaign events. Organizational chores provided an opportunity for PRI members to demonstrate the degree to which they could back up their loyalty with political power and their ability to work. The candidate's power as the future president and the Mexican social structure explain the common characteristic found in all campaign events: its vertical orientation. Events were organized primarily to impress the candidate and secondly to impress the public. As one of the people interviewed stated, politicians always "look to the top" where their immediate superiors are situated, while the designated candidate is the only one who "has nowhere to look" other than "down." The knowledge that the candidate could potentially decide the political futures of all political groupings of the PRI—directly or indirectly—created a campaign mechanism where the candidate, far from trying to gain a majority vote from the electorate, received proofs of unconditional support, loyalty, and efficiency. Salinas's campaign formally introduced a democratic discourse with downward accountability—with phrases such as "Facts, Not Words" and "Let Mexico Speak." Informally, the campaign was organized so that resources were mobilized from the top down, while accountability took place from the bottom up.

All involved were evaluated (their capabilities, their willingness to work with the president, and their political strength) on the basis of the success or failure of events. Politicians mobilized their respective teams, intermediaries, and resources (be it the control over economic resources, over employment opportunities, and/or over networks of personal loyalties) to ensure a large-scale attendance at events and thus to be seen as successful. The ability to control and to mobilize large groups of "clients" was seen as an expression of the internal power exerted by every leader. As a result, there was a constant reference to numbers throughout the campaign. Under the guise of quantity of voters, what was really presented were the number of subordinates who, thanks to the intervention of the leader, provided their loyalty to the regime. The expression of "as a single person" was not gratuitous in reference to contingents. The transfer of orders took place in a descending manner until they reached the carpenter and the protestor. Conversely, any failure (technical or even in the degree of enthusiasm expressed by those in attendance) was reason for being discredited in the eyes of one's immediate superior. Therefore, each event represented a fragment of the Mexican political structure and its social pyramidal organization. Rehearsals of cheerleaders before the candidate's arrival at an event were not meant as psychological techniques used on masses, but instead were intended to communicate the strength and organization of the group, sector, or region that had been convoked. All participants knew that meetings had nothing to do with electoral passions, but rather with negotiating positions.

The fear of being *quemado* [burnt] or of "failing" the candidate or the boss was an incentive to make special efforts to comply with the obligations assigned to everyone. To be quemado meant that a good opportunity for promotion was annulled for the following six-year term and that the potential position had to be handed over to another more competent person. This was clear in the event organized on science and technology that was discussed in chapter 6, where the person responsible was supposedly very close to the candidate but did not pass the test of being able to manage organizational tasks which the campaign assigned to him. Responsibility for a failure was also transferred vertically downward, with the leader closest to the candidate protected from suffering the consequences of mistakes. According to participating political actors, the greater the social distance that existed between a person and the candidate, the greater the possibility for that person to make upward or downward movements related to his performance in the campaign. Consequently, people in the middle and upper levels were interested, if not in becoming members of the candidate's inner circle (perhaps passing from being a person of the system to one of the president's people), in at least retaining their positions. The possibilities for movement were an incentive to show one's loyalty and efficiency.

This was as much true for popular events as it was for in-depth discussions, such as those organized by the IEPES. The discussion themes selected and the competence and exhaustiveness of those attending were not designed as carefully as they were because they helped to elaborate a better government program, but rather because the person in charge of organizing the event was accountable to the team closest to the candidate and he/she believed that this raised his/her potential to access a government position in the future (or at least not to reduce these chances).

There was a substantial difference between popular events geared toward the sectors, federal groups, and entities and those that involved technical and cultural elites, such as the forums organized by the IEPES and the meeting organized with intellectuals in Cuernavaca. In the former, those who attended (at least those who had been mobilized) largely belonged to one of the pyramidal structures and were members of a vertical order. In contrast, events that included intelligentsia were more egalitarian, with horizontal relationships. This is a reflection of the resources, interests, and expectations used by each group to formulate relationships with the political regime. Popular sectors strengthened their immediate leader's position in an effort to uphold a continuous relationship that provided them with benefits. Technocrats, specialists, and intellectuals sought more vague benefits, which included the opportunity to socialize with other individuals from their same strata or access to the future circle of power, as well as the positive image that its members could create. Each stratum tried to generate or obtain resources, but according to their own means.

In chapter 5, we showed that in the organization of various events there were struggles and negotiations that took place among diverse actors that at a minimum included the candidate's team, the party, the governors, and the sectors. Each group promoted its own interests, trying to gain benefits by presenting an image of strength at these events. In negotiations, the candidate and his network had to reward abilities, loyalty, and the strength of each group according to their performance in the campaign, while the candidate learned how to exercise his power and discovered its limitations in relationship to these groups. These groups would become their most important intermediaries in the upcoming six-year presidential term. The candidate used the campaign to reinforce his abilities to manage power and make decisions.

In a more indirect form, Salinas's campaign also provided the population in general with selective incentives. It did so by opening up some spaces for the average citizen to issue his/her concrete demands and address these directly to the candidate. The "candidate's mailbox" was one such example, as was the possibility for "spontaneous" participation in IEPES and Center for Political, Economic, and Social Studies (Centro de Estudios Políticos, Económicos y Sociales–CEPES) forums. The purpose of the spontaneous participation was so that the synthesized documents (and with them the government plan) incorporated social needs starting at the municipal level. In several cases, the intention to open these spaces as participative democratic instruments could be seen, in which the audience was not limited to expressing personal needs but could provide proposals that would solve problems in general. Regardless of how far these requests were or were not translated into government actions, calls for the population to express themselves in the presence of the (future) authorities worked to build up the presidential figure by inspiring the idea that the candidate had the ability to disburse resources such as jobs or public service projects if he was made aware of needs. On several occasions, we were able to witness how Salinas provided expectations for solutions to concrete problems such as housing conditions and the regularization of property holdings. In this way, the candidate presented himself not only as a leader of professional politicians but also as a leader of almost all voters. On the other hand, one should not underestimate the informational role that these communication channels between the candidate (or the candidate's team) and the population played, since they provided data about the sentiments of citizens who were not directly members of some political network.

Within this framework, criticisms gained a very specific connotation. The PRI's campaign encouraged participants to express their feelings about circumstances that created discontent, which provided the candidate with materials that allowed him to present himself as the person who would resolve these problems. Nevertheless, complaints were not allowed to reach such levels that they accused a specific member of the political structure of causing the problem, although references to actors outside of the structure were allowed, such as the intermediaries or the businesspeople who benefited from protectionism (if these remained within categorical margins). When on the exceptional occasion criticism reached these levels, it was not interpreted as being a spontaneous expression of discontent, but rather an indication of the incompetence or disloyalty of the people involved in the organization, or as a manipulation by someone wishing to make the organizers look bad. The parallelism in the manner in which criticisms in the press were interpreted prior to the destape is noticeable: functionaries who were criticized were seen as politically incompetent for their inability to prevent the issuance of the criticism, rather than seen as inefficient in complying with their regular duties.[5]

Consequently, criticisms were issued only in opposition party campaigns, so that the PRI candidate and his party could claim ignorance. In this case, the opposition's need to continuously point out the failures and the negative results of the governing party in their campaigns, combined with the somber nature of their events, contrasted greatly with the festive and complacent environment surrounding the PRI. This could very well have led to an association of opposition criticism with everything somber and negative,[6] while PRI events led to associations of the PRI with continuity and abundance and the joy of being Mexican. However, criticisms of the political system that arose parallel to the battles launched by opposition parties opened the way up to publicity, particularly of radio shows (see chap. 7). In the same way that the print media served to communicate codified messages among members of the political elite, the radio provided a possibility for the population to express its discontent in an explicit fashion.

Symbolic Resources and PRI Identity

The candidate was not only the reference point for the distribution of resources to promote political careers but also the provider of collective resources during his campaign through a dual process. On the one hand, he became the symbolic representative of the country as the incarnation of unity. On the other hand, he became the center and reference point for the national image in relationship to which each part found its corresponding place within the whole. As stated by one of Miguel de la Madrid's campaign members, the electoral campaign "is a process in which a man is transformed into a god." This symbolic operation was based on a holistic conception of the country that was formed on the basis of sectarian and regional axes—just like the PRI's organization.

In the absence of real electoral competition, one has to take into account that governors lacked incentives to watch over the population's interests adequately. The campaign compensated for the lack of political representation with the construction of a symbolic representation.[7] During his campaign, the candidate toured all of Mexico and received support, complaints, and petitions, reaching many diverse groups and individuals who demanded privileged negotiating positions. In this process of identification with and demands made to the candidate, his personal identity was manipulated to convert him into a public figure that simultaneously was very closely linked to his followers. The candidate was made to fit in as a member of all the state and sectarian groups of the country. The structure of the Mexican political culture helped to make this method highly efficient. The campaign process, gestures, and the candidate's presence or absence with regard to different people, groups, and regions were interpreted in terms of his relative closeness to each one of these. As a result, each sector tried to position itself symbolically in a relationship of identification with the candidate so that diverse leaders could project a privileged image to their followers and other leaders.

At the same time, the persona of the candidate was modified, since his personal history was transformed into a part of national history and society: personal anecdotes and the candidate's curriculum vitae were appropriated by the nation, and each part was magnified and connected (metaphorically and metonymically) with "national" sectors and groups. The candidate himself intentionally promoted this transformation by different means, among which the constant changes in clothing stand out. In events with ranchers, he wore a leather jacket without a tie; with peasants he wore a guayabera; with businesspeople and women's groups he wore a suit and tie, etc. Negotiating positions vis-à-vis the candidate did not only modify and/or consolidate the position of the groups or individuals involved but also transform the negotiator-candidate into the president of the republic. In other words, he became a fetish whose uniqueness lay in the fact that the history of his personal relations was equal to the political relations of the state.

The fetishism surrounding the future president of the republic was based on his identification with each part of the nation. The central piece of Mexican holism was the president, and each social group's place was determined by its relative position in relationship to him. During the campaign, the "fetishizing" of the candidate not only served to confirm to groups their position within the nation's whole but also placed the candidate at the axis of this distribution. By using signs easily identifiable with each part of the nation, the candidate showed all of them that he would not change their place within the system, as we were told by a political veteran we interviewed.

This process was correlated with the transformation of the candidate by means of the campaign: his rising sense of security was a product of the metamorphosis from a simple powerful politician to a man-symbol—a transformation that was marked by valor and security in his public presentation and even in his posture and way of speaking (including, as we discussed, his sex appeal). As a fetish, the candidate generated fascination: "Wherever he went . . . people wanted to get close to him, look at him from up close, touch him when they could, pat his back or reach out their hand" (Portilla 1992, 328). Particularly through television, millions of people received appropriate images to introduce him as the man who decided the nation's destiny.

As a part of his created image, it should also be noted, the candidate started to acquire the respectful manners used by patrons, especially when it came to providing verbal recognition of the abilities of subordinates who were in reality lacking these abilities. On several occasions, Salinas conditioned the implementation of his government projects or the fulfillment of his offers to the will of the electorate; frequently, he started his proposals with the following words "if you favor me with your vote." More than irony, these types of phrases were meant to satisfy the informal requirements of clientelistic subordination not to make people's subordination that obvious. Courtesy is an integral part of all hierarchical social systems.

The place that each person held within the whole, as expressed in campaign rituals, was by no means arbitrary or based on the candidate's whims. On the contrary, the placement responded rigorously to an image of the nation that had been historically forged by the PRI regime and was implicit in the institutional order of the country and in educational contents. Every moment of the campaign not only expressed the situation of people who were in front of the candidate but also the placement of the group, sector, or region that was symbolically in front of the national order (which is equally present in the symbol of the candidate/leader of the state). Each one of these events consolidated or reinforced what Anderson (1983) has called the "imaginary community." In this case, the imaginary community is the one that was constructed together with the organization of the Mexican state: the federal entities and all the social categories that were created by the state bureaucracy, which simultaneously represent the dual structural axes of the PRI. The pertinent recognition that the candidate made to the contribution of each one of the states in their composition of the nation was to express in words what the rituals produced in facts: the revitalization of the national myth where the parts of the imaginary community that form the nation are recognized.

The myth of Mexican nationality, as updated by campaign rituals, contained two sides: one was cosmogenic and gave unity to the country with an explanation of origin; the other was cosmological and defined the groups that made up the country and the relative places that they occupied. The former is explicative, while the latter is descriptive. The cosmological part is reaffirmed in the organization of each event, where the strengths of various groups that are a part of the imaginary community are measured in concrete terms. The cosmogenic part is revitalized to explain and give order to the events.

The historic or cosmogenic side recreated the myths of origin of the Mexican peoples—the conquest, the fusion of races, the independence struggle, and the battles against the reactionary forces of the conservatives and the Catholic Church, and finally the rise to power of the "true" Mexicans (the mestizos) starting with the Mexican Revolution.[8] The descriptive side is linked to the organization of civil society (workers, peasants, "popular groups," entrepreneurs) based on an idea of what the national community is, so that these can be integrated at different levels and places within the spatial structure of the government (the federal government, the state governments, municipal governments, the party).

The relationship between the concrete political power and the national ideology (within the context of "myths of origin" and of "national order") provided a framework to negotiate the positioning of groups and individuals within or before the state. There were groups that had a real and strong organizational base within the daily functioning of national order, as well as groups whose political weight depended on the symbolic position they occupied within the cosmogenic order (such as the indigenous people and the "Mexican women"). Even though the latter could find places within the organizational structure of the state, the importance and strength of these positions followed a different logic than the positions that were fought over by groups that enjoyed independent political power. In one way or another, the groups that stood out as a part of the imaginary community during the 1988 campaign included the three sectors of the PRI, the entrepreneurs, the large unions or federations of unions (Federation of Unions of Workers in the Service of the State [Federación de Sindicatos de Trabajadores al Servicio del Estado–FSTSE], the National Union of Workers in Education, and the Petroleum Workers Union), the states and the municipalities,[9] the intellectuals, the state bureaucracy, the Indians, the youth, and the women. Analyzing these groups within the ritualistic context shows that they formed a three-dimensional map where the central axis contained the sectors, the entrepreneurs, and the large unions; this axis culminated in the real politics of the federal government, with the representation that each group had within the legislative branch and their cabinet positions. There were smaller such structures within the federal states and even within municipal governments.

On the horizontal level, groups that represented regional power were located. In Morelos, for example, the National Confederation of Peasants (Confederación Nacional Campesina–CNC) traditionally controlled the majority of municipal governments (even though not the most important ones) and the federal congressional positions. When confronted with the true weakness of the Morelos peasantry compared to the workers and popular sectors, the spaces reserved for their organization reflected first the importance of the myth of origin (the CNC received these spaces because Morelos was the state of Emiliano Zapata, not because of the CNC's strength within the state), and secondly, Morelos's weakness within the federation (Morelos did not have a regional political elite that could incorporate its members within the federal government). In contrast, the strong regional groups (the followers of Carlos Jonguitud in San Luis Potosí or of Joaquín Hernández Galicia in Tampico, the businesspeople in Monterrey, the ranchers in Veracruz) were able to access government through their independent power. Sectorial powers were located in regional entities: weak regions or those regions with limited power were generally dominated by cosmogenic logic. The same happened to groups that had limited abilities to pressure the state but that occupied an important place within the myth of origin or in the regime's utopia: this was the case with indigenous people and those who fought in the revolution (such as the Old Guard). Their importance within the imaginary community was highlighted in campaign rituals based on the place that they were assigned within the myth of origin (and not vice versa).

There is another notable difference in observing the meetings with groups that did not form a part of the corporatist structure, but that were considered significant in defining nationality. We are specifically referring to indigenous people and women. In both cases, the atmosphere at the meetings and the treatment they received were neither as formally rigid as in the IEPES forums nor as supportive and festive as were found in sectorial events and those organized during state visits. In the case of the Indians of Yucatán, the PRI ritual was abandoned in favor of a pre-Hispanic ritual with the acceptance of the candidate and his team. These events were marked by respectful treatment that often was emotional, where participants found themselves on a more egalitarian level. It is likely that this exceptional closeness was precisely possible because women and indigenous people were not a part of the pyramidal power structure and therefore lacked the ability to pressure or provide support (unless they were incorporated into one of the sectors and as a result assumed the identity of another group, as was the case of young people), and they were exempt from the traditional political ceremony. The candidate and social group were able to enjoy these interludes because such events would not have direct consequences on the structure of power. Both situations represent cases of symbol reversal, which is quite common in rituals. At the same time, groups such as women and the youth organizations began to explore new positions in order to gain access to places within the political system: they highlighted their numerical strength as an important electoral segment, to which the candidate responded with verbal concessions.

The situation was very different for businesspeople, since they enjoyed autonomous power and functioned outside of the corporatist structure of the political pyramid (even though they had informal ties by means of social networks). The candidate's meetings with these groups did not fulfill any expressed functions of any kind, and they were held behind closed doors. This social group, which did not participate directly in campaign rituals, was the only group actively courted by the candidate.

The campaign rituals in their totality represented a dramatization of the idea of nation, exactly in the way that it had been forged by the state. Many people in various positions within this national structure felt a sense of belonging during these rituals, while others saw themselves as playing a role made up specifically for the purpose of the dramatization of national power: women dressed in traditional regional clothes that they never wore in normal life; bricklayers dressed up as peasants; people who essentially did not identify themselves with the group that they had been assigned to for ritualistic purposes. Of course, there were also people who were not pleased with the place that they were allocated within the national cosmology or who felt the enormous disparity between the place that they occupied during the ritual and the one they held in the country for the rest of the time (for example, indigenous people who were listened to only during the campaign). Despite the difficulties confronted by the PRI to situate all Mexicans within the "national whole" that the PRI itself had helped construct, there is no doubt that the campaign events were dramatized—giving life to that whole and evoking emotional responses (positive and negative ones) related to the specific national proposal of the PRI. The party and its candidate seemed to be the providers of the places within the national whole (the idea itself of the nation as the ultimate instance of solidarity among the Mexican inhabitants is, of course, a creation of the state). The relational traditions of Mexico that were based on principles of family relations, friendships, trust, godparents, loyalty, and rivalry helped structure collective actors of different types and helped create a communal mentality that probably reinforced the use of nationalism (in the shape of national unity) as the ultimate and main *raison d'état*.

This brings us to another aspect of the campaign related to the regime's message to the population. As noted in Linz (1982) concerning elections held within totalitarian systems, campaigns in Mexico were a celebration of unity where unity was being reconstructed by the campaign itself. Campaign events were festive (even if forcefully so), with music, dancing, and food. The entertainers or emcees fulfilled an essential function by transforming party acts into national fiestas. With this, the regime authenticated its populist character and its belief in redistribution, while simultaneously providing those in attendance with a sense of "centralism" with regard to the totality of the imaginary community. But it particularly focused on celebrating the unity of the (future) president and his party, the unity within the party before the president, and with this, national unity. The phase prior to the destape was marked by a call for discipline, while during the campaign unity was emphasized.

Note that this gives a negative connotation to fragmentation, which in the extreme version of war between irreconcilable groups had threatened the country in reality, but that in the form of peaceful competition between different parts (the parties) for the preference of a majority could only threaten the regime. In their speeches and interventions, the candidate, the leaders, the party bases, and even the entertainers stressed the positive value of unity and its benefits for the proper path of the country. In an election in which discontent with the informal rules of succession had led to the ouster of a group that afterward challenged the PRI's hegemony through elections, the rhetoric of unity was in and of itself a disqualifier of the dissidents, who, from this perspective, did not demand their rise to power through the electorate, but who attacked national stability.

Using the campaign acts to transform the image of the presidential candidate in the terms discussed above brings with it a high degree of artificiality among participants: the candidate as well as those in attendance at every event played a role and followed a written script out of habit. The rituals in the end have a high theatrical content, and campaign acts were not an exception. In these, the candidate and participants behaved according to the imposed guidelines because of the interpretation the other would give to his/her conduct. If those in attendance observed the candidate as if he were the central reference point of the national whole, the candidate also observed those in representation of a sector, with their loyalty and their force, as a specific political group. The supposed spectators of the ritual were not really spectators, but rather active participants. Campaign rituals did have spectators even if they were not recognized as such formally. With the presence of communications media, the rituals were observed by the political class not present who could follow the development of negotiations through media transmissions. The population in general could also observe the symbolic rise to power of the candidate. In a middle point between participation and observation were the so-called "special guests," a group that was made up of renowned personalities (former governors, former municipal mayors of important cities, intellectuals, distinguished actors or artists, entrepreneurs, party or government people, collaborators close to the candidate, television anchors, and important journalists) who were usually seated at the end of the podium, where they could be observed and recognized (demonstrating the candidate's ability to summon people) while they could directly watch the event in question at the same time (thus becoming an elite public).[10] One of the people we interviewed when referring to the care taken in organizing these events said: "All of this, in the end, is a script."

The Internal Campaign

The events of Election Day and those that followed proved that the PRI in 1988 was no longer an invincible force within the electoral arena and that the opposition forces fought for votes against the party that until then had been hegemonic. However, the PRI's campaign was not competitive in the sense of presenting the public with a better electoral option. During the process, references to the opposition were sparse. For example, there were no calls for voters to take the comparative advantages of the ruling party into consideration. It was as if there were no other forces that were different from the official party that were also aspiring to hold elected positions. Remember that the media, especially television, basically ignored the opposition campaigns. In fact, as soon as the Democratic Current separated from the PRI it was immediately relegated to a position of political marginality. The presence of an opposition was only felt with the rage expressed in the Comarca Lagunera, when Cárdenas supporters came close to physically attacking Salinas. Thus, one of the most notable elements of the process was that despite recent changes the campaign continued to be by and for PRI members.

The two sources of uncertainty during the phases of the presidential succession process (the candidate's identity and his relationship with the party) share the fact that they are both part of the internal relationships of the dominant coalition, composed in general terms of the duality of the PRI government. Taking into consideration the constitutional aspects of the regime, real politics and relationships of power took place within this coalition, and it is not surprising that under traditional norms, stability within the dominant coalition implied stability of the political system. Once the PRI's triumph was certain, the major sources of conflict could only arise within the struggle for the PRI candidacy and within the president's relationship to the party: all efforts focused on preventing and avoiding all conflicts which, as the regime's politicians saw it, in effect did represent a risk. As a result, to address the systemic needs that the PRI campaigns had to confront, it was irrelevant whether there were other competitors or not (as happened in the 1976 campaign). Therefore, the presidential campaigns were not only geared upward but also inward.

In these terms, the adequate distribution of material and ideological incentives among the members of the dominant coalition meant that the succession crisis would be over by the time the actual takeover of power occurred, with the political class and the nation in general accepting its new leader. The candidate in turn became extremely aware of the reach and limitations to his power and how best to exercise this power. The political system, at this time, would enter into a new phase of stability— at least that is what was expected.

Recent Successions (I)
The Last Elections under PRI Rule (1994–2000)

Since Salinas's presidential campaign, the Mexican political system has undergone important changes that have transformed the roles of the Institutional Revolutionary Party (Partido Revolucionario Institucional–PRI) and of the presidency. The most significant one was the transition from an authoritarian political regime to a democratic one, with its corresponding impact on the separation of powers. The nature and style of the technocratic government of Carlos Salinas and Ernesto Zedillo also led to acts of indiscipline that brought about changes in the mechanisms applied to the succession process. Changes had an impact on inter-party relations and on the internal relations within the governing coalition. However, there were still behaviors that demonstrated that society's cultural patterns continued, especially since groups did not clearly understand their position within the new political context.

Structural Adjustment and Party Discipline

This study has looked at the relationship of different presidents and the PRI according to an informal agreement that is analogous to a clientelistic relationship. The president used his powers while respecting the permanent interests of the party (its sectors, local leaders) and did not hamper political mobility (following the norm of no reelection), and the party provided the president with subordination and loyalty and with the guarantee that its members would respond in a disciplined manner to his directives even when they were not happy about them. This type of discipline was the mainstay of the informal rights that PRI presidents enjoyed.

The six-year term of Salinas was marked by an intensive use of party discipline in an effort to deepen the structural adjustment program that had been initiated by Miguel de la Madrid. In Congress, the PRI approved the constitutional reforms that made it possible for communal landholdings to be sold or rented to private interests, the legal recognition of churches, a loosening of nationality requirements for parents of presidential candidates, and the privatization of banks. The Senate ratified the terms of the North American Free Trade Agreement immediately, in contrast to the intense debates that took place over this agreement within the Congress of the United States. The three PRI sectors were effective in containing the discontent that arose among those affected by these policies. The peasant bases and the official unions were negatively impacted by the termination of protectionist policies for rural areas (Fox 1996), the greater flexibility in collective contracts that went against the model of labor protectionism, and the decrease in purchasing power of salaries (de la Garza Toledo 1996). However, their leaders managed the situation well, preventing these issues from leading to social conflicts. Their participation in policies such at the Pact for Stability and Economic Growth (Pacto para la Estabilidad y el Crecimiento Económico),[1] designed to combat inflation, and the design of the constitutional reform with regard to landed property (Article 27 of the constitution) were circumscribed once information on agreements made in other spheres became known, which guaranteed the compliance of their respective members (Fox 1996, 319–21; Valdés Ugalde 1996, 385–88). Without traditional PRI discipline, it would have been very hard for Salinas to give his projects the depth and reach they achieved.[2]

The PRI not only supported a program that it was adverse to but also suffered from presidential wrath due to the negative results of the 1988 elections. The Federal Electoral Commission (Comisión Federal Electoral–CFE) interrupted the flow of electoral results, leading to questions about the legality of Salinas's triumph and protests that demanded that the elections be annulled.[3] The electoral college in the end confirmed the final results, giving Salinas 50.7 percent of the vote, Cuauhtémoc Cárdenas 30.1 percent, and Manuel de Jesús Clouthier 16.8 percent. The disputed winner was able to take over the presidency on December 1, 1988. Salinas's response to the crisis of legitimacy was to blame the PRI for the resentment voters expressed through their ballots and to present himself as the person who would correct all of the PRI's defects. "Salinas . . . tried 'to leave the system' to change it after the 1988 elections. By doing so . . . he transferred the population's perception that his government was illegitimate to the PRI and managed to present himself as a reformist who fought against the interests of the party hardliners" (Cook, Middlebrook, and Molinar Horcasitas 1996, 81). This is what led to the arrest of La Quina and the departure of Carlos Jonguítud from the teachers' union—measures that increased the president's rating in the public's opinion while also showing the hierarchies of the workers sector that opposition and incompetence would have serious consequences.

The transformation of the PRI became part of Salinas's modernization project, and in this process, he took on the informal role of leader of the party. He tried to implement reforms to the organizational structure that would have decreased the control exerted by the sectors on the administrative entities of the PRI and make it a party of "citizens" (Cook, Middlebrook, and Molinar Horcasitas 1996, 70; Dresser 1996, 230–32; González Compeán, Lomelí, and Salmerón Sanginés 2000, 582–93 and 607–9). The project included updating the PRI's ideology and adapting it to new realities by substituting revolutionary nationalism with a call for "social liberalism" in its statutes (González Compeán, Lomelí, and Salmerón Sanginés 2000, 596–97). He also used his abilities to choose party leaders to send messages to the opposition—a reformist was named to send conciliatory messages; a hardliner was named if negotiations were being shut down (Guerrero Gutiérrez 2001)—which meant that there was a lesser need to maintain internal balance.

The president took on his party's powers so that local groups would accept negotiations between the executive and those who opposed him. In return for their collaboration with Salinas, the National Action Party's (Partido Acción Nacional–PAN) gubernatorial triumphs in the states of Baja California and Chihuahua were recognized. Post-electoral mobilizations led to the resignation of the governor-elect and the designation of a substitute by the president in the states of San Luis Potosí, Michoacán, and Guanajuato (where the designated governor was a member of PAN).[4] The same process was repeated in various municipal elections. The advances made by the opposition did not mean that the regime was becoming more competitive, since recognition depended on the president's will. The president based his recognition on his informal rights by applying a selective criterion (it is known that the Party of the Democratic Revolution [Partido de la Revolución Democrática–PRD] was not as fortunate as PAN) in political rather than legal terms. It was never quite clear if the opposition's claims were justified (Villa 1994, 30–31).

Finally, Salinas sought alternative communication channels between the executive and society, displacing the party structures that handled these functions. The program to combat poverty implemented in his six-year term (the National Solidarity Program; Programa Nacional de Solidaridad) created a national management network that was directly tied to the executive, which prevented the PRI from acting as an intermediary in satisfying social needs.[5] A rumor that arose during that time was that the approximately eighty thousand Solidarity committees (Aziz Nassif 1997, 71) would form the basis of a third refounding of the party. In parallel manner, he authorized a privileged position of interlocution to the Federation of Goods and Services Unions (Federación de Sindicatos de Bienes y Servicios–Fesebes), an organization that was born out of the intention to challenge the hegemony of the Confederation of Mexican Workers (Confederación de Trabajadores de México–CTM) and that focused its discourse on productivity (Hernández Juárez and Xelhuantzi López 1993; Bizberg 2003, 229–35).

Even though Zedillo did not develop a strategy to transform the party, his policy of a "healthy distance"—at least as he demonstrated it in public—negated the benefits that the PRI usually gained by having a member of its ranks in the presidency (Hernández Rodríguez 2003, 55). Nevertheless, he was still able to count on PRI support in Congress to approve unpopular measures that had to be implemented to confront the economic crisis of 1995—measures such as an increase in the value added tax and the use of public funds to rescue the banking system. The PRI also approved the 1996 electoral reform, which included many of the demands made by the opposition and greatly limited the advantages that the PRI had enjoyed by being the governing party. He removed municipal presidents and governors (Chiapas, Guerrero, Morelos) in response to opposition demands and continued to nominate members for administrative positions in the PRI. However, his decisions led to certain outbursts of indiscipline: the PRI refused to support his project to reform the electrical sector. In Tabasco, local PRI bases prevented him from provoking the governor's resignation. The last president of the PRI whom he designated faced enormous competition that his rivals based on the party's statutes (González Compeán, Lomelí, and Salmerón Sanginés 2000, 666–67). The greatest show of indiscipline took place during the XVII National Assembly held in May 1996 when statutes were changed so that PRI presidential and gubernatorial candidates were forced to show that they were members of the party's leadership and had held a position of popular election, requirements that are commonly known as "chains."

In summary, the two presidents that continued with the structural adjustment program leaned heavily on their informal rights and on party discipline. However, their concrete measures went against the existing structures of interests that had to be satisfied, since these were at the root of the pact between the president and the party and of the identity of PRI nationalism. The neo-liberal governments "gave the impression that the party was a non-operational and inefficient burden"; the fiscal restrictions prevented them from upholding the full dimensions of their old operational style; public institutions weakened local party entities in the same way that the government imposed candidacies and negotiated electoral triumphs (González Compeán, Lomelí, and Salmerón Sanginés 2000, 650–52). As stated by one analyst, the PRI "was, as it had always been, an entity at the president's service with the difference that on this occasion the president's interests were not those of the party's"; the hegemonic party "saw the president as an enemy" (Hernández Rodríguez 2003, 57).

The economic restrictions and the social impacts of public policies, the negotiated modifications to electoral results, presidential disdain for the PRI, and the decreased certainty of electoral victories, due to electoral reforms, were all factors that slowly decreased PRI members' motivation to respond to presidential decisions with discipline. Discipline was essential for the adequate functioning of succession mechanisms; in fact, one of the most outstanding effects of the decrease in discipline within the PRI was the change in the traditional terms of the succession process.

Succession and Electoral Campaigns

If the measures taken and the style of the technocratic elite that gained access to the executive power created problems, the prospect of its continuity into the future was another source of discomfort for the PRI. This prospect led to the formation of PRI splinter groups in the time periods covered by our study, and because of it, events followed that would eventually transform the nature of presidential successions in Mexico—before a change in government occurred and even before the PRI lost its absolute majority in Congress in 1997.

Salinas and Zedillo concentrated decision making within the economic cabinet, which in both cases was composed of members of their respective circles of trust and excluded traditional PRI members. Salinas made sure that this group was well represented in his political cabinet and in lesser positions (which gave them access to the administrative apparatus). Zedillo, however, reduced the participation of "politicians" to a minimum (Camp 1995a; Hernández Rodríguez 2003, 46–54).

As stated by Castañeda (1998, 570–73), Salinas made the decision to name Luis Donaldo Colosio as his successor in the beginning of his presidential term and did everything to make this nomination viable. He thus showed his intentions to continue with neo-liberalism, while also making sure that Colosio would be acceptable to conservative PRI members. Colosio had a less technocratic and more "populist" profile than other cabinet members; he was the first candidate since Lázaro Cárdenas to have been a senator and have presided over PRI; and finally, his incorporation into the list of potential candidates when he headed the Ministry of Social Development linked him to the fight against poverty and not with neo-liberal economic policies. The presidential candidate's characteristics were summarized in the following terms by Camp (1996, 314): "His [Colosio's] victory in the voting booths would ensure a rebirth in the importance of experience in the party and elected office as precedents for political figures to rise to the highest national level, but it would not prevent the continuation of the predominance of the executive, especially concerning the economy."

Custom dictated that the presidential decision had to be accepted and celebrated by everyone, winners and losers alike, without letting any specific event overshadow it: this meant that the president was in control of the process. That expectation was not met. One of the aspiring candidates, Camacho Solís, refused to congratulate Colosio without previously speaking with the president; the following day, he called for a press conference in which he stated that he too wanted to run for the presidency.

The rise of the Zapatista Army of National Liberation (Ejército Zapatista de Liberación Nacional–EZLN)[6] had an impact on the candidate's campaign, as described below. Camacho Solís was named as the government's negotiator with the rebels (for which he resigned from the cabinet),[7] and his constant appearance in front page news was detrimental to diverse campaign activities, including Colosio's, and gave way to rumors about the candidate's weakness (even though he led in the polls) and the possibility that he would be replaced (Aguilar Camín 2004). The uncertainty and the speculations that surrounded the candidate's identity after he had already been unveiled represented a change in the traditional mechanisms and forced the president to clarify the situation in mid-January and Camacho Solís to do the same two months later.

The assassination of Colosio on March 23, 1994, far beyond the issue of the uncertainty that surrounded the identity of those who ordered his killing and their motivations, represented a fracture in the ultimate historic objective in the succession mechanism: to avoid its association with violence.[8] Although Salinas was able to use his power to designate another PRI candidate to the presidency, he had to face the activities launched by a group of politicians and congresspeople who belonged to a sector that had been displaced by the technocracy and who favored the candidacy of Fernando Ortiz Arana, a politician of the old guard, president of the party, and a person who was far removed from the neo-liberal economic model. Ortiz Arana himself was very involved in these activities (Castañeda 1998, 618–20).[9] The elections eventually favored a pure technocrat—Ernesto Zedillo—but the shows of indiscipline made the tensions between the party and the technocracy clear.

For the following succession process, the statutory changes that the party bases had promoted and that required that presidential candidates of the PRI had to have "political" experience excluded Zedillo's inner circle from being nominated. Additionally, Roberto Madrazo, who was the governor of the state of Tabasco, a man of the system, and Zedillo's political enemy, managed to launch a separate movement in favor of his candidacy that led to internal party elections in which he competed against Francisco Labastida—the only member of Zedillo's cabinet who fulfilled the new statutory requirements. Madrazo's campaign openly challenged the process of deciding on a candidacy based on presidential preferences. In the end, the presidential choice won, and Labastida became the PRI's candidate.[10] Restrictions on the range of options available to the president, open and explicit competition of formal pre-candidates for internal elections, and the fact that Zedillo had to openly negotiate with governors in order for his favorite to win (Hernández Rodríguez 2003, 61) were all factors that contradicted the patterns of unilateral decision making, informal competition, a single pre-candidacy, and the unanimous acceptance of the candidate that had been a part of the era of the *tapadismo*.

The erosion of the process in which the decision centered on the president had an impact on the way that campaigns were handled. The 1987–1988 succession process had demonstrated that campaigns designed to satisfy internal needs were of little use in gaining new votes. There was a slow transformation in the ritualistic patterns of campaigns. In the intermediary elections of 1991, Salinas implemented professional criteria in campaigns for federal congressional seats (Dresser 1996, 242–43). Although Colosio followed the traditional path of state campaigning, the uncertainty about whether he would continue as the candidate, combined with the perception that the executive exerted too much influence on the organization of the campaign, must have created problems in construing Colosio's persona as the highest patron of the country. Zedillo, in the words of PRI's president at the time, Ignacio Pichardo Pagaza, completely excluded the party from involvement in his campaign (Hernández Rodríguez 2003, 55). Colosio's campaign lasted only four months, half the time that Salinas spent on creating his presidential image. These factors probably contributed to the fact that Zedillo, who won the elections with 50.1 percent of the votes and without there being any significant doubts raised regarding his victory, was seen as a weak president internally. Nevertheless, there is evidence that the belief that the PRI would win the 1994 electrion with certainty was still widespread, which had an impact on the decisions made by the population during elections (Magaloni 2002, 260–68).

During the next electoral rounds, the threat of losing was even greater, placing the PRI candidate in greater difficulties. On the one hand, it seems that Labastida made decisions based on an attempt to maximize the number of votes during his campaign—attempts that were resisted by the traditional PRI (Aguirre 2002). On the other hand, Labastida distanced himself from the president, which was not beneficial in electoral terms, since the public had a positive opinion of Zedillo because of his economic management programs (Beltrán 2003).[11] The 2000 campaign, contrary to traditional ones, was marked by a competition for votes and uncertainty about the winner. Its importance did not lie in the degree to which the dominant coalition could or could not gain cohesion, but in the determining effects it had on electoral results. As stated by Jorge Domínguez (2004, 323): "Were it not for the campaign, the PRI's Labastida might have become president instead of PAN's Fox."

Regime Change and the End to the Meta-constitutional Presidency

Since 1989, the government and the opposition have agreed to four electoral reforms that slowly improved the conditions for competition and increased levels of impartiality among the authorities responsible for elections. The 1996 reforms completely removed the executive from the organization of elections and gave full authority to an autonomous electoral tribunal to make decisions regarding controversies arising from electoral results.[12] Due to these reforms, no political group was guaranteed victory anymore, and electoral outcomes contained a high degree of uncertainty. By 2000, what used to be a system of a hegemonic party rule had become a multi-party system with two parties (PRI and PAN) fighting over dominance by means of courting votes, with the PRD in a third consolidated position.

The legislative elections of 1997, 2000, and 2003 created a Congress in which there was no absolute majority by any party. The phenomenon of divided government activated the mechanisms of balance of power and limits placed on the presidential power in such a way that the relationship between the executive and the legislative branches awoke from what Silva-Herzog Márquez (2002) called the "constitutional siesta."[13] For the 2000 elections and thereafter, the legislative power exercised the formal obligations that it had informally renounced, and neither Zedillo nor Vicente Fox had the privileges of the grand legislator that their predecessors enjoyed.[14] In the same way, both branches became limited by a more autonomous and strengthened judiciary (Cossío 2001, 98–102).

The change in presidential power finally made obvious the degree to which PRI cohesion was a function of presidential leadership. The formal leadership of the party still has not been consolidated as a real leadership, and to date its divisions have led to unprecedented events, such as PRI congressional members voting differently on budgetary issues. These internal divisions were largely caused by the dispute that arose about the 2006 presidential candidacy. The PRI's situation in 2004 was summarized by a commentator in the following manner: "Today, the PRI has no tutelage. . . . The culture of following a specific line, obedience, and discipline has been left behind, but in its place there is no mechanism or procedure that can uphold unity and give direction. The great pyramid has become fragmented into many small pyramids. The struggle among all of them is disorganized, and no one can appeal to a referee who will act with impartiality" (Sánchez Susarrey 2003, 13A).

Political Culture and Elements of Continuity

The great ruptures of the past can be explained by (1) PRI's indiscipline vis-à-vis the president, which arose from discontent with the technocracy and which modified the traditional presidential succession mechanisms; and (2) the transition from an authoritarian to a democratic regime, primarily at the institutional level with electoral competition and changes in the relationship between the executive and the legislative branches.

Faced with these new conditions, a detailed observation shows that there are still aspects of hierarchical culture and authoritarianism that prevail in diverse areas. We will now discuss some cases and reflect on their implications for the future evolution of the Mexican political system.

The print media exemplifies the readjustment of old practices under new conditions. Its reduced number of readers[15] and concomitant economic dependence on paid publicity makes it susceptible to co-optation by different powers and to self-censorship. The difference from previous times is that co-optation is not concentrated in the federal government, but rather the federal government fights over control for informative content with other groups (political parties, businesspeople, local governments). Contrary to what Scherer García and Monsiváis (2003) have stated, the press did not largely contribute to democratic transition in Mexico. Instead, changes in the country allowed certain media to be more openly critical. A reader who understands where paid advertisements come from will have a good idea of the people who will not be covered in a critical manner, for example in some cases where the governor of the state of Mexico published bulletins in various newspapers. Because of these and other sources of control, the political class finds it useful to speculate on the identity of the political and economic interests that are behind the print media. There were rumors, for example, that Carlos Salinas financed the newspaper *La Crónica* or that a personal relationship existed between Rosario Robles, the mayor of Mexico City, and Carlos Ahumada Kurtz, the owner of *El Independiente*.

The journalistic style in and of itself has retained certain past characteristics, specifically in the spreading of rumors. The sections Trascendió in the newspaper *Milenio*, Bajo Reserva in *El Universal*, and Templo Mayor in the *Reforma* are all spaces dedicated to the publication of versions of unconfirmed events. The three have an explicit purpose, and the reader knows that they deal with "hallway gossip," but their high level of readership shows that a certain audience finds it very important to have such spaces available and to interpret their meaning. In other media, this phenomenon finds a more pernicious expression in headlines, accusations, and filtering of information without offering the reader reliable sources. The fulfillment of former functions is also reflected in the work of various columnists who serve as interpreters of national politics and who are in turn interpreted by the political class.

Another sign that can be considered folkloric but is nevertheless important is the use of terms in competitive contexts that were originally created to describe authoritarian processes. When someone mentions that a certain politician has the possibility of competing for the presidency, the headline in question will include the word *destape*; if a politician refers to his own aspiration, the headline will include the word *autodestape*. *Futurismo* is another term used frequently. In *El Independiente* (Jan. 24, 2003), the article that talked about the presentation of pre-candidates for the Democratic Party in the United States called the event a *pasarela*.

The origin of these words, and the added financial motives, lies in the fact that the political class continues to see the print media as an arena for debate, communication, and the launching of controversies. To interpret information is no longer considered viable with regard to candidates' probabilities in running for the presidency: in this regard, the credibility of certain newspapers such as the *Reforma* and *El Universal* is based on their publication of survey results that closely reflect actual election outcomes. However, the tendency to search for hidden indicators of correlation between the strength of the political factions and members of the cabinet continues. Because of this, the presidency of the republic continues to grant more privileges to the print media than to electronic media in terms of their access to privileged information. There seems to be a division of tasks in which the print media continue to function as arenas for the political class, while television has abandoned its role in diffusing the presidential image of the candidate and has become a vehicle for politicians and parties to communicate with the masses and gain their electoral votes.

The power of television has led to at least two presidential interventions that create doubt about the willingness of political powers to count on an information source that is independent and varied. On the one hand, the 2006 communication law introduced by the executive guarantees and perpetuates the existence of television monopolies. On the other hand, the dispute between TV Azteca and Channel 40 that led in mid-2000 to the takeover of Channel 40's facilities by a private army, with President Fox refusing to enforce the law, did not so much give a message related to the censorship of a small independent television channel as it gave a "warning" to the big television stations of the possible consequences they could face if they proved critical of the president.

The use of ambiguous language seems to be another characteristic of the political culture that has survived the change of government. Vicente Fox, for example, benefited from the desire for a "change" by a large portion of the electorate, presenting himself as the agent of this change (Moreno 2003, 180–86; Camp 2004, 33–36). However, he was careful (and successful) in avoiding a definition of the meaning of such change beyond removing the PRI from power (Magaloni and Poiré 2004), which left everyone to decide what meaning of the concept best suited him/her. A clearer definition could lead to electoral abandon if voters were not satisfied with one or the other definition. It also allowed Fox to conceal the intended content of his political actions until he reached the presidency. In relation to the 2006 presidential elections, many politicians who felt cornered made use of expressions such as "I accept but do not concede" to make their intentions of running for the candidacy known. Juan Carlos Romero Hicks, PAN governor of the state of Guanajuato, made the following statements when asked directly about his willingness to compete for the nomination: "For now, don't eliminate anyone . . . anyone who wishes to run should do so, including the one who is speaking" (*El Independiente*, Jan. 24, 2003). There are many other examples, but the point is that the political class adds ambiguities to its messages in competitive conditions in an effort to avoid commitments or a hasty cancellation of several possible action venues.[16]

Practices associated with the hierarchical political culture can be found in unexpected spheres. The intellectuals, a group based on a cacique system, with their pyramidal organization and relationships of loyalty and protection of the group, are a group that deserves further study. In the political arena, some of the states of the country, such as Oaxaca, Veracruz, or Tabasco, show similar characteristics as those described for the 1988 presidential election, especially when analyzing the governors' unchallenged powers.

In its electoral presence, political clientelism may have lost its usefulness. Cornelius (2004) reports that in the 2000 elections all the parties— especially the PRI—in one way or another used clientelistic relationships to gain votes. However, this strategy's impact on electoral outcomes was minimal. Nevertheless, Heredia (1997a, 26–32) noted that electoral competition has forged new forms for local governments to attend to social demands. Where populations enjoy a higher standard of living, clientelism has been reduced, but in depressed economic situations, the relationship between government and society follows clientelistic patterns. Also, when party activities are not regulated in the way that internal elections are, the clientelistic vote is commonly practiced and tends to be decisive in outcomes.[17] The political parties generally have difficulties

in abiding by their own statutory rules: in the PRD, the informal negotiations and the arbitrage of Cuauhtémoc Cárdenas were for years the
basis of internal political dynamics (Prud'homme 2003, 116–29); while
in PAN, which is by far the most institutionalized of the three dominant
parties, an exception had to be made with regard to Fox's strategy, who
gained access to the nomination by bypassing the procedures established
in his party's statutes by creating a parallel organization—"The Friends
of Fox" (Loaeza 2003). The pyramidal structure of factions within the
parties forms part of its informal structure.

It can be argued that the structure of Mexican society is based on elements of continuity within the Mexican political system. Adler-Lomnitz
and Melnick (2000, 6–9) proposed that there was a correlation between
the predominance of horizontal relationships and the multiparty system
with limited leaderships on the one hand, and a predominance of vertical
relationships and a single-party system with a centralized and authoritarian leadership on the other. According to this model, Chile represents
the first extreme and the Mexico under PRI hegemony the second. In
the 1988 electoral campaign, the traditional political culture (clientelistic, holistic, authoritarian, vertical) is seen in itself as encompassing the
whole; in its actions, it represented the dominant political culture of the
nation. However, after these elections and through electoral participation, new groups were incorporated, such as the educated middle-class
urban electorate with its individualistic ideology that favored democratic rules (Klesner and Lawson 2001; Méndez de Hoyos 2003). This
phenomenon led Adler-Lomnitz, Lomnitz, and Adler (1993) to propose
that tensions existed between the modernization of the country and the
permanence of hierarchical interpersonal relations.

The tensions between two national subcultures have still not been
fully resolved. The "modern" electorate has lost the character of marginalization that it had prior to 1988, but the social groups that are susceptible to patron-client relationships and that uphold the symbolic system
of these relations continue to be a majority.[18] These groups have proven
to be the mainstay of the PRI's and the PRD's electorate (Klesner 1993;
Moreno 2003, 63–76), both parties that on average in the last three elections received close to three-fifths of the vote. If the political culture of
a society presents a greater resistance to change than formal political
institutions (Elster, Offe, and Preuss 1998, 293–96), the culture of the
most traditional sector of the population may stop influencing current
political activities. This is true even under the new scheme of political

regime and of separation of powers.[19] President Fox recognized this, saying: "The battle in favor of a democratic political culture has not been easy. After many years of dominance by an authoritarian and paternalistic culture, it is difficult for politics to be perceived in any other manner" (*Reforma*, Jan. 27, 2004).

Returning to the model of the relationship between culture and government, it is possible to provide three alternative scenarios about the changes in one or the other: (1) the traditional political culture will impede the stabilization of the democratic regime and lead to the formation of a new variant of an authoritarian-clientelistic system; (2) the changes in the political regime will impel further transformations at the cultural level in such a way that the horizontal models will progressively substitute for the hierarchical ones until they reach a point similar to Chile; and (3) on a middle ground between these two scenarios, the traditional political culture is adapted to the competitive regime in such a way that even if the single party corporatist structure is abandoned, the three parties that compete against one another for the citizens' preferences present a pyramidal structure internally with hierarchical, clientelistic relations of loyalty, which of course will have an impact on the nature of democracy. Assertions on which one of the alternative paths will prevail fall within the realm of another study.

10

Recent Successions (II)
The 2006 Election

On July 2, 2006, the first elections were held during which the PRI was not the ruling party. From the moment that the formal electoral campaign started, there were two events that caught everyone's attention. The first was that Andrés Manuel López Obrador, the candidate for the Party of the Democratic Revolution (Partido de la Revolución Democrática–PRD), was seen as the frontrunner, which made people believe that Mexico would follow other Latin American voters who had led left-leaning candidates to the presidency (Schamis 2006). The other notable event was that PRI's candidate, Roberto Madrazo, was in third place according to polls, a place that he would retain in the actual elections.

In the 2000 elections, the fact that Vicente Fox won although he was originally in second place showed that electoral campaigns met their democratic function—they influenced electoral preferences. In 2006, Felipe Calderón, who was the candidate for the ruling National Action Party (Partido Acción Nacional–PAN), made use of the time allotted for the presentation of the government's platform to overtake the ten point advantage López Obrador had over him. And, in the end, he won the elections with a small margin of less than one percentage point.

For the second consecutive time, the electoral campaign lacked those elements that defined the 1988 campaign, as discussed in this study. In the first place, uncertainty about who would win marked the process throughout. The possibility that the ruling party's candidate could lose the elections was very real, and only the events that occurred during the campaign determined the final results—such as strategic errors of the opposition candidate and Calderón's positive approach. In the second place, and precisely because there was no a priori winner, an electoral victory depended on the candidates' abilities to present themselves as the best choice, and none of the campaigns were geared toward the internal party structures, as had been the case with Salinas. In a democratic context, a format that focuses on accommodating internal forces and mediating party conflicts would amount to electoral suicide.

On the contrary, the message of the campaigns and the political speeches tended to highlight contrasts, and as a result, rivals were mentioned constantly. It went so far that two controversial television spots were launched by PAN that discussed only López Obrador without even mentioning Calderón's name.

However, the events that followed Election Day were reminiscent of the time when the opposition mobilized people as the only means of countering the hegemony of the PRI and its control over the electoral apparatus (Eisenstadt 2007). At the end of the voting, electoral authorities announced that the distance between the two first places was so close that it was not possible to give any estimates of results. López Obrador declared himself the winner and warned that he would not allow anyone to steal his triumph from him. A short time later, when preliminary results showed Calderón ahead, López Obrador denounced the elections as a fraud orchestrated by a group of corrupt entrepreneurs and politicians.

The PRD submitted a complaint to the Electoral Tribunal with incompatible demands: (1) the total recount of votes, (2) the annulment of results in certain voting booths since they had presented numeric inconsistencies, and (3) declaring the entire election invalid since irregularities in the process made the election unfair. Parallel to his legal strategy, López Obrador called for protest marches by multitudes of people in support of his demands, which included the permanent blocking of one of Mexico City's main avenues.

The electoral court ordered a partial recount of the votes of those booths that the PRD claimed had considerable inconsistencies in calculations. The recount of approximately 3.5 million votes reduced the distance between López Obrador and Calderón by 0.02 percent, which was not enough to change the entire electoral outcome.[1] The court recognized that irregularities had existed during the process, specifically the statements made by Fox with more or less hidden insinuations against the PRD candidate and the television spots that had been paid for by entrepreneurial groups that told people not to risk their stability by voting for López Obrador, which are prohibited under Mexican regulations. However, the judges did not see sufficient irregularities to justify the annulment of the results.

López Obrador did not accept the court's verdict, and amid new protests, he had his followers proclaim him the "legitimate president." He named a cabinet and proposed the reestablishment of the country through the creation of a new constitution.

In the following pages, we will present some of the implications of recent events with regard to the main themes of our study. We believe that despite López Obrador's insistence and the number of followers he has within society, there is insufficient evidence to support the hypothesis of a purposeful manipulation of popular will that would imply a return to the hegemonic party system's electoral processes, now under PAN rule.[2] On the contrary, we will argue that in the last election and throughout its processes, new forms of interaction between the traditional political culture and the competitive political regime were revealed. Even though our observations are of a provisional nature, we believe that sufficient indicators are available regarding the coexistence and mutual adaptation between the competitive regime and the traditional and clientelistic culture. These factors can at least somewhat explain certain aspects of the campaign strategy chosen by the main competitors, voting patterns, and the tensions that arose once the results became known.

In general terms, the discourse and the attitudes of PAN had a modernizing approach that was largely indebted to the project initiated by the technocratic group headed by Carlos Salinas. On the other hand, the discourse as well as the behavior of López Obrador presented a more or less explicit vindication of how to do politics through public policies associated with the traditional PRI.[3] In this way, the 2006 elections could be seen as a re-edition of the battle that marked the 1987–1988 succession process with the important difference that in this case the arbiter of the conflict was not the omnipotent president, but the electoral majority. The PRI, for its part, although seeking an intermediate position, seems to have been unable to find mechanisms that could guarantee internal unity to compensate for the loss of an undisputed leadership to the presidency.

The Candidates and Their Campaigns

One notable quality of the 2006 election is that the three principal candidates were true party representatives, and not people trained mainly in public office (vid. Adler-Lomnitz, Pérez Lizaur, and Salazar Elena 2007). All three had held the presidency of their respective parties. However, the process by which each one gained the presidential nomination of his party was different and had its own peculiarities.

Calderón had to defeat Santiago Creel, the secretary of the interior, in primary elections to obtain the nomination. Creel was definitely

Fox's and the PAN president's favorite (Berman 2006; Camarena 2007). Zedillo's case was similar since he also had to confront an internal challenger. But it was only under the presidency of Fox that the selection of the candidate by the president (the *dedazo*) was completely overcome in the sense that the president's favorite had to face internal competition and the president had to accept a result that went contrary to his preferences.

The internal processes of the PRI and the PRD suggest a more centralized pattern. In the PRI's case, Roberto Madrazo headed the party as of January 2002 when he started preparing his candidacy. Given the new conditions, it is not surprising that various individuals publicly announced their own intentions of running for the presidency. Among these, a group of five governors stood out who agreed to confront Madrazo as a unified block, supporting the person who was preferred by a majority in a national survey. The winner was the governor of the populous state of Mexico, Arturo Montiel. Madrazo, who wanted to avoid the risk of losing in internal elections, implemented a PRI model: a process of systematic discrediting in the print media. In a few days, several news articles linked Montiel's fortunes to the inappropriate use of public funds. The pre-candidate announced his withdrawal from the race, which made the internal process of the PRI a simulation, since Madrazo only had to face one rival who was completely unknown to the public (Langston 2007).

This and other events gave the PRI candidate a reputation for being an unscrupulous politician, which without a doubt had an impact on his electoral possibilities. Significantly, his negative reputation was apparently widespread within his own party. Several people interviewed by Torres (2005) described him as a person who was excessively pragmatic and who did not hesitate in going against commitments he had made when they were contrary to his personal interests (or with less subtlety, he was described as a traitor). There are two considerations that need to be stressed. On the one hand, this type of description fits poorly with the image of the patron that we have been discussing previously. In the patron-client relations, the patron gains loyalty from the client as long as he continues to take care of his responsibilities related to the constant flow of resources from the top down. Madrazo, however, may have failed in the ethical obligations of a patronage that had been forged for decades by the hegemonic party. On the other hand, these failures could also have been related to changing conditions. Madrazo was expelled from the presidency of the PRI, and while the party's leader, he faced a scarcity of resources, which made it impossible to satisfy the demands of diverse party factions, as presidents had been able to do during the party's golden years.

Madrazo was unable to gain a higher position than third place in surveys, which reduced his credibility on promises for future benefits in exchange for support during his campaign. Under these conditions, the seventeen governors of the PRI lacked incentives to mobilize their own clients for these elections. One should take into account that currently governors enjoy their own political power and resource stability, based on the rules that regulate budgetary transfers from the federation (Langston 2007). When combining these factors, one would expect field research to show that the events of the PRI candidate's campaign were a pale remembrance of what we reported for the 1988 campaign.

López Obrador, on the other hand, began to construct his presidential candidacy once he became the head of the Mexico City government in 2000. From this position, he initiated a media-based strategy that combined the completion of highly visible public works and of socially beneficial public policies with daily press conferences in which he gave his opinion on a variety of topics. They included systematic criticisms of the Fox government (Pliego Carrasco 2007, 162).

The success of his behavior was reflected in the constant strengthening of López Obrador´s public image, and he from very early on was mentioned by the press as one of the presidential candidates of 2006. His popularity was heightened thanks to his adversaries. In 2005, PAN and PRI legislators voted to impeach López Obrador because they claimed that he had violated a judicial order related to an embattled plot of land. If these legal procedures would have continued, he would not have been able to compete for the presidency. The judicial process was seen as an opposition attempt to get rid of their rival who had strong possibilities for victory. The Fox government eventually had to withdraw the charges (Lawson 2007).

As the possibility of an electoral triumph for López Obrador increased, the leadership of his party went through a restructuring. Since its formation in 1991, all the members of the PRD acknowledged the informal leadership of Cuauhtémoc Cárdenas, who was sometimes referred to as the "moral leader" and whose insights were sought in resolving internal conflicts. In many ways, Cárdenas reproduced the role that the presidents of Mexico under the PRI had played, but within the PRD.

Cárdenas's power was not only evident in the fact that he had run for the presidency three times (1988, 1994, 2000) but also in that his support was essential in determining the political careers within his party (see Chávez Gutiérrez 2007).

Based on this logic, Cárdenas intervened so that López Obrador would become the leader of the party in the state of Tabasco and, later, the president of the National Executive Committee (1996–1999). In 1999, he promoted him for the candidacy to head the government of the Federal District. As the date approached by which the presidential candidate had to be determined, Cárdenas explored the possibility of once again running, but decided to withdraw from the race. He accused López Obrador and his group of refusing to discuss the candidacy when it was clear that Cárdenas had no chance of winning internal elections at that moment. During almost the entire campaign, Cárdenas was an absent personage. He would later criticize the platform of the PRD's candidate for not "being of the left" and for his ambiguity concerning the United States and the defense of national petroleum (Camacho and Almazán 2006).

These programmatic differences are more apparent than real. In fact, López Obrador explicitly situated himself within the ideological left (which Cárdenas always hesitated to do), and as we will see, his proposals had a strong nationalist and left-leaning component. It is probably better to conceptualize their differences as a manifestation of internal struggles over power. The fact that López Obrador was perceived as a candidate with real possibilities of winning, as well as his access to enormous amounts of resources based on his position, led to a transference of loyalties within the PRD which ended up displacing Cárdenas in favor of the group of people close to López Obrador.[4]

It is worthwhile to look at how the PRD's candidate built his support network utilizing those resources available to him from the local executive power. According to anthropologist Roger Bartra (2007, 67), López Obrador "wove together his force thanks to a structure of social mediations copied from the model that was the traditional base of the PRI." The description that he makes of this model is analogous to the model we have presented in this work:

> It refers to an intensive clientelistic network of organizations that are more or less informal and linked to the "barrios," or political bands linked to marginalized sectors, to groups of merchants, taxi drivers, bus chauffeurs, and vendors in the informal sector. A web that

includes the management of investments, the distribution of economic aid to the elderly and the physically challenged, the legalized takeover of squatter lands that belonged to construction companies, or of suppliers by unions and low-level leaders of pressure groups. This whole constitutes a pyramid of mediations . . . and at the top sits the head of the Mexico City government. (Ibid.)

At the level of political discourse, there was a division between those who in one way or another alluded to the virtues of the old regime on the one hand, and those who focused on the necessity to immerse the country into the current of globalization on the other. Calderón's message corresponded to the need for globalization, since he referred to himself as a candidate who was a political expert, modern, honest, well-educated, and able to preserve macroeconomic stability (Estrada and Poiré 2007, 78). The generation of employment was central to his platform, as was globalization, understood as accessing international investments (Berman 2006, 34–35).

Calderón's discussion strategy began to change over the course of his campaign: changing his emphasis to pay more attention to negative elements, warning against fiscal irresponsibility and the authoritarian personality of López Obrador, and not risking the advances that had been made in the area of economic policies. This strategy was viable thanks to the recent economic recuperation of the country, impelled by the increased international price for oil (Moreno 2007). The same message in essence was reproduced by President Fox in public interventions as well as by the Corporate Coordinating Council in television spots (Camacho and Almazán 2006).

Madrazo tried to strengthen his image on the one hand by presenting himself in the middle of two extremist and potentially radical candidates, and on the other as the candidate with the ability to make decisions and follow through on them. His slogan, So That Things Will Get Done, had a very clear intention. Madrazo alluded to the problems faced by Fox in getting congressional approval for his policies, since the majority in Congress opposed Fox. In a clear way, the candidate offered voters an idealized version of the period in which the president could count on the legislative power by controlling it through the party so that it would not resist his decisions.

As seen in the election results, Madrazo's focus on the past because of its efficiency was not a very appropriate strategy. López Obrador enjoyed much greater success, since he appealed to the values upheld by the political class and by a large part of the population during the PRI regime. This also included the symbolic arena. For example, while he was the head of the capital city and throughout his campaign, López Obrador continuously identified himself with the figure of Bénito Juárez, the Mexican president who during the nineteenth century led the liberal party in its battle against conservative factions, a battle that took place as much within the purely political arena as on the actual battlefield. As mentioned before, it was common for the PRI's presidential candidates to be inspired by some prominent figure from Mexico's history. In this particular case, the characterization of PAN as the direct descendent of the conservatives of the nineteenth century was a rhetoric commonly used by the PRI for decades.

Confronted by the cosmopolitan nature of the technocratic elite, López Obrador supported his nationalist position by exposing his lack of contact with the external world. His only experience outside of the country was a few days spent in the United States and vacation visits to Cuba. Questioned on this topic by the historian Enrique Krauze, he affirmed (2006, 15): "One has to concentrate on Mexico. For me the best foreign policy is a good domestic policy."

The style of his discourses and the message of López Obrador's campaign were categorized by Bartra (2007) with the term "conservative populism," referring to the direct relationship of the leader with the people outside of the representative institutions. This term was also based on his intentions to restore practices and ideals of the PRI regime. Bartra describes López Obrador's electoral platform as "a mixture of conservative (lowering taxes), nationalist (limit the in-bond industries) and antiquated economic measures (basing development on petroleum, electricity, and construction). It also implies a regression to government assistance. . . . It is a project where the only thing that is said about Mexican culture, pathetically, is that it has 'survived all the disgraces of its history,' which 'is our sign of identity'" (Bartra 2007, 75).

He began to emphasize government assistance programs in his proposals toward the end of his campaign. López Obrador offered to increase the income of everyone with a salary below nine thousand pesos by 20 percent, which represented approximately 64 percent of the population. The plan included price reductions for gas, electricity, and gasoline, as well as economic transfers, all of which would be financed by austerity measures (Estrada and Poiré 2007, 77).

In his speeches, López Obrador became the people's representative with his stated antagonistic relationship with "those above"—an expression he used to refer to a homogenous group formed by those who spearheaded economic and political power. The message is similar to populist presidential candidates of other Latin American countries who experienced greater electoral success, such as Venezuela's Hugo Chávez and Bolivia's Evo Morales (Salazar Elena 2007).

The premise of a struggle between the elite and the people permitted the PRD's candidate to present himself as the victim of a machinated conspiracy launched by the privileged sectors. From the very start of the campaign, but more insistently as Calderón gained greater electoral preference, he affirmed that he had to confront an "election of state" led by Fox, as well as a "dirty war" conducted by PAN (Schedler 2007, 89). In incremental fashion, his discourse became increasingly anti-institutional. A clear example is seen when one looks at his perspective on legality: "The court can not be above the sovereignty of the people. Jurisprudence precisely has to do with popular sentiments. In other words, if a law does not reflect the feelings of the people, it can not function effectively" (Krauze 2006, 18).

López Obrador's continuation of the traditions of the old regime was even more noticeable in the venues he used to diffuse his campaign proposals among the population.

Pliego Carrasco (2007, 161–69) shows the contrasts that existed between the privileged venues of campaign strategies used by Madrazo and Calderón on the one hand and López Obrador on the other. The PRD's candidate focused exclusively on direct contact with the population in municipal rallies organized with the poorest segments of the population and did not make use of massive communications media either in the form of paid publicity or of interviews with newspapers and news programs. Madrazo, and later Calderón, produced a series of television announcements in which they explicitly criticized López Obrador personally beyond his proposals or platform. These attacks had the desired impact, but López Obrador continued with his strategy "at the ground level," which later proved to be less effective.[5] As Pliego Carrasco (2007, 167–69) demonstrates, the poorest municipalities where López Obrador focused his efforts were rural and sparsely populated, while Calderón's media strategy served to diffuse his message in urban areas where a larger concentration of voters existed.

These strategic differences coincided with the styles of conduct found in each campaign. In López Obrador's campaign, decisions were made by the candidate together with a small circle of people, who developed relationships of loyalty and trust with López Obrador, relied in a very limited fashion on professionalism, and lacked sensitivity toward changes that occurred in the electoral environment. It was very difficult for this group to take on positions that were not simply a reiteration of the candidate's views (Camacho and Almazán 2006). In contrast, Calderón's campaign style was closer to what could be considered a modern campaign. It must be noted that he too had a close circle of collaborators made up of people who had worked with him in his position as the minister for energy and during his nomination process. However, decision making had a more equitable character, and the campaign strategy was based on measuring public opinion and giving marketing criteria considerable weight (Camarena 2007).

The Bases of Support

Recent analyses of surveys show a characterization of voters' profiles that correspond to each one of the three strongest candidates and in many ways to the dividing lines that have been discussed above.[6]

It must be stressed that in this election decisions were largely made according to ideological differences, identification with the party, and the diverse evaluations that the voters made about the country's economic situation: the voters that thought that the economy had improved in comparison to 2000 strongly favored Calderón, while those who saw the economy as deteriorating supported López Obrador.

If the impact of these factors is taken as a constant, the distribution of preferences according to the socioeconomic characteristics of voters seems to indicate that the breach of modernity/tradition seen in the candidates had an effect on society. Calderón received a disproportionate number of ballots from the younger voters, who were more educated, urban, and belonged to higher-income brackets. The PRD's candidate, López Obrador, received more votes from rural sectors and people from lower-income brackets. People involved in the urban informal sector also showed a greater propensity to vote for the PRD's candidate.

Without taking into consideration the effect that differences in opinion had, the sociodemographic profile that characterized the voters for each one of the parties seems to indicate a division that separates the bases of support for PAN from those of the PRI and the PRD. If one accepts that the urban, educated, and young sectors are less likely to uphold and reproduce the values of a clientelistic culture, it seems that the highly traditional campaign styles and messages of Madrazo and López Obrador are consistent with the values and cultural norms of their respective electoral bases.

The weight of leadership on political attitudes of Mexicans should also be added. When he managed the Mexico City government, López Obrador launched a publicity campaign in which he promoted his social policy actions, presenting them as personal donations toward those less privileged. The success of this strategy may explain the findings by Estrada and Poiré (2007, 83–86), which showed the citizens' propensity to mobilize if their chosen candidate decided to denounce electoral outcomes. It is interesting that the willingness to answer the candidate's calls was particularly strong among the following groups: (1) the older voters with low incomes in the Federal District (the clients of López Obrador's social policies), and (2) those who supported López Obrador and were quite certain that he would win (an impact that was not found among the voters for Calderón). These relations are consistent with the idea that López Obrador, within a democratic context, had as a distinctive feature the ability to gain social support generated by a sense of loyalty and subordination appropriate for a patron-client relationship in contrast to his competitors.

Continuity in Change

Even though the candidates of the PRI and the PRD coincided in their positioning and in their traditional styles of working with the population, only the latter knew how to evoke images and make implicit and explicit commitments associated with the patron figure among the traditional sectors of voters. Madrazo, who was seen as a person without scruples and without access to government resources that could be distributed in a visible manner among sectors that did not belong to his inner circle, could not offer anything other than efficiency and modernization. López Obrador, on the other hand, constructed an image of honesty that was even resistant to corruption scandals that affected the members of his inner circle. Taking advantage of the national attention that television gave his activities as the head of the Mexico City government, he knew how to present himself as a disinterested ruler who was concerned with the well-being of his followers. He also presented himself as a person who—with credibility—could offer a flow of resources to those "below" who, in turn, could provide him with electoral support.

If systematic research confirms these impressions, then it would be shown that clientelism has a place in Mexican democracy that is as preponderant as the one that existed under the authoritarian regime—if not more so. It represents both a useful mechanism in forging a coalition of support and an attractive image in electoral terms for those sectors of the population that have been less exposed to modernization and that appropriate as their own the values of a hierarchical and a holistic culture. The degree to which these values represent a source of votes can be appreciated if one notes, for example, that during the 1990s when most of the neo-liberal reforms were instituted, nationalist values and deference toward authority were reinforced among the Mexican population (Moreno 2005).

Even though López Obrador stated that "PRI-ism is a disease that goes away over time" (Camacho and Almazán 2006, 39), in practice, certain forms, ethics, and the discourse of the traditional political culture that had been forged over seven decades of PRI hegemony were revived through him. This is not surprising if one takes into account that his first political training took place in the 1970s in the primarily agricultural state of Tabasco (Krauze 2006). His formative stage affects his economic platform but, as we have argued here, also transcends in his relational style as a leader of the masses.

Clientelism as a means of attending to social demands was a constant element of the government of the Federal District even though it used different modalities than those found in the old regime. The corporatist structure of the PRI included the large workers and peasants sectors. The structure was influenced by an ideological division of society into social classes that fought over the distribution of the product (León and Marván 1985). The PRD tried to establish close ties with some of the unions of the services sector but was unable to take workers' representation away from the PRI. However, in Mexico City, it has been successful with marginalized urban sectors that arose as a consequence of the crisis of the 1980s and the economic adjustment of the 1990s (Adler-Lomnitz 1994; Portes 1995). This new marginalized class, which survives through activities that border on illegality (i.e., informal sector merchants, squatters), has a conflictive relationship not only in the capital city but also with the bureaucratic structure in charge of enforcing regulations. Several PRD leaders of Mexico City have based their power on their relationship with these marginalized sectors, taking advantage of their positions of authority to condone the enforcement of laws in return for political support. It is not surprising that at the protests against López Obrador's impeachment process there were five hundred vehicles that belonged to the Pantera organization, which organizes taxi drivers who do not have the appropriate operational licenses. The ties between the PRD and the Francisco Villa Popular Front (Frente Popular Francisco Villa), a group that represents residents living on squatter properties in marginalized areas of Mexico City, are also well known.

Of course, the events of the past elections also demonstrate that a renewed clientelism does not guarantee a victory in the competitive arena. There could even be contradictions between traditional mechanisms of campaigning and electoral efficiency. For example, López Obrador's preference for holding rallies with rural populations is a return to a time period when these events served the purpose of cementing the power of the person who was known to be the sure winner. In contrast, it is a rather inefficient method in a time when there is uncertainty as to who will win and the imperative goal is to access a greater number of voters in the least time possible. The same can be said about López Obrador's openness in providing candidacies and decision-making positions to several former PRI members who saw him as better serving their own professional goals (Camacho and Almazán 2006). The candidate thought that he could use their abilities in mobilizing their clients to gain electoral advantages; however, by supporting them, his reputation paid a high price, especially among undecided voters.

The candidate who represented traditional values may have read incorrectly some of the aspects of the culture he represented. In several rallies, López Obrador insulted the president, which was transmitted by television and radio and also in PAN spots. It is precisely during this time that the intentions to vote for López Obrador began to fall. Beyond the fact that Fox was a president who received high levels of approval during most of his term, it is also possible that the PRD candidate may have harmed his own possibilities by going against one of the values of traditional culture: to show respect for the presidential figure.

Even though the PRD's case is clearer in its adaptation of a culture of clientelism to democratic conditions, one can not say that it is unique to that party. PRI upheld its organic ties with several of the most powerful unions of the country, while the governor's internal power is based on their capacity to gain access to the top of the clientelistic pyramid within their respective states. Lastly, PAN also responded to competitive pressures by making commitments with some of the PRI governors and with the teachers' union of the country, which has the highest number of affiliated members (Camarena 2007).

The division of Mexican society into traditional and modern sectors that in 1988 provoked political fragmentation with far-reaching and long-term consequences survives and is reflected within the current Mexican political system. In 1988, the confrontation between these two visions primarily occurred within the hegemonic party. In 2006, and consistent with the transformation of the political regime, these positions competed within the electoral arena in the organization of parties other than the PRI. The close electoral victory of PAN can be seen as an opportunity for the modernizing project (individualistic and globalizing). The completion of this project is hindered by the continuation of the traditional culture (holistic and hierarchical). Those who promote modernization will have to show that they can attend to social demands without giving up the electoral benefits of clientelism. If the contrary takes place, a future edition of this dispute could lead to the victory of a strong clientelistic patron who, as has been the case in other countries of Latin America, reveals himself largely antagonistic toward the system of separation of powers and democratic rule.

Appendix A
A 1987–1988 Presidential Succession Timeline

Mid-1986	The Democratic Current of the PRI is formed.
June 17, 1986	Jesús Silva Herzog resigns as secretary of finance and public credit.
October 8, 1986	Jorge de la Vega replaces Lugo Verduzco as president of the PRI.
March 2–4, 1987	XIII PRI General Assembly
August 13, 1987	Jorge de la Vega makes public the names of "six distinguished members of the PRI" as potential candidates: Ramón Aguirre, Manuel Bartlett, Alfredo del Mazo, Sergio García Ramírez, Miguel González Avelar, and Carlos Salinas.
August 17–27, 1987	Each of the potential candidates addresses the most prominent PRI leaders.
September 22, 1987	The director of the IEPES hands over the project for the Basic Electoral Platform to the head of the PRI, after more than a full year of forums and consultations.
September 23–24, 1987	National Extraordinary Council held.
October 2, 1987	Miguel de la Madrid tells Salinas, privately, that the party favors his candidacy.
October 3, 1987	The National Extraordinary Council of the CEN of the PRI issues the convocation for the Seventh National Ordinary Convention.
October 4, 1987	Carlos Salinas is "unveiled" as the PRI's presidential candidate.
October 6, 1987	Salinas registers his pre-candidacy.
October 12, 1987	Cuauhtémoc Cárdenas accepts the nomination as PARM's presidential candidate.

November 6, 1987	The workers sector declares Salinas the candidate of the proletariat.
November 7–8, 1987	PRI's Seventh National Ordinary Convention held. Salinas is sworn in as the PRI's presidential candidate.
December 1, 1987–July 2, 1988	Salinas's presidential campaign
July 6, 1988	Election Day
September 10, 1988	The electoral college declares Carlos Salinas president-elect.
December 1, 1988	Carlos Salinas is sworn in as constitutional president of the United Mexican States.

Appendix B
Glossary of People and Institutions

This section draws on information provided by Musacchio (1989, 2002).

Aguirre, Ramón (1935–). A member of the PRI since 1956. He was one of the six contenders for the presidential nomination in 1987–1988. He served as head of the government of the Federal District from 1982 to 1988 and directed the National Lottery from 1988 to 1991. In 1991, he ran as the PRI candidate for the governorship of the state of Guanajuato. Although he won according to official results, opposition demonstrations charging fraud precluded him from taking office.

Bartlett, Manuel (1936–). One of the six contenders for the PRI presidential nomination in 1987–1988, the party of which he was a member since 1963. He coordinated Miguel de la Madrid's presidential campaign. He served as secretary of the interior from 1982 to 1988 and, as such, presided over the Federal Electoral Commission (CFE) in 1988. From 1988 to 1992, he served as secretary of education and, from 1993 to 1999, as governor of the state of Puebla.

Camacho Solís, Manuel (1946–). Undersecretary of regional development of the Ministry of Programming and Budgeting under Salinas (1982–1986) and secretary of urban development and ecology from 1986 to 1988. In 1988, he headed the general secretariat of the PRI. He served as head of the government of the Federal District from 1988 to 1993. When Colosio was nominated as the PRI presidential candidate, Camacho publicly rejected the decision. He was appointed secretary of foreign affairs from 1993 to 1994 and government commissioner for the peace in Chiapas in 1994.

Cárdenas, Cuauhtémoc (1936–). The son of former president Lázaro Cárdenas (1934–1940), he served as governor of the state of Michoacán from 1980 to 1986. He and other PRI politicians formed the Democratic Current, demanding a more open process to nominate the presidential candidate. In 1988, he ran as the National Democratic Front's candidate. He founded the left-wing Party of the Democratic Revolution (Partido de la Revolución Democrática–PRD) in 1989.

Castillo, Heberto (1928–1997). Political left-wing activist, he ran as presidential candidate for the Mexican Socialist Party (Partido Mexicano Socialista–PMS), but withdrew his candidacy to support Cuauhtémoc

Cárdenas. He co-founded the Party of the Democratic Revolution (Partido de la Revolución Democrática–PRD) in 1989.

CEN. Comité Ejecutivo Nacional (National Executive Committee). Governing body of the PRI. The president and the secretary general of the CEN are the party's top leaders.

CEPES. Centro de Estudios Políticos, Económicos y Sociales (Center for Political, Economic, and Social Studies). Affiliate offices of the IEPES in each state of the republic.

CEU. Consejo Estudiantil Universitario (University Student Council). Organization created by students of the National Autonomous University of Mexico (Mexico's most important public university) during the strike of 1986–1987, resisting a plan of academic reforms designed by the university's authorities.

CFE. Comisión Federal Electoral (Federal Electoral Commission). State agency in charge of organizing national elections from 1973–1990.

Chirinos, Patricio (1939–). General director of delegations of the Ministry of Programming and Budgeting under Salinas (1982–1987). During the campaign, he was head of electoral action of the PRI. He served as secretary of urban development and ecology (1988–1992) and as governor of the state of Veracruz (1992–1998).

CIM. Consejo para la Integración de la Mujer (Council for the Integration of Women). A PRI office responsible for coordinating the participation of women in the three party sectors.

Clouthier, Manuel de Jesús (1934–1989). Leader of the Council for the Coordination of Business in 1982. Presidential candidate for PAN in 1988. He died in a car accident.

CNC. Confederación Nacional Campesina (National Confederation of Peasants). Founded in 1938, the CNC represents the peasants of communally owned lands. It makes up the peasants sector of the PRI.

CNOP. Confederación Nacional de Organizaciones Populares (National Federation of Popular Organizations). Founded in 1943, the CNOP is a federation of unions of public employees, informal workers, and small business owners, among others. It represents the so-called "popular" sector of the PRI.

Colosio, Luis Donaldo (1950–1994). General director of regional programming of the Ministry of Programming and Budgeting under Salinas (1982–1985). He served as deputy minister from 1985 to 1988. In 1988, he was appointed Salinas's campaign manager. He served as senator from 1988 to 1994. He was president of the PRI from 1988 to 1992 and secretary of social development from 1992 to 1993. In 1994, he was chosen the PRI's presidential candidate, but was assassinated in a campaign rally.

Córdoba Montoya, Joseph-Marie (1950–). Chief assessor and general director of social and economic policy of the Ministry of Programming and Budgeting under Salinas (1982–1987). During the campaign, he became the candidate's advisor on special issues. He served as head of the Office of the Presidency between 1988 and 1994.

CONACYT. Consejo Nacional de Ciencia y Tecnología (National Science and Technology Council). State agency for the promotion of scientific development.

CROC. Confederación Revolucionaria de Obreros y Campesinos (Revolutionary Confederation of Workers and Peasants). Federation of unions founded in 1952. Since then it has been affiliated with the PRI.

CROM. Confederación Regional Obrera Mexicana (Regional Confederation of Mexican Workers). Federation of labor unions founded in 1918. The CROM held considerable political power during the 1920s, but it was eclipsed after the creation of the CTM.

CTM. Confederación de Trabajadores de México (Confederation of Mexican Workers). The largest confederation of labor unions in Mexico. Founded in 1936, it represents the workers sector of the PRI.

de la Madrid, Miguel (1934–). President of Mexico from 1982 to 1988. A PRI member since 1963, he graduated with a bachelor's degree in law from the National Autonomous University of Mexico. He served as secretary of programming and budgeting from 1979 to 1981. During his presidency, de la Madrid introduced several market-oriented reforms in order to tackle inflation and fiscal deficit. He was director of the Fondo de Cultura Económica (a state-owned publishing house) from 1990 to 2000.

de la Vega, Jorge (1931–). President of the PRI from 1986 to 1988, which included the time period of Salinas's presidential campaign. He served as secretary of agriculture from 1988 to 1989.

del Mazo, Alfredo (1943–). A PRI member since 1962, he was one of the six contenders for the presidential nomination in 1987–1988. He served as governor of the state of Mexico from 1981 to 1986, and then as secretary of energy, mines, and government-owned industries. During Salinas's term, he was appointed ambassador to the European Community.

EZLN. Ejército Zapatista de Liberación Nacional (Zapatista Army of National Liberation). An armed group based in Chiapas. It went public in 1994 with revolutionary goals, that later transformed into the demand of autonomy for the indigenous groups that make up its rank.

Fonseca, Guillermo (1934–). Leader of the National Federation of Popular Organizations (CNOP) from 1982 to 1988.

FSTSE. Federación de Sindicatos de Trabajadores al Servicio del Estado (Federation of Unions of Workers in the Service of the State). Union of state employees. It is affiliated with the CNOP.

Gamboa Patrón, Emilio (1950–). Personal secretary of President de la Madrid (1982–1988) and member of Salinas's clique. During the latter's term, he was general director of Infonavit (1988–1991) and of the Mexican Social Security

Institute (1991–1993), as well as secretary of communication and transportation (1993–1994).

García Ramírez, Sergio (1938–). One of the six contenders for the PRI presidential nomination in 1987–1988, the party of which he was a member since 1961. He served as attorney general from 1982 to 1988.

García Sainz, Ricardo (1930–). Head of the Mexican Social Security Institute from 1982 to 1991.

González Avelar, Miguel (1937–). A PRI member since 1964, he was one of the six contenders for the presidential nomination in 1987–1988. He was Senate Speaker from 1982 to 1985, and secretary of education from 1985 to 1988. During Salinas's presidency, he headed the Instituto Matías Romero of the Ministry of Foreign Affairs (1988–1991) and then was elected deputy (1991–1994).

González Guevara, Rodolfo (1918–2003). Founded the Democratic Current of the PRI while serving as Mexican ambassador to Spain. Unlike Muñoz Ledo, Cárdenas, and others, he did not leave the party until 1994.

González Pedrero, Enrique (1930–). Governor of the state of Tabasco from 1982 to 1987, when he resigned to head the IEPES during Salinas's campaign. He served as director of the state-owned publishing house Fondo de Cultura Económica (1988–1990) and as ambassador to Spain (1989–1991).

Granados, Otto (1956–). Head official of the Ministry of Programming and Budgeting under Salinas (1986–1987). During the campaign, he became press secretary of the PRI. Between 1988 and 1992, he served as spokesman for the President's Office and, from 1992 to 1998, as governor of the state of Aguascalientes.

Hernández Galicia, Joaquín (1922–). Also known as La Quina. Leader of the Petroleum Workers Union. Allegedly, he opposed Salinas's candidacy before and after his nomination and secretly supported Cárdenas. In 1989, he was charged with several crimes and imprisoned.

Ibarra de Piedra, Rosario (1927–). A renowned civil rights activist, she was the presidential candidate for the PRT in 1988.

IEPES. Instituto de Estudios Políticos, Económicos y Sociales (Institute for Political, Economic, and Social Studies). Research center belonging to the PRI, created for the study of national issues and oriented to the formulation of policy proposals based on the party's ideology.

Infonavit. Instituto del Fondo Nacional de la Vivienda para los Trabajadores (National Workers' Housing Fund Institute). State institution in charge of financing housing for the working class.

INI. Instituto Nacional Indigenista (National Indigenist Institute). State institution with the goal of improving the living conditions of the indigenous peoples and communities.

Jonguitud Barrios, Carlos (1922–). Leader of the teachers' union. He served as senator from 1988 to 1994. In 1989, Salinas managed to end his long-time leadership position.

La Quina. *See* Hernández Galicia, Joaquín.

Lugo Gil, Humberto (1934–). General secretary of the party from 1986 to 1988. He served as senator from 1988 to 1994.

Lugo Verduzco, Adolfo (1933–). President of the PRI from 1982 to 1986. During his term, the PRI faced electoral defeats, and the Democratic Current was formed. He served as governor of the state of Hidalgo from 1987 to 1993.

Magaña Negrete, Gumersindo (1939–). A former member of the National Synarchist Union, he was presidential candidate for the Mexican Democratic Party (Partido Demócrata Mexicano–PDM) in 1988.

Manzanilla Schaffer, Víctor (1924–). Governor of the state of Yucatán from 1988 to 1991, when he was forced to resign due to his opposition to Salinas's policies.

Muñoz Ledo, Porfirio (1933–). President of the PRI from 1975 to 1976, secretary of labor from 1972 to 1975, and secretary of education from 1976 to 1977. He was considered a possible successor to Luis Echeverría (1970–1976). He was one of the leaders of the Democratic Current and then of the National Democratic Front.

Olivares, Héctor Hugo (1954–). Leader of the PRI peasants sector from 1986 to 1988. He was elected senator from 1988 to 1994.

PAN. Partido Acción Nacional (National Action Party). Right-wing political party founded in 1939. Until 1988, it was considered the strongest opposition party in Mexico.

PARM. Partido Auténtico de la Revolución Mexicana (Authentic Party of the Mexican Revolution). Founded in 1954 by a group of veterans of the Mexican Revolution. A government-controlled party, from 1958 to 1982, it supported the PRI presidential candidate. In 1988, the PARM formed part of the coalition that nominated Cuauhtémoc Cárdenas. It lost its legal registry in 2000.

PDM. Partido Demócrata Mexicano (Mexican Democratic Party). Catholic, right-wing party founded in 1971. It lost its legal registry in 2000.

Petricioli, Gustavo (1928–1998). Secretary of finance and public credit from 1986 to 1988, and Mexican ambassador to the United States from 1989 to 1993.

PFCRN. Partido del Frente Cardenista de Reconstrucción Nacional (Party of the Cardenist Front of National Reconstruction). Nationalist party, controlled by the government, founded in 1973 as the Socialist Workers' Party. In 1988, the PFCRN nominated Cuauhtémoc Cárdenas as its presidential candidate. It lost its legal registry in 1997.

PMS. Partido Mexicano Socialista (Mexican Socialist Party). Founded in 1987 from the merger of several left-wing parties and organizations. In 1988, it joined the coalition that nominated Cuauhtémoc Cárdenas. A year later, the PMS and other groups formed the PRD.

PNR. Partido Nacional Revolucionario (National Revolutionary Party). Founded in 1929 to unify the political factions and the regionally based parties that emerged after the Mexican Revolution. It is considered the forerunner of the PRI.

PPS. Partido Popular Socialista (Popular Socialist Party). Left-wing party founded as Partido Popular in 1948 by Vicente Lombardo Toledano. A government-controlled party, from 1958 to 1982, it supported the PRI candidate. In 1988, it made up the coalition that nominated Cuauhtémoc Cárdenas. It lost its legal registry in 1997.

PRD. Partido de la Revolución Democrática (Party of the Democratic Revolution). Left-wing party founded in 1989 by Cuauhtémoc Cárdenas and other members of the Democratic Current, as well as several groups and parties that supported his candidacy in 1988.

PRI. Partido Revolucionario Institucional (Institutional Revolutionary Party). Political party that wielded power from 1929 to 2000. Its current name was adopted in 1946, when the PRM was reorganized.

PRM. Partido de la Revolución Mexicana (Party of the Mexican Revolution). Name adopted by the former PNR in 1938, when the party acquired its corporatist structure by integrating the workers, peasant, and popular sectors within its ranks.

PRT. Partido Revolucionario de los Trabajadores (Workers' Revolutionary Party). Trotskyist party founded in 1976. Some of its members split to support Cuauhtémoc Cardenas's candidacy. It lost its legal registry in 1997.

Robledo, Eduardo (1947–). Federal deputy from 1985 to 1988. During the campaign, he served as deputy general secretary of the PRI. He served as senator from 1991 to 1994. In 1994, he contested, successfully, for the governorship of the state of Chiapas. He was forced to resign in 1995.

Salazar Toledano, Jesús (1940–). President of the PRI's Administrative Committee of Mexico City from 1985 to 1986. As such, he was the first to mention a list of potential presidential candidates.

Salinas de Gortari, Carlos (1948–). President of Mexico from 1988 to 1994. A Harvard-trained economist, he headed the Ministry of Programming and Budgeting during de la Madrid's term (1982–1988) and was widely perceived as the head of a group advocating neo-liberal reform. In November 1987, he was sworn in as the PRI's presidential candidate. He was declared the winner of the 1988 election amid accusations of massive fraud.

Silva Herzog, Jesús (1935–). Economist with a master's degree from Yale University. Secretary of finance and public credit from 1982 to 1986. An early contender to succeed de la Madrid, he was eventually discarded after a debate with Salinas over economic policy. During the latter's term, he was appointed ambassador to Spain and secretary of tourism.

SNTE. Sindicato Nacional de Trabajadores de la Educación (National Union of Workers in Education). Formed in 1949, this union represents public school teachers around the country. Affiliated with the CNOP, the SNTE is the largest trade union in Latin America.

Soberón, Guillermo (1925–). President of the National Autonomous University of Mexico from 1973 and 1981. Between 1982 and 1988, he served as secretary of health.

Velázquez, Fidel (1900–1997). One of the founders of the CTM, which he led from 1941 until his death. He was said to have preferred del Mazo over Salinas as the presidential candidate.

Appendix C
Glossary of Spanish Terms

acarreados. Literally, the carried people. People brought in for a specific purpose—generally to attend a rally or a demonstration—in exchange for favors or services.

acarreo. Literally, carrying. *See* acarreados.

besamanos. Literally, hand kissing. *See* salutaciones.

cargada de los búfalos. Literally, the charging of the buffaloes. *See* salutaciones.

carrusel. Literally, carrousel. An organized group of individuals that place their votes in several ballot boxes.

chayote. Literally, mirliton. *See* embute.

dedazo. Literally, pointing out. The informal method by which the Mexican president handpicked his successor.

destape. Literally, unveiling. The public announcement of the identity of the PRI's presidential candidate.

embute. Literally, stuffing. A form of bribe made by politicians to journalists in order to get positive media coverage.

futurismo. Literally, futurism. The speculation about the true identity of the PRI's presidential candidate.

gallera. Literally, cockfight. A group of people fighting with each other.

hueso. Literally, bone. Any position in the public administration.

madruguete. Roughly, early rising. An unforeseen event planned by any prospective candidate or his followers in order to force the nomination decision in their own favor.

pasarela. Literally, catwalk. The public presentation of a political platform by the six contenders for the PRI presidential nomination.

placeo/placeado. Roughly, taking a walk in a square. A form of early political promotion by which someone is given an assignment of a public nature, in order to became known.

presidenciable. Roughly, presidential material. A politician perceived as having a chance to obtain the PRI presidential nomination.

quemado. Literally, burnt. A politician with no promotion prospects in the near future.

ratón loco. Literally, crazy mouse. The closing down or opening up of voting booths without prior notice; the sending of a voter from one booth to the other.

salutaciones. Literally, salutations. As soon as the identity of the PRI's presidential candidate is known, the most prominent members of the political class (including the unlucky contestants) congratulate him personally.

satélite. Literally, satellite. A formal opposition party that, in fact, was subservient to the president's and the PRI's interests.

sexenio. Literally, six-year period. The six-year presidential term.

tapadismo. Roughly, practice of veiling. The expression refers to the custom of keeping the PRI candidate's name secret, letting different politicians think that they could be picked.

tapado. Literally, veiled. The expression refers to the true, yet unknown, PRI candidate amongst the list of contenders.

taqueo de votos. Literally, making tacos of votes. A voter submitting more than one ballot.

urna embarazada. Literally, pregnant ballot box. A ballot box filled with ballots before the election begins.

Notes

Part I. The Mexican Political System and Its Actors

1. As described by Böröcz (2000, 351), we consider formal rules to include all those that are set, explicit, part of a larger group, professionally documented, known to the general public, and obligatory for all those belonging to a given organization. Informal actions arise parallel to formal regulations in areas that have not been regulated yet or in direct opposition to established rules. When an informal behavior or action is generally, regularly, and consistently pursued within a society, it becomes an informal "rule" or "norm."

Chapter 1. The Mexican Political System: A Structural Analysis

1. Andreas Schedler (2002) has identified seven conditions throughout an electoral process that reflect its competitiveness. Among these is "equitable competition," which can be seen as a prerequisite for all others.

2. Because these governments are in a borderline position, they have been described using numerous terms such as pseudo-democracies (Diamond 1997), systems with restricted democratic practices (Fukuyama et al. 1999), semi-democratic regimes (Gasiorowski 1996; Colomer 2000), bureaucracies (Przeworski et al. 2000), and electoral authoritarianism (Diamond 2002), among others.

3. Authoritarian regimes with a hegemonic party system have become the most common form of non-democratic rule over the years. At the beginning of the third wave of authoritarianism in 1974, only half a dozen countries (including Mexico) permitted the participation of opposition parties in electoral processes. All others were military, one-party, or dictatorial systems. Currently, at least forty-five and perhaps as many as sixty countries (between one-fourth and one-third of all political regimes worldwide) follow this type of authoritarianism (Diamond 2002, 27).

4. As one observer has stated: "[T]he fact that these regimes decide to organize elections although mostly not obligated to do so makes one believe that they expect specific and precise outcomes that are produced only in trivialized competitive elections and within a given timeline" (Hermet 1982, 43). The voluntary decision to call for elections implies that those in power "definitely obtain some benefit" (Hermet, 1982, 44). For a more detailed analysis of this topic, see Salazar Elena (2003).

5. Game theory argues that in times of crises a change from a one-party system to a democracy is expected to bring great utility to a population. However, a shift from a democracy to hegemonic party authoritarianism makes no difference, since such a shift is expected to produce only a small degree of utility (if the possibility to transition toward democracy by means of mobilization remains constant). Hardin (1989) argues that political institutions do not need a generalized consensus to retain their stability. It is enough that a "sufficiently strong opposition" is non-existent.

6. As Juan Linz (1982, 137) states: "It is appealing to contribute to a peaceful transition toward a competitive or semi-competitive democracy within a liberalizing process.... To reject all offers to participate in competition against the governing party, even if this is without any hope of winning, is a difficult choice to make for all those who hope for the return of pluralist political practices. Apart from the distant possibility that an opposition party could gain sufficient electoral strength to force the existing authoritarian coalition from power, by competing even in a subordinate position, the opposition gains access to institutional space (Congress) where it can assemble, organize, and publicly denounce the regime (Levitsky and Way, 2002, 55–56).

7. See above.

8. For the 1988 elections, the Electoral Disputes Tribunal (Tribunal de lo Contencioso Electoral) was created. This, however, did not change the scheme of operations, since the tribunal's resolutions had to be sent to the electoral college, which then determined whether or not it paid attention to these resolutions and what consequences, if any, these actions should have (Valdés 1993, 153–58).

9. The main source for the following information is Garrido (1982).

10. The hegemonic party passed through two important transformations in 1938 and 1946, which were also accompanied by changing the party's name to the Mexican Revolutionary Party (Partido de la Revolución Mexicana–PRM) and then the Institutional Revolutionary Party (Partido Revolucionario Institucional–PRI) respectively.

11. Although the 1946 legislation did not prevent Padilla from leaving the ranks of the PRI and Henríquez from forming his own party within the time limit, the new legislation presented enough obstacles so that these types of candidates and potential defectors, when weighing their chances of success within this system, opted to not follow the previous examples. Until 1988, the PRI's control over the presidency would not be challenged by anyone from within its own ranks.

12. See Molinar Horcasitas (1991, 34–37, 66–169) for a detailed explanation of the dynamics that ruled party registrations in this time.

13. PAN was formed in 1939 by Manuel Gómez Morín, a previous president of the National Autonomous University of Mexico (Universidad Nacional

Autónoma de México–UNAM), who had also been the minister of finance under Obregón and was one of the founders of the Bank of Mexico during the Calles administration. The first PAN presidential candidate was the dissident Juan Andrew Almazán (Guillén Vicente 1982a, 126; Loaeza 1999, 113n). The founder of the PPS in 1948 was Vicente Lombardo Toledano, who also created the CTM and who played an essential role in integrating this party with the PRM (Rodríguez Araujo 1982, 142–43). The PARM arose in 1958 as a token concession by the Ruiz Cortines government to ex-revolutionary military officers who were upset at their political marginalization and by the path taken by post-revolutionary governments (Guillén Vicente 1982b, 156–57).

14. The electoral system is a body of rules that determines the number of seats that each party obtains as a function of elections (Lijphart 1994, 1). In a system that is based on a majority with proportional representation, the negative effects of pure majority-based systems are attenuated vis-à-vis small parties. In proportional representative systems, these small parties receive greater representation, but the larger parties also benefit in such a system by often becoming overrepresented. See Salazar Elena (2003) for an explanation of the characteristics and structures of majority rule systems with proportional representation, as well as their application in Mexico that would allow the participation of opposition groups. Molinar and Weldon (2001) and Weldon (2001) provide a complete explanation of every electoral system that has been implemented in Mexico since 1964.

15. See Molinar Horcasitas (1991, 178–200) for a description of party divisions in Mexico during the 1980s.

16. See also Klesner (1993).

17. This section is based on research done by Adler-Lomnitz (1971, 1975, 1977, and 1994) and Adler-Lomnitz and Melnick (1991) on the Chilean middle class, the Mexican urban sectors, and the informal market of the former Soviet Union.

18. A model of a society that is predominantly egalitarian is what Sartori (1988, 26, 200–201) calls a poliarchy, using a semantic interpretation of the word coined by Robert Dahl. Instead of a pyramidal structure where power is concentrated at the top, society is a "constellation of multiple groups of power" where power is diffused. When combined with competitive elections, the power base has responsibilities toward those below.

19. For more information on the "diffusion" of certain types of social relations, see Knight (1992). His "mutatis mutandis" explanation argues that the distribution of resources in any given society determines the relative power of those involved in their exchange. After a period of trial and error, those on an equal footing will learn that their "best strategy" is to create relationships of reciprocity. Those on an "inferior" level will see that loyalty is the only means to take advantage of the exchange. These strategies arise spontaneously, without a

formal legal structure. Over time, these structures become the model followed by everyone who wishes to participate in the system without having to pay the costs of "learning" (Knight 1992, chap. 5).

20. The origins of the concept of a holistic political culture, according to Richard Morse (1982), can be found in the neo-Thomist philosophies that ruled Spain's unification. According to these, each part of the empire maintained a position within the whole that was specific, particular, and good from an ethical standpoint. Each position resulted from divine will. Harmony between the parts extended to esthetic criteria of beauty (Eco 1986). Historians such as Liss (1975) and Machlan and Rodríguez (1980) furthered this concept within the context of Mexico's political and cultural system. The idea of a hierarchical society in contrast to an individualistic society is based on Louis Dumont's (1970) work, which influenced studies on totalitarianism by Lefort (1986) and Castoriadis (1987). The relationship in Latin American societies of the legal/individualistic on the one hand and the holistic/relational on the other is discussed in Adler-Lomnitz (1975), Adler-Lomnitz and Pérez Lizaur (1987), DaMatta (1978, 1985), and Guerra (1985). For further details on this topic, see Adler-Lomnitz, Lomnitz, and Adler (1993, 237–41).

21. The PRI's organizational structure is discussed in chapter 2.

22. According to Centeno's report (1997, 132–40), each ministry or group of homogenous ministries is composed of personnel with similar profiles as related to their educational level, their professional experience, and their level of specialization. These bureaucrats are essentially promoted within the same governmental structure until they head an important office within the bureaucracy. Once this level has been reached, the institutional continuity is ruptured. This trajectory demonstrates the transition of a power group to a larger network, since promotions within the bureaucracy increases a person's responsibilities and diversifies his/her activities. Thus, the leader needs to create an action group whose members have a more diversified and heterogeneous professional profile. See Centeno (1997, 146–47) for a description of power groups as pyramidal structures based on loyalty. See also Smith (1979) and Camp (1995b, 1996). The dynamics of political networks with formal models are also discussed by Gil Mendieta and Schmidt (1999).

23. This discussion on the representative model and its relationship to democratic practices is based on Manin (1998), Pitkin (1985), and Sartori (1988). See also Przeworski et al. (2000, 33).

24. See also Gruzinski (1990). Among the pioneers who studied political rituals in complex societies are Roberto DaMatta in Brazil (1978, 1985), Clifford Geertz in Bali (1981), David Kertzer in Italy (1988), and Mona Ozouf in France (1988).

25. This discussion on the role placed by print media is taken from Adler (1993b).

26. In 1982, the president's Social Communications Office (Coordinación de Comunicación Social de la Presidencia) ordered all federal government entities, all state governments, and the PRI to cancel their publicity contracts with *Proceso* magazine. As an explanation, President José López Portillo said: "I don't pay so they can attack me."

27. For a more in-depth analysis, see Scherer García and Monsiváis (2003).

Chapter 2. The President and His Party: Informal Networks in a Formal System

1. The positions of the cabinet secretaries and the heads of the administrative departments ended up being the same in practice. From here on in the text, unless indicated otherwise, both will be considered integral parts of the president's cabinet and will be called generically "cabinet secretaries." For more information on this topic, see Tena Ramírez (2001, 457–60). The administrative offices at the time included the Department of the Federal District, which meant that the governor of Mexico City was appointed at will by the president.

2. The powers enjoyed by the president, according to the aforementioned authors, include the ability to approve regulations that are legally sanctioned without legislative approval (decrees); the exclusive power to implement laws in certain areas; limited intervention of the legislature in the development of the budget; the ability to veto laws passed by the legislature, partially or wholly combined with the legislature's power to revert vetoes; and the ability to send a project to be approved by referendum rather than submitting it to the general assembly.

3. For a detailed discussion on the legislative powers of the Mexican president that indicate his relative weakness, see Casar (1999, 2002) and Weldon (1997). Both authors juxtaposed the Mexican constitutional structure against the actual functioning of the Mexican presidency, which made the PRI discipline toward the president a function of the configuration of the party system and the political regime.

4. For an explanation on the power and functioning of each of the legislative chambers, see Lijphart (1999, chap. 11) and Stepan (1999).

5. On the use of parliamentary structures in Communist systems to subject the head of state to party decisions, see Shugart and Carey (1992, 37) and Verney (1961, chap. 4).

6. The constitution's language on this point is ambiguous, and the use of this process has often been abused. See Tena Ramírez (2001, 424–25) for an interpretation of this law.

7. In his *Confesiones políticas*, Víctor Manzanilla Schaffer (1998), who was governor of the state of Yucatán for three years, lengthily and emotionally explains the removal of various governors (voluntarily or not), including his own impeachment under the Salinas presidency. It should be mentioned that

several governors resigned from their positions to join the presidential cabinet, which is exactly opposite to the cases we are discussing here, since these were promotional moves that gave people access to the circle from which the future president of Mexico would be selected.

8. There were, however, official limitations to this right. As of 1988, an executive decision or a law could be abrogated only through an appeal process, which contemplates reparations only vis-à-vis the affected party, without being able to make declarations in direct reference to the law or the unconstitutional act. Only in 1994 did the judiciary become empowered to revoke a law. For a discussion on the judicial and political conditions that guarantee the impartiality of the judiciary, see Negretto and Ungar (1997). On the limits set for appeals to ensure constitutionality, see Tena Ramírez (2001, 512–19). The evolution of Supreme Court roles and methods of integrating these are discussed in Cossío (2001) and Finkel (1998).

9. The military sector was suppressed on December 16, 1940, and thereafter was no longer taken into consideration. For a summary of the evolution of the relationship between the armed forces and the civil authorities under PRI rule, see Serrano (1996).

10. The CTM was the most important and strongest organization in the workers sector within the PRM. Apart from it, the sector was also composed of the Regional Confederation of Mexican Workers (Confederación Regional Obrera Mexicana–CROM), the National Union of Mine and Metal Workers of the Mexican Republic (Sindicato Nacional de Trabajadores Mineros y Metalúrgicos de la República Mexicana–SNTMM), the General Confederation of Workers (Confederación General de Trabajadores), and the Mexican Electrical Workers Union (Sindicato Mexicano de Electricistas).

11. The communal landholding system in Mexico had specific characteristics and was called a "ejido" system. From here on, the term ejido will be used in reference to this specific and legally sanctioned land-ownership structure.

12. For more information on the differences between corporatism and clientelism, see Heredia (1997a, 6).

13. The private sector was subject to semi-corporatist legislation, according to which every entrepreneur or merchant who had a certain level of capital had to be associated with one of the four big business confederations: CONCANACO, CONCAMIN, Canacintra, and Coparmex. From a legal standpoint, the first two were considered government "consulting groups"; however, unlike the workers and peasants committees, none were officially affiliated to the PRI. In reality, they functioned as relatively independent pressure groups. See Adler-Lomnitz (1994, 245–49), Basáñez (1990, 96–126), and Centeno (1997, 68–71) for a further discussion. In 1975, the Business Coordination Council (Consejo Coordinador Empresarial), a civil association with a voluntary membership that was not linked to the laws of chambers, was created, which brought together the

more important corporate/business organizations of the country and became the arbiter between the private sector and the government (Valdés Ugalde 1996, 382–85).

14. Fidel Velázquez, for example, was the general secretary of the CTM without interruption from 1950 until he was forced to leave due to ill health in 1997. Another practice of continuity that took place among confederations was represented in the "moral leadership." The leader hands over the general secretariat to a "loyal" person and exerts power over the organization from outside of his formal role or from a minor position.

15. The distinction between "the president's people" and "people of the system" arose during various interviews with those in charge of organizing the presidential campaign, especially upon discussing the distribution of responsibilities and the reasons for this distribution. The differences, as proposed by Adler-Lomnitz, Lomnitz, and Adler (1993, 224–29), refer to relationships of trust that crosscut those between "technocrats and politicians" in reference to the divisions within the state bureaucracies. This means that there will be technocrats and politicians that are of the president's trust, while other technocrats and politicians function as "people of the system." For a classification of the members of the bureaucracy, see Centeno (1997, 104–7).

16. As explained by Serrano (1998, 17), "in essence [discipline] was an agreement among politically active actors in an effort to share and distribute power according to mutually agreed upon and accepted rules ... it resulted from a combination of incentives, pressures, and sanctions."

17. The comment made by Miguel de la Madrid (2004, 834) in reference to his relationship as president with the party is significant: "[The PRI] is like a girlfriend that one has to enamor: one has to call her, send her flowers, visit her; in other words, one has to pay attention to her to ensure her reciprocity."

18. The National Action Party on that occasion did not nominate a candidate due to internal problems, while the PPS and the PARM supported the candidate chosen by the PRI, José López Portillo. The Communist Party, which did not have legal registry at that time, presented the dissident union leader, Valentín Campa, as a symbolic candidate.

19. The fact that the purpose of campaigns was not to compete for votes was so evident that presidential candidates preferred to look at campaigns as an opportunity to get to know "the realities" of the country. See de la Madrid (2004, 26–27).

Part II. The Succession Process and the *Destape*

Chapter 3. The Structure of Presidential Succession in Mexico

1. For example, in the electoral process of the Díaz Ordaz–Echeverría succession, the governor of Nayarit announced one list, then a senator in his role as

a "simple citizen interested in the problems of Mexico" reduced the list to four names "with their respective surnames" (*El Universal*, Aug. 6, 1969). In the following elections, the president of the Association of Industrialists (Asociación de Industriales del Estado de México–AIEM) of the state of Mexico listed four names that later on would be expanded to six names by the secretary for hydraulic resources (*El Universal*, Oct. 8, 1974). In 1980, the governor of the state of Guerrero proposed four names (Garrido 1987, 90).

2. One has to remember, however, that González Casanova explains the average annual strikes by presidential period in relation to the workers' characteristics or in terms of how each president favored private capital (1976, 26–29).

3. Presidential declaration made before the Commission of the Chamber of Deputies (*Excélsior*, Sept. 25, 1987).

4. See González Casanova's work (1986, 62–70) on the role played by ambiguity.

5. The political arena for this battle was the print media, a topic that will be discussed in chapter 4.

6. Until the convention took place, the person announced by the sectors was called the "pre-candidate," since officially each sector could present their own pre-candidate and the delegates to the convention had to choose among all nominees. The mechanisms of the *dedazo* led to a reality in which the pre-candidate, the candidate, and the future president were one and the same person from the moment that the sitting president communicated his decision. Article 152 of the PRI statutes stated that for candidates to be nominated to positions of popular election at any level of government, the following had to be done: "Invariably apply the formula of an individual and secret vote, public and open selection in assemblies and conventions that were made up of delegates who had been elected for this purpose." This article ended up in some way legalizing the ambiguity of the system's structure: the election of candidates will be done "according to the degree of the party's evolution and the political, social and cultural conditions of each corresponding region" (Partido Revolucinario Institucional 1987, 292).

7. For an initial exploration of the transition rituals, see Van Genneph (1969). For a more in-depth theoretical analysis, see Turner (1974).

8. The displacement of the electoral and party experience was in the making since the 1960s, and the background history of each president illustrates this evolution. Since 1929 (the year in which the first candidate of the hegemonic party was nominated) until the 1960s, all presidents, with the exception of Ávila Camacho, had held one or more positions determined by popular vote. Echeverría had never been elected, but he had held various positions within the party. José López Portillo and Miguel de la Madrid (as was also the case with the two presidents who followed them) did not correspond with either one of the traditional backgrounds (Garrido 1987, 106).

9. The transformations that took place within the Mexican political system induced by globalization are explained in greater detail in Adler-Lomnitz (2002).

10. There was a story behind Cárdenas's "indiscipline." In 1974, Echeverría had offered the governorship of Michoacán to Carlos Torres Manzo. Cárdenas, who wanted the position, responded with a paid ad in which he denounced the PRI for not selecting him when he had the support from social organizations in that state. On that occasion, however, there was room for negotiation, and in 1976, Cárdenas became a senator for his state. Almost immediately thereafter, he was named as an undersecretary. In 1980, he finally became governor of Michoacán (Camacho Alfaro 1989, 43–44).

11. González Guevara abandoned the dissident group at the end of August 1986 (Garrido 1993, 36–37).

12. Carlos Salinas de Gortari was the son of Raúl Salinas Lozano, a distinguished member of Adolfo López Mateos's cabinet (1958–1964) and a presidential hopeful. While a student of economics at the National Autonomous University of Mexico (1966–1969), he came into contact with influential professors in the public sector such as David Ibarra Muñoz, future secretary of finance and public credit; Jesús Silva Herzog, former secretary of finance and public credit; Leopoldo Solís, mentor to a group of technocrats; and Miguel de la Madrid, who would help him get a scholarship for post-graduate studies at Harvard, where he eventually completed doctoral studies. Throughout the 1970s, he held positions within the Ministry of Finance and Public Credit, becoming the general director of programming while de la Madrid was the sub-secretary of credit. When the latter was named secretary of programming and budgeting (1979), Salinas took over the general directorship of that department. Between 1981 and 1982, he headed the IEPES, and between 1982 and 1988, he was the secretary for programming and budgeting (Camp 1996, 290–93).

13. This position is argued and substantiated in González Graf (1989, 147–53).

14. The meetings between the PRI and the Democratic Current were called by the president of the CEN of the PRI, Lugo Verduzco. The first such meeting took place on August 22, 1986, between Muñoz Ledo and the PRI leaders at PRI headquarters. Meetings were held more frequently throughout September. Under the leadership of Jorge de la Vega, the PRI met with Muñoz Ledo fourteen times. In October 1986 and in January and February 1987, Cuauhtémoc Cárdenas and Porfirio Muñoz Ledo were received by Miguel de la Madrid separately, who said that their questioning was essentially correct, but who tried to discourage them in favor of party unity (Garrido 1993).

15. In his memoirs, Miguel de la Madrid (2004, 642–43) affirms that he "chose" de la Vega for his conciliatory nature and gave him the mission to prepare the PRI for a presidential successor.

16. See the notice to the XIII National Assembly, February 12, 1987.

17. The comment made by the president about this demonstrative show illustrates the caution that must be taken when signals are sent that will be interpreted differently depending on who the recipient is. De la Madrid states that when he asked the former presidents to accompany him, it definitely had the purported effect within the party; externally, however, it irritated the private sector that still was offended by the nationalization of the banks (de la Madrid 2004, 703).

18. The dispute between the PRI as the legitimate heir to the revolution and the dissident fight against its use of certain symbols would continue in various forms. For example, on March 18, 1988, on the fifieth anniversary of the oil expropriation, Cárdenas and his people organized a commemorative march, which forced the government to mobilize to bring together 120,000 people for an event that had been previously scheduled at the Zócalo for the same purpose and that was headed by de la Madrid.

19. For a discussion on the battle between Silva Herzog and Salinas, see Castañeda (1998, 500–11).

20. Ignacio Ovalle, Mexico's ambassador to Cuba (*Excélsior*, Sept. 25, 1987).

21. Antonio Mena Brito (*Excélsior*, Sept. 25, 1987).

22. Ibid.

23. Lorenzo Meyer (*Excélsior*, Oct. 1, 1987).

24. In 1991, the IEPES was transformed into the Cambio XXI Fundación Mexicana, today called the Luis Donaldo Colosio Foundation.

25. The platform was made up of ten chapters referring to the future tasks of the revolution; the strengthening of the social pact; the defense of national sovereignty; political and democratic renewal; social justice; economic modernization; the meeting of basic needs; education; national culture and identity; the decentralization of national life; the administration of justice; public security; and policies for economic and social growth.

26. It seems that Federico, the oldest son of de la Madrid, had stated at a dinner the previous night that the *tapado* was "SG" (which could be the initials both of Salinas de Gortari and Sergio García Ramírez). The young man had received this information from Gamboa Patrón, the personal secretary of the president, but was considered an irrefutable source himself. In a telephone conversation, the president is said to have stated to the frustrated erroneous candidate: "Hey, Alfredo, since when do you think that I use my son Federico to transmit my decisions?" García Ramírez remained discreet in these moments, and the rest of the political class, who sensed that there was something strange in the way that the candidacy was announced, waited for clarification (Castañeda 1998, 250–51 and 529–32). For a more detailed version of this event, see the research of Herrera Valenzuela (1988), which shows the intensity of the speculations and interpretations surrounding the destape.

27. That same afternoon, García Ramírez told de la Madrid that his own discretion was based on the fact that he had never been told about this by the president of the republic or by the PRI (de la Madrid 2004, 759).

28. The emcees or entertainers (*jilgueros*), as far as we could tell from interviews, were party members, mostly young people, who had years of experience as political activists in local structures. They were specialized in providing entertainment at events and even taught this as a vocation. They were protagonists at all campaign events, and as will be seen later, they fulfilled an unexpectedly important function.

29. This account of events has been taken from Castañeda (1998, 185–86, 300, and 533–34) and de la Madrid (2004, 754–56).

30. Jorge de la Vega; Fidel Velázquez, head of the workers sector; Héctor Hugo Olivares, leader of the peasants sector; Guillermo Fonseca, leader of the popular sector; Antonio Riva Palacio, Senate representative; Nicolás Reynés Berezaluce, congressional representative; and Guillermo Jiménez Morales, representative of the territorial committees, met with the president.

31. Joaquín Hernández Galicia, also known as La Quina, was the secretary of social work and the "moral leader" of the petroleum workers union. He would become one of the protagonists of this campaign. As secretary of programming and budgeting, Salinas had suspended the handing over of construction contracts of the government-owned oil company PEMEX to this union, forcing them to compete for these contracts. In response, it is said that La Quina secretly supported the candidacy of Cárdenas, telling his support bases to vote for him (Dresser 1996, 229). President de la Madrid states that before his nomination La Quina had rejected Salinas as the presidential candidate; afterward, he officially accepted the candidacy, but continued "politicking under the table." At the time, he believed that the potential electoral damage would be low (at the most, half a million votes) and was more concerned with La Quina's financing of the opposition and the payment for news articles that issued criticisms against Salinas (de la Madrid 2004, 785).

32. From very early on, the banners were being prepared to add the candidate's name as soon as it was announced. The statements of "unanimous" support were difficult to make, and some PRI members wanted to take all possible precautions. The governor of Campeche, for example, arrived in Mexico City with banners that showed every one of the possible candidates as being his favorite (Centeno 1997, 12n).

33. This organization was formed in 1963 and grouped together union organizations that belonged to the PRI (from both the workers and the popular sectors) and the National Confederation of Workers union, which made it the country's largest union. The Workers' Congress was quickly overtaken by the CTM's hegemony. See Xelhuantzi López (1986).

34. That afternoon, the president of the republic also received personally various politicians who expressed their support; the first was Rojas, followed by the defeated potential candidates, who in this manner showed their discipline, with the exception of the embattled del Mazo who came in the following day. Other well-known people who visited with the president included Bernardo Sepúlveda, secretary of foreign relations; Gustavo Petricioli, secretary of finance and public credit; and Fernando Gutiérrez Barrios, governor of the state of Veracruz (de la Madrid 2004, 759).

35. For a list of Salinas's inner circle collaborators, see Camp (1996, 305).

36. Surrounding the creation of the candidate's political team, there were battles that initially seemed to demonstrate Salinas's political weakness, since the "people of the system" held various important positions and candidacies. For examples of these speculations, see *Proceso* (no. 613, 16–17: "Madruguete de De la Vega a los priistas. Sus líderes camerales, no modernos pero habilidosos") and *Excélsior* (Oct. 7, 1987: "Forjar consensos").

37. Many started using the term "candidate" even though he was still officially the pre-candidate.

38. National Union of the Ministry of Communication and Transportation (*Excélsior*, Oct. 9, 1987).

39. The PRI members of Michoacán as quoted in *Excélsior*, Oct. 6, 1987.

40. In Mexican folklore, such emphatic negations express precisely the opposite; in this case, it meant that there had been distancing.

41. The reforms to the composition of the Federal Electoral Commission had made the so-called *satelites* (satellite parties) superfluous, since their votes were no longer required by the PRI representatives and the government to form a majority of votes. With this in mind, these parties had foreseen that their votes would no longer be artificially inflated (González Graf 1989, 139–41). Other political groupings that did not have their own registration and that formed a part of the National Democratic Front were the Socialist Revolutionary Party, the Social Democratic Party, and the Democratic and Green Union (González Sandoval 1989, 164–65).

42. See Camacho Alfaro (1989) for a write-up on all of the candidates.

43. According to the narration given by the Conventions Commission of the CEN of the PRI, sectarian delegates were chosen in plenary municipal sessions and then participated in the state-based assemblies and later attended the national convention of the party.

Chapter 4. The Press Prior to the *Destape*

1. López Portillo began the six-year term of Luis Echeverría as the undersecretary of national heritage. In 1972, he was named director of the National Electricity Commission, and on June 1, 1973, he became the secretary of finance and public credit. Miguel de la Madrid under López Portillo was undersecretary of finance until 1979 and thereafter secretary of programming and budgeting.

2. In this regard, it is said that *Fortune*'s mention of him as the "Minister of Finance of the Year" in 1983 was pivotal.

Part III. Carlos Salinas's Presidential Campaign

Chapter 5. Touring the Federal States

1. See Aziz Nassif (1997, 63–65) and Avramow Gutiérrez (1989, 178–86) for a summary of the government's program provided by Salinas in these speeches.

2. Miguel de la Madrid's campaign slogan, The Moral Renovation of Society, arose from the great disillusion people had with the previous government based on their perception of corruption. José López Portillo, who had to face an angered business class due to Luis Echevarría's populism, used We Are All a Part of the Solution. Echeverría, who aimed to reconstruct popular and middle class alliances after the 1968 repression, was made famous for his slogan Up and Forward.

3. For more details on the characteristics of the new political culture, see Salinas's speech given at the Seventh National Ordinary Convention of the PRI on November 8, 1987 (Salinas 1987).

4. In comments made a little after the elections, Miguel de la Madrid (2004) talked in quite clear terms about the distancing that had taken place between Salinas and his team regarding the party: "Jorge de la Vega, who represents the point of view of the majority of the PRI members, does not feel close to Salinas or Camacho" (831); "the hardcore membership is led by Jorge de la Vega, by the leaders of the three sectors and by all the governors; the less committed PRI members are headed by Salinas and Camacho" (832).

5. A leader of the CNOP commented in an interview that Salinas effectively planned voluntary participation of those attending his events, believing that the people "would come towards him." The leader expressed his skepticism vis-à-vis the candidate's good intentions, basically for pragmatic reasons: "In this way, people will not go."

6. The tortilla bonus program (*tortibonos* program) consisted of the free distribution of tortillas to low-income urban families. The program was in effect from 1985–1990.

7. Ruta 100 is the government-owned enterprise that offers public transportation services in Mexico City.

8. The National Institute of Statistics and Geography (INEGI) is a governmental organ charged with handling the national census, among other duties.

9. This was a highly devalued market exchange. Even though our research did not incorporate a systematic analysis, the payments that we were able to observe fluctuated between two and four dollars, to which eventually a small amount of food was added.

10. This program was an innovation to Salinas's campaign. According to what we were told, the forms that were filled out by those in attendance were collated by the CEPES, so a first systematization process could take place, and from there they were transferred to the CEN of the PRI. When a return address was provided, the person submitting the comment would receive a written response signed by the candidate. The program's operation was based on the municipal party structure, from where the people came (usually young people and housewives) who requested that those present write up their petitions. The messages that were sent to the candidate could be "tacky, recommending recipes for the hair," but most of them were job requests, and in second place, items related to local problems. Even though they were few in number, there were also some that provided government action proposals.

11. The press reported the incident in the following manner: The priest was preparing the ceremony when "an ill-humored security agent arrived and yelled, to the Indians' surprise: 'Take all of this away. There will be no ceremony.' And with eyes that were welling up, an Indian asked: 'Why don't you want the ceremony to take place?' 'Because that is what I have been ordered.' Immediately following, he called several of his assistants, and he ordered them to 'Take away all of these old pieces of ceramics, immediately.' The indigenous person immediately began to pick up his receptacles and his jugs and to pour the sacred water into a jar. . . . But how great was the joy of the old priest when, upon the arrival of the candidate, someone told him that it was indispensable that the ceremony take place. Proudly, with a triumphant air, he received authorization to perform a ceremonial act. He did it with great devotion before the respectful observation of SG."

12. This federal organization is in charge of providing housing credits to unionized workers.

13. The reaction by those attending, and later the candidate's reaction, was due to the fact that Saturnino Cedillo (1890–1938) was the cacique of San Luis Potosí and a member of the Lázaro Cárdenas's cabinet who ended up heading an armed uprising in an effort to become president.

14. Charro is a type of horse person in Mexico who wears a similar costume to that worn by mariachi musicians.

15. The LINCONSA program distributed subsidized milk to impoverished families.

16. After the candidate had left, it was common for fiestas to be held. Sometimes, raffles were organized or food was simply distributed. There was always a reference to "prizes" for those who had attended an event and been present for the candidate's speech.

17. This quote is from the general secretary of the Revolutionary Youth Front, organizer of the youth assembly and candidate to a federal congressional position, in an interview with the news program *Ocho en Punto*.

Chapter 6. The Role Played by the Institute for Political, Economic, and Social Studies (IEPES)

1. The IEPES had twelve sub-entities: political studies, social studies, legal studies, regional coordination, development programs, strategy and development, state affairs, economic studies, agricultural studies, organization, information systems, and documentation and analysis systems.

2. The CONACYT is a government entity that is in charge of promoting and coordinating activities related to science and technology.

3. A tlatoani was the healer and/or community leader of pre-Hispanic indigenous communities.

Chapter 7. The Press and the Presidential Campaign

1. This chapter is based extensively on Adler (1993a).

2. This refers to a North American tradition, which became a legal requirement after the U.S. Supreme Court's 1969 ruling, which basically stated that information provided by reporters on any given subject had to provide "both sides" of the argument. For example, an opposition party must be able to transmit its discourse immediately following the presidential discourse.

3. *Excélsior* had a circulation of between 175,000 and 185,000. It was considered to be the main newspaper, extensively read by the political class. *La Jornada*, with a circulation of 25,000, was the favorite newspaper of intellectuals—its readership was low in number but considered politically important. *Siempre!* had a circulation of 100,000 and was a traditionally important political magazine read by the political class. It was linked to the PRI in editorial terms, although it regularly allowed critical articles to be published. *Proceso* had a circulation of 200,000 and was seen as the country's most critical publication as it had a good reputation among journalists (United Nations 1990).

4. The analysis is limited to news coverage and excludes propaganda defined as paid inserts that were usually published as statements of support from private and public associations, institutions, party factions, and others. It is difficult to differentiate propaganda in the form of news stories sponsored by parties from regular journalistic articles. Since this presentation is not so obvious, it was treated in the same way as regular articles. Photographs were not taken into consideration for this analysis, since the authors of this book received trustworthy information that all of them in their totality were provided by the PRI and therefore need to be treated as propaganda. This includes only news reports directly related to the campaign. General news items about the elections have been excluded (technical explanations, etc.) as have political op-ed pieces that were not directly linked to the campaign.

5. The decentralized structure (territorially and reference to the source of resources) of the campaign costs at that time makes it difficult to estimate

expenses by specific categories; however, some informal calculations derived from interviews show that approximately 25 percent of the total was allocated to the press.

6. This statement is debatable if one takes into account that as of this time opposition parties greatly insisted on informational fairness as a means of guaranteeing electoral fairness. Buendía Laredo (2002, 299–303) states in this regard that the degree of knowledge that the electorate had about each candidate had an impact on its voting decisions; however, while Cárdenas and Clouthier were especially affected by the fact that voters did not know them, the probability of votes going to the PRI was very high regardless of the levels of knowledge about Salinas's candidacy.

7. In 1976, *Excélsior* confronted the presidential power of Luis Echeverría, but found his force to be too strong. In the end, the system of co-optation brought with it threats of financial sanctions. As a result of the battle for power, *Excélsior* was forced to fire its director, Julio Scherer García, who later founded and published the renowned weekly *Proceso*. That *Proceso* was able to survive without the traditional sources of funding (government advertisements, bribes, etc.) is a famed chapter in the history of Mexican journalism. This does not mean, however, that other publications could have reproduced *Proceso*'s success.

Part IV. Continuity and Change in Presidential Politics

Chapter 8. Conclusions: Ritual and Stability in the Presidential Succession

1. Some of the following ideas are discussed in Adler-Lomnitz, Lomnitz, and Adler (1993).

2. See his own evaluation of the adjustment program in de la Madrid (1995).

3. See Avramow Gutiérrez (1989, 178–86) and Salinas (1989b).

4. According to the formulae presented by Angelo Panebianco (1990), all parties that need nominal voluntary participation by their followers and structures are required to distribute selective and collective incentives. The former primarily consist of material goods and status, which motivate participation based on individual interests; collective incentives are linked to ideological and official goals of the organization, promoting participation by providing party members with an identity.

5. Miguel de la Madrid referred to this dynamic when he skeptically commented on the participative strategy adopted by Salinas in his campaign: "In a campaign one can not speak too frankly about those topics that have the greatest impact on society," which prevents "reaching the heart of what is of interest to the people, of that which we all know is of extreme importance" (de la Madrid 2004, 788 and 789, respectively).

6. In the campaigns of the two main opposition leaders, criticisms and denouncing of wrongdoings were common. Both were accompanied by terms

associated with instability, such as "civil resistance" in Clouthier's case and "insurrection" and "rebellion" in Cárdenas's case. See Cándano Fierro (1989, 58–64).

7. Pitkin explains the difference between political and symbolic representation (1985, chaps. 5 and 10). Even when governors have the freedom to decide on more appropriate policies without a need to consult citizens or obey their wishes, there is the possibility that they will be replaced by a competitor through elections, providing an incentive to better meet the interests of the electorate so that the electorate will approve of their decisions and vote for them for reelection. Symbolic representation, in contrast, is based on the population's belief that the leader is "incarnate" through subjective and emotional connections that can be manipulated by the leader. Very much in line with our research, Pitkin comments: "If the main goal is to integrate the nation as a unified whole . . . then one is tempted to conclude that one dramatic symbolic act can achieve this goal in a much more efficient manner than an entire legislature of representatives" (ibid., 117).

8. See Bartra (1987) and Lomnitz (1987) for a discussion on the myths of origin of the Mexican nation.

9. Institutional Revolutionary Party nationalism gave limited importance to the regions that were not a part of the administrative divisions such as the Bajío, the Laguna, the Isthmus, the Huastec, the Mixteca, and the northern frontier, despite the fact that they were noted in their diagnostic studies and political analyses.

10. For a more in-depth analysis of the similarities between the campaign acts and the theater, see Lomnitz and Adler-Lomnitz (2003). The relationship between rituals and the theater is explained in Turner (1992).

Chapter 9. Recent Successions (I): The Last Elections under PRI Rule (1994–2000)

1. This policy was implemented in December 1987 under the name of the Pact of Economic Solidarity and remained in effect throughout the Salinas administration.

2. This can be compared to the application of economic reforms in other countries. In Bolivia, for example, adjustment programs were accompanied by martial law called for by Congress (Gamarra 1997); in Argentina, the adjustment program lacked coherence because its approval required that the provinces be compensated where governors were in a position to grant votes to the members of Congress elected in their respective provinces (Benton 2003). The Chilean dictatorship was able to implement its neo-liberal economic program without any pressures since social protest was prohibited. Salinas was aware of the difficulties in implementing his project under democratic conditions. In an interview with *Newsweek*, he stated that the simultaneous implementation of

economic and political reforms could lead to a complete absence of reforms and the disintegration of the country, using the case of the Soviet Union as an example (Centeno 1997, 224–25).

3. The first firm electoral results received came from the Valley of Mexico and favored Cuauhtémoc Cárdenas. With this information, and as a result of Salinas's doubts (he did not want to show himself as the victor without official results), Jorge de la Vega, with the president's authorization, hastily declared his candidate as the winner to prevent Cárdenas from presenting himself as the likely victor. Cárdenas, Clouthier, and Ibarra de Piedra called for the reestablishment of legality in the process on the night of Election Day, threatening that they would not accept the electoral results. Three days later, Cárdenas said that he was the winner and warned that upholding the fraud would be equivalent to a coup. For a detailed account of the events that took place during Election Day, see Madrid (2004, 814–17) and Castañeda (1998, 541–51); the events of the days and weeks that followed are recounted in Sánchez Gutiérrez (1989).

4. The resignations of the governors of Tabasco and Jalisco, whose incompetence produced political problems, must be added to the list, together with the departure of governors who were not close to Salinas's policies, such as Manzanilla Schaffer in Yucatán. Salinas's solution to local crises of removing the heads of the executive meant that at the end of his six-year term, seventeen out of thirty-one states were headed by interim governors (Serrano 1998, 34).

5. In other aspects, the Solidarity Program followed the traditional mechanisms of patron-client relations in the allocation of resources to the new actors that had been promoted by Salinas. See Braig (1997).

6. The EZLN had begun to organize prior to the structural adjustment policies. When it made its public appearance, it alluded to the fraudulent presidency of Salinas and stated that its existence (an army formed by indigenous, poor peasants) represented the hidden image that lay behind modernization. The EZLN showed a tremendous ability to challenge the regime's symbols, continuously referring to the 1910–1917 Mexican Revolution and its pure ideals, represented in the figure of Emiliano Zapata (a historic emblem that Salinas had taken on). This reference to a popular aspiration that had been betrayed by neoliberalism had a clear precedent in the discourse launched by the Democratic Current six years earlier. For a general history on these matters, see Tello Díaz (1995) and Meyer (2003).

7. With his resignation, Camacho had been out of a government position for more than six months prior to the elections—and thus did not meet with the requirements mandated by the constitution for potential presidential candidates.

8. There were two other assassinations in addition to Colosio's that took place during the succession process: the death of the Guadalajara-based Cardinal Posadas Ocampo in May 1993 and of the general secretary of the PRI, José Francisco Ruiz Massieu, in September 1994.

9. This was the most notorious *madruguete* but not the only one. A group of governors mobilized in favor of Emilio Gamboa Patrón, while Raul Salinas, the president's brother, apparently grouped people together in support of Manlio Fabio Beltrones (Castañeda 1998, 621–22).

10. Internal elections were held on November 7, 1999. Labastida won with 54.8 percent of the vote against 28.4 percent received by Madrazo (González Compeán, Lomelí, and Salmerón Sanginés 2000, 669–79). Manuel Bartlett and the former president of the PRI Humberto Roque Villanueva also competed in these elections. From 1998 on, the PRI used the same procedures to determine the candidacies of governors. In some cases (Tlaxcala, Baja California Sur, Zacatecas), those who lost competed under the banner of opposition parties and were elected governors, which definitely contradicted the foundations on which PRI discipline had been built (González Compeán, Lomelí, and Salmerón Sanginés 2000, 661–65).

11. The description provided by Bruhn (2004) of the campaigns of the three most important parties explains that Fox's success was largely due to the fact that he was able to control the party and focus his campaign entirely on gaining votes, while Labastida and Cárdenas were cornered by internal factors since they followed more traditional campaigning models.

12. For a detailed analysis of the evolution and terms of the different electoral reforms implemented as of 1977, see Becerra, Salazar, and Woldenberg (2000).

13. See Carrillo and Lujambio (1998), Casar (1999), and Nacif (1999) for an analysis of these transformations.

14. See Lujambio (2000a) for a discussion of the legislature of 1997–2000 and Pérez Correa (2003) for a history on the relationship between the executive and the legislature since 1997.

15. In a 2003 survey, only 8.3 percent of the adult population mentioned newspapers as their most used source for information on political events, while 61 percent stated that they watched television for this purpose (Secretaría de Gobernación and Instituto Nacional de Estadística Geografía e Informática 2003).

16. When asked during a television interview by Brozo about his stubborn denial of being a presidential candidate when everyone believed him to be a competitor, the head of the Federal District, Andrés Manuel López Obrador, answered: "I don't want to be a slave of my words."

17. See a discussion on the elections for PRI leadership in Garrido (2002).

18. As stated by Rouquié (1982, 69–76), economic vulnerability and unemployment stand out as social conditions that favor the rise of clientelistic relations. According to the calculations made by Julio Boltvinik and Enrique Hernández, which are more reliable than official ones, poverty affected 70.6 percent of the population at the end of the 1990s (quoted in Alba Vega 2003, 173).

19. Different analyses based on surveys also raise these questions. Moreno and Méndez (2002) found that for 2000 the upholding of values generally associated

with what has been called the democratic political culture (tolerance, empathy, rejection of strong leaderships and of military governments, support of democracy, respect for human rights) is not spread through the whole population. Within Mexican society, these values are primarily upheld by the most educated sectors. See also Temkin, Ramírez, and Salazar Elena (2005).

Chapter 10. Recent Successions (II): The 2006 Election

1. According to official results, Calderón of PAN received 35.89 percent of the votes; López Obrador of the PRD, 35.33 percent; Roberto Madrazo of the PRI, 22.23 percent; Patricia Mercado of Alternativa, 2.71 percent; and Roberto Campa of Nueva Alianza, 0.96 percent. Annulled votes and votes cast for candidates who were not registered totaled 2.89 percent (www.ife.org.mx).

2. The accusations of fraud launched by the PRD started when preliminary results were being announced at the end of Election Day. During that day, none of the parties reported any irregularities, and international observers called the elections exemplary. Suspicions about electoral manipulation were primarily based on how the results were received from the voting booths and the mathematical inconsistencies that were revealed in various registries at the voting booth level. See Schedler (2007) for an explanation of those elements that make the Mexican electoral system reliable, and also procedural aspects that make the occurrence of mathematical errors almost inevitable. The most systematic analyses to date have shown that there are no systematical associations that would be seen should there have been an intentional manipulation of the votes. See Pliego Carrasco (2007) and Aparicio (2006a, 2006b). For a statistical analysis of data that support the version of fraud, see Mochán (2006).

3. This part requires some clarification. In the first place, the classification of projects as "modernizing" or "traditional" has an analytical purpose and is by no means normative. On the other hand, it refers strictly to their relationship with the model that predominated during the PRI years, as has been described in the first part of this study. Therefore, we refer to "traditional" as the statist, nationalist, and hierarchical model, while a modernizing model or project stands for individualism, the market, and insertion into the global realm. We do recognize that in terms of other dimensions, these labels could be deceiving. For example, the positions of PAN with regard to sexuality and religion can hardly be seen as part of a modernizing idea, while the proposed social reforms of the PRD are closer to what one would generally term progressive positions.

4. It is naturally not unusual that a person who is identified as the candidate acquires more power within the party. What stands out in this case is the extent of López Obrador's power, who gained access to the main position within his party's leadership without any major problems. This can be contrasted to Calderón whose differences with the president of PAN were relatively public. Calderón tried to ensure the appointment of people of his circle to the positions of general

secretary, treasurer, and to two ministries of PAN. However, the president of the party opposed him and agreed only to some minor nominations (Camarena 2007, 170–72).

5. See also Camacho and Almazán (2006, chap. I) where the PRD candidate's resistance to using the media is discussed. López Obrador even stated: "I will be the first candidate to win without using television" (17).

6. The following paragraphs are based on the results presented by Estrada and Poiré (2007), Klesner (2007), and Moreno (2007).

References

Adler, Ilya. 1986. Media uses and effects in a large bureaucracy: A case study in Mexico. PhD diss., University of Wisconsin–Madison.

———. 1993a. The Mexican case: The media in the 1988 presidential election. In *Television, politics and the transition to democracy in Latin America*, ed. Thomas E. Skidmore, 147–73. Baltimore: Johns Hopkins University Press.

———. 1993b. Press-government relations in Mexico: A study of freedom of the Mexican press and press criticism of government institutions. *Studies in Latin American Popular Culture* 12:1–30.

Adler-Lomnitz, Larissa. 1971. Reciprocity of favors in the urban middle class of Chile. In *Studies in Economics and Anthropology*, ed. George Dalton, 93–106. Washington, D.C.: American Anthropological Association.

———. 1975. *Cómo sobreviven los marginados*. Mexico City: Siglo XXI.

———. 1977. *Networks and marginality: Life in a Mexican shantytown*. San Francisco: Academic Press.

———. 1994. *Redes sociales, cultura y poder: Ensayos en antropología latinoamericana*. Mexico City: M.A. Porrúa; FLACSO.

———. 2002. Los efectos de la globalización en la estructura de poder en México. *Revista de Antropología Social* 11:185–200.

———. 2003. Los usos del miedo. Pandillas de porros en México. In *Jóvenes sin tregua: Culturas y políticas de la violencia*, ed. Francisco Ferrándiz and Carles Feixa, 85–94. Barcelona: Anthropos.

Adler-Lomnitz, Larissa, and Frida Gorbach. 1998. Entre la continuidad y el cambio: El ritual de la sucesión presidencial. *Revista Mexicana de Sociología* 60 (3): 61–83.

Adler-Lomnitz, Larissa, Claudio Lomnitz, and Ilya Adler. 1993. El fondo de la forma: Actos públicos de la campaña presidencial del Partido Revolucionario Institucional, México 1988. In *Elecciones y sistemas de partidos en América Latina*, ed. Dieter Nohlen, 223–66. San José, Costa Rica: IIDH; CAPEL.

Adler-Lomnitz, Larissa, and Ana Melnick. 1991. *Chile's middle class: A struggle for survival in the face of neoliberalism*. Boulder, CO: Lynne Rienner Publishers.

———. 2000. *Chile's political culture and parties: An anthropological explanation*. Notre Dame, IN: University of Notre Dame Press.

Adler-Lomnitz, Larissa, and Marisol Pérez Lizaur. 1987. *A Mexican elite family*. Princeton, NJ: Princeton University Press.

Adler-Lomnitz, Larissa, Marisol Pérez Lizaur, and Rodrigo Salazar-Elena. 2007. Globalización y nuevas élites en México. In *Élites en América Latina*, ed. Piter Birle, Wilhelm Hofmeister, Günther Maihold, and Barbara Potthast, 143–68. Madrid: Iberoamericana; Frankfurt, Germany: Vervuert.

Aguilar Camín, Héctor. 2004. *La tragedia de Colosio: Según el testimonio de sus propios actores, tal como puede hallarse en los ordenados infiernos de la fiscalía especial del magnicidio: Una novela sin ficción.* Mexico City: Alfaguara.

Aguirre, Alberto. 2002. La caída del PRI. Los dinosaurios derrotaron a Labastida. *Enfoque* (November 24). http://www.reforma.com.

Alba Vega, Carlos. 2003. México después del TLCAN. El impacto económico y sus consecuencias políticas y sociales. *Foro Internacional* 43 (1): 141–91.

Anderson, Stephen C. 1983. Tone and morpheme rules in Ngyemboon-Bamileke. PhD diss., University of Southern California.

Aparicio, Javier. 2006a. Errores aritméticos en actas: Análisis comparativo para 2000, 2003 y 2006. http://www.cide.edu/investigadores/aparicio/elecciones.

———. 2006b. La evidencia de una elección confiable. *Nexos* 346 (October): 49–53.

Avramow Gutiérrez, Jacqueline. 1989. La promesa salinista. In *Las elecciones de 1988 y la crisis del sistema político*, ed. Jaime González Graf, 173–90. Mexico City: Editorial Diana.

Aziz Nassif, Alberto. 1997. El rompecabezas salinista: Recuento político de un gobierno. In *México en el desfiladero: Los años de Salinas*, ed. Marcelo Cavarozzi, 59–88. Mexico City: FLACSO; Juan Pablos.

Babb, Sarah. 1997. Money doctors, international constituencies, and the legitimation of expert knowledge: Mexican economics, 1929–present. Paper presented at the annual meeting of the American Sociological Association, Toronto, Ontario, Canada, August 11.

Badie, Bertrand, and Guy Hermet. 1993. *Política comparada.* Mexico City: Fondo de Cultura Económica.

Bartra, Roger. 1987. *La jaula de la melancolía.* Mexico City: Grijalbo.

———. 2007. *Fango sobre la democracia: Textos polémicos sobre la transición mexicana.* Mexico City: Planeta.

Basáñez, Miguel. 1990. *La lucha por la hegemonía en México 1968–1990.* Mexico City: Siglo XXI.

Becerra, Ricardo, Pedro Salazar, and José Woldenberg. 2000. *La mecánica del cambio político en México: Elecciones, partidos y reformas.* Mexico City: Cal y Arena.

Beltrán, Ulises. 2003. Venciendo la incertidumbre: El voto retrospectivo en la elección presidencial de 2000 en México. *Política y Gobierno* 10 (2): 325–58.

Benton, Allyson Lucinda. 2003. Presidentes fuertes, provincias poderosas: La economía política de la construcción de partidos en el sistema federal argentino. *Política y Gobierno* 10 (1): 103–37.

Berman, Sabina. 2006. Felipe Calderón: Las tribulaciones de la fe. *Letras Libres* 90 (June): 29–38.

Bizberg, Ilán. 2003. El sindicalismo en el fin de régimen. *Foro Internacional* 43 (1): 215–48.

Böröcz, József. 2000. Informality rules. *East European Politics and Societies* 14 (2): 348–80.

Braig, Marianne. 1997. Continuity and change in Mexican political culture: The case of PRONASOL. In *Citizens of the pyramid: Essays on Mexican political culture*, ed. Wil G. Pansters, 247–78. Amsterdam: Thela Publishers.

Brandenburg, Frank. 1964. *The making of modern Mexico*. Englewood Cliffs, NJ: Prentice Hall.

Bruhn, Kathleen. 2004. The making of the Mexican president, 2000: Parties, candidates, and campaign strategy. In *Mexico's pivotal democratic election: Candidates, voters, and the presidential campaign of 2000*, ed. Jorge I. Domínguez and Chappell Lawson, 123–56. Stanford, CA: Stanford University Press; San Diego: Center for U.S.–Mexican Studies, University of California, San Diego.

Buendía Laredo, Jorge. 2002. Incertidumbre y comportamiento electoral en la transición democrática: La elección mexicana de 1988. In *Lecturas sobre el cambio político en México*, ed. Carlos Elizondo Mayer-Serra and Benito Nacif Hernández, 281–311. Mexico City: Centro de Investigación y Docencia Económicas; Fondo de Cultura Económica.

Camacho, Óscar, and Alejandro Almazán. 2006. *La victoria que no fue. López Obrador: Entre la guerra sucia y la soberbia*. Mexico City: Grijalbo.

Camacho Alfaro, Carlos. 1989. Los candidatos contendientes. In *Las elecciones de 1988 y la crisis del sistema político*, ed. Jaime González Graf, 31–52. Mexico City: Editorial Diana.

Camarena, Salvador. 2007. La conquista del poder. In *El presidente electo. Instructivo para sobrevivir a Calderón y su gobierno*, ed. Salvador Camarena and Jorge Zepeda Patterson, 11–190. Mexico City: Planeta.

Camp, Roderic Ai. 1995a. El gabinete de Zedillo: ¿Continuidad, cambios o revolución? *Este País* 51 (June): 46–54.

———. 1995b. *La política en México*. Mexico City: Siglo XXI.

———. 1996. *Reclutamiento político en México, 1884–1991*. Mexico City: Siglo XXI.

———. 2004. Citizen attitudes toward democracy and Vicente Fox's victory in 2000. In *Mexico's pivotal democratic election: Candidates, voters, and the presidential campaign of 2000*, ed. Jorge I. Domínguez and Chappell Lawson, 25–46. Stanford, CA: Stanford University Press; San Diego: Center for U.S.–Mexican Studies, University of California, San Diego.

Cándano Fierro, Mónica. 1989. Las campañas electorales. In *Las elecciones de 1988 y la crisis del sistema político*, ed. Jaime González Graf, 53–71. Mexico City: Editorial Diana.

Cárdenas, Cuauhtémoc. 1989. Fragmentos del discurso de Cuauhtémoc Cárdenas, gobernador de Michoacán, en el que critica la desviación de la Revolución
Mexicana (Jiquilpan, 30 de agosto de 1985). In *Las elecciones de 1988 y la crisis del
sistema político*, ed. Jaime González Graf, 201–8. Mexico City: Editorial Diana.

Carpizo, Jorge. 1978. *El presidencialismo mexicano*. Mexico City: Siglo XXI.

Carrillo, Ulises, and Alonso Lujambio. 1998. La incertidumbre constitucional:
Gobierno dividido y aprobación presupuestal en el congreso mexicano.
Revista Mexicana de Sociología 40 (2): 239–63.

Casar, María Amparo. 1999. Las relaciones entre el poder ejecutivo y el legislativo: El caso de México. *Política y Gobierno* 6 (1): 83–128.

———. 2002. Las bases político-institucionales del poder presidencial en
México. In *Lecturas sobre el cambio político en México*, ed. Carlos Elizondo
Mayer-Serra and Benito Nacif Hernández, 41–78. Mexico City: Centro de
Investigación y Docencia Económicas; Fondo de Cultura Económica.

Castañeda, Jorge G. 1998. *La herencia: Arqueología de la sucesión presidencial en
México*. Mexico City: Punto de Lectura.

Castoriadis, Cornelius. 1987. *The imaginary institution of society*. Cambridge,
MA: MIT Press.

Centeno, Miguel Ángel. 1997. *Democracy within reason: Technocratic revolution
in Mexico*. University Park: Pennsylvania State University Press.

Chapela, Ignacio. 1983. Planning conflict and the power structure in a Mexican
public organization. Unpublished manuscript.

Chávez Gutiérrez, Héctor. 2007. El liderazgo de Cuauhtémoc Cárdenas y sus
efectos en la institucionalización de la izquierda mexicana. Paper presented
at the International Colloquium on Political Leadership in Modern Societies, Xalapa, Mexico, November 12–14.

Colomer, Josep M. 2000. *Strategic transitions: Game theory and democratization*.
Baltimore: Johns Hopkins University Press.

Cook, María Lorena, Kevin Middlebrook, and Juan Molinar Horcasitas. 1996.
Las dimensiones políticas del ajuste estructural: Actores, tiempos y coalicio-
nes. In *Las dimensiones políticas de la reestructuración económica*, ed. María
Lorena Cook, Kevin Middlebrook, and Juan Molinar Horcasitas, 39–105.
Mexico City: Cal y Arena.

Córdova, Arnaldo. 1974. *La política de masas del cardenismo*. Mexico City: Era.

Cornelius, Wayne A. 1975. *Politics and the migrant poor in Mexico City*. Stanford,
CA: Stanford University Press.

———. 2004. Mobilized voting in the 2000 elections: The changing efficacy of
vote buying and coercion in Mexican electoral politics. In *Mexico's pivotal
democratic election: Candidates, voters, and the presidential campaign of 2000*,
ed. Jorge I. Domínguez and Chappell Lawson, 47–65. Stanford, CA: Stanford
University Press; San Diego: Center for U.S.–Mexican Studies, University of
California, San Diego.

Corriente Democrática. 1989a. Documentos de trabajo (1 y 2) para la fundación de la Corriente Democrática del PRI. In *Las elecciones de 1988 y la crisis del sistema político*, ed. Jaime González Graf, 209–15. Mexico City: Editorial Diana.

———. 1989b. Propuesta de la Corriente Democrática para ser integrada en la plataforma electoral del PRI. In *Las elecciones de 1988 y la crisis del sistema político*, ed. Jaime González Graf, 217–53. Mexico City: Editorial Diana.

Cossío, José Ramón. 1998. *Dogmática constitucional y régimen autoritario*. Mexico City: Fontamara.

———. 2001. La Suprema Corte y la teoría constitucional. *Política y Gobierno* 8 (1): 61–115.

Dahl, Robert. 1983. Federalism and the democratic process. *Nomos* 25:95–108.

DaMatta, Roberto. 1978. *Carnavais, malandros e herois: Para una sociologia do dilemma brasileiro*. Rio de Janeiro: Zahar.

———. 1985. *A casa e a rua: Espaço cidadania, mulher e mort no Brasil*. São Paulo, Brazil: Brasiliense.

de la Garza Toledo, Enrique. 1996. La reestructuración del corporativismo en México. In *Las dimensiones políticas de la reestructuración económica*, ed. María Lorena Cook, Kevin Middlebrook, and Juan Molinar Horcasitas, 403–32. Mexico City: Cal y Arena.

de la Madrid, Miguel. 1995. Doce años de cambios en México. *Este País* 53 (August): 22–32.

———. 2004. *Cambio de rumbo. Testimonio de una presidencia, 1982–1988*. With Alejandra Lajous. Mexico City: Fondo de Cultura Económica.

de la Vega Domínguez, Jorge. 1988. Palabras pronunciadas por el C. Lic. Jorge de la Vega Domínguez, presidente del CEN del PRI, en el desayuno de la Unidad Revolucionaria, efectuado en la Sala de Armas de la Magdalena Mixhuca, México, D.F., 5 de septiembre de 1988. In *Desayuno de la Unidad Revolucionaria*, ed. Partido Revolucionario Institucional, 9–22. Mexico City: Secretaría de Divulgación Ideológica.

Delgado, René. 2003. Subproductos políticos. *Reforma* December 6:12A.

Diamond, Larry. 1997. Is the third way of democratization over? An empirical assessment. Working Paper 236. Hellen Kellog Institute for International Studies, University of Notre Dame.

———. 2002. Thinking about hybrid regimes. *Journal of Democracy* 13 (2): 21–35.

Díaz Cayeros, Alberto, and Beatriz Magaloni. 1998. Autoridad presupuestal del poder legislativo en México: Una primera aproximación. *Política y Gobierno* 5 (2): 503–28.

Domínguez, Jorge I. 2004. Conclusion: Why and how did Mexico's 2000 presidential election campaign matter? In *Mexico's pivotal democratic election:*

Candidates, voters, and the presidential campaign of 2000, ed. Jorge I. Domín-guez and Chappell Lawson, 321–44. Stanford, CA: Stanford University Press; San Diego: Center for U.S.–Mexican Studies, University of California, San Diego.

Dresser, Denise. 1996. Muerte, modernización o metamorfosis del PRI: Neolib-eralismo y reforma partidaria en México. In *Las dimensiones políticas de la reestructuración económica*, ed. María Lorena Cook, Kevin Middlebrook, and Juan Molinar Horcasitas, 211–50. Mexico City: Cal y Arena.

Dumont, Louis. 1970. *Homo hierarchicus: The caste system and its implications.* Chicago: University of Chicago Press.

Eco, Umberto. 1986. *Art and beauty in the Middle Ages.* New Haven: Yale University Press.

Eisenstadt, Todd A. 2007. The origins and rationality of the "legal versus legiti-mate" dichotomy invoked in Mexico's 2006 post-electoral conflict. *PS: Political Science and Politics* 40 (1): 39–43.

Elster, Jon, Claus Offe, and Ulrich K. Preuss, with Frank Boenker, Ulrike Goetting, and Friedbert W. Rueb. 1998. *Institutional design in post-communist societies: Rebuilding the ship at sea.* Cambridge: Cambridge University Press.

Estrada, Luis, and Alejandro Poiré. 2007. Taught to protest, learning to lose. *Journal of Democracy* 18 (1): 73–87.

Etzioni, Amitai. 1975. *A comparative analysis of complex organizations: On power, involvement, and their correlatives.* New York: Simon and Schuster.

Fernández Baeza, Mario, and Dieter Nohlen. 2000. Elecciones. In *Diccionario Electoral*, ed. Centro de Asesoría y Promoción Electoral. San José, Costa Rica: IIDH. http//www.iidh.ed.cr/siii/diccelect/_private/default.asp.

Finkel, Jodi. 1998. Judicial reform in Latin America: Market economies, self-interested politicians, and judicial independence. Paper presented at the XXI International Congress of the Latin American Studies Association, Chicago, September 24–27.

Fox, Jonathan. 1996. Cambio político en la nueva economía campesina de México. In *Las dimensiones políticas de la reestructuración económica*, ed. María Lorena Cook, Kevin Middlebrook, and Juan Molinar Horcasitas, 295–332. Mexico City: Cal y Arena.

Fukuyama, Francis, Seymour Martin Lipset, Orlando Patterson, Mark Plattner, and Fareed Zakaria. 1999. *Democracy's century: A survey of global political change in the 20th century.* New York: Freedom House. http://216.119.117.183/reports/century.pdf.

Gamarra, Eduardo A. 1997. Hybrid presidentialism and democratization: The case of Bolivia. In *Presidentialism and democracy in Latin America*, ed. Scott Mainwaring and Matthew Soberg Shugart, 363–93. Cambridge: Cambridge University Press.

García Castro, María. 1997. Mujer y poder: Las mujeres diputadas. Las transformaciones de los modos de vida de la mujer en México. MD diss., UAM–Iztapalapa.

García Pelayo, Manuel. 1993. *Derecho constitucional comparado*. Madrid: Alianza.

Garrido, Luis Javier. 1982. *El partido de la revolución institucionalizada: La formación del nuevo estado en México (1928–1945)*. Mexico City: Siglo XXI.

———. 1987. Las quince reglas de la sucesión presidencial. In *La sucesión presidencial en 1988*, ed. Abraham Nuncio, 85–106. Mexico City: Grijalbo.

———. 1993. *La ruptura: La Corriente Democrática del PRI*. Mexico City: Grijalbo.

———. 2002. La democracia imposible. *Proceso* 1322 (February 24): 8–11.

Gasiorowski, Mark J. 1996. An overview of the political regime change dataset. *Comparative Political Studies* 29 (4): 469–83.

Geddes, Barbara. 1999. Authoritarian breakdown: Empirical test of a game theoretic argument. Paper presented at the annual meeting of the American Political Science Association, Atlanta, September 2–5.

Geertz, Clifford. 1981. *Negara*. Princeton, NJ: Princeton University Press.

Gil Mendieta, Jorge, and Samuel Schmidt. 1999. *La red política en México: Modelación y análisis por medio de la teoría de gráficas*. With Jorge Castro and Alejandro Ruiz. Mexico City: UNAM.

Gómez Tagle, Silvia. 1986. Democracia y poder en México: El significado de los fraudes electorales en 1979, 1982 y 1985. *Nueva Antropología* 9 (October): 127–57.

González Casanova, Pablo. 1976. *La democracia en México*. Mexico City: Era.

———. 1986. *El estado y los partidos políticos en México*. Mexico City: Era.

González Compeán, Miguel, Leonardo Lomelí, and Pedro Salmerón Sanginés. 2000. *El partido de la revolución: Institución y conflicto (1928–1999)*. Mexico City: Fondo de Cultura Económica.

González Graf, Jaime. 1989. La crisis del sistema. In *Las elecciones de 1988 y la crisis del sistema político*, ed. Jaime González Graf, 137–57. Mexico City: Editorial Diana.

González Sandoval, Juan Pablo. 1989. La emergencia del neocardenismo. In *Las elecciones de 1988 y la crisis del sistema político*, ed. Jaime González Graf, 159–71. Mexico City: Editorial Diana.

Graber, Doris. 1989. Content and meaning: What is it all about? *American Behavioral Scientist* 33 (2): 135–52.

Gruzinski, Serge. 1990. *La guerre des images: De Christophe Colomb a "Blade Runner."* Paris: Fayard.

Guerra, François-Xavier. 1985. *Le Mexique: De l'ancien régime à la révolution*. Paris: L'Harmattan.

Guerrero Gutiérrez, Eduardo. 2001. Competencia partidista e inestabilidad del gabinete político en México. *Política y Gobierno* 8 (1): 13–60.

Guillén Vicente, Alfonso. 1982a. Partido Acción Nacional. In *La reforma política y los partidos en México*, ed. Octavio Rodríguez Araujo, 125–41. Mexico City: Siglo XXI.

———. 1982b. Partido Auténtico de la Revolución Mexicana. In *La reforma política y los partidos en México*, ed. Octavio Rodríguez Araujo, 156–67. Mexico City: Siglo XXI.

Gutiérrez Espíndola, José. 1989. Información y necesidades sociales: Los noticieros de Televisa. In *Televisa: El quinto poder*, ed. Raúl Trejo Delabre, 62–98. Mexico City: Claves Latinoamericanas.

Haber, Paul Lawrence. 1996. El arte de la reestructuración y sus implicaciones políticas: El caso de los movimientos urbanos populares. In *Las dimensiones políticas de la reestructuración económica*, ed. María Lorena Cook, Kevin Middlebrook, and Juan Molinar Horcasitas, 333–70. Mexico City: Cal y Arena.

Hardin, Russell. 1989. Why a constitution? In *"The Federalist Papers" and the new institutionalism*, ed. Bernard Grofman and Donald Wittman, 100–120. New York: Agathon Press.

Heredia, Blanca. 1997a. Clientelism in flux: Democratization and interest intermediation in contemporary Mexico. Paper presented at the XXth International Congress of the Latin American Studies Association, Guadalajara, Mexico, April 17–19.

———. 1997b. La transición al mercado en México. Desempeño económico e instituciones políticas. In *México en el desfiladero: Los años de Salinas*, ed. Marcelo Cavarozzi, 151–74. Mexico City: FLACSO; Juan Pablos.

———. 2002. Estructura política y reforma económica: El caso de México. In *Lecturas sobre el cambio político en México*, ed. Carlos Elizondo Mayer-Serra and Benito Nacif Hernández, 175–226. Mexico City: Centro de Investigación y Docencia Económicas; Fondo de Cultura Económica.

Hermet, Guy. 1982. Las elecciones en los regímenes autoritarios: Bosquejo de un marco de análisis. In *¿Para qué sirven las elecciones?* ed. Guy Hermet, Alain Rouquié, and Juan J. Linz, 18–53. Mexico City: Fondo de Cultura Económica.

Hernández Juárez, Francisco, and María Xelhuantzi López. 1993. *El sindicalismo en la reforma del estado*. Mexico City: Fondo de Cultura Económica.

Hernández Rodríguez, Rogelio. 2003. Ernesto Zedillo: La presidencia contenida. *Foro Internacional* 43 (1): 39–70.

Herrera Valenzuela, Jorge. 1988. *La radio, el PRI y el destape*. Mexico City: Editorial Diana.

Hirschman, Albert O. 1970. *Exit, voice and royalty: Responses to decline in firms, organizations, and states*. Cambridge, MA: Harvard University Press.

Huntington, Samuel P. 1994. *La tercera ola: La democratización a finales del siglo XX*. Mexico City: Paidós.

Kertzer, David. 1988. *Ritual, politics, and power*. New Haven, CT: Yale University Press.

Klesner, Joseph L. 1993. Modernization, economic crisis, and electoral alignment in Mexico. *Mexican Studies* 9 (2): 187–223.

———. 2007. The 2006 Mexican elections: Manifestation of a divided society? *PS: Political Science and Politics* 40 (1): 27–32.

Klesner, Joseph L., and Chappell Lawson. 2001. Adiós to the PRI? Changing voter turnout in Mexico's political transition. *Mexican Studies* 17 (1): 17–39.

Knight, Jack. 1992. *Institutions and social conflict*. New York: Cambridge University Press.

Krauze, Enrique. 2006. El Mesías tropical. *Letras Libres* 90 (June): 15–24.

Langston, Joy. 1996. *Why rules matter: The formal rules of candidate and leadership selection in PRI, 1978–1996*. Working Paper 54. Mexico City: CIDE.

———. 2002. Los efectos de la competencia electoral en la selección de candidatos del PRI a la Cámara de Diputados. In *Lecturas sobre el cambio político en México*, ed. Carlos Elizondo Mayer-Serra and Benito Nacif Hernández, 387–430. Mexico City: Centro de Investigación y Docencia Económicas; Fondo de Cultura Económica.

———. 2007. The PRI's 2006 electoral debacle. *PS: Political Science and Politics* 40 (1): 21–25.

Lassman, Peter. 2000. The rule of man over man: Politics, power and legitimation. In *The Cambridge companion to Weber*, ed. Stephen Turner, 83–98. New York: Cambridge University Press.

Lawson, Chappell. 2007. How did we get here? Mexican democracy after the 2006 elections. *PS: Political Science and Politics* 40 (1): 45–48.

Lefort, Claude. 1986. *The political forms of modern society: Bureaucracy, democracy, totalitarianism*. Cambridge, MA: MIT Press.

León, Samuel, and Ignacio Marván. 1985. *La clase obrera en la historia de México: En el cardenismo (1934–1940)*. Mexico City: Siglo XXI; IIS.

Levitsky, Steven, and Lucian A. Way. 2002. The rise of competitive authoritarianism. *Journal of Democracy* 13 (2): 51–65.

Lijphart, Arend. 1994. *Electoral systems and party systems: A study of twenty-seven democracies, 1945–1990*. Oxford: Oxford University Press.

———. 1999. *Patterns of democracy: Government forms and performance in thirty-six countries*. New Haven, CT: Yale University Press.

Linz, Juan J. 1982. Funciones y disfunciones de las elecciones no competitivas: Los sistemas autoritarios y totalitarios. In *¿Para qué sirven las elecciones?* ed. Guy Hermet, Alain Rouquié, and Juan J. Linz, 90–146. Mexico City: Fondo de Cultura Económica.

———. 1997. Democracia presidencial o parlamentaria: ¿Qué diferencia implica? In *La crisis del presidencialismo: Perspectivas comparativas*, ed. Juan J. Linz and Arturo Valenzuela, 25–147. Madrid: Alianza.

———. 2000. *Totalitarian and authoritarian regimes*. London: Lynne Riener Publishers.

Linz, Juan J., and Alfred Stepan. 1996. *Problems of democratic transitions and consolidation: Southern Europe, South America, and post-communist Europe.* Baltimore: John Hopkins University Press.

Liss, Peggy. 1975. *Mexico under Spain, 1521–1526: Society and the origins of nationality.* Chicago: University of Chicago Press.

Loaeza, Soledad. 1999. *El Partido Acción Nacional: La larga marcha, 1939–1994. Oposición leal y partido de protesta.* Mexico City: Fondo de Cultura Económica.

———. 2003. Acción nacional en la antesala del poder: 1994–2000. *Foro Internacional* 43 (1): 71–102.

Lomnitz, Alberto, and Larissa Adler-Lomnitz. 2003. La teatralidad de las campañas electorales del PRI en México: Un estudio de caso. Unpublished manuscript.

Lomnitz, Claudio. 1987. Cultural relations in regional spaces. PhD diss., Stanford University.

———. 2000. Ritual, rumor y corrupción en la conformación de los "sentimientos de la nación." In *Vicios públicos, virtudes privadas: La corrupción en México,* ed. Claudio Lomnitz, 241–74. Mexico City: CIESAS; M.A. Porrúa.

Loza Otero, Nicolás. 2008. *Legitimidad en disputa: Zedillo, Fox, Calderón.* Mexico City: FLACSO.

Lujambio, Alonso. 2000a. Adiós a la excepcionalidad: Régimen presidencial y gobierno dividido en México. *Este País* 107 (February): 2–16.

———. 2000b. *El poder compartido: Un ensayo sobre la democratización mexicana.* With Horacio Vives Segl. Mexico City: Océano.

Lujambio, Alonso, and Ignacio Marván Laborde. 1997. La formación de un sistema electoral "netamente mexicano": La reforma de los "diputados de partido," 1962–1963. *Diálogo y Debate* 1 (April–June): 41–75.

Machlan, Collin M., and Jaime E. Rodríguez. 1980. *The forging of the cosmic race: A reinterpretation of colonial Mexico.* Berkeley, CA: Berkeley University Press.

Magaloni, Beatriz. 2002. Dominio de partido y dilemmas duvergerianos en las elecciones presidenciales de 1994 en México. In *Lecturas sobre el cambio político en México,* ed. Carlos Elizondo Mayer-Serra and Benito Nacif Hernández, 229–80. Mexico City: Centro de Investigación y Docencia Económicas; Fondo de Cultura Económica.

Magaloni, Beatriz, and Alejando Poiré. 2004. The issues, the vote, and the mandate for change. In *Mexico's pivotal democratic election: Candidates, voters, and the presidential campaign of 2000,* ed. Jorge I. Domínguez and Chappell Lawson, 293–319. Stanford, CA: Stanford University Press; San Diego: Center for U.S.–Mexican Studies, University of California, San Diego.

Mahan, Elizabeth. 1985. Mexican broadcasting: Reassessing the industry-state relationship. *Journal of Communication* 35 (1): 60–75.

Manin, Bernard. 1998. *Los principios del gobierno representativo*. Madrid: Alianza.

Manzanilla Schaffer, Víctor. 1998. *Confesiones políticas. Síntesis de mis memorias.* Mexico City: Océano.

Méndez de Hoyos, Irma. 2003. Competencia y competitividad electoral en México, 1977–1997. *Política y Gobierno* 10 (1): 139–82.

Meyer, Lorenzo. 2003. La sorpresa: Una rebelión indígena al final del antiguo régimen. *Foro Internacional* 43 (1): 249–67.

Middlebrook, Kevin J. 1996. El trabajo y la política en el México contemporáneo. *Este País* 67 (October): 35–43.

Mochán, Luis. 2006. PREP: Un análisis científico de los resultados. http://analisisprep.wordpress.com.

Molinar Horcasitas, Juan. 1991. *El tiempo de la legitimidad: Elecciones, autoritarismo y democracia en México.* Mexico City: Cal y Arena.

Molinar Horcasitas, Juan, and Jeffrey A. Weldon. 2001. Reforming electoral systems in Mexico. In *Mixed-member electoral systems: The best of both worlds?* ed. Matthew Soberg Shugart and Martin P. Wattenberg, 209–30. New York: Oxford University Press.

Moreno, Alejandro. 2003. *El votante mexicano: Democracia, actitudes políticas y conducta electoral.* Mexico City: Fondo de Cultura Económica.

———. 2005. *Nuestros valores: Los mexicanos en México y Estados Unidos a inicios del siglo XXI.* Mexico City: Banamex.

———. 2007. The 2006 Mexican presidential election: The economy, oil revenues, and ideology. *PS: Political Science and Politics* 40 (1): 15–19.

Moreno, Alejandro, and Patricia Méndez. 2002. Actitudes hacia la democracia: México en perspectiva comparada. In *Deconstruyendo la ciudadanía: Avances y retos de la cultura democrática en México*, ed. Secretaría de Gobernación, 119–43. Mexico City: SEGOB; SEP; IFE; M.A. Porrúa.

Morlino, Leonardo. 1991. Estabilidad política. In *Diccionario de política*, ed. Norberto Bobbio, Nicola Matteucci, and Gianfranco Pasquino, 533–41. Mexico City: Siglo XXI.

Morse, Richard. 1982. *El espejo de próspero*. Mexico City: Siglo XXI.

Musacchio, Humberto. 1989. *Diccionario enciclopédico de México. Ilustrado.* Mexico City: Andrés León.

———. 2002. *Quién es quién en la política mexicana.* Mexico City: Plaza & Janés.

Nacif, Benito. 1996. Electoral institutions and single party politics in the Mexican Chamber of Deputies. Working Paper 48. Mexico City: CIDE.

———. 1999. La lógica de la parálisis y el cambio bajo gobiernos sin mayoría. Unpublished manuscript.

———. 2002. La rotación de cargos legislativos y la evolución del sistema de partidos en México. In *Lecturas sobre el cambio político en México*, ed. Carlos Elizondo Mayer-Serra and Benito Nacif Hernández, 79–114. Mexico

City: Centro de Investigación y Docencia Económicas; Fondo de Cultura Económica.

Negretto, Gabriel, and Mark Ungar. 1997. Independencia del poder judicial y estado de derecho en América Latina: Los casos de Argentina y Venezuela. *Política y Gobierno* 4 (1): 81–114.

O'Donnell, Guillermo. 1998. *Accountability* horizontal. *La Política* 4 (October): 161–88.

Olson, Mancur. 1992. *La lógica de la acción colectiva: Bienes públicos y la teoría de grupos.* Mexico City: Limusa.

Ozouf, Mona. 1988. *Festivals and the French Revolution.* Cambridge, MA: Harvard University Press.

Panebianco, Angelo. 1990. *Modelos de partido: Organización y poder en los partidos políticos.* Mexico City: Alianza.

Partido Revolucionario Institucional. 1987. *Documentos básicos: Declaración de principios, programa de acción, estatutos.* Mexico City: Secretaría de Divulgación Ideológica.

Pérez Correa, Fernando. 2003. La alternancia y el gobierno dividido. *Este País* 152 (November): 33–44.

Pitkin, Hanna Fenichel. 1985. *El concepto de representación.* Madrid: Centro de Estudios Constitucionales.

Pliego Carrasco, Fernando. 2007. *El mito del fraude electoral en México.* Mexico City: Pax.

Portes, Alejandro. 1995. *En torno a la informalidad: Ensayos sobre la teoría y medición de la economía no regulada.* Mexico City: FLACSO; M.A. Porrúa.

Portilla, Santiago. 1992. *Crónica del gobierno de Carlos Salinas de Gortari. Antecedentes: Campaña electoral y elecciones federales, 1987–1988.* Mexico City: Unidad de la Crónica Presidencial, Fondo de Cultura Económica.

Prud'homme, Jean François. 2003. El Partido de la Revolución Democrática: Las ambivalencias de su proceso de institucionalización. *Foro Internacional* 43 (1): 103–40.

Przeworski, Adam. 1995. *Democracia y mercado: Reformas políticas y económicas en la Europa del Este y América Latina.* Cambridge: Cambridge University Press.

Przeworski, Adam, Michael Alvarez, José Antonio Cheibub, and Fernando Limongi. 2000. *Democracy and development: Political institutions and well-being in the world, 1950–1990.* Cambridge: Cambridge University Press.

Robinson, Michael, and Margaret A. Sheehan. 1983. *Over the wire and on TV: CBS and UPI in campaign '80.* New York: Sage.

Rodríguez Araujo, Octavio. 1982. *La reforma política y los partidos en México.* Mexico City: Siglo XXI.

Rouquié, Alain. 1982. El análisis de las elecciones no competitivas: Control clientelista y situaciones autoritarias. In *¿Para qué sirven las elecciones?* ed. Guy

Hermet, Alain Rouquié, and Juan J. Linz, 54–89. Mexico City: Fondo de Cultura Económica.

Salazar-Elena, Rodrigo. 2003. La elección de instituciones electorales en un régimen autoritario: Una aplicación a México. *Revista Mexicana de Estudios Electorales* 1 (January–June): 67–91.

———. 2007. Confianza política, instituciones y populismo en Bolivia y Venezuela. In *Vox Populi: Populismo y democracia en Latinoamérica*, ed. Julio Aibar Gaete, 213–65. Mexico City: FLACSO.

Salinas, Carlos. 1987. *Discurso de Carlos Salinas de Gortari al protestar como candidato del PRI a la presidencia de la república durante la VII Convención Nacional Ordinaria del PRI, el 8 de noviembre de 1987.* Mexico City: FENASE/CNOP.

———. 1989a. Discurso de Carlos Salinas de Gortari en el Zócalo, durante su cierre de campaña (2 de julio de 1988). In *Las elecciones de 1988 y la crisis del sistema político*, ed. Jaime González Graf, 307–11. Mexico City: Editorial Diana.

———. 1989b. Síntesis de discursos pronunciados en Cuatrociénagas, Puebla, Chalco y Monterrey. In *Las elecciones de 1988 y la crisis del sistema político*, ed. Jaime González Graf, 257–68. Mexico City: Editorial Diana.

Sánchez Gutiérrez, Arturo. 1989. La contienda electoral. In *Las elecciones de 1988 y la crisis del sistema político*, ed. Jaime González Graf, 105–35. Mexico City: Editorial Diana.

Sánchez Susarrey, Jaime. 2003. Hora final. *Reforma* December 6:13A.

Sartori, Giovanni. 1988. *Teoría de la democracia.* Madrid: Alianza.

———. 1998. *Homo videns: La sociedad teledirigida.* Madrid: Taurus.

———. 1999a. *Elementos de teoría política.* Madrid: Alianza.

———. 1999b. *Partidos y sistemas de partidos: Marco para un análisis.* Madrid: Alianza.

Schamis, Hector E. 2006. Populism, socialism, and democratic institutions. *Journal of Democracy* 17 (4): 20–34.

Schedler, Andreas. 2002. The menu of manipulation. *Journal of Democracy* 13 (2): 36–49.

———. 2007. The mobilization of distrust. *Journal of Democracy* 18 (1): 88–102.

Scherer García, Julio, and Carlos Monsiváis. 2003. *Tiempo de saber: Prensa y poder en México.* Mexico City: Nuevo Siglo, Aguilar.

Secanella, Petra. 1984. *El periodismo político en México.* Mexico City: Prisma.

Secretaría de Gobernación and Instituto Nacional de Estadística Geografía e Informática. 2003. *Encuesta nacional sobre cultura política 2003.* CD-ROM.

Serrano, Mónica. 1996. Estado y fuerzas armadas en México. In *México en el desfiladero: Los años de Salinas*, ed. Marcelo Cavarozzi, 117–49. Mexico City: FLACSO; Juan Pablos.

———. 1998. El legado del cambio gradual: Reglas e instituciones bajo Salinas. In *La reconstrucción del estado: México después de Salinas*, ed. Mónica Serrano and Víctor Bulmer-Thomas, 13–43. Mexico City: Fondo de Cultura Económica.

Shugart, Matthew Soberg, and John M. Carey. 1992. *Presidents and assemblies: Constitutional design and electoral dynamics.* New York: Cambridge University Press.

Shugart, Matthew Soberg, and Stephan Haggard. 2001. Institutions and public policy in presidential systems. In *Presidents, parliaments and policy,* ed. Stephan Haggard and Matthew D. McCubbins, 64–104. Cambridge: Cambridge University Press.

Shugart, Matthew Soberg, and Scott Mainwaring. 1997. Presidentialism and democracy in Latin America: Rethinking the terms of the debate. In *Presidentialism and democracy in Latin America,* ed. Scott Mainwaring and Matthew Soberg Shugart, 12–54. New York: Cambridge University Press.

Silva-Herzog Márquez, Jesús. 2002. El fin de la siesta constitucional. In *Gobernar sin mayoría: México 1867–1997,* ed. María Amparo Casar and Ignacio Marván, 369–87. Mexico City: CIDE; Taurus.

Smith, Peter H. 1979. *Labyrinths of power: Political recruitment in twentieth-century Mexico.* Princeton, NJ: Princeton University Press.

Stepan, Alfred. 1999. Toward a new comparative analysis of democracy and federalism: Demos constraining and demos enabling federations. Paper presented at the Conference on Federalism, Democracy and Public Policy, Mexico City, June 14–15.

Sunstein, Cass R. 1993. *The partial constitution.* Cambridge, MA: Harvard University Press.

Tello Díaz, Carlos. 1995. *La rebelión de las Cañadas.* Mexico City: Cal y Arena.

Temkin, Benjamín, Gustavo Ramírez, and Rodrigo Salazar-Elena. 2005. Explorando la dinámica del abstencionismo electoral: ¿Valores, identificación partidista o evaluación de instituciones políticas? In *Demos ante el espejo: Análisis de la cultura política y las prácticas ciudadanas,* ed. Leticia Aguiar Meugniot, 261–79. Mexico City: UNAM.

Tena Ramírez, Felipe. 2001. *Derecho constitucional mexicano.* Mexico City: M.A. Porrúa.

Torres, Jonathan. 2005. Roberto Madrazo Pintado: El candidato tricolor. *Enfoque* (May 29). http://www.reforma.com.

Turner, Victor. 1974. *Dramas, fields and metaphors.* Ithaca, NY: Cornell University Press.

———. 1992. *From ritual to theater: The human seriousness of play.* New York: PAJ Publications.

United Nations. 1990. *World media handbook.* New York: United Nations Department of Public Information.

Valdés, Leonardo. 1993. Las consecuencias políticas de las reformas electorales en México: 1978–1991. PhD diss., El Colegio de México.

Valdés Ugalde, Francisco. 1996. De la nacionalización de la banca a la reforma del estado: Los empresarios y el nuevo orden mexicano. In *Las dimensiones políticas de la reestructuración económica*, ed. María Lorena Cook, Kevin Middlebrook, and Juan Molinar Horcasitas, 371–402. Mexico City: Cal y Arena.

Van Genneph, Arnold. 1969. *Rites of passage*. New York: Johnson Reprint.

Verney, Douglas V. 1961. *Análisis de los sistemas políticos*. Madrid: Tecnos.

Villa, Manuel. 1994. El fin de la política del estatismo. In *México: El voto por la democracia*, ed. Antonio Argüelles and Manuel Villa, 11–32. Mexico City: M.A. Porrúa.

Weldon, Jeffrey. 1997. Political sources of "presidencialismo" in Mexico. In *Presidentialism and democracy in Latin America*, ed. Scott Mainwaring and Matthew Soberg Shugart, 225–58. New York: Cambridge University Press.

———. 2001. The consequences of Mexico's mixed-member electoral system, 1988–1997. In *Mixed-member electoral systems: The best of both worlds?* ed. Matthew Soberg Shugart and Martin P. Wattenberg, 447–76. New York: Oxford University Press.

———. 2002. The legal and partisan framework of the legislative delegation of the budget in Mexico. In *Legislative politics in Latin America*, ed. Scott Morgenstern and Benito Nacif, 377–410. Cambridge: Cambridge University Press.

Williamson, John. 1990. What Washington means by policy reform. In *Latin American adjustment: How much has happened?* ed. John Williamson, 5–20. Washington, D.C.: Institute for International Economics.

Xelhuantzi López, María. 1986. El Congreso del Trabajo. Los primeros diez años: Formación y desarrollo en una época de insurgencia obrera (1966–1976). In *75 años de sindicalismo mexicano*, ed. Alejandra Moreno Toscano and Samuel León González, 659–95. Mexico City: INEHRM.

Index

Sindicato Nacional de Trabajadores de la Educación (SNTE), 91; leadership, 149; power of, 35; Salinas campaign events with, 189–190; Salinas support by, 172, 180
SNTE. *See* Sindicato Nacional de Trabajadores de la Educación (SNTE)
Soberón, Guillermo, 77, 111
Social discontent. *See also* Protests; Strikes: in authoritarian regimes, 7; Democratic Current and, 70; economy and, 241; prim at PRI meetings, 214–216; with technocracy, 101
Social relationships, 13–16, 146
Society, 12, 271, 286
Solidarity committees, 262
Solís, Camacho, 97, 264
Special guest, 257
Stability, 198, 241; attacks on, 256; Democratic Current and, 72; dominant condition of, 258; economic, 37, 279; employment, 34, 36; factors insuring, 20; mechanisms for, 18–19; preconditions for, 245; preserving, 242, 279; presidential selection process and, 40–48, 58; risks to, 274
STIRT. *See* Sindicato de Trabajadores de la Industria de la Radio y la Televisión (STIRT)
Strikes, 55–56
Subordination. *See also* Loyalty: clientelistic, 252; government needs, 241–242; political parties, 42–44, 49–50; submission *versus*, 50; union, 39
Succession process. *See also* Candidates: "distinguished priistas" saga, 75–81; author in authoritarian regimes, 40; characterization of, 2; contextual framework of, 12–13; Democratic Current and, 69–75; destape, 86–95; divergence from, 52; dual leadership during, 60–61; erosion of, 265–266; formal rules of, 43, 48–49; legitimacy

in, 47–48; national convention, 103–108; nomination period in, 51, 244; overview, 65–66; people of the system and, 41–42; phrases of: campaigns, 62–63; destape, 60–62; elections, 64; prior to destape, 53–60; takeover of power, 64; platform preparation, 81–85; political actors in, 49; political context of, 48; power groups in, 55; pre-campaign activities, 96–99; press role in, 118–119; problem resolution, 43; proselytizing activities during, 99–101; salutaciones, 95–96; structural adjustment during, 66–68, 74–75; structural problems in, 40–41; subordinate party and, 49–50; unity breakfast, 85–86
Suprema Corte de Justicia de la Nación, 31–32
System of accountability. *See* Representative political system

T
Tapadismo, 107–108, 265
Tapado (veiled candidate), 82–83
Taqueo de votos, 9
Tarahumaras, 134
Teachers: demands of, 188–189, 191; image of, 188; modernizing role of, 191; vote oath of, 185–186
Technocrats: benefits for, 248; characterization of, 68; sector displacing, 265
Technology and science, 211–216
Televisa, 227–228
Television: campaign coverage by, 236–237; candidates' image on, 251–252; PAN use of, 285; power of, 269; PRI use of, 232; regulation of, 224
Tetecala, Morelos, 183–184
Tlaxcala tour, 177–179
Toledano, Salazar, 102
Tortibonos, 137

About the Authors

Larissa Adler-Lomnitz (PhD) is a sociocultural anthropologist specializing in social networks analyses. She is a full-time professor and researcher at the Institute for Applied Mathematics at the National Autonomous University of Mexico (IIMAS–UNAM). In 1995, she received the National Prize for Arts and Sciences in the Humanities, awarded by the Mexican government. She is the author of several books including *Networks and Marginality* (New York: Academic Press, 1977); *A Mexican Elite Family, 1820–1980* (Princeton, NJ: Princeton University Press, 1988); *Becoming a Scientist in Mexico* (University Park: Pennsylvania State University Press, 1994); and *Chile's Political Culture and Parties* (Notre Dame, IN: University of Notre Dame Press, 2000). She has also written several articles including "Informal Networks in Formal Systems" (*American Anthropologist* 1998, 90: 42–55). Her latest book is *Lo formal y lo informal en las sociedades contemporáneas* (Santiago: Centro de Investigaciones Diego Barros Arana, 2008). Currently, she is conducting research on Mexican plastic artists' acquisition of identity.

Rodrigo Salazar-Elena (MD) is a political scientist. He is a full-time professor and researcher at the Latin American Faculty of Social Sciences (FLACSO) in Mexico. He has authored and co-authored papers on Mexican electoral dynamics, Latin American politics, and political culture. His current research interests involve populism in Latin America, the causes and consequences of presidential reelection, and social science methodology.

Ilya Adler (PhD) held a master's degree in public communication and a PhD in mass communication, and he specialized in international and intercultural communications. He was a professor for many years, teaching in the areas of communications, and business and international relations at Mexican and U.S. universities, including the University of Illinois–Chicago, the Tecnológico de Monterrey, the Universidad Nacional Autónoma de México, and Alliant International University. He also held several academic administrative positions. He authored a number of articles and a book dealing with social, political, and cultural issues in Mexico and had been a regular columnist of *Mexconnect*, an electronic magazine dedicated to Mexico, writing about the cultural challenges faced in the Mexican business world. He was also a successful consultant to business and public institutions both in the U.S. and Mexico as a principal of Kochman, Mavrelis Associates, Inc., a Chicago-based firm that specializes in cross-cultural management, where he worked with a long list of important corporate and educational clients. He passed away in September 2007.

CPSIA information can be obtained at www.ICGtesting.com
Printed in the USA
241657LV00002B/1/P

9 780816 527533